# Grassroots Environmental Governance

T0298662

Grassroots movements can pose serious challenges to both governments and corporations. However, grassroots actors possess a variety of motivations, and their visions of development may evolve in complex ways. Meanwhile, their relative powerlessness obliges them to forge an array of shifting alliances and to devise a range of adaptive strategies.

*Grassroots Environmental Governance* presents a compilation of in-depth ethnographic case studies, based on original research. Each of the chapters focuses specifically on grassroots engagements with the agents of various forms of industrial development. The book is geographically diverse, including analyses of groups based in both the global North and South, and represents a range of disciplinary perspectives. This allows the collection to explore themes that cross-cut specific localities and disciplinary boundaries, and thus to generate important theoretical insights into the complexities of grassroots engagements with industry.

This volume will be of great interest to scholars of environmental activism, environmental governance, and environmental studies in general.

**Leah S. Horowitz** is Assistant Professor of Environmental Studies at the University of Wisconsin–Madison, USA.

**Michael J. Watts** is Professor of Geography at the University of California, Berkeley, USA.

# Routledge Research in Global Environmental Governance

Series Editors:

Philipp Pattberg, *VU University Amsterdam and the Amsterdam Global Change Institute (AGCI), the Netherlands.*

Agni Kalfagianni, *VU University Amsterdam, the Netherlands.*

Global environmental governance has been a prime concern of policy-makers since the United Nations Conference on the Human Environment in 1972. Yet, despite more than nine hundred multi-lateral environmental treaties coming into force over the past forty years and numerous public-private and private initiatives to mitigate global change, human-induced environmental degradation is reaching alarming levels. Scientists see compelling evidence that the entire earth system now operates well outside safe boundaries and at rates that accelerate. The urgent challenge from a social science perspective is how to organize the co-evolution of societies and their surrounding environment; in other words, how to develop effective and equitable governance solutions for today's global problems.

Against this background, the *Routledge Research in Global Environmental Governance* series delivers cutting-edge research on the most vibrant and relevant themes within the academic field of global environmental governance.

# Grassroots Environmental Governance

# Community engagements with industry

Edited by Leah S. Horowitz
and Michael J. Watts

LONDON AND NEW YORK

First published 2017 by Routledge

2 Park Square, Milton Park, Abingdon, Oxfordshire OX14 4RN
52 Vanderbilt Avenue, New York, NY 10017

*Routledge is an imprint of the Taylor & Francis Group, an informa business*

First issued in paperback 2019

*British Library Cataloguing in Publication Data*
A catalogue record for this book is available from the British Library

*Library of Congress Cataloging in Publication Data*
A catalog record for this book has been requested

ISBN: 978-1-138-12302-1 (hbk)
ISBN: 978-0-367-25580-0 (pbk)

Typeset in Goudy
by Apex CoVantage, LLC

This book is dedicated to the memory of Berta Cáceres, a Honduran environmental activist who was murdered in 2016, one year after receiving the Goldman Environmental Prize for successfully organizing the indigenous Lenca people against a dam that would have cut off their water supply. May her legacy live on.

All royalties from sales of this book will be donated to Ensemble pour la Planète, a grassroots environmental organization in New Caledonia.

# Contents

# Illustrations

## Figures

## Tables

# Contributor biographies

**Eleanor Andrews** is a PhD student in Development Sociology at Cornell University, USA, with a Master's in geography from Pennsylvania State University, USA. Her research addresses social learning and collective action for sustainable natural resource management in the United States, with particular attention to the politics and micropolitics of environmental knowledge.

**Patrick Bond** is Professor of Political Economy at the University of the Witwatersrand (Johannesburg, South Africa) and Honorary Professor at the University of KwaZulu-Natal's Centre for Civil Society, South Africa. Recent books include *Elite Transition* (2014, 3rd edn), *South Africa – Present as History* (2014, with John Saul), and *Politics of Climate Justice* (2012).

**Julia Freeman** is a faculty lecturer for the McGill School of Environment, Canada. She holds a PhD in resource management and environmental studies from the University of British Columbia, Canada, and an MA in anthropology from McGill University, Canada. She's most interested in sustainable human-plant relationships, particularly when those relationships are controversial.

**Leah S. Horowitz** is Assistant Professor of Environmental Studies at the University of Wisconsin–Madison, USA. Her research explores how social relationships and networks shape grassroots engagements with environmental issues. Her primary field sites are in New Caledonia (Kanak responses to mining) and Wisconsin (Native American encounters with unconventional fossil fuel development).

**Milind Kandlikar** is Professor at the Liu Institute for Global Issues and the Institute of Resources, Environment and Sustainability, Canada. His current projects include cross-national comparisons of regulation of agricultural biotechnology, air quality in Indian cities, risks and benefits of nanotechnology, new technologies for sustainable transportation, and development and climate change.

**Joan Martinez-Alier** is a senior researcher at ICTA, Universitat Autonoma de Barcelona, Spain, ex-president of the International Society for Ecological Economics, and author of *Ecological Economics: Energy, Environment and Society* (1987) and *The Environmentalism of the Poor* (2002). In 2016–2021, with an

ERC Grant, he will direct the ENVJUSTICE project on global movements for environmental justice.

**James McCarthy** is Professor of Geography at Clark University, USA. His research examines the intersections of political economy and environmental politics, with emphases on neoliberalism and environmental governance, rural areas and industries, property relations, and social movements. His current research examines the political economies and ecologies of potential renewable energy transitions.

**Tom Perreault** is Professor of Geography at Syracuse University, USA. His research interests include political ecology, environmental governance, rural development, and indigenous/campesino social movements in Andean South America. He was lead editor of the *Handbook of Political Ecology* (Routledge) and edited *Minería, Agua y Justicia Social en los Andes* (PIEB).

**Terre Satterfield** is Professor of Culture, Risk and the Environment, and Director of the University of British Columbia's Institute for Resources, Environment and Sustainability, Canada. Her research concerns sustainable thinking and action in environmental management and decision-making. Recently, she has studied tensions between indigenous communities and the state and/or regulatory dilemmas regarding new technologies.

**Leah Temper**, ICTA, Universitat Autonoma de Barcelona, Spain, is Founder and Director of the Global Atlas of Environmental Justice and Director of the International Seeds of Survival Program at USC-Canada. She is co-PI of ACKnowl-EJ (Activist-Academic Co-production of Knowledge for Environmental Justice), a project within the Transformations to Sustainability Initiative, which runs from 2015–2018.

**Caroline Upton** is a senior lecturer in the Department of Geography, University of Leicester, UK. An environmental geographer and political ecologist, she has been working with herders and activists in Mongolia since 1999. Her collaborative research focuses on issues of environmental governance, activism and justice, pasture management, conservation, and environmental values.

**Gabriela Valdivia** is Associate Professor in the Geography Department at UNC Chapel Hill, USA. She examines resource governance, environmental mobilization, and frontiers of nature-society relations in Latin America, with attention to everyday formations of national and regional communities. Her most recent work focuses on oil and environmental injustices in Ecuador.

**Michael J. Watts** is Class of '63 Professor of Geography, and Co-Director of Development Studies at the University of California, Berkeley, USA, where he has taught for almost 40 years. His recent research has focused on the political economy of development and on the relations between oil and the field of conflict in Nigeria in particular.

# 1 Introduction

## Engaging with industry and governing the environment from the grassroots

*Leah S. Horowitz and Michael J. Watts*

### The governance of industrial expansion

Industry provides us with the products upon which we have grown to rely and which we take for granted as necessary for survival, yet it pollutes our air, water, and soil, contributes significantly to climate change, causes biodiversity loss, and leads to the exploitation of workers. Economic growth, fuelled by the productivity increases associated with the rise of industrial manufacturing since the eighteenth century, has however been seen as both the source of and the solution to modernity's devastating ecological footprint as cleaner, more efficient technologies emerge, environmental regulations increase, and more highly-educated populations gain greater environmental awareness. The famous Environmental Kuznets Curve, an inverse U-shaped arc, depicts the rise, peak, and fall of environmental degradation as a modern society increases its regulatory capacity and the self-reflexive knowledge and expertise to pursue, as Ulrich Beck calls it, "ecological modernization". But the Kutznets Curve masks the fact that wealth is correlated with ever-increasing consumption, and that domestic regulations are no indicators of the environmental impacts of imported products (Atıl Aşıcı and Acar 2016). In other words, wealthier countries simply allow poorer nations to engage in the dirty industries to which their own citizens no longer wish to be exposed. The export of environmental and social harms, such as pollution and resource depletion, associated with industrial expansion, represents a type of "spatial fix" (Harvey 1982) in which global inequities are the twin of "pollution havens" (Rauscher 2005), the repositories of exported toxic electronic waste and other detritus from the global North. Industrial wastes, in turn, result from capitalism's "treadmill of production" (Schnaiberg 1980), the constant and inevitable drive toward overproduction and overconsumption as companies continually seek new markets simply to survive. The global division of labor regarding industrial waste is of course replicated within the advanced industrial states: polluting industries preferentially locate their facilities in neighborhoods that lack the economic and political clout that would afford them support from decision-makers within national or local governments. These are usually poor communities, and often comprised of people of color (Mohai, Pellow, and Roberts 2009). Environmental injustice, in short, is multi-scalar.

As economic operations increasingly compete in a global arena, governments lose much incentive or indeed ability to regulate corporations, which simply regime-shop for the most favorable regulatory environment. This pressures governments into a neoliberal "race to the bottom," a competition to attract industry and the jobs and tax revenue it represents, not to mention campaign donations and other financial support for politicians, by loosening environmental standards. Fearing businesses' emigration, states shift from a position of regulator toward a position of "facilitator" or "enabler" of firms' own self-regulation (Gouldson and Bebbington 2007), effectively "subcontracting" regulatory responsibilities to the corporations themselves (Ayres and Braithwaite 1992, 103). Simultaneously, "socially responsible" investors have begun to screen, and pressure, potential funding recipients. For instance, in 1998 the International Finance Corporation adopted "Environmental and Social Safeguard Policies" directed at clients, and in 2001 the Financial Times Stock Exchange created an index, FTSE4Good, which listed companies that met criteria for environmental and social performance.

Corporations, meanwhile, have embraced the opportunity to demonstrate self-regulation, as a means of pre-empting formal regulation through voluntary codes of conduct. These efforts have translated into a discourse and practice of Corporate Social Responsibility (CSR), the idea that businesses should protect, or even benefit, local communities and ecosystems. The notion that businesses have moral duties can be traced back to nineteenth century debates about industry's social role (Sadler 2004), but CSR fully emerged in the early 1980s (Hilson 2012). CSR can be seen as a type of "roll-out neoliberalism" (Peck and Tickell 2002), part of a wider movement consisting of reforms designed to address the social and environmental harms that had resulted from "roll-back neoliberalism," which had exclusively aimed to free markets from regulation. However, this move toward CSR stemmed not from altruism but from the profit motive, as corporations had identified a "business case" for being a good "corporate citizen" (Zadek 2001): The costs of ignoring community demands had begun to outweigh the costs of addressing them, as openly admitted by industry representatives (Humphreys 2000).

Clearly, governments and corporations are not the only entities governing corporate practices. Extra-governmental organizations, groups, and individuals play a growing role in influencing decision-making processes, particularly regarding environmental concerns, as recognized by a burgeoning scholarship of environmental governance (Reed and Bruyneel 2010). In response, industry – like neoliberalization (Springer 2011), or capitalism itself (Gibson-Graham 2006 (1996)) – seeks to create a context that can support and enable its operations. This context is not only political and economic, in the form of a favorable regulatory environment and bailouts on an as-needed basis (a continual process of "rescheduling the crisis" [Harvey 1989]), but also social. Companies need to show that they have obtained a "social license to operate," a "critical mass of public consent" for their operation – or at least the appearance thereof, in the eyes of governments, activists, and funding bodies (Owen and Kemp 2013, 31). In the process, CSR must adapt to local circumstances, articulating in each instance with local politico-economic conditions, as well as with cultural ideologies and practices (Horowitz 2015). One means of demonstrating this "social license" is the Impact and Benefit Agreement (IBA), a company-community contract that may include sponsoring community activities, providing local jobs, ensuring environmental safeguards and/or making efforts to preserve cultural heritage (O'Faircheallaigh 2012). However, these attempts to win hearts and minds may stand in lieu of more far-reaching changes to environmentally damaging industrial processes. Furthermore, corporations are keenly aware of the socio-economic context in which they operate. They will expend less effort in communities that possess less political influence (Pellow and Brulle 2005; Gouldson 2006), and where possible may manipulate or intimidate vulnerable communities into putatively accepting the project in spite of its environmental and social harms (Calvano 2008), often in exchange for desperately needed jobs (Auyero and Swistun 2009).

In what has become a "risk society" (Beck 1992), publics increasingly mistrust governments' and corporations' ability or willingness to protect citizens from industrial risks. They may feel the need to take matters into their own hands through processes of "informal regulation" (Pargal and Wheeler 1996, 1315) – social pressure, threats to corporations' reputations (increasingly important in a globalized world), and even the threat or use of violence. The emergence of "multi-stakeholder initiatives" is precisely an index of how civic groups, governments and capitalist enterprises have been drawn together into complex new configurations, typically promoted as the sorts of governance mechanisms required by the globalization of capital (see Burca et al. 2014; Carothers and Brechenmacher 2014).

## Grassroots and the rise of multi-stakeholder initiatives: the case of the extractives sector

When viewed from the perspective of globalization and the new forms of environmental governance, the extractives sector is an especially rich and compelling domain to explore how local grassroots organizations are drawn into multi-stakeholder initiatives. What is especially striking is the degree to which not just the oil and gas industry but the entire extractive and minerals industry has become one of, if not *the* most significant sector in which both voluntary and mandatory governance structures have been promoted by intentional interventions over the last three decades. A five-hundred-page book like *Blood Oil* authored by legal theorist Leif Wenar and published in 2015 – devoted to anti-corruption laws, voluntary transparency institutions, resource validation and certification systems, commercial and multilateral embargoes and sanctions, and direct revenue distribution mechanisms in the global extractive industries – is a striking example of the density, complexity and multi-scalar character of contemporary governance mechanisms that inhere in the oil complex. The fact that a moniker such as "blood diamonds" or "blood oil" now has such worldwide currency – supported now by a considerable array of national and international NGOs devoted to extractives, and bolstered by global business modalities such as the UN Global Compact – confirms the fact that from the late 1990s a new set of global norms have arisen around oil and gas, minerals, and natural resources. Far from being exclusively or primarily addressing extractive regimes, the rise of these transnational multi-stakeholder initiatives (MSIs) – voluntary partnerships between government, civil society and the private sector – points to an increasingly prevalent strategy for promoting governmental and corporate responsiveness and accountability to citizens (Brockmeyer and Fox 2015). While most MSIs involve voluntary social and environmental standards – the proliferation of Corporate Social Responsibility programs for global companies is a parallel development – a handful of global instruments, like EITI (the Extractive Industries Transparency Initiative) in the extractives sector but also entities like COST (the Construction Sector Transparency Initiative) and GIFT (the Global Initiative on Fiscal Transparency) focus on information disclosure, public governance and participation in the public sector. How then do we account for the rise of a new international transparency norm now widely espoused by the world's largest mining and oil corporations, governments and international financial and aid institutions alike and how do civil society and grassroots organizations participate? This question is especially interesting insofar as it arose at a time when resource commodity prices were booming, capital flows deepening and the prevailing ideological ethos was unsympathetic to the very idea of regulation.

The emergence of this norm in the global oil and gas industry is particularly puzzling for several reasons (see Gillies's 2010 excellent account). First, the industry is vast and institutionally complex. Disclosure and transparency would logically encompass everything from *revenue flows* (payments from companies to governments, communities, civic organizations as well as flows between government entities such as tax entities and sub-national states and local governments), *revenue management* (investment strategies, windfall accounts, oil savings funds), *revenue expenditures* (budgetary processes, sub-national revenue formulae, contracting), and *industry operations* (from bid round criteria to contracts to production and reserve data to legal, regulatory and operating structures). The regulatory terrain capable of taking on the oil complex is potentially vast. Second, the period in which these norms arose was one, generally speaking, of buoyant oil prices in which oil states enjoyed leverage and power, as did the petro-elites who benefitted from increased oil revenues. The post 9/11 US strategy to diversify supply stimulated the expansion of a number of oil-suppliers in West Africa, the Caucasus and elsewhere, many of which were hardly models of probity and good governance. Third, transparency and disclosure is advocated as a means to enhance government accountability among a class of resource-dependent producers – "petro-states" – which are customarily seen not just as exemplars of poor governance, systemic state deficits and endemic corruption, but the toughest and most demanding of political environments in which any reform effort might be prosecuted: they are limit cases and exceptionally hard nuts to crack. Furthermore, all of the classic traits of the resource curse would logically increase the political costs associated with adopting a new transparency norm. Fourth, political analysts (see Gillies 2010) suggest that international norms arise when they are likely to prevent bodily harm and protect personal liberties or protect vulnerable groups. A norm devoted to budgets, disclosure and auditing is therefore not intuitively plausible, or at the very least would demand the difficult task of linking, say, transparency to protection. Indeed a norm purporting to link transparency to development outcomes such as education or health indices would have to identify both causal mechanisms and a set of indicators deployed for prescriptive purposes. And not least, the world of "Big Oil" has, for almost all of its history, been viewed with deep popular suspicion, has operated often with high degrees of secrecy, is a highly "securitized" industry in which local and international security forces protect its assets, and in its operations in the Global South has for the most part been able to operate, in virtue of its technological capability and corporate and political power, with impunity. The same might be said of the national oil companies (NOCs), many of which through joint ventures with international oil companies (IOCs) have emerged as powerful players. Which is to say, why might large, powerful IOCs and NOCs voluntarily sign up to become more transparent and in theory more accountable in view of the sorts of exclusive political settlements constructed in and around petro-states?

If norms are typically seen to arise through a process of "grafting" (building upon and benefitting from their adjacency to more established norms), and to "norm entrepreneurs" who advocate for and are capable of assembling coalitions (and ultimately signatories) to a set of institutional arrangements (Gillies 2010), then how might one explain the emergence (and widespread adoption) of a transparency norm in the oil and gas industry, and the emergence of its institutionalized form as the global EITI in 2003? And how might we account for a certain sort of rapid success? In a little over ten years, 48 countries had become signatories (31 certified as compliant) supported by 88 major oil and gas and mining companies and in 35 countries disclosure audits had occurred for 1.2 trillion dollars in government revenues. And not least, how and in what ways has the norm spawned a massive institutional proliferation – in effect a dense global network of institutions and organizations – which now populate the extractives sector as part of what one might call the "multi-stakeholder initiatives universe"?

The founding moment – the critical juncture – of the transparency norm, and what came to be EITI, was the decade of the 1990s. A confluence of forces and trends proved to be crucial and all linked in complex ways to globalization. First, the global extractive industries – over four billion people reside in what are termed "extractive economies" – became an object of academic and policy scrutiny operating under the moniker of the "resource curse". A body of research dating back to the 1980s (examining the Dutch disease, and the costs of mineral-based boom-and-bust cycles) garnered attention and strength through the work of distinguished economists Richard Auty, Terry Karl, Jeffrey Sachs, Paul Collier and others which linked resource dependency to not only poor economic performance but governance, transparency and accountability failures and the increased likelihood of costly civil war and political violence.

As the resource curse model rapidly entered the world of policy prescription, it met up with two other trends that together comprise the second aspect of the conjuncture. One was a deepening interest among aid agencies in governance as seen through the lens of dominant neoliberal prescriptions in which poor governance and corruption were fetters on market operations. And the other was the mainstreaming of corporate social responsibility (CSR) as a response to the increased scrutiny of corporate activity in which Western consumers (and shareholders) and NGOs were able to pry open the black box of off-shoring, poor working conditions and human rights violations within the global value chains of manufacturing and resourced-based industries. For example, in the United States the National Labor Committee brought sweatshops into the mainstream media in the early 1990s when it exposed the use of sweatshop and child labor to sew clothing for Wal-Mart and the United Students Against Sweatshops became active on college campuses. CSR became a means by which increasingly contested social licenses to operate were to be secured.

In the extractive sector, resources (and oil and gas in particular) have characteristics which brought these issues into the bright light of day: many resources are seen as national assets for development, a priority area for foreign direct investment (FDI), a significant source of state revenues, and carry a large ecological, social and economic footprint. These developments were not unrelated to two other sorts of global norms that gathered steam during the 1990s: one was the link between human rights and development that had been triggered both by growing indigenous rights movements and by the horrors of a number of brutal civil wars (Sierra Leone, Angola, Liberia) during the 1990s. Another was a focus on corruption and bribery especially in relation to global business operations. In the United States, the Foreign Corrupt Practices Act had been signed in 1977 but it is not accidental that in 1998 it was amended – and its capacities enhanced – through the International Anti-Bribery Act which was designed to implement the Organisation for Economic Co-operation and Development (OECD) Anti-Bribery Convention.

The third force was the globalization of the extractives sector itself. Oil and gas had been a global industry from its birth of course and it had been compelled to restructure its operations and value chains in the wake of OPEC's catellization and the assertive nationalism of the 1970s. But by the 1990s, it was confronted by a series of legitimacy crises which brought into question the IOCs' (and mining companies' too) "social license to operate" and their rhetoric of corporate social responsibility. Crises of legitimacy of course translated into reputational losses for global brands, as was thrown into sharp relief by the controversy surrounding Shell in Nigeria (the Ogoni trials ending in the hanging of Ken Saro-Wiwa); the Elf investigation begun in 1994 which ensnared the French government, the state-owned oil company and several African governments in corruption cases; and other high-profile cases (for example, UNOCAL in Burma, and pipeline controversies in the Caucasus and Chad). The admission in 2001 of large payments by BP to unnamed officials in Angola was especially critical in pushing forward the momentum toward more formal voluntary arrangements like EITI which had built up during the 1990s.

The fourth process was an unprecedented inquiry into the World Bank Group's extractive industry operations. Multilaterals often insist that part of their mission is to promote and inculcate global values and best practices and after 1996, when the World Bank's president pledged to commit to fighting "the cancer of corruption", the Bank's remit was reinterpreted in favor of robust engagements around issues of corruption and fiscal transparency (Craig and Porter 2006, 69–71). In the IMF and World Bank cases, interest in transparency was certainly enhanced by their own legitimacy crises sustained in the wake of the 1997–98 Asian Financial Crisis, but the ground had been laid during contentious relations with civil society groups during the early 1990s over the Bank investments and technical assistance to both large-scale engineering projects (dams most obviously) and the extractives sector. NGOs questioned the Bank's record in protecting mining communities, environmental protection, and the degree to which it funded undemocratic and corrupt governments. The resource curse literature, of course, bolstered such arguments. In 2000, the Bank conducted a participatory review of its activities in extractives followed by the independent Extractive Industry Review (EIR) in 2001. While there were important points of disagreement between the Bank's internal review and EIR (notably on sequencing), the Bank aggressively promoted transparency in extractives. Both before and after, other international financial institutions (IFIs) (the IMF for example in Angola) pushed transparency and all multilateral banks followed suit.

Finally, there is the crucial role of the agents ("entrepreneurs") who assertively promoted the cause of opening up the black box of extractives and of creating a discourse which grafted transparency onto other emergent norms and debates. In the case of extractives and EITI, the role of Global Witness and their early 1990s work on illegal logging in SE Asia and subsequently their pathbreaking report on Angola – *Crude Awakening* published in 1999 – proved to be instrumental (Weinar 2016). Transnational civil society groups focused particularly on "breaking the links between exploitation of natural resources, conflict and corruption" and targeted multinational companies, foreign banks and host country governments. In the case of Angola, Global Witness prioritized for the first time the question of transparency and the responsibility to publish information on revenues, payments, and operations. Human Rights organizations were also important – a case of norm grafting – especially around the Niger Delta. In 1999 the Human Rights Watch Report *The Price of Oil* linked the operations of oil companies to Nigerian security forces and to wider issues of democracy, conflict and social justice. Campaigning around controversial pipelines in Chad and Turkey-Georgia (the BTC pipeline) put pressure on governments, companies and IFIs alike and promoted the idea that revenue flows should be publicly disclosed. Such advocacy gained strength from the fact that robust social movements within host communities in oil and mineral states gained a prominence during the 1990s – whether the Ogoni movement in Nigeria or the struggles of Papuans around Ok Tedi – and often became part of powerful transnational coalitions of actors linking up with organizations like Greenpeace, the Rainforest Action Network, and so on. Global Witness through funding from the Open Society Institute established

Publish What You Pay (PWYP) in 2002; a coalition of 30 organizations in Europe and America joined forces with and provided capacity building and a degree of protection for local activists working in authoritarian settings. Global Witness was especially influential in the United Kingdom, midwifing what became EITI. Indeed the UK government was a crucial ally in the confluence of forces which gave birth to EITI. Discussions began in 2001 with DFID and Prime Minister Blair. The former was well resourced at the time and included high-ranking transparency supporters. For the government, criticism over BP's illicit payments in Angola and the BTC pipeline, coupled with DFID's and Tony Blair's growing concern with African governance (what was to become the Commission for Africa), all conspired to make transparency highly serviceable for their collective interests.

In sum, it was this constellation of five forces – all traceable in some way to the character of globalization in a post-Cold War world – which contributed to the consolidation of a set of collective interests around the norm of transparency. A powerful set of actors – IOCs, IFIs, Western governments – were brokered by a coalition of civil society entrepreneurs (many of who had direct links to local grassroots community organizations) around an emergent norm of transparency within the extractives sector. Faced with growing public scrutiny regarding the operations of oil companies and the questionable relations between governments and donors and corrupt, and often conflicted, resource-dependent states, questions of reputation, legitimacy, and human rights provided a common ground on which a coalition could be built. But this network was also shot through with quite different sets of powers, capabilities, and interests which did not gravitate toward an "equilibrium" point of mutual agreement.

If it was in the interest of these actors to endorse the notion of disclosure, the question of under what conditions and through what institutional arrangements, was a source of bitter contention. When EITI was announced by Blair in 2002 at the World Summit for Sustainable Development in Johannesburg, it placed the onus of disclosure squarely on the host government, and rested upon a system of voluntary compliance rather than international enforcement. The early 2000s then represented a space within which there was bargaining among all of the actors regarding what sort of transparency system was to emerge. On offer were two models (Gillies 2010; O'Sullivan 2013). One promoted by PWYP primarily targeted North American and European IOCs and their home governments: they called for full corporate disclosure of payments made to petro-states and disclosure was to be mandatory through home country legislation. Oil companies were divided on this issue at first but rising oil prices and competition from non-Western oil companies conspired to make IOCs wary of mandatory revenue disclosures. The UK Department for International Development (DFID) and the UK government pushed for implementation to be the responsibility of individual countries. This "middle way" transferred the onus to host country governments who moreover were, along with the IOCs and civic groups, to become voluntary signatories. All major oil companies immediately signed up as "supporters" and governments, IFIs, and multilaterals jumped on board.

In short order a governance structure for compliance was designed, a World Bank-run Multi-Donor Trust Fund was established in 2004, by 2005 the compliance rules had been laid out in a Validation Guide, a secretariat opened in 2007 in Norway, and two key signatories from each of the focus regions (Nigeria and Azerbaijan) were the first to implement the process, thus affording considerable credibility. In 2009, the first batch of countries were certified as compliant. EITI represented for governments, IFIs and IOCs alike a low cost mechanism to back transparency and improve reputations, to rebuild the social license to operate – without threatening commercial or political interests. The bargaining space which emerged around the emergence of the transparency norm in the 1990s and early 2000s struck a particular "settlement". The crisis of legitimacy facing global extractive industries was resolved by shifting the transparency burden onto resource-dependent governments of the Global South who voluntarily became signatories. For the likes of the IFIs and multilaterals a relatively toothless and tightly circumscribed EITI served their interests of promoting good governance.

The attractiveness of EITI's "big tent" approach was facilitated by its voluntary nature, low compliance standards and a structure that permitted a number of countries to participate without committing them to either compliance or implementation (Shaxson 2009). EITI in this way retained donor and IOC support because it could offer a veneer of respectability by being part of an entity in which the worst, highest reputational risk offenders (Equatorial Guinea, for example) could be seen to be part of a transparency discourse. Compliance was to hinge on two interventions, each containing enormous challenges: first, revenue disclosure within a hugely complex set of structures (from bidding to contracts to marketing and sale and so on) by focusing on a *single node* in the oil complex: the transfer of funds from oil companies to host governments. And second, the creation of a multi-stakeholder body to oversee implementation which demanded civil society involvement in monitoring, often in political circumstances in which NGOs are weak, under-resourced and facing intimidating political conditions. The challenge was "how to be meaningful while retaining as many country participants as possible" (Gillies 2010, 120).

This is not the place to provide a full accounting of EITI to date (see David-Barrett and Okamura 2013; Brockmyer and Fox 2015; Sovacool et al. 2016). If EITI has matured, deepened its remit, and grown some teeth, the fact remains that it is voluntary, depends upon the efficacy of reputation as a basis for compliance, and cannot in its current form do much to ensure that the audits and disclosure have consequences for either public sector governance or corporate behavior. The connection between transparency and accountability is weak. In short, EITI rests on a particular theory of social change which would demand the existence of multiple levels of democratic institutions, and forms of deliberative democracy rooted in a robust civil society in order for the EITI to meet the expectations of its promoters.

The presumption is that the EITI standards and systems of compliance can start from the lowest common denominator – revenue disclosure – with the idea that information triggers a virtuous cascade of events – public understanding, policy debate, enhanced public management, accountability, and business operating environment which translate into development outcomes. In so many cases transparency is simply performed and the disclosure "bounces" off governance structures that are hard to shift; at best one discovers isomorphic mimicry and a naive belief that information and its public circulation (often big questions in themselves) will do "political work". A recent comprehensive review of 16 EITI compliant countries concludes as follows:

> We analyze the performance of the first 16 countries to attain EITI Compliance Status over the period of 1996–2014. We find, interestingly, that in most metrics EITI countries do not perform better during EITI compliance than before it, and that they do not outperform other countries. We postulate four possible explanations behind the relative weakness of the EITI: a limited mandate, its voluntary nature, stakeholder resistance, and dependence on strong civil society.
>
> (Sovacool et al. 2016, 1)

From the perspective of this book, the adequacy of EITI as a new form of voluntary governance turned on the degree to which civil society groups (including grassroots organizations) were included, and with what powers, in the 'multi-stakeholder' coalition. The EITI program is part of a raft of forms of governance in extractives of course. The mining sector has instituted all manner of community-company governance institutions all of which, like EITI, purportedly offer a bargaining space in which local concerns (whether disclosure, or environmental compensation, or community benefits) can be adjudicated (Kirsch 2014; Welker 2014). The moral of the EITI story as an example of "grassroots" involvement in the new voluntary structures, is that the structure of power – the bargaining – which produced the new norms of disclosure placed the onus on particular actors within the extractives complex. The civil society groups, to the degree they could be effective, required capacities and organizational and funding structures they often did not possess. Even when they did, the mere fact of disclosure could not, under most circumstances, shift the existing ordering of power in signatory countries. Civil society groups often became complicit with what was in effect "performing disclosure" without in any meaningful way addressing the deep structural problems in the extractives sector.

## Theoretical engagements

The chapters in this edited volume contribute to cutting-edge scholarship on grassroots movements – in the context of a global intensification of environmentally-oriented mobilizations – by focusing on community engagements, in both the developed and developing world, specifically with a variety of forms of industrial expansion. The authors draw upon a range of theoretical perspectives from anthropology, economics, environmental studies, geography, and sociology to describe and analyse case studies from Africa, Asia, the Pacific, and both North and South

America. Despite this diversity, the contributors' aims coalesce around a single set of questions: Under what circumstances do such engagements arise? How do relationships with outsiders, as well as internal power dynamics, shape grassroots goals and strategies, and how do these evolve in response to changing conditions? Finally, what internal characteristics and external factors inform the outcomes of grassroots engagements? Below, we outline some theoretical framings for these questions. We find that research to date has not adequately examined micropolitical tensions both within and between groups involved in grassroots environmental governance. In conversation with this literature, then, our contributions demonstrate the diversity and complexity of grassroots engagements with industry.

### Grassroots environmental governance: defining the terms

We begin this discussion of grassroots environmental governance with a definition of each term, and a recognition of the difficulties inherent to defining each one, as the chapters demonstrate. First, "grassroots" connotes action by a loosely defined and fluid group of people addressing a locally-relevant issue through "essentially democratic" processes (Gould, Schnaiberg, and Weinberg 1996, 3). The grassroots organizations (GROs) into which these activists form, in contrast to larger, better-funded non-governmental organizations (NGOs), are relatively small and tend to rely entirely on volunteers (see Mercer 2002), although they may receive support from donors and wider networks (Temper and Martinez-Alier, this volume). While NGOs possess far vaster resources and connections, allowing them to engage in more high-profile actions such as large-scale campaigns and lobbying activities, grassroots activists are often driven by a deeply personal and passionate engagement with the matter of concern, rather than a desire for career advancement which often motivates NGO employees. Meanwhile, GROs may benefit from other types of resources that NGOs lack, including special legal rights, public sympathy for the "underdog," or the political and moral legitimacy associated with indigeneity (Horowitz 2012). Ultimately, a grassroots organization is, by definition, "an authentic and legitimate representative of community [ . . . ] an organic and living organization with its roots in the lifeworld of the community" (Brulle 2000, 91).

This definition is complicated, however, by the existence of "astroturf" organizations. Like the vividly verdant plastic carpet that masquerades as lawn, astroturf groups are "synthetic creation[s]" (Brulle 2000, 91) that are not structured so as to allow true representation of the community's voice but are instead controlled by the corporations or governments against which genuine grassroots groups are struggling. Often created by a public relations firm, these "front groups," like a ventriloquist's dummy, can make it appear that the community is publicly promoting the corporation's message and aims (Beder 1998). This can sow doubt in people's minds and thus call into question the grassroots movement's legitimacy (Cho et al. 2011). However, instead of a strict dichotomy between grassroots and astroturf, the reality is a complex continuum, with most groups falling, or sliding, somewhere between the two extremes (Brulle 2000), due to a reliance on at least some sources of funding or political support, or a sensitivity to political pressure, whether exogenous or endogenous, that make them vulnerable to co-optation (see Horowitz this volume).

The term "environmental," in this context, seems an obvious reference to a concern for the biotic and abiotic elements that compose one's natural surroundings. However, it too is subject to controversy as different groups have different conceptions of the "environment" and its value. The environmental concerns of rural communities, especially in the developing world, revolve around availability of the natural resources upon which they rely heavily for subsistence and livelihood. In industrialized or industrializing nations, parallel environmental concerns emerge regarding the availability of clean air and water, which are threatened by polluting industries (see Andrews and McCarthy, this volume; Valdivia, this volume). Poor and minority neighborhoods bear a disproportionate burden of these threats, as hazardous facilities are more likely to be located in their communities (Mohai, Pellow, and Roberts 2009; Bond, this volume). However, relatively wealthy communities, whether in the Global North or South, may also face threats to their own environmental health and well-being. These may include the siting of locally unwanted land uses (LULUs), but may also encompass more generalized anxieties stemming from what has increasingly become a "risk society" (Beck 1992) – a world filled with mysterious hazards generated by novel technologies (see Freeman et al., this volume).

Finally, the term "governance" has been defined in many ways within many different disciplinary fields, but generally refers to the "steering, managing, controlling or guiding" of some aspect of society (Kooiman 1993, 2). This concept emerged in recognition of a progressive "hollowing-out" of the nation-state (Jessop 1993) – a shift from "government" to "governance," from purely formal to a mixture of formal and informal systems of rule (Rosenau 1992). In the 1990s, scholars began to recognize that regulatory power was shifting simultaneously toward both supra-national and local scales, through a process termed "glocalization" (Swyngedouw 2000). Agencies operating at a global level – including international financial institutions such as the World Bank and the International Monetary Fund, but also non-governmental organizations like WWF and Greenpeace, and transnational corporations like BP and Monsanto – were accumulating wealth and influence and thus becoming ever more salient on the world scene. Meanwhile, sub-national scales of government, such as municipalities and regions, were gaining their own voice on the international stage (Hobbs 1994; Fry 1998). Its powers usurped from both above and below, the state was further subjected to pressure from within. On one side were the advocates of neoliberalism, who sought – often successfully – to encourage a transition to a minimalist state that would embrace deregulation and privatization, along with reductions in taxes (and, concomitantly, the social services they fund). This move was facilitated by a severe financial crisis that hit nations around the world in the 1980s and '90s, leaving governments with less fiscal and political power.

On the other side was civil society, with which the government had begun to share responsibility for provision of the public services that it could no longer afford (Pierre 2000), and which had begun to view the nation-state as unable to cope with the demands traditionally made of it (Birch 1984). Many of these grassroots actors also viewed the state as ill placed to address urgent challenges that were revealing themselves to be global in scale, such as world hunger and environmental degradation. While some activists envisioned a world government, others advocated greater decentralization of power (Wapner 1996). Social movements have largely bypassed the government by placing pressure directly on corporations and international institutions while taking advantage of the increased opportunities for networking with other activists around the world (Keck and Sikkink 1998; Upton, this volume) and for the rapid public dissemination of information, all facilitated by the "Internet age" (Castells 1996). At the same time, as non-government actors build their own capacity to govern, states have begun governing through them by funding, encouraging, and supporting their actions (Sending and Neumann 2006). Because of the increasing "disaggregation" of authority structures, including not only governments but also a variety of non-governmental institutions, it is no longer possible to envision a purely top-down solution to governance problems, particularly environmental issues (Rosenau 2005).

Environmental governance involves decision-making, by both state and non-state actors, about the management and distribution of natural resources and their associated ecological services, as well as of environmental harms such as pollution and the risk of industrial disaster (see Lemos and Agrawal 2006; Watts, this volume). Because of their complexity and the diversity of interests, concerns, and perspectives involved, environmental issues tend to be "wicked problems" (Rittel and Webber 1973) with no clear-cut or widely agreed-upon solutions. Efforts to address such multi-faceted issues require engaging a wide range of stakeholders, including governments at a range of scales, NGOs, corporations, and civil society (Newell, Pattberg, and Schroeder 2012). In the wake of widespread perceptions of governments' failure to address social problems adequately, as discussed earlier, non-state actors have begun to play a greater role in environmental governance. This, in turn, has raised questions about the legitimacy of such institutions (Biermann and Gupta 2011; Horowitz, this volume), which emerge through unofficial and generally non-democratic processes. On the other hand, grassroots action can sometimes mobilize more citizens than formal procedures (Bulkeley and Moser 2007).

### Emergence, relationships, outcomes of grassroots engagements

What sparks grassroots mobilizations, and what forms do grassroots movements take? Social movement theory has long explained the emergence of collective action as couched in deep discontent with social, economic and/or political conditions, and often triggered by particular "precipitating factors" (Smelser 1962), such as a sudden event, "imposition," or "demand" that clashes with socio-cultural norms and that affects many people (Moore 1966, 474). Leadership, too, is often important in catalysing grassroots action (Allport 1924; Smelser 1962), particularly when it can build on newly emerging identities and a sense of solidarity based in shared grievances (Tarrow 2011). Given the complexities of communities, composed of "multiple and contradictory constituencies and alliances" (Watts 2000, 268), and including members with various, contingent identities (Robertson 1984), a common identity may need to be forged, or "imagined" into existence (Anderson 1983). Such solidarity may emerge when communities come together, in the face of industrial expansion, to claim rights (e.g. to employment or compensation), or to demand justice (e.g. for social and/or environmental impacts) (Ballard and Banks 2003).

However, environmental resistance does not always arise. Development, particularly of lucrative natural resources like petroleum or diamonds, may also lead to communities to be "unimagined" (Watts 2004) as tensions flare over the unequal distributions of benefits, or even expectations that this will occur (Hirsch 1996; Bebbington et al. 2008). Community members may disagree about the relative merits of jobs and of the natural resources that the industrial activity places at risk, and which may represent to them not only a source of long-term livelihood security but also the basis of their cultural identity (Horowitz 2010). Meanwhile, where industries provide the community with a meagre income, people may feel that they have no choice but to accept the associated pollution (Auyero and Swistun 2009). Village elites may even attempt to suppress local activism against a corporation that they see as promising development (Welker 2009). A pragmatic "environmentalism of the poor" (Martinez-Alier 2014), depending on circumstances, may manifest itself as resistance to the environmental impacts of industry, or acquiescence to them (Auyero and Swistun 2009). Poor people's environmental engagements, driven by basic needs, stand in contrast to the "ecology of affluence," characterized as a "luxury, leisure-time concern" (Guha 1997). A mainly urban and middle-class form of environmentalism, it often centers on distant ecosystems (Brockington 2008), viewed as "wilderness" with intrinsic value independent of its usefulness to humans. However, relatively affluent communities may also be concerned about the health implications, for themselves or others, of industrial expansion.

Sometimes these different types of environmentalism encounter one another. Different groups, defined by class, location, and often ethnicity, may seek to work together toward overlapping goals, such as resistance to industrial activity (Bond, this volume). Indeed, grassroots activists' relative powerlessness obliges them to forge an array of shifting alliances. However, these alliances may encounter obstacles due to differences in environmental understandings (West 2006), economic needs (Freeman et al., this volume), agendas (Kosek 2006; Upton, this volume), positionalities (Perreault, this volume), or power dynamics (Baviskar 1995), or simply a sense of cultural incompatibility (Little 2012). Yet they may also succeed in achieving shared objectives (Grossman 2003). Successful collaborations require the development, over time, of mutual understanding, trust, and respect, along with a willingness to "hybridize" discourses and even identities (Pirkey

2012), in favor of collaborative strategies that recognize both the intrinsic value of species and spaces and also local groups' "intertwined environmental, cultural, and political concerns" (Willow 2012).

Finally, grassroots structures and strategies, and the politico-economic context within which they operate, all play a part in determining the outcomes of grassroots engagements with industry. One important tool in movement-building is framing: talking about grievances and proposing solutions in ways that earn others' sympathies, unite people from disparate backgrounds and forge new identities in the process, and ultimately motivate people to participate in collective actions (Benford and Snow 2000). Grassroots campaigns often encompass a wide array of strategies, including media outreach (vastly facilitated by the Internet), lawsuits, and demonstrations. Perhaps the most important approaches are innovative, quickly-adapting actions that directly disrupt the opponent's normal activities (McAdam 2010), such as road blocks or destruction of equipment. These types of disruption require a great deal of energy and entail significant personal risk, and so as time wears on they tend to die down in favor of more institutionalized, legally acceptable actions such as lobbying and publicity (Tarrow 2011). On one hand, a loose, non-hierarchical, "rhizomic" structure is able to act quickly and adapt flexibly, and is free from the constraints that inhibit more hierarchical, "arborescent" institutions that often depend upon relationships with state governments or corporations (Horowitz 2016). On the other hand, as grassroots organizations grow, they build infrastructure that allows continuity, streamlines decision-making, and can attract resources and support. However, as organizations become increasingly bureaucratized, sometimes even seeking funding from the very elites they target, they lose the ability to aggressively pursue their original goals (Michels 1962 [1911]; Piven and Cloward 1977; Schwartz, Rosenthal, and Schwartz 1981). Meanwhile, a more radicalized subgroup may split apart and continue to engage in direct actions (see Upton, this volume), which can grow increasingly violent. Violence, while a useful threat, runs the risk of discouraging sympathy for the cause (Horowitz 2009), and also of attracting severe repression (Tarrow 2011). Of course, the degree of repression will depend upon the extant socio-political context, or "political opportunity structure" (Meyer 2004), including the degree of openness of the government and broader society – or the degree to which activists are able to frame their struggles so as to create openness – to the proposed changes.

## The chapters

The chapters in Part 1, Strategies, examine some forms that grassroots engagements with industry can take, tactics that they may involve, and the outcomes of these approaches. In Chapter 2, "Mapping Ecologies of Resistance," Leah Temper and Joan Martinez-Alier provide an overview of grassroots activism, with a focus on strategies and their effects within the different contexts in which this activism occurs. Temper and Martinez-Alier describe the Global Atlas of Environmental Justice (EJ Atlas; accessible online at ejatlas.org), a compilation of data from approximately (as of 2016) 1,700 socio-environmental conflicts around the world. This atlas is the product of Environmental Justice Organisations, Liabilities and Trade (EJOLT), a research project that aims to document and analyze conflicts over the distribution of environmental "goods" and "bads" in order to combat environmental racism at a global scale. As Temper and Martinez-Alier show, in analyzing the data in the EJ Atlas, several patterns become clear. First, environmental justice (EJ) struggles involve a disproportionate number of indigenous communities. Additionally, indigenous communities involved in these struggles are far more likely to suffer violent responses to their actions than are non-indigenous communities. However, the EJ Atlas also points to positive changes in approaches to fighting environmental injustices. For one, although groups in resistance commonly draw upon "classic and traditional protest methods", they are also using more innovative strategies, which are able to spread through activist networks and the media. These new techniques include community-organized consultations or referenda, court cases involving legal appeals to the rights of nature (recognized in Ecuador's constitution since 2008), financial divestment and shareholder activism. Further, activists have created a new vocabulary to frame their actions, with terms such as "ecological debt", "popular epidemiology", and "*Buen Vivir*". This new terminology has entered into the popular consciousness, and in particular has been accepted by academics and policy makers, playing a role in the reconceptualization of EJ concerns. Meanwhile, the EJ Atlas also demonstrates that projects that are relatively mobile, such as tourism or waste management projects, are easier for activists to stop, and that the conflicts that arise around these mobile projects are lower in intensity than conflicts over projects involving immobile resources, such as mines or hydroelectric projects. Not surprising, but important to highlight, is the EJ Atlas's insight that for any project, the earlier the resistance begins, the more likely the project is to be stopped. Finally, the EJ Atlas reveals that resource politics are no longer implemented along party lines, especially in Latin America; even "post-neoliberal leftist politicians" have pursued a neo-extractivist model of economic development, although this may lead to inequitable distribution of environmental harms. Ultimately, as Temper and Martinez-Alier claim, the EJ Atlas points to the global nature of the environmental justice movement, through shared concerns and ever-tightening linkages.

Next, in Chapter 3, "Red–Green Alliance-Building against Durban's Port-petrochemical Complex Expansion," Patrick Bond discusses strategies used to counter a proposed project in South Africa that would expand Durban's port-petrochemical complex to eight times its current capacity, vastly worsening the already-serious health threats to neighboring residents, who are mainly people of color – Africans, Indians, and Colored people. These residents have banded together into the South Durban Community Environmental Alliance (SDCEA). They strive to counter the government's framing of the project as providing desperately needed jobs with their own framing of the project as causing devastating social and environmental disruption. These communities have already endured environmental racism; in 2007–2014, the South African rail, port and pipeline company Transnet doubled its oil pipeline capacity and also re-routed it away from mostly-white Durban suburbs through mostly black, low-income neighborhoods. SDCEA has highlighted this injustice, along with a general lack of opportunity for public input regarding industrial expansion. More recently, in fighting the port-petrochemical complex expansion, they have pointed to its potential displacement of farming communities, the damage to the estuarine bay that would result, government failure to cope with the risk or reality of pipeline leaks, the implications of such large-scale industrialization for climate change, and the economic irrationality of creating more infrastructure than is ever likely to be used. In addition to informing the public, SDCEA has testified in court against Transnet, organized peaceful protests, and – most powerfully – campaigned for financial sanctions against the company. The activist group can boast of several past successes, including shutting down toxic landfills and forcing oil refineries to install $SO_2$ scrubbers; however, they were unable to stop Transnet's pipeline rerouting and expansion, and are generally up against far more powerful forces than they can muster themselves. In conclusion, Bond calls for greater attempts to forge alliances among local residents, labor movements, and environmentalists in combatting not only this but all instances of capitalism's social, environmental, and economic excesses.

In Chapter 4, "Indigenous by Association: Legitimation and Grassroots Engagements with Multinational Mining in New Caledonia," Leah Horowitz discusses the strategic use of such alliances, but also the pitfalls they may entail, through a study of conflicts over a multinational mining and refinery project in New Caledonia, a French possession in the South Pacific. In the early 2000s, environmental concerns led to the formation of several grassroots organizations, including Rhéébù Nùù, an indigenous Kanak group that formed specifically to "keep an eye on" this mining and refinery project, then known as Goro Nickel and run by the Canadian multinational, Inco. While not seeking to shut the project down, the group aimed to ensure it would minimize harm to the environment while providing the maximum number of jobs for local residents. Its actions ranged from distributing pamphlets to legal action, and even roadblocks that turned violent when armed police arrived. Rhéébù Nùù needed to establish its legitimacy in the eyes of fellow Kanak, as well as in the international arena. It did so through a strategic association with customary authorities. Even after the two local chiefs who had founded the group in 2002 both passed away in 2004, Rhéébù Nùù continued to claim that it represented local chieftainships. In a context of deep distrust of the government, which many Kanak saw as failing to protect them from a rapacious multinational, the customary authorities' legitimacy was paramount. However, Rhéébù Nùù leaders were not the only ones to realize the importance of customary legitimacy. Non-indigenous environmental grassroots groups also tried to capture this legitimacy, by associating themselves with Rhéébù Nùù, thus – unconsciously – forming a "chain" of legitimacy that originated with the customary authorities. In 2008, Vale, who two years earlier had purchased Inco and taken over the project, realized that it could undercut Rhéébù Nùù's legitimacy by negotiating directly with the customary authorities themselves. Indeed, over the last few years, the customary authorities had begun to feel that the group no longer represented them. Younger members, sometimes acting independently of their leaders, often expressed a goal of shutting the project down; this contrasted with their elders' interest in the employment opportunities the project offered, for these very youth. Taking advantage of this growing rift, Vale brought the customary authorities to the negotiating table. Their presence effectively silenced Rhéébù Nùù, which still based its legitimacy in the claim that it simply represented the customary authorities. These negotiations also excluded the non-indigenous environmentalists, who were not invited to participate. In 2008, all three parties signed an agreement in which the company pledged to fund local development initiatives, to create a "Consultative Customary Environmental Committee" (CCCE), to train local "environmental technicians", and to reforest other companies' long-abandoned mine sites, without addressing any of its own environmental impacts, in exchange for Rhéébù Nùù's promise not to engage in any further violent actions. Thus, this chapter shows that alliances, particularly with indigenous authorities, may confer legitimacy in very powerful ways, yet may also leave their allies (here, the non-indigenous environmentalists) vulnerable to shifting power dynamics and social relationships.

This leads us into Part 2, Relationships, whose chapters share a concern with the factors that shape connections among activists, communities, governments, and corporations, and ways that these interactions and mutual perceptions – whether friendly, hostile, or a mixture of both – in turn shape the activism itself. Chapter 5, "Governing from the Ground Up? Translocal Networks and the Ambiguous Politics of Environmental Justice in Bolivia," focuses on the often-strained relationships between communities and the activists who aim to represent their concerns about environmental damage from industry. Tom Perreault examines a grassroots environmental justice network, CORIDUP (Coordinadora en Defensa de las Cuencas del Río Desaguadero y Lagos Uru Uru y Poopó), in Bolivia's Oruro department. CORIDUP formed in the early 2000s to protest the release of untreated waste, over nearly a century, into the Huanuni River by the state mining corporation COMIBOL (Corporación Minera de Bolivia), which has resulted in extreme soil and water contamination. CORIDUP organized various actions, including a march from Oruro to the capital, La Paz. CORIDUP's very emergence, not to mention its legal recognition in 2006, marked the beginning of a sea change in the Bolivian government's approach to grassroots resistance to mining, given the state's long-standing support for mining regardless of environmental and social costs, and its repression of earlier protest actions. Yet at the same time, an ambiguous and tense relationship to mining is characteristic of the country as a whole, even at the grassroots. Thus, CORIDUP found itself struggling not only to oppose the harmful effects of mining, but also to negotiate the tensions between the various stakeholder groups involved. Pressured by communities to force the government to take action, and by the government to urge communities to be patient with the process, CORIDUP is also dependent upon international NGOs, foreign researchers, and even the Catholic Church. These latter relationships provide the organization with funding, information, technical and logistical support, and legitimacy, but also elicit community members' suspicions that the activists are receiving personal benefits or at least are in league with government officials or "outsiders". Most importantly, the group is forced to walk a fine line between environmental activism and recognition of mining's economic and historico-political importance to this poverty-stricken region. Indeed, social mobilization in the Bolivian Andes has not been to oppose mining but rather to demand more control over it. This translates into communities' mixed feelings regarding CORIDUP; many local residents, in a context of governmental neglect and scarce employment alternatives, have tacitly accepted severe ecological degradation in return for a meagre livelihood. Meanwhile, miners' unions are hostile to CORIDUP and have accused it of threatening the local, mining-based, economy. This context has forced CORIDUP to insist that it is not advocating an end to mining but, rather, "responsible mining" that follows environmental laws. Nonetheless, CORIDUP's organizing efforts played a key role in securing, in 2009, a presidential decree of "environmental emergency" in the department's Huanuni River Valley, which mandated environmental remediation. This was a first for anthropogenic pollution in Bolivia. Thus, Perreault's chapter illustrates the ways that politico-economic factors can shape communities' multiple and conflicting concerns about industrial activity, and their relationships with even local, working-class, grassroots activists who seek to represent them.

Chapter 6, "Between Sacrifice and Compensation: Collective Action and the Aftermath of Oil Disaster in Esmeraldas, Ecuador," provides insights into how apparent tensions within an activist community can obscure oppression by governments and corporations. The community that Gabriela Valdivia describes – La Propicia Uno, a neighborhood within Esmeraldas, a coastal city in northwest Ecuador – suffered tremendous environmental pollution from a refinery operated by the state-owned oil company, Petroecuador. The refinery was built in 1977, and beginning in the 1980s, people settled right up to the boundaries of the refinery property, in informal – and often illegal – shantytowns. There, they suffer from a lack of municipal services and pollution from the refinery, but have nowhere else to go. Many depend on employment with the company for a meager livelihood. Although most neighborhoods remain informal, La Propicia Uno used patronage networks to achieve incorporation as an urban parish in 1996. Two years later, a gasoline leak from the refinery resulted in a devastating fire that destroyed 60 homes and killed over 100 people. Survivors sued Petroecuador; over time, nearly all of the neighborhoods renounced their struggle, but La Propicia Uno persisted. Like the Bolivian activists that Perreault describes (this volume), La Propicia Uno residents also scored a "first" for environmental justice. In 2002, for the first time in Latin America, grassroots activists won a lawsuit against an oil company, as Petroecuador was sentenced to pay $11 million in compensation and mitigation projects. However, La Propicia Uno's story swung from great victory to tragedy as the compensation was fought over within the community, misused, and remained largely unallocated. At first glance the cause seems to be "internal heterogeneities" within the community, which is part of the story. Able to join together against the company, the community later suffered from vicious infighting and individuals' personal leadership styles became a source of controversy. Scratching the surface, though, we discover that the community's relationships with outsiders played a key role in inhibiting proper use of the compensation. The government and Petroecuador ultimately retained crucial decision-making power over how the funds could be used. Community members were not allowed to provide any funds to individuals, nor to use them for anything that could change the prevailing socio-economic system. Instead, they could only request public works, and could not even decide who would provide these services, so that the monies were largely frittered away by a mishmash of misguided contractors. These restrictions maintained the community's dependency on the company in the same way that people's need for employment with the company prevented them from seeking more radical change (cf. Auyero and Swistun 2009). Meanwhile, NGOs allied with the community, just like Petroecuador, used community tensions as an excuse to step away from the struggle. Thus, Valdivia's contribution points to the importance of political and economic forces in constraining the outcomes of activism into maintenance of the status quo, while making this result appear to be due to the choices, and the failings, of the activists themselves.

In Chapter 7, "From Contested Cotton to the Ban on Brinjal: India's Shifting Risk Narratives in Opposition to Genetically Engineered Agriculture," Julia Freeman, Terre Satterfield, and Milind Kandlikar also explore relationships between activists and communities, through an analysis of debates over the risks and benefits of genetically engineered (GE) crops in India. Concerned about declining agricultural yields and rising production costs, the government of India has embraced the promise of a technological solution offered by GE crops that are resistant to pests, but this has faced resistance from civil society. The authors analyze three "risk narratives" that have arisen around GE crops and examine how these narratives have evolved, particularly in relation to urban activists' descriptions of the rural farmers they claim to represent, and the two groups' often very different concerns and agendas. The first narrative, social justice, began with a portrayal of the farmers as helpless victims of multinational biotechnology and agri-chemical companies, particularly Monsanto. However, the farmers in fact eagerly embraced GE crops, illegally planting or hybridizing Bt cottonseed before its regulatory approval, which they demanded. In response, the narrative shifted to a depiction of the farmers as manipulated and misled. As Bt cotton became commercialized, the narrative shifted again, to one of agronomic integrity, i.e., debates over crop yields and environmental impacts. Pointing to the poor performance of Bt cotton, despite farmers' ever-increasing cultivation of it in the hope of economic benefits, urban activists continued to paint these farmers as victims of aggressive corporate tactics. Failing to gain much traction, the anti-GE focus finally switched from cotton to food, in particular eggplant – widely grown and consumed by poor farmers – and to a narrative of health risks and the importance of consumer choice. This narrative did achieve more purchase than had the others and resulted in a moratorium on Bt eggplant; ironically, this may have been because it touched upon the anxieties of middle-class consumers, and because the eggplant farmers were too poor and too dispersed to pressure the government into authorizing this GE crop. Freeman et al. argue that, in line with the economic transition it is experiencing, India is going through a "risk transition" in which concerns about traditional risks, i.e. conditions that threaten people's ability to fulfill their basic needs, are gradually giving way to anxieties surrounding "late modern risks" from newer technologies related to various industries. However, not all social sectors are transitioning simultaneously, with urban middle classes worrying about the latter form of risk while poorer rural citizens need to focus on the former. In the case of GE crops, the two types of risk are at odds; acting on their fears of the late modern risks associated with biotechnology, urban activists claim to represent farmers' interests, yet ignore the very real concerns and desires of the rural poor who struggle to make ends meet. Thus, like those discussed in Perreault's and Valdivia's chapters, the communities described in this chapter need to provide for their basic needs first; environmental concerns are important to them but, by necessity, a secondary priority. Here, Freeman et al. demonstrate that in their struggles against the environmental risks posed by industry, activists' agendas may compete with, and conceal, communities' interest in the relief from severe poverty that this industry promises.

The chapters in Part 3, Internal Dynamics, reveal the diversity of backgrounds, opinions, and motivations among seemingly similar or homogeneous communities' engagements with instances of industrial expansion. Caroline Upton's Chapter 8, "Contesting Development: Pastoralism, Mining and Environmental Politics in Mongolia," focuses on tensions internal to grassroots mining resistance in Mongolia. Uranium mining is currently transforming the country's economy, but seriously impacting herders by degrading pastureland, cutting off migration routes, and restricting access to winter pastures and shelters. Resistance first emerged in 2001, with the Onggi River Movement (ORM). Five years later, ten more grassroots groups had appeared, and they united to form the Mongolian Nature Protection Coalition (MNPC). As the movement expanded, so did its area of concern. Activists moved from demands for the restoration of local river basins to broader and more politically charged issues regarding pastureland governance and citizens' rights in the context of mining, and to more politically engaged strategies. The movement also forged relationships internationally. In 2006, in response to a variety of environmental and economic concerns about mining from investors, activists, government officials, and mining companies, the Asia Foundation organized a Multi-Stakeholder Forum on Responsible Mining (MSF). However, a larger and broader movement also provided scope for differences of opinion. By 2008, the MNPC had split. A small subset of more radical groups rejected the Asia Foundation's discourse of "responsible mining", broke with the MSF, began to threaten violence against company property, and formed a new umbrella organization, the United Movement of Mongolian Rivers and Lakes (UMMRL). Others, who continued to embrace more mainstream approaches, created the Mongolian Nature Protection Civil Movement Coalition (MNPCM). Nonetheless, these irreconcilable differences concerned tactics rather than goals. All of the various grassroots groups sought not to ban mining but rather to see it regulated appropriately, and all agreed that this would involve several crucial elements: land rights, particularly for herders; the creation of active, engaged "environmental citizens" with rights to the land and its mineral and natural wealth, but also responsibilities toward these; community participation in decision-making, couched in culturally-inflected understandings of shared stewardship of the "motherland"; and respect for the spiritual dimensions of the landscape, including both Buddhist and Shamanic belief systems, which were re-emerging in the post-Soviet era. Ultimately, Upton's chapter highlights micropolitical disagreements that can occur within grassroots movements, but also points to the importance of shared cultural values, interests, and concerns in shaping engagements with industrial expansion.

In Chapter 9, "Micropolitics in the Marcellus Shale," Eleanor Andrews and James McCarthy provide a crucial reminder that grassroots actors do not always unite to pressure corporations to reduce the environmental impacts of their activities; they may instead come together to negotiate better financial outcomes for themselves, and to exert more control over industrial expansion. Andrews and McCarthy examine the landowner coalitions that emerged in rural Pennsylvania in response to extraction of natural gas through hydraulic fracturing ("fracking") in the Marcellus Shale. Landowners formed these coalitions in order to bargain collectively when the gas industry came knocking on their doors looking to lease land for drilling. However, despite this apparent unity, the most salient characteristic of these coalitions was their diversity. They varied greatly in many dimensions, particularly in number of coalition members, area of land owned, and leadership styles and modes of organization, and they also operated within a variety of local politico-legislative contexts. Similarly, the outcomes of their negotiations varied tremendously, notably in terms of monetary compensation. Meanwhile, homeowners who did not own enough land, or land the drilling companies wanted to lease, were excluded from negotiation processes and from the coalitions. These coalitions were composed of individuals with different views on fracking; some saw it as an economic and environmental boon, many were indifferent to the environmental effects and sought financial advantage, and a few were unenthusiastic about the drilling but hoped to gain more control over the process or at least earn some money if they could not stop it. Within the groups, individuals had varying degrees of influence, due in part to the group's leadership (whether more democratic or autocratic) and in part to social relations within the community. Despite this diversity, all coalitions – even those whose members harbored concerns about fracking – ended up taking a pro-drilling stance, in some cases by ostracizing members who opposed it. Reasons for this included the region's relatively high rates of poverty and unemployment, and its low incomes, educational levels, and alternative economic opportunities. Perhaps more pertinent was the looming threat of "forced pooling", a process similar to eminent domain, by which land may be seized for development. Additionally, fracking benefited from a favorable regulatory environment in Pennsylvania (unlike neighboring New York), possibly because the corporations had contributed generously to politicians' campaigns. These two factors led landowners to feel that drilling was inevitable. Nonetheless, the coalitions did succeed in gaining higher royalties, stronger protections for the environment and for landowners, and more influence in the way the development was carried out. Thus, Andrews and McCarthy remind us that local residents may sometimes embrace environmentally-harmful industrial expansion, and that there are economic and political factors behind their decisions, but also that their engagements must be analyzed in light of the diversity and micropolitics inherent to local communities.

Finally, in Part 4, Politics, Michael Watts provides a broader vision of social issues surrounding industrial expansion in Chapter 10, "Accumulating Security and Risk Along the Energy Frontier." He discusses how energy, and particularly oil, became entangled in the national security debate in ways that, ironically, led to extreme risk-taking and ultimately environmental disaster. On April 20, 2010, the Macondo oil well in the Gulf of Mexico exploded into flames, killing 11 workers, and proceeded to leak oil into the gulf for nearly three months until it was finally sealed. Clean-up efforts, to the tune of billions of dollars, continued over the next four years. Yet less than a year after the disaster, the Obama administration announced its new American energy security "blueprint", of which oil and gas development was a cornerstone. Moreover, a moratorium imposed on drilling in the Gulf had lasted only six months. Watts points to the irony of the fact that "securitization" – putatively the deliberate avoidance of risk, here the threat of a dearth of cheap oil – actually led to the neoliberalization of risk, through the weakening of regulatory oversight accompanied by corporate corner-cutting to minimize safety-related costs in the pursuit of profit. Ultimately, lives (of the oil rig workers) and livelihoods (of Gulf Coast fisherfolk) were sacrificed on the altar of the oil-dependent American lifestyle.

## Conclusions

*Grassroots Environmental Governance* paints a picture of the diversity of community responses to industry, yet also indicates patterns and commonalities in grassroots engagements. Here, we return to the core questions that animate the chapters. First, what motivates grassroots engagements with industry? The contributions demonstrate that these engagements may arise from a variety of motivations. Several of the chapters describe poor communities that suffer from, and resist, industrial pollution. Often, as Bond's chapter exemplifies, these are communities of color fighting environmental racism. In particular, Temper and Martinez-Alier's chapter highlights how indigenous communities are often involved in environmental justice (EJ) struggles, fighting for lands and resources that represent not only economic but also cultural and spiritual value. Theirs is a special form of EJ activism, as they are demanding not equal treatment with mainstream society but recognition of their unique knowledge and rights, including the right to self-determination as acknowledged by the United Nations and other international bodies.

Second, what happens when different groups, whose engagements with industry stem from different motivations, come into contact? Notably, the concerns of the poor may differ sharply from those of the relatively affluent. As the chapters by Horowitz, Perreault, and Valdivia make clear, poor communities often must prioritize daily needs in their struggles simply to get by. While community members might have deep-seated anxieties about the environmental impacts of industry, their resistance is often constrained by its economic importance, particularly in terms of the employment opportunities it represents. Relatively affluent groups, in contrast, such as those described by Freeman et al., have the "luxury" of worrying about more long-term effects of industry, such as potential health risks from new technologies. Sometimes, these concerns coincide, allowing groups from different backgrounds to work together, such as in the case of the South Durban Community Environmental Alliance described by Bond. However, these different concerns may also come into conflict. In such cases, as the contributions show, power dynamics at the national scale help determine the outcomes of such tensions. Sometimes, poor communities' needs for the economic benefits of industrial development take precedence over environmental activists' concerns. As in the Bolivian community that Perreault discusses, environmental activists may have to temper their message in response to local communities' and labor unions' insistence on the economic importance of industry. Environmentalists may even be excluded from the debate, particularly when negotiations about industrial activity involve indigenous communities, which have widely recognized political and moral legitimacy, as Horowitz's chapter demonstrates for New Caledonia. Similarly, Freeman et al. show that activists may be unable to counter communities' demands when these match industry's goals, as anti-GE activists in India discovered. However, in some cases, the balance of power may favor urban anti-industry activists; in Freeman et al.'s study, the purchasing power of middle-class consumers proved stronger than the voices of impoverished eggplant farmers. Finally, the chapter by Andrews and McCarthy implicitly calls into question any clear-cut divide between "wealthy" and "poor" communities. The grassroots mobilization they describe takes place in rural Pennsylvania, not as destitute as many places in the developing world, yet where people are eager to improve their modest incomes. This chapter shows that even when communities are not desperate for employment, they may still choose to dismiss the risk of environmental harm in favor of their desires for control over industrial expansion – which they may view as inevitable – and for favorable financial outcomes for themselves, in the absence of many viable alternatives.

Third, how do relationships, both between grassroots communities and other actors, and within grassroots groups themselves, influence goals and strategies? The economic incentives promised by industry play a huge role in shaping grassroots engagements, but this volume's contributions show that companies may use other strategies to manipulate communities into accepting their activities, such as the ideological capture (in this case, of indigenous legitimacy) portrayed in Horowitz's chapter. Meanwhile, political power – which almost always involves industry as well as government actors – also comes to the fore. The regulatory environment, often at least partially shaped by industry contributions to politicians' campaigns, can set parameters that in turn strongly shape grassroots engagements with industry, as the chapter by Andrews and McCarthy makes clear. Moreover, governments may team up with companies to repress grassroots activism, as is widely known; Valdivia's chapter, however, provides a new angle on these tripartite relationships, showing that what appear to be conflicts internal to a grassroots organization – inhibiting action that would benefit the community – may actually mask a refusal by the government and company to relinquish control.

Intra-community conflicts, though, as these chapters demonstrate, can indeed be important determinants of grassroots outcomes. Even in the community Valdivia studied, micropolitical quarrels formed part of the explanation of the grassroots activists' failure to turn an unprecedented victory over an oil company into material benefits for the community. Upton, too, shows how internal disagreements can plague grassroots movements, impelling groups to split apart when they are unable to agree on strategies (e.g. more mainstream vs. more radical approaches) even when they largely agree on goals (in this case, appropriate regulation of uranium mining and land rights for herders) and values (here, land stewardship and spirituality-based respect for the land). Furthermore, as Horowitz's chapter shows, companies can capitalize on internecine tensions, practicing a "divide-and-conquer" diplomacy in which, by strengthening their own relationships with one community sector (here, customary authorities), they can severely weaken the position of other sectors that oppose the project – even if these opponents comprise the majority of community members. On a more optimistic note, as Bond's chapter illustrates, positive relationships within and among grassroots communities can be essential in building strong resistance to environmental injustices.

Beyond examining relationships within or among communities, and those between communities, governments, and companies, the chapters provide insights into the crucial, yet often problematic, nature of alliances among different interest groups, such as between GROs and international institutions. Inevitably, these relationships are fraught with power imbalances; as Perrault's chapter makes clear, international NGOs and institutions can share some of their – far greater – resources with grassroots groups, but can also make the latter dependent on these "outsiders," of whom community members may harbor suspicions. At a national scale, relationships between rural and urban or between indigenous and non-indigenous activists are similarly infused with power relations. Valdivia's chapter shows us that NGOs may abandon grassroots groups just when their assistance is urgently needed. Moreover, while urban-based NGOs often claim to represent poor rural communities, their interests and concerns do not always coincide. When this happens, as Freeman et al.'s chapter evidences, urban activists may push their own agendas, while still discursively portraying themselves as fighting for the interests of rural communities. However, as Horowitz's chapter explains, this strategy may backfire when the impoverished rural groups actually possess sources of legitimacy – such as indigeneity – that the urban activists lack.

Finally, what are the ways that internal and external factors shape outcomes? On one hand, the contributions all include examples of successful activism, i.e.

the attainment of some important goals, despite other disappointments. As the chapter by Temper and Martinez-Alier informs us, some of these successes can be traced to the implementation of cutting-edge strategies, many of which build on increased opportunities provided by the Internet for activists to network and draw attention to their cause. Additionally, their data confirms that resistance that begins earlier in the lifecycle of a project has a greater chance of achieving its goals. However, Temper and Martinez-Alier's chapter also show how conditions that lie beyond grassroots actors' immediate control – e.g. the type of industry involved, or the willingness of the government to use violence – may play a decisive role in determining the results of their actions. Similarly, Horowitz's chapter highlights the company's part in these interactions, and the fact that it may outmaneuver its opponents.

The book argues for the importance of a micropolitical analysis of grassroots environmental governance issues. As a set, the chapters offer a highly nuanced understanding of the motivations of grassroots actors in their engagements with the agents of industry. Community members may be driven by multiple – and often conflicting – needs, not only for natural resources, clean air and water but also for a living wage and sometimes for recognition of indigenous rights. The contributions also emphasize the importance of relationships: power dynamics between relatively poor and relatively affluent citizens; ways that companies attempt to take control of the situation, often in league with governments; the pitfalls of disagreements within the community; and the difficulties of alliances between groups with different interests and agendas. Ultimately, this collection delves into the debates generated by community mobilizations around industrial expansion, at a range of locations around the world and through a variety of disciplinary perspectives, in order to paint a broader picture of grassroots engagements as critical forces in shaping industrial activities on both a local and a global scale. It is our hope that a greater understanding of the politico-economic contexts, social relationships, strategies, and motivations that in turn shape these movements may help to foster further social change.

## References

Allport F. H. (1924) *Social psychology* Houghton Mifflin, Boston.

Anderson B. (1983) *Imagined communities: Reflections on the origin and spread of nationalism* Verso, London.

Atıl Aşıcı A., and Acar S. (2016) "Does income growth relocate ecological footprint?" *Ecological Indicators, 61* 707–14.

Auyero J., and Swistun D. A. (2009) *Flammable: Environmental suffering in an Argentine shantytown* Oxford University Press, Oxford.

Ayres I., and Braithwaite J. (1992) *Responsive regulation: Transcending the deregulation debate* Oxford University Press, Oxford.

Ballard C., and Banks G. (2003) "Resource wars: The anthropology of mining" *Annual Review of Anthropology, 32* 287–313.

Baviskar A. (1995) *In the belly of the river: Tribal conflicts over development in the Narmada Valley* Oxford University Press, Delhi and New York.

Bebbington A., Bebbington D. H., Bury J., Lingan J., Muñoz J. P., and Scurrah M. (2008) "Mining and social movements: Struggles over livelihood and rural territorial development in the Andes" *World Development, 36* 2888–905.

Beck U. (1992) *Risk society: Towards a new modernity* Sage, London.

Beder S. (1998) "Public relations' role in manufacturing artificial grass roots coalitions" *Public Relations Quarterly, 43* 21–23.

Benford R. D., and Snow D. A. (2000) "Framing processes and social movements: An overview and assessment" *Annual Review of Sociology, 26* 611–39.

Biermann F., and Gupta A. (2011) "Accountability and legitimacy in earth system governance: A research framework" *Ecological Economics, 70* 1856–64.

Birch A. H. (1984) "Overload, ungovernability and delegitimation: The theories and the British case" *British Journal of Political Science, 14* 135–60.

Brockington D. (2008) "Powerful environmentalisms: Conservation, celebrity and capitalism" *Media Culture & Society, 30* 551–68.

Brockmyer M., and Fox J. (2015) *Assessing the evidence* Transparency and Accountability Initiative, London.

Brulle R. J. (2000) *Agency, democracy, and nature: The US environmental movement from a critical theory perspective* The MIT Press, Cambridge, MA.

Bulkeley H., and Moser S. C. (2007) "Responding to climate change: Governance and social action beyond Kyoto" *Global Environmental Politics, 7* 1–10.

Burca G., Keohane R., and Sabel C. (2014) *Global experimental governance* Public Law and Legal Theory Working Paper #14–393, Columbia Law School, New York.

Calvano L. (2008) "Multinational corporations and local communities: A critical analysis of conflict" *Journal of Business Ethics, 82* 793–805.

Carothers T., and Brechenmacher S. (2014) *Accountability, transparency, participation and inclusion: A new development consensus?* Working Paper, Carnegie Endowment for Peace, Washington, DC.

Castells M. (1996) *The rise of the network society* Blackwell Publishers, Cambridge, MA.

Cho C. H., Martens M. L., Kim H., and Rodrigue M. (2011) "Astroturfing global warming: It isn't always greener on the other side of the fence" *Journal of Business Ethics, 104* 571–87.

Craig D., and Porter D. (2006) *Development beyond neoliberalism? Governance, poverty reduction and political economy* Routledge, London.

David-Barret L., and Okamura K. (2013) *The transparency paradox* Working Paper 38, European Research Center for Anti-Corruption and State Building, Berlin.

Fry E. H. (1998) *The expanding role of state and local governments in US foreign affairs* Council on Foreign Relations, New York.

Gibson-Graham J. K. (2006 [1996]) *The end of capitalism (as we knew it): A feminist critique of political economy* University of Minnesota Press, Minneapolis.

Gillies A. (2010) "Reputational concerns and the emergence of oil sector transparency as an international norm" *International Studies Quarterly, 54* 103–26.

Gould K. A., Schnaiberg A., and Weinberg A. S. (1996) *Local environmental struggles: Citizen activism in the treadmill of production* Cambridge University Press, Cambridge.

Gouldson A. (2006) "Do firms adopt lower standards in poorer areas? Corporate social responsibility and environmental justice in the EU and the US" *Area, 38* 402–12.

Gouldson A., and Bebbington J. (2007) "Corporations and the governance of environmental risk" *Environment and Planning C, 25* 4–20.

Grossman Z. (2003) "Cowboy and Indian alliances in the northern plains" *Agricultural History, 77* 355–89.

Guha R. (1997) "The environmentalism of the poor" in Fox R. G. and Starn O. eds, *Between resistance and revolution: Cultural politics and social protest* Rutgers University, New Brunswick, New Jersey, and London 17–39.

Harvey D. (1982) *The limits to capital* University of Chicago Press, Chicago.

———. (1989) *The condition of postmodernity: an enquiry into the origins of cultural change* Blackwell, Oxford and New York.

Hilson G. (2012) "Corporate social responsibility in the extractive industries: Experiences from developing countries" *Resources Policy, 37* 131–37.

Hirsch P. (1996) "Dams and compensation in Indo-China" in Howitt R. with Connell J. and Hirsch P. eds, *Resources, nations and indigenous peoples: Case studies from Australasia, Melanesia and Southeast Asia* Oxford University Press, Oxford 212–22.

Hobbs H. H. (1994) *City hall goes abroad: The foreign policy of local politics* SAGE, Thousand Oaks, CA.

Horowitz L. S. (2009) "Environmental violence and crises of legitimacy in New Caledonia" *Political Geography, 28* 248–58.

———. (2010) "Twenty years is yesterday: Science, multinational mining, and the political ecology of trust in New Caledonia" *Geoforum, 41* 617–26.

———. (2012) "Translation alignment: Actor-network theory, resistance, and the power dynamics of alliance in New Caledonia" *Antipode, 44* 806–27.

———. (2015) "Culturally articulated neoliberalization: Corporate social responsibility and the capture of indigenous legitimacy in New Caledonia" *Transactions of the Institute of British Geographers, 40* 88–101.

———. (2016) "Rhizomic resistance meets arborescent assemblage: UNESCO World Heritage and the disempowerment of indigenous activism in New Caledonia" *Annals of the Association of American Geographers, 106* 167–85.

Humphreys D. (2000) "A business perspective on community relations in mining" *Resources Policy, 26* 127–31.

Jessop B. (1993) "Towards a Schumpeterian workfare state? Preliminary remarks on post-fordist political economy" *Studies in Political Economy, 40* 7–39.

Keck M. E., and Sikkink K. (1998) *Activists beyond borders: Advocacy networks in international politics* Cornell University Press, Ithaca, NY.

Kirsch S. (2014) *Mining capitalism* University of California Press, Berkeley.

Kooiman J. (1993) "Socio-political governance: Introduction" in Kooiman J. ed, *Modern governance: New society-government interactions* SAGE, London 1–8.

Kosek J. (2006) *Understories: The political life of forests in northern New Mexico* Duke University Press, Durham and London.

Lemos M. C., and Agrawal A. (2006) "Environmental governance" *Annual Review of Environment and Resources, 31* 297–325.

Little P. C. (2012) "Environmental Justice discomfort and disconnect in IBM's tainted birthplace: A micropolitical ecology perspective" *Capitalism Nature Socialism, 23* 92–109.

Martinez-Alier J. (2014) "The environmentalism of the poor" *Geoforum, 54* 239–41.

McAdam D. (2010) "Tactical innovation and the pace of insurgency" in McAdam D. and Snow D. A. eds, *Readings on social movements: Origins, dynamics, and outcomes.* Second edition Oxford University Press, New York 478–98.

Mercer C. (2002) "NGOs, civil society and democratization: A critical review of the literature" *Progress in Development Studies, 2* 5–22.

Meyer D. S. (2004) "Protest and political opportunities" *Annual Review of Sociology, 30* 125–45.

Michels R. (1962 [1911]) *Political parties: A sociological study of the oligarchical tendencies of modern democracy* Free Press, New York.

Mohai P., Pellow D., and Roberts J. T. (2009) "Environmental justice" *Annual Review of Environment and Resources, 34* 405–30.

Moore B. (1966) *Social origins of dictatorship and democracy: Lord and peasant in the making of the modern world* Beacon Press, Boston.

Newell P., Pattberg P., and Schroeder H. (2012) "Multiactor governance and the environment" *Annual Review of Environment and Resources, 37* 365–87.

O'Faircheallaigh C. (2013) "Community development agreements in the mining industry: An emerging global phenomenon" *Community Development, 44*(2) *1–17*.

O'Sullivan D. (2013) What's the point of transparency. (www.laohamutuk.org/Oil//// EITI/2013/WhatPointTransparencyEn.pdf).

Owen J. R., and Kemp D. (2013) "Social licence and mining: A critical perspective" *Resources Policy, 38* 29–35.

Pargal S., and Wheeler D. (1996) "Informal regulation of industrial pollution in developing countries: Evidence from Indonesia" *Journal of Political Economy, 104* 1314–27.

Peck J., and Tickell A. (2002) "Neoliberalizing space" *Antipode, 34* 380–404.

Pellow D. N., and Brulle R. J. eds. (2005) *Power, justice and the environment: A critical appraisal of the Environmental Justice movement* MIT, Cambridge, Massachusetts and London.

Pierre J. (2000) "Introduction: Understanding governance" in Pierre J. ed, *Debating governance: Authority, steering, and democracy* Oxford University Press, Oxford 1–12.

Pirkey W. M. (2012) "Beyond militant particularisms: Collaboration and hybridization in the 'contact zones' of environmentalism" *Capitalism Nature Socialism, 23* 70–91.

Piven F. F., and Cloward R. A. (1977) *Poor people's movements: Why they succeed, how they fail* Vintage books, New York.

Rauscher M. (2005) "International trade, foreign investment, and the environment" in Mäler K. G. and Vincent J. R. eds, *Handbook of environmental economics* Elsevier, Amsterdam 1403–56.

Reed M. G., and Bruyneel S. (2010) "Rescaling environmental governance, rethinking the state: A three-dimensional review" *Progress in Human Geography, 34* 646–53.

Rittel H. W. J., and Webber M. M. (1973) "Dilemmas in a general theory of planning" *Policy Sciences, 4* 155–69.

Robertson A. F. (1984) *People and the state: An anthropology of planned development* Cambridge University Press, Cambridge.

Rosenau J. N. (1992) "Governance, order, and change in world politics" in Rosenau J. N. and Czempiel E. O. eds, *Governance without government: Order and change in world politics* Cambridge University Press, Cambridge 1–9.

———. (2005) "Globalisation and governance: Sustainability between fragmentation and integration" in Petschow U., Rosenau J. N. and von Weizsäcker E. U. eds, *Governance and sustainability: New challenges for states, companies and civil society* Greenleaf Publishing, Sheffield 20–38.

Sadler D. (2004) "Anti-corporate campaigning and corporate 'social' responsibility: Towards alternative spaces of citizenship?" *Antipode, 36* 851–70.

Schnaiberg A. (1980) *The environment: From surplus to scarcity* Oxford University Press, New York.

Schwartz M., Rosenthal N., and Schwartz L. (1981) "Leader-member conflict in protest organizations: The case of the Southern Farmers' Alliance" *Social Problems, 29* 22–36.

Sending O. J., and Neumann I. B. (2006) "Governance to governmentality: Analyzing NGOs, states, and power" *International Studies Quarterly*, 50 651–72.

Shaxson N. (2009) *Just a glorious audit? Nigeria's Extractive Industries Transparency Initiative* Chatham House, London.

Smelser N. J. (1962) *Theory of collective behavior* The Free Press, New York.

Sovacool B. K., Walter, G., Van de Graaf, T. and Andrews, N. (2016) "Energy governance, transnational rules, and the resource curse: Exploring the effectiveness of the Extractive Industries Transparency Initiative (EITI)" *World Development*, 83 179–92.

Springer S. (2011) "Articulated neoliberalism: The specificity of patronage, kleptocracy, and violence in Cambodia's neoliberalization" *Environment and Planning A*, 43 2554–70.

Swyngedouw E. (2000) "The Marxian alternative: Historical-geographical materialism and the political economy of capitalism" in Sheppard E. and Barnes T. J. eds, *A companion to economic geography* Blackwell, Oxford 41–59.

Tarrow S. G. (2011) *Power in movement: Social movements and contentious politics* Cambridge University Press, Cambridge.

Wapner P. (1996) *Environmental activism and world civic politics* State University of New York Press, Albany.

Watts M. (2000) "Political ecology" in Sheppard E. and Barnes T. J. eds, *A companion to economic geography* Blackwell, Oxford and Malden 257–74.

———. (2004) "Antinomies of community: Some thoughts on geography, resources and empire" *Transactions of the Institute of British Geographers*, 29 195–216.

Welker M. A. (2009) "Corporate security begins in the community: Mining, the corporate social responsibility industry, and environmental advocacy in Indonesia" *Cultural Anthropology*, 24 142–79.

———. (2014) *Enacting the corporation* University of California Press, Berkeley.

Wenar L. (2016) *Blood oil* Oxford University Press, London.

West P. (2006) *Conservation is our government now: The politics of ecology in Papua New Guinea* Duke University Press, Durham, NC.

Willow A. J. (2012) "Re(con)figuring alliances: Place membership, Environmental Justice, and the remaking of indigenous-environmentalist relationships in Canada's boreal forest" *Human Organization*, 71 371–82.

Zadek S. (2001) *The civil corporation: The new economy of corporate citizenship* Earthscan, London.

# Part I
# Strategies

# 2 Mapping ecologies of resistance

*Leah Temper and Joan Martinez-Alier*

## Introduction

The environmental movement has been described as "the most comprehensive and influential movement of our time" (Castells 1997: 67), representing for the 'post-industrial' age what the workers' movement was for the industrial period. Yet while strike statistics have been collected for many countries since the late nineteenth century (van der Velden 2007),[1] until the present no administrative body tracks the occurrence and frequency of mobilizations or protests related to environmental issues, in the way that the World Labour Organization tracks the occurrence of strike action (http://laborsta.ilo.org/) and thus it is impossible to properly document the prevalence and incidence of contentious activity related to environmental issues or to track the ebb and flow of protest activity.

There is not a single "environmental movement" as such. Broadly speaking, three major streams have been identified (Martinez-Alier 2002): the conservationist movement of the IUCN, the WWF, nature conservancy; the eco-efficiency or ecological modernization movement with slogans such as "sustainable development" or even "green growth"; and the movement for environmental justice and the environmentalism of the poor and the indigenous. This chapter focuses on this third stream.

There is a growing interest in the fields of sociology, anthropology, ecological economics, and political ecology, among others, in the study of environmental conflicts and social protest. Some within this line of scholarship highlight how environmental conflict is a fundamental part of social conflict, rooted in the basic reproduction of human society, and demonstrate how historically it has often been at the core of what were viewed as class conflicts (Gonzalez de Molina et al, ND). Other scholars emphasize that we are currently witnessing a further "environmentalization" of social struggles, whereby ecological issues are increasingly used to both legitimate and contest political and scientific structures and practices (Acselrad 2010).

We argue that that there is a growing number of ecological distribution conflicts or, equivalently, socio-environmental conflicts born from increasing resource extraction at the "commodity frontiers" (Moore 2000) and also because of increasing waste disposal, including excessive production of greenhouse gases.

While there may not (yet) exist an organized "global" environmental justice movement to speak of, and much less a central committee or "politburo", the relevance of groups mobilizing over interlinked environmental issues is gaining traction, and they are experiencing greater cohesion. We also would argue that among the several environmentalisms, the environmental justice (EJ) movement, composed of a coalition of anti-toxics, labour, civil rights, indigenous, radical scholars, environmental, and feminist movements, among others, is gaining prominence globally. Such movements share a common conviction that environmental problems are political issues that cannot be solved apart from social and economic justice and that these call for a transformative approach and the restructuring of dominant social relations and institutional arrangements (Martinez-Alier et al. 2016). Furthermore, these movements defend specific uses of the environment against encroachment by the market or state forms of resource use (Gadgil and Guha 1993) manifesting as confrontations between more sustainable uses and industrial forms of resource extraction, transport, and waste disposal.

EJ is a powerful lens through which to make sense of many struggles over the negative impacts that the changing social metabolism imposes on human livelihoods and nature conservation worldwide (Gottlieb 2009). By "social metabolism" is meant the flows of energy and materials in the economy, which are increasing and changing in their composition. The economy can be seen as a process of extraction and transport of resources, production and exchange of commodities, and waste disposal (and Fischer-Kowalski and Haberl 2015). As early as 1991, at the Washington DC "People of Color Environmental Leadership Summit" ties were forged so as "to begin to build a national and international movement of all peoples of color to fight the destruction and taking of our lands and communities." (www.ejnet.org/ej/principles.html)

This paper contributes to a theoretical framework on environmental justice, drawing from our Global Atlas of Environmental Justice (www.EJ Atlas.org) with an inventory of about 1700 socio-environmental conflicts worldwide, as well as experiences from collaborative research on EJ in the EJOLT project (2011–15) (www.ejolt.org) involving activists and scholars to examine dynamics, trends and identify novelty through a systematic analysis of environmental conflicts. It opens up the following lines of research: What are the general contours of the Global EJ movement? Are socio-environmental movements of the poor and the indigenous gaining strength in their struggles, or are they being further marginalized? And what is the role and relative strength of appeals to identity politics? Are there scientific debates in these struggles? Are new "repertoires of action" appearing and diffusing among networks?

## Background: the conflictual metabolism of industrial societies

To provide for their material welfare, nutrition, housing and other needs, societies organize a continuous flow of energy and materials from their natural environments, extracting resources, transforming them and discharging them again as waste (Fischer-Kowalski and Haberl 2007). A socio-metabolic view of societies thus allows us to examine them from a physical perspective: as systems of material and energy stocks and flows regulated by biological, cultural, technological and economic processes (Fischer-Kowalski and Haberl 2015).

Today's global economy has a colossal appetite for materials and energy. Even a non-growing industrial economy would need "fresh" supplies of fossil fuels (because energy is not recycled) and also new supplies of materials which are recycled only in part. Such requirements increase with economic growth. The world social metabolism (the flows of energy and materials) is increasing and it is changing. The economy uses more inputs and it produces more waste. The inputs often come from the "commodity extraction frontiers" (Moore 2000), and the waste is dumped locally or internationally. Increased amounts of carbon dioxide are deposited in the atmosphere (increasing the greenhouse effect, or finding their way to the acidifying oceans). The economy is not circular; it is entropic (Haas et al. 2015). Even the renewable resources such as water from aquifers, timber, and fisheries are overexploited, the fertility of the soil is jeopardized and biodiversity is depleted.

Depletion occurs, or as metabolic growth is required, mining, dams, gas fracking, plantations and industries are on the march. They are little by little reaching every remaining corner of the planet, undermining the environment in ever more regions as well as the conditions of existence of local populations who complain accordingly. The growth dynamics of capitalism generates ecologically unequal exchange between nations and gives rise to local and regional ecological distribution conflicts.

Ecological distribution conflicts (Martinez-Alier 1995; Martinez-Alier and O'Connor 1996) is a term for environmental injustices which has its origin in ecological economics. It refers to struggles over the burdens of pollution or over the sacrifices made to extract resources, which overlap with inequalities of income, social status and power. Sometimes the local actors claim recognition before they can claim redistributions.

For instance, a factory may be polluting the river (which belongs to nobody or belongs to a community that manages the river – as studied by Ostrom (1990) and her school). This is not a damage valued in the market. The same happens with climate change, observable already in sea-level rise in some Pacific islands or in the Kuna islands in Panama. More than market failures (a terminology that implies that such externalities could be valued in money terms and internalized into the price system) these are "cost-shifting successes" (Kapp 1950) which, oftentimes lead to complaints from those bearing them. If such complaints were effective (which is not the rule), some activities could be banned, or, if we would accept economic commensuration and reject incommensurability of values (Munda et al. 1998), "equivalent" eco-compensation mechanisms could be introduced. The economy would change accordingly.

Thus, this changing social metabolism of industrial economies gives rise to a growing number of ecological distribution conflicts that sometimes overlap with other social conflicts on class, ethnicity or indigenous identity, gender, caste, or territorial rights.

Such conflicts are today as historically significant if not more than the classic struggles between capital and labour, with which they sometimes overlap (Barca 2012). The ecological distribution conflicts arise from what James O'Connor (1988) called the "second contradiction of capitalism". We might speculate whether such conflicts would also exist in a non-capitalist, a planned industrial economy such as that in Russia and Eastern Europe until 1990; the fact is that such an economy does no longer exist. The economy of China, whether we call it state capitalism or any other name, certainly causes domestic and international ecological distribution conflicts.

However, these conflicts do not result from metabolic patterns per se, as if such patterns were disconnected from the economy and society. First, protests are also directed against institutional configurations that define the room for manoeuvre of private or state-owned companies and of environmental movements. Secondly, these conflicts are expressed as struggles over valuation, in two senses: which values are relevant for decision making on the use or abuse of nature in particular projects (e.g. market values including fictitious money values through contingent valuation or other methods; livelihood values; sacredness; indigenous territorial rights; ecological values in their own units of account . . .), and even more importantly, who has the power to include or exclude the relevant values, to give weights to them, to allow or not to allow trade-offs. For instance, does sacredness imply a veto power? (Munda et al. 1998, Martinez-Alier 2002).

## The EJ Atlas – coverage and data

Many such ecological conflicts are being gathered in the Global Atlas of Environmental Justice, EJ Atlas (reaching 1700 cases by January 2016, www.EJ Atlas. org) (for more details, Temper et al. 2015). Currently most research on such conflicts is undertaken at either the case study level or sometimes at the national or regional level or sectoral level. While such in-depth case study analyses and thematic mapping yields valuable analytical inputs, the EJ Atlas offers a tool that transcends individual cases to identify patterns, relationships among cases and actors and how such conflicts are shaped by the larger political economy. We believe this exercise will enable the consolidation of a general theory of resource extraction and waste disposal conflicts, which is still under construction.

Further, the methodology for the data gathering of EJ Atlas is built on data entered by activists from their own inventories, as well as by scholars of these movements. This participatory form of data collection has created a space of interaction that enabled collaborative research on EJ conflicts at a global scale.

The unit of analysis in the EJ Atlas is a well-documented project-based campaign or place-based struggle, which sometimes results in influential national protest-events or broader campaigns. These contestations are made visible through press reports and court cases, campaigning, petitions, meetings, demonstrations, boycotts, strikes, threats, civil disobedience, collective violence, and other action forms.

Conflicts are classified in the first instance in only one of ten primary categories, and then also on all relevant 2nd level categories, which describe the disrupting activity in more detail (see Table 1). For instance a conflict on waste management (1st level), can be a conflict on incineration of urban waste or a conflict on ship-breaking overseas (2nd level). Similarly, a conflict born from a project for copper mining would be classified under Mineral Ores (1st level) although it also involves land acquisition (2nd level) and has consequences on water and air pollution (2nd level).

- **Nuclear (1st level):** i.e., uranium extraction; nuclear power plants; nuclear waste storage (2nd level)
- **Mineral ores & building materials extraction (1st level):** i.e., mineral extraction; mineral processing; tailings; building material extraction (2nd level)
- **Waste Management (1st level):** i.e., e-waste & other waste import zones; ship-breaking; waste privatization; waste pickers; incinerators; landfills; uncontrolled dump sites; industrial; municipal waste (2nd level)
- **Biomass and land conflicts (1st level):** i.e., land acquisition; tree plantations; logging; non-timber products; deforestation; agro-toxics; GMOs; agrofuels; mangroves vs. shrimps; biopiracy and bio-prospection; intensive food production (monoculture & livestock); fisheries (2nd level)
- **Fossil Fuels & Climate Justice/ Energy (1st level):** i.e., oil and gas extraction; oil spills; gas flaring; coal extraction; climate change related conflicts (glaciers & small islands); REDD/CDM; windmills; gas fracking (2nd level)
- **Infrastructure & Built Environment (1st level):** i.e., mega-projects, high-speed trains, airports, urban development (2nd level)
- **Water management (1st level):** i.e., dams, water transfers, aquifers, hydroways, desalination (2nd level)
- **Biodiversity conservation conflicts (1st level):** invasive species, damage to nature, conservation conflicts (2nd level)
- **Industrial & utilities conflicts (1st level):** factory emissions, industrial pollution (2nd level)
- **Tourism conflicts (1st level):** establishment of national parks; tourism facilities (hotels, marinas . . .) (2nd level)

Table 2.1 shows the distribution of conflicts by 2nd level category. The table could be prolonged to types of conflicts appearing only one or two times. It shows that beyond the historical EJ emphasis on urban exposure to toxics, due emphasis is given to rural conflicts in which diminished or denied access to local environmental resources, their degradation and corporate enclosures dramatically affect local communities and their livelihood security. EJ for rural people and their communities has to do with whether they have and are able to exercise rights to own, access and use the natural resources on which their livelihoods depend. It also has to do with preserving the quality of the resources themselves (IUCN 2007). Brown issue agendas such as access to sanitation and poor waste management issues are also represented. Further, while most conflicts in the EJ Atlas refer to the extraction

*Table 2.1* Distribution of environmental justice cases by main 2nd level category.

*Number of environmental conflicts per 2nd level categories*

| | | |
|---|---|---|
| Land acquisition conflicts 371 | Pollution related to transport (spills, dust, emissions) 94 | REDD/CDM 44 |
| Mineral ore exploration 273 | | Other industries 41 |
| Water access rights and entitlements 243 | Intensive food production (monoculture and livestock) 88 | Agro-toxics 40 |
| | | Oil and gas refining 39 |
| Dams and water distribution conflicts 201 | Establishment of reserves/ national parks 72 | Aquaculture and fisheries 37 |
| Deforestation 177 | | Incinerators 35 |
| Tailings from mines 151 | Urban development conflicts 71 | Water treatment and access to sanitation (access to sewage) 35 |
| Oil and gas exploration/ extraction 145 | Thermal power plants 67 | |
| Landfills, toxic waste treatment, uncontrolled dump sites 130 | Chemical industries 54 | Manufacturing activities 34 |
| | Coal extraction and processing 53 | Building materials extraction (quarries, sand, gravel) 34 |
| Plantation conflicts (incl. Pulp) 127 | Tourism facilities (ski resorts, hotels, marinas) 47 | |
| Mineral processing 107 | Wetlands and coastal zone management 46 | Interbasin water transfers/ transboundary water conflicts 31 |
| Transport infrastructure networks (roads, railways, hydroways, canals and pipelines) 105 | Agro-fuels and biomass energy plants 46 | Ports and airport projects 31 |

Source: authors' elaboration, based on EJ Atlas data as of April 2015 (n =1354). Note conflicts can be categorized by several second level types.

phase, local conflicts related to urban and industrial waste, as well as those arising from CO2 emissions related to REDD or CDM projects, and transnational waste disposal conflicts in ship-breaking and e-waste are represented.

The atlas has a global purview – emphasizing the spatial organization of the global economy and how it entrenches geographies of injustice and how apart from singular and historical patterns of social inequality and ethnic discrimination, socio-environmental conflicts should be seen as produced through the insertion of countries and communities into the international economy.

## Theorizing ecological conflicts – reflections on actors, forms of mobilization, frames and outcomes

### Actors

The EJ Atlas database forms include a space to list social actors mobilizing in conflicts (Figure 2.1, which refers to 1345 cases, April 2015). Several actors can be listed simultaneously in the same conflict. For instance, in a conflict the protagonists could be pastoralists, who are also indigenous, and they can be led by women, and supported by a religious group. What can be seen in Figure 2.1, is

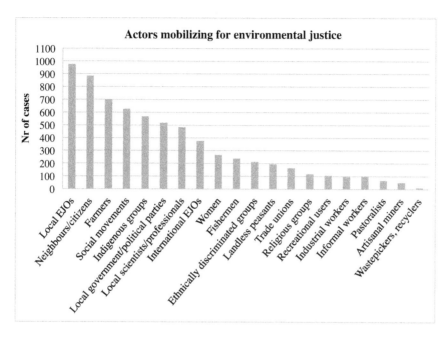

*Figure 2.1* Frequency of social actors involved in mobilizations (n = 1354).

that most often, actors mobilizing against projects appear as locally organized groups (local EJOs, environmental justice organizations). The atlas documents collective mobilizations, and groups that are more highly organized such as formal environmental justice organizations, are more likely to succeed in bringing attention to their cause. A wide variety of local groups participate in environmental mobilizations. Based on their level of organization and the political, symbolic and material resources available to them, they are able to pick different tactics and leverage different forms of influence.

One primary group of actors includes subsistence, marginalized or what has sometimes been termed subaltern communities, including landless peasants, indigenous groups, pastoralists, etc.

"Environmental justice" originally emerged as a movement and as a term in environmental sociology in the United States in the early 1980 (Bullard 1990) to bring attention to the inequality of environmental burdens and benefits along racial lines – hence the term "environmental racism". The cases in the atlas, however, bring our attention to the multiple and often overlapping forms of difference that are subject to marginalization, and which can be along lines of race, gender, class, caste or other forms of difference.

Particularly the atlas draws attention to the high occurrence of cases involving indigenous communities – who are involved in over one third of the cases documented with wide regional variation. While some estimates have put indigenous peoples at over 370 million globally (five per cent of world population), such a perspective is complicated by the fact that there is no universally accepted definition of indigenous and no global map outlining indigenous territories. Indigenous peoples, according to the UN, occupy 20% of the global territory and are stewards of 80% of the biodiversity which goes a long way towards explaining why government and corporate targeting of these lands is thus one of the primary drivers of conflicts in the atlas. Indigenous communities impacted will often appeal to their territorial rights, or special protections such as the Right to Free Prior and Informed consent afforded to them through ILO 169.

Environmental injustice against indigenous and other subsistence communities can perhaps be considered different to the traditional view of environmental racism against racial minorities in the United States. Whereas in the case of minorities, the demand was for an end to segregation and equality, indigenous communities are often forcibly assimilated by the colonial or dominant powers. This would also apply to indigenous groups in the United States – such as the Navajo in New Mexico who suffered from uranium mining. Remedies for environmental injustice in these cases thus must often transcend a simplistic approach of "equal burdens of pollution" and adequate participation to recognition of indigenous sovereignty, self-government and their own lifeworlds and relationship with the territory. Much work remains to be done to develop a theory of EJ that takes this into account.

Further, not only is the representation of indigenous communities in the EJ Atlas disproportionate, but cases involving indigenous and minority communities are up to twice as likely to suffer violent repression, criminalization, and persecution.

Nancy Fraser's work has grappled with the current dilemma in understanding social movements, which she refers to as the contradiction between claims for recognition and distribution – or in other terms the politics of equality and the cultural politics of difference, and attempts to reconcile them (Fraser 1996, 1999). Fraser notes that increasingly claims regarding social justice are dividing into two types: redistributive claims, which have for over a century and a half been paradigmatic for theorizing social justice, and the newly ascendant "politics of recognition."

EJ offers a particularly interesting application of this dilemma. Environmental justice requires both redistribution and recognition and those claiming for EJ are making bivalent claims that include class inequalities as well as cultural oppression. In several instances we can see how claims-makers are combining the two, to interesting effect.

EJ is different than mainstream environmentalism because it concerns issues of power and privilege. By acknowledging that "pollution is not colour blind" it has led to numerous identity-based sub-groups (black and Latinos in the United States, indigenous groups, "rural residents" in different places, etc.) that often use environmental justice to bring attention to issues of misrecognition and group rights through bivalent claims for both misdistribution and cultural misrecognition.

Further, as EJ expands to new groups staking claims under shared identities, they increasingly ask not only for social recognition, but for recognition of the environmental and reproductive functions they provide, across multiple scales from the local up to the global. For example, groups are contesting the "green economy" and capitalistic logics of the environment by foregrounding how their reproductive and regenerative work sustains the basis for capitalist markets.

They thus claim recognition of the contribution of their livelihoods through representing themselves as the stewards of social and natural "capitals". Small farmers in the Via Campesina point out to the environmental movement that their reproductive mode of production actually "cools down the earth." (Martinez-Alier 2011).

Although many of the cases recorded refer to resource extraction conflicts, there are also struggles on waste disposal. The waste pickers documented in several conflicts in the EJ Atlas highlight their contribution to reducing the waste stream as well as reducing carbon emissions. Waste pickers have been active at the United Nations Climate Change Conferences arguing that they contribute to the conservation of natural resources and energy while reducing air and water pollution. They also reduce greenhouse gas emissions through the reuse of materials. Around the globe, waste pickers are organizing and fighting for recognition of their significant environmental contributions in recycling and the role this plays in climate change mitigation and a healthy economy. To this end, they are demanding a Global Climate Fund to invest in resource recovery programs that will ensure decent livelihoods for all workers, and that are directly accessible by waste pickers and other informal economy groups and the exclusion of waste disposal technologies (such as incinerators) from the Clean Development Mechanism (CDM) that destroy valuable reclaimable materials and take income from workers (Demaria and Schindler 2015).

The role of women as leaders of EJ social movements has been well documented (Newman et al. 2004). In Figure 2.1, "Women" are shown as social actors for environmental justice only in about 250 cases (out of 1354). This requires an explanation. Women are present along men in practically all cases, and are often at the forefront and many would go so far as to say that all environmental struggles are feminist struggles over social reproduction (Di Chiro 2008). They are however listed as a particular actor when women's organizations have been prominent and where gendered patterns of environmental justice are explicitly expressed.

While the indigenous movement is perhaps the most successful example of global identity-based activism, an ascendant mobile pastoralist identity is also gaining discursive and material ground as "custodians of the commons" (Upton 2014). In the past, pastoralist land practices were portrayed as environmentally destructive with herders particularly prone to land loss through conservation-based exclusion (Neumann 2002). Yet new scientific knowledge is recasting the impact of pastoralism on drylands as policy fashions turn towards devolution in resource management and a growing recognition of the efficacy of communal tenure (Upton 2014).

Such new communities of interest increasingly make use of such "eco-political" capital to defend their livelihoods and press for justice. While they engage in conversations sometimes using language based on capitalist valuation of nature and "human and natural capital", this does not signify that they are buying into the ideology of commodifying nature to save it. What it demonstrates is that those most directly impacted at the places where commodity chains and capitalism "touch down" are assuming a more direct role and voice in activism to defend their interests, express their grievances and press for remedies and are using material as well as symbolic arguments or appeals to justice to stake their claims.

As Reitan (2007: 63) argues, "under conditions of neoliberal globalization, redistributive gains are not perceived as achievable without also winning a genuine recognition of diverse individuals' and communities' rights to exist and to determine – or at the very least to have a voice regarding – the pace and nature of change."

Yet, the identity politics inherent in EJ need not be a divisive force but rather entail a more mature analysis of actual power relations and inequalities within society than mainstream environmentalism. In this way EJ holds the potential for environmentalism to be a much more potent force that seeks unity through diversity and can succeed in incorporating disparate struggles of minority and marginalized communities under a common master frame.

*Forms of mobilization*

Figure 2.2 shows the frequency of mobilization forms, as reported in April 2015 (n. 1354). Most commonly reported forms of mobilizations include classic and traditional protest methods, such as complaint letters, public campaigns, street

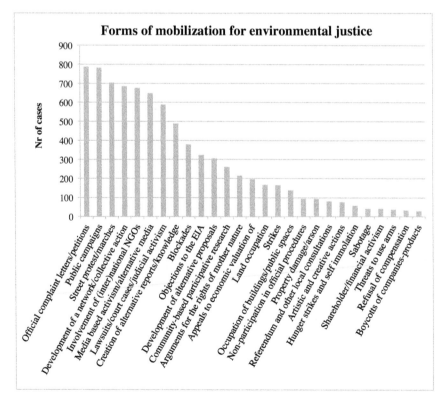

*Figure 2.2* Frequency of mobilization forms (n = 1354).

protests, the development of a network for collective action and furthermore, the involvement of national and international NGOs (Keck and Sikkink 1998).

In social movement theory (SMT), according to McAdam and Snow (1997: 326) social movements eschew politics through "proper" channels, often because their participants lack access to political institutions and other conventional means of influence or because they feel that their voices are not being heard. An important line of enquiry in SMT is what factors influence a social movement's selection of tactics? And what kinds of tactics are most likely to achieve successful outcomes?

One of SMT's major theoretical propositions is that a movement's effectiveness in bringing about social change is linked to its ability to disrupt or threaten a social order (McAdam 1982; Tarrow 1998). Protest for example is deemed to be most effective in forcing concessions when it manages to de-legitimize existing policies and impose direct material and political costs on their target. Yet an ongoing debate is whether "disruptive or violent" actions lead to more successful campaign outcomes. Here Sharp's (1973) distinction between nonviolent protests that are mainly symbolic (e.g., demonstrations) from nonviolent actions that impose sanctions on the target (e.g., strikes, sit-ins, blockades, and civil disobedience) and violent forms of mobilization (such as arson) is useful. Groups generally increase the contentiousness of their actions when milder forms of protest prove ineffective. Tarrow (1998: 98) argues that conventional actions are too easily ignored while violence divides potential supporters and generates strong repression. Thus, according to many theorists, the intermediate form of contention – non-violent disruption (strikes, blockades) is the strongest weapon of social movements and most likely to lead to concessions (Gamson 1990).

Actors employ a range of tactics to confront processes of dispossession, contamination and other forms of environmental processes that negatively affect them to the benefit of others. These tactics will be shaped by the nature of the processes of dispossession and entail physical, political and legal means against the coercive forces of the state and corporate actors.

Certain forms of dispossession may privilege more overt forms of resistance. One question is which types of activities and actors engender more contentious actions. Figure 2.3 shows the intensity level of conflict per activity category. Tourism and waste management appear on average to provoke fewer high-level intensity conflicts (around 15% of cases within their categories). They are also the most likely to be successfully stopped. On the other hand, mining conflicts and water management conflicts (i.e., hydroelectric dams) seem to provoke the largest number of highly intense conflicts (around 35%).

One hypothesis for further research is that point resources, including mines and hydroelectric projects are both more strategic for state interests and more conflictive, as opposed to landfills or tourism projects that are more mobile.

Whether contention is increasing in environmental conflicts generally is another interesting line of enquiry. Some authors argue that there is increasing intensity of resistance at the point of enclosure, deriving from the fact that the ecological contradictions that are being thrown up now seem to be more "existentially threatening" and frightening than previously (Levien 2012).

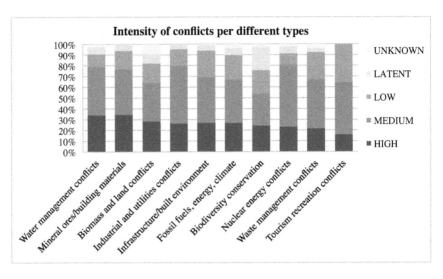

*Figure 2.3* Conflict intensity levels per conflict category (1st level category).

In 1993, O'Connor argued that "today's environmental problems represent not only a major economic crisis of supply, they also represent a crisis of legitimacy for the market system" (O'Connor 1993). Recently, (Levien 2013) has taken this up in the Indian context arguing that the success of current struggles against Special Economics Zones (SEZs) can be attributed to the fact that the current neo-liberal regime of dispossession has been proven to be based on corruption and profit-seeking and can no longer viably be understood to represent the public or national interest. The resistance is also driven by the non-materialization of benefits from previous development projects that have derailed the promise of the hegemonic development narrative. As Levien argues, when the state's justifications for expropriation do not resonate, and material concessions prove inadequate, anti-dispossession struggles will multiply and become more powerful.

Taking blockades as one form of disruptive action, the high prevalence of blockades in India (present in 50% of cases) bears out Levien's theory. In contrast, blockades can be evidenced in 30% of cases in Western Europe and a similar proportion on Latin America. Another observation is that almost 60% of cases with blockades also include indigenous communities. Further work remains to be done teasing out, confirming and interpreting such differences as they are shown in the EJ Atlas as well as their relation to the underlying biophysical limits.

Other forms of contention are apparent in Europe, under very different conditions but perhaps stemming from a similar growing disenchantment with government corruption and differences over public interest. The Forum against

Unnecessary Imposed Mega Projects (*Grands Projets Inutiles Imposés*) actively opposes massive infrastructure projects such as the HS2 rail scheme in the UK, the new Lyon-Turin rail line, the airport of Notre-Dame-des-Landes in Nantes, the Stuttgart 21 train station, the Bordeaux-Spain high-speed train, and more. The forum argues not in terms of direct threats to the livelihood of local populations but because such unnecessary projects " divert vital public funds to mega schemes that are first and foremost about generating private mega profits, and Imposed because citizens are excluded from real influence in both the analysis of the transport problem, and in the democratic identification of ways to address that."[2]

Such projects have led to large-scale protests. One emblematic case is that of Gezi Park in Turkey (Özkaynak et al. 2015a). Another well-known one is the TAV case in Italy on the railway between Turin and Lyon (Greyl et al. 2012), which demonstrates how the effect of the recent economic crises and the deteriorating economic situation in the country, the slashing of public funds, and the imposition of austerity measures from the European "troika" in the absence of public support have served to further catalyze resistance. The Italian state responded to protests by declaring the TAV to be a site of "strategic national interest", opening the way for the militarization of the valley and criminalization of the activists. The effect of such repression, that can also be seen in reaction to the waste crisis in Campania (D'Alisa et al. 2010), has further delegitimized the state and shown that it is either unable or unwilling to coherently address the complex, multi-faceted aspects of these contestations. Yet the TAV case also shows how faced with the failure of representative democracy, citizen movements enact alternative forms of participation.

## Innovation in action forms

Rather than simply being "defensive and reactionary" as some authors have claimed, EJ movements are also proactive and propositional in nature (Agyeman 2005). This can be evidenced by the introduction of new forms of governance across multiple scales as well as new forms of participatory democratic decision-making.

One example of the former includes the Yasuni initiative to leave oil in the soil (Martinez-Alier and Temper 2007) that aimed to design a global mechanism for financing a transition to a post-fossil fuels economy from the bottom-up, founded on principles of local respect for biodiversity and indigenous populations and of global climate justice, and rejecting false solutions like carbon trading that in practice "displace" environmental burdens (Sachs 1995) that benefit northern polluters.

Innovation in tactical repertoire has also proven effective in leading to desired outcomes. Tactical innovations occur because of linkages between activist networks and movement organizations, as the same protest tactics spread from one campaign to another. This is often spurred by success in media attention (Soule 1997), but also by other means. For example, recently waves of popular community-organized consultations or referenda have taken place across Latin America to oppose and open democratic spaces against mining projects (Urkidi and Walter 2011; Walter and Urkidi 2015). The authors show how the spread and diffusion of these popular consultations happened thanks to activists' connections, documentary video screenings and international meetings on the matter at regional level. In both these examples, we see a process of transformation of the scale of governance, in the first case, upwards to the international level, at the second, downwards to the local (municipal) level.

Local consultations or referenda appear in 98 cases so far in the EJ Atlas. We also see that the ability to challenge EIAs has improved in some countries and is increasingly widespread, with some 355 cases entailing such challenges. Groups are also using new strategies such as legal appeals to the Rights of Mother Nature in court cases in some Latin American countries. Financial divestment campaigns and some forms of shareholder activism have become more prevalent in recent years yet we only see this in some 40 or so cases (all as of May 2015).

As the EJ Atlas expands, further diffusion studies through network analysis will shed insight into how patterns of apparent influence reflect alliances and shared collective actions between disparate groups as well as how meanings are constructed and why some symbols, tactics and practices flourish and expand while others languish.

### Articulation

Marginalized groups negatively impacted will often build alliances or coalitions with more powerful actors that may exert more influence. They come together in networks against particular companies, for instance, as the *Articulaçao Internacional dos Atingidos e Atingidas pela Vale* (international articulation of those affected by the Vale company, a multinational iron ore company of Brazilian origin). The atlas currently documents 20 conflicts with the involvement of Vale, 20 from Chevron, 19 from Río Tinto and 38 from Royal Dutch Shell, just to give a few examples.

At the local level, these "articulations" may include local scientists, recreational users, organized NGOs, or trade unions. In particular, links with sympathetic local government and political parties can help increase the leverage of contentious actors. Another important source of support entails alliances with extra-local actors such as scientific consultants who are experts, for instance, on hydrogeology, environmental chemistry or low level radiation (Conde 2014) and with conservationist organizations from northern countries, in temporary coalitions through "boomerang strategies", Keck and Sikkink's (1998) term for activist attempts to try to bring external pressure to bear when states prove non-responsive to domestic pressure.

A cogent example of how local movements are expanding their discourse and tapping into broader and structural critiques is embodied by the Fracktivist movement. While born over a concern over gas extraction taking place literally "in their backyards" in primarily middle-class communities in America, Combes describes (in Temper et al. 2013) how part of the struggle keeps a local defensive attitude, deepening the mobilization and promoting dissemination to the general public while another line is focused more on proactive work to broaden the mobilisation to support global energy issues.

Another relevant example is how anti-incineration movements, with a genesis in local place-based mobilizations, have amplified their discursive frame in recent years through the formation of coalitions with waste-picker and recycling movements. This allows them to tap into wider debates about climate change and resource use generally, rather than a focus on the politics of consumption.

The case of Foil Vedanta for example is an interesting illustration of the articulation of multi-scale movements for environmental justice. Kumar (2014) has previously highlighted the tensions between local and international EJOs around the Niyamgiri conflict in India. Yet the historical development of the case shows how activism born in one location can exert influence and reappear in sometimes unexpected quarters.

When the case in India was resolved against the company, the transnational UK-based social justice group Foil Vedanta broadened its activism to other sites in Vedanta's supply chain. A video released in 2014 by Foil Vedanta shows Vedanta boss Anil Agarwal mocking the Zambian parliament and bragging that he makes $500 million per year from Konkola Copper Mines (KCM), after having bought the company for $25 million, against a $400 million asking price. The video caused outrage in Zambia, where KCM has failed to pay taxes, and is indebted to contractors. A few days later hundreds protested in the streets of Lusaka demanding that Vedanta pay taxes and improve the conditions for workers. The Zambian government is now undertaking an audit of the companies' financial records. This story demonstrates how even small, resource-strapped radical groups can leverage knowledge and social media to effect change by turning the capitalist production-consumption exchange system in on itself.

## Frames

Social movement actors direct a large part of their activities to the creation, institutionalization, and monitoring of norms. They do this through the strategic creation and recreation of meanings or "framings". According to Sidney Tarrow (1998), frames are not ideas but ways of packaging and presenting ideas. Movements then use these frames to attempt the "mobilization of consensus," that is, persuasive communication aimed at convincing others to take their side. In this way, frames aim to produce a shared understanding of the problems they seek to address, how the problems should be handled, and the motivation behind their actions (often called diagnostic, prognostic, and motivation frames, respectively) (Snow and Benford 1988).

Since the early 1980s in their own battles and strategy meetings (Martinez-Alier et al. 2014), the EJOs (environmental justice organizations) and their networks have introduced several concepts and proposals of political ecology and ecological economics which have been taken up also by academics and policy makers, who have applied them and further supplied in turn other related concepts, working in a mutually reinforcing way with EJOs (Table 2). We argue that these processes and dynamics build an activist-led and co-produced social sustainability science. The EJ Atlas, through its description of conflicts, is a good source to find other terms and slogans of the global EJ movement.

*Table 2.2* Vocabulary of the global environmental justice movement

|  | EJOs PROMOTING IT | SHORT DESCRIPTION |
|---|---|---|
| Environmental Justice (EJ) | USA Civil Rights Movement, North Carolina 1982 against environmental injustices (Bullard 1990). | "People of color" and low-income populations suffer disproportionate harm from waste sites, refineries and incinerators, transport infrastructures. |
| Environmental racism | Rev Benjamin Chavis, c. 1982 | The fight for EJ, against pollution in Black, Hispanic, Indigenous areas, was seen as a fight against *environmental racism*. |
| Ecological debt | Instituto Ecología Política, Chile, 1992, Acción Ecológica 1997 | Rich countries' liability for resource plunder and disproportionate use of space for waste dumping (e.g. GHG). |
| Popular epidemiology | Brown, P. , 1992, 1997 | "Lay" local knowledge of illnesses from pollution may be more valid than official knowledge (sometimes absent). |
| Environmentalism of the poor | A. Agarwal/S. Narain (CSE, Delhi) c. 1989 | Struggles by poor/ indigenous peoples against deforestation, dams, mining. . . ; proactive collective projects for water harvesting, and forest conservation |
| Food sovereignty | Via Campesina, c. 1996 | People's right to healthy, culturally appropriate, sustainably produced food. Right to define own food and agriculture systems. |
| Biopiracy | RAFI (Pat Mooney) 1993, popularized by Vandana Shiva | Appropriation of genetic resources (in medicinal or agricultural plants) without recognition of knowledge and property rights of indigenous peoples. |
| Climate justice | CES (Delhi), 1991, Durban Alliance, CorpWatch 1999–2002 | Radically reduce excessive per capita emissions of carbon dioxide and other GHG. "Subsistence emissions vs. luxury emissions". |
| Water justice, hydric justice | Rutgerd Boelens, EJOs in Latin America (e.g. CENSAT) 2011 | Water should not run towards money, or towards power. It should go to those needing it for livelihood. |
| Water as human right | Pablo Solon (Bolivian envoy to UN), Maud Barlow (Council of Canadians), 2001 | Human Right to Water recognized at UN level in 2011, as an independent human right. |

|  | EJOs PROMOTING IT | SHORT DESCRIPTION |
|---|---|---|
| "Green Deserts" | Brazil, network against eucalyptus plantations, *Rede Alerta contra o Deserto Verde*, 1999 | Brazilian local term for eucalyptus plantations, used by networked CSO and communities, also by researchers and activists for any tree plantation. |
| Tree plantations are not forests | *Pulping the South*, 1996 by R. Carrere, L. Lohmann, World Rainforest Movement | The WRM collects and spreads information on tree plantation conflicts. It proposes a change in the FAO definition of forest, to exclude tree monocultures. |
| Land grabbing | GRAIN ( small pro-peasant EJO), 2008 | The wave of land acquisitions in Southern countries for plantations for exports, leading to first statistics on land grabbing. |
| Resource caps | Resource Cap Coalition, RCC Europe, c. 2010 | It advocates reduction in global resource use and in poverty. It calls for a *European energy quota scheme* and the ratification of the *Rimini protocol*. |
| To Ogonize / Yasunize | ERA Nigeria, Acción Ecológica, Oilwatch, 1997–2007 | Leave oil in the soil to prevent damage to human rights and biodiversity, and against climate change. Adopted by anti-shale gas fracking, tar sands and open cast coal-mining movements. |
| Rights of Nature | Ecuador, Constitutional Assembly, 2008 | In Constitution of Ecuador 2008, art 71, pushed by Acción Ecológica and Alberto Acosta. Actionable in court. |
| Corporate accountability | Friends of the Earth International, 1992–2002 | At UN Johannesburg summit, FoE proposed the adoption of a Corporate Accountability Convention, against lukewarm CSR principles. |
| "Critical mass", cyclists' rights | San Francisco 1992 (Chris Carlsson) | International reclaiming the streets with cyclists marching to impose cyclists' rights. |
| Urban waste recyclers movements | c. 2005, GAIA against incineration and "energy valorization" of urban waste. | Unions or cooperatives of urban waste gatherers, with their positive environmental impact, including climate change (movements in Delhi, Pune, Bogota). |
| Urban "guerrilla food gardening" | c. 2000, started by "food justice" networks? | Vacant lot food growing, permaculture, community gardening movements in cities around the world. |

*(Continued)*

*Table 2.2* (Continued)

|  | EJOs PROMOTING IT | SHORT DESCRIPTION |
|---|---|---|
| Toxic colonialism, toxic imperialism | BAN, Basel Action Network, c. 2000 | Fighting the long-distance export of waste from rich to poor countries, forbidden by the Basel Treaty. E.g. ship-breaking in India or Bangladesh, chemical residues or nuclear waste, electronic waste. |
| Post-extractivism | Latin America, 2007, Eduardo Gudynas (CLAES), Alberto Acosta, Maristella Svampa | Against the reprimarization of LA economies. Transition to a sustainable economy based on solar energy and renewable materials. Impose quotas and taxes on raw materials exports. |
| *Buen Vivir, Sumak Kawsay* | Ecuador and Bolivia 2008 | Adopted in Constitutions of both countries, inspired by indigenous traditions and by the "post-development" approach. |
| Indigenous territorial rights, and prior consultations | Convention 169 of ILO, 1989; adivasi forest rights in India. . . | In conflicts on mining, oil exploitation, dams . . . communities ask for applying legislation defending indigenous rights. |
| "Sand mafias" | Name given c. 2005 by environmental movement, journalists. | The illegal "mining" of sand and gravel in India in many rivers, driven by the growing building and public works industry. |
| "Cancer villages" | In China, popular name adopted by academics, officials (Lora-Wainright 2013) | Rural villages where industry has caused pollution (e.g. heavy metals), where lay knowledge of illness is relevant, and subdued protests take place. |

Many of these terms are applied in several contexts. In other words, terms born in the struggles for EJ travel between communities and continents – thus, Lora-Wainright finds that the term of "popular epidemiology" born in the USA is useful to interpret the acquired knowledge of industrial illnesses and the muted responses in some villages in China. The term "sacrifice zones" (Lerner 2010) has travelled well beyond the United States. The "ecological debt" from north to south (a term born in 1991 in Latin America) was recently included and carefully defined in paragraph 51 of Pope Francis's encyclical Laudato si. In 2014–15, new terms related to climate justice and to prevention of local damage from fossil fuel extraction have been introduced, such as Blockadia (by Naomi Klein, referring to struggles in North America against oil and gas pipelines such as Keystone XL) and Annex 0 (by Oilwatch, in Paris in December 2015) for support for local EJOs stopping fossil fuel extraction (while Annex 1 listed the rich countries in the Climate Change Treaty of 1992 committed in principle to reductions in emissions).

*Outcomes*

The EJ Atlas also tracks outcomes. One conflict case can of course have different outcomes. "Strengthening of participation" across affected stakeholders has been observed as the most common positive outcome of environmental conflicts in the EJ Atlas database forms, followed by compensations; however, we do not know in how many cases compensations were perceived as adequate or not. There follows moratoria or other successful ways of stopping projects. Negotiated alternative solutions, as well as environmental improvement, representing a set of compromise responses to environmental injustice, follow. On the negative outcomes, the most common cases are displacement, followed by criminalization of activists, repression, corruption, violent targeting of activists, and deaths (which occur in 12 per cent of all cases, n. 1345 by April 2015).

The chance of stopping a project may vary with the timing of the resistance, with the type of social actors and their allies, with the type of commodity in question. While tourism and waste management projects are those most often stopped (over 30% 'stopped'), fossil fuel (e.g. oil explorations) and water management (e.g. hydroelectric dams) projects are those that most rarely have been stopped (in less than 15% of cases). We hypothesize that this is because point resources such as mines are less mobile than factories and agricultural projects which can more easily be displaced to new locations when encountering resistance.

Figure 2.4 shows the relationship between project status and start of the mobilizations. A clear difference becomes visible regarding proactive versus reactive mobilizations, both in terms of percentage of project stopped, as well as percentage of projects in operation. For the cases reporting preventive resistance, around 27% of projects could be stopped, while for cases showing resistance in reaction to the implementation, only around 17% of projects were stopped with 55% in operation. While this may be somewhat evident, the results underline the importance of early response and mobilization.

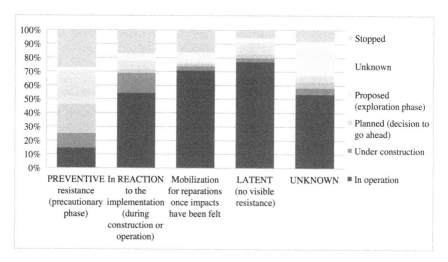

*Figure 2.4* Project status and mobilization start.

In the EJ Atlas a field offers the contributor (the one entering the conflict) the possibility to provide, either as involved actor or expert having substantial knowledge on the case, a classification of the outcome in terms of EJ success or failure. The field asks the question, "Do you consider this an environmental justice success? Was environmental justice served?", for which there are three possible answers: 'Yes', 'I'm not sure' and 'No', accompanied by an open-ended text field in which the contributor is asked to explain the answer. Of all cases contributors have chosen so far to answer the question with 'not sure' in over 30% of cases while almost 50% are characterized as EJ failures, in which from the perspective of the contributor, environmental justice was not served.

In nearly 20 per cent of conflicts, movements have succeeded in stopping or significantly stalling the projects. In many conflicts, the mobilizers have no interest in the forms of development proposed for their land and are fighting to stop the project; others are fighting to be incorporated into it on better terms, while still others are fighting for environmental remediation.

The cases in in the EJ Atlas can be mobilized to argue against the supposed "post-political" turn in environmental politics as argued recently by geographers such as Žižek (1992) and Swyngedouw (2010). While these authors have tended to see the nation-state as the privileged place for the political, as noted by Routledge (2003), environmental politics are often taking specific forms at scales below and above the nation-state. Such forms are not immediately recognized as being political. First, they are not engaging with party politics the way movements did in the past. For example, while many authors equate neoliberalism and capitalism as the driving force behind dispossession (McMichael 2010), authors such as Acosta (2011) and Svampa (2013) point out that even post-neoliberal leftist politicians in Latin America were adopting (until 2015) what they term the "commodities consensus" to describe economic policies in countries such as Argentina, Brazil, Bolivia and Ecuador that escaped the neoliberal "Washington Consensus" imposed by the World Bank and the IMF, but became trapped in a neo-extractivist model. Regardless of the specific ideological characteristics of each government, and despite their hostility toward neo-liberal structures of power, these governments continued to rely on and expand extractive growth models based on the appropriation and excessive exploitation of non-renewable natural resources for export. According to the South American post-extractivist school of Acosta, Gudynas and Svampa, the escalation of socio-environmental conflicts is one of the consequences of this, accompanied by the emergence of new forms of mobilization and civic participation focusing on defending the commons, biodiversity, and the environment. An analysis of cases in the EJ Atlas in Ecuador by (Latorre et al. 2015) compares their distribution and intensity before and 2007, the year Correa's presidency started.

This emerging environmentalism may also be termed "environmentalism of the dispossessed" (Temper 2014), a term appropriate for people impoverished because they are dispossessed through projects threatening the environment, and thus their sources of livelihood; and one that calls attention to the fact that environmentalism centered on opposition to capitalist "accumulation by dispossession" is motivated by but not limited to personal material concerns, but also by opposition at broader scales to dispossession of self-governing authority, spiritual and ethical values, and that these are not limited to the poor.

## Conclusion

The increasingly interlinked and globally integrated nature of contemporary EJ struggles can provide a powerful answer to Harvey's critique that painted place-based EJ movements as enacting "militant particularisms" (Harvey 1996: 400–401) that are unable to "transcend the narrow solidarities and particular affinities shaped in particular places" and to confront the "fundamental underlying processes . . . that generate environmental and social injustices": that is, the asymmetrical power relations embedded in "unrelenting capital accumulation". Harvey's critique in terms of "militant particularisms" (based on analyses of working-class action in Welsh social history by Raymond Williams) led him and other scholars to miss the birth of the global environmental justice movement (Sikor and Newell 2014).

Latin American political ecologists, such as Escobar (2008) and Leff (2012), posit that an effective grassroots political strategy should entail the re-appropriation of knowledge and space through the reinvention of cultural identities and through the reshaping of territories. Yet they affirm that real world projects erecting 'strong' boundaries around places need not necessarily be seen as regressive. As Castree (2004: 163) argues,

> it is perfectly possible for inward looking localisms to be founded on an explicit and conscious engagement with extra-local forces. That is, the trans-local can be strategically harnessed for purely local needs (as captured in the following reversal of a hackneyed phrase 'think locally, act globally') and this is not at all paradoxical.

Thus in conclusion, the EJ movement conversely can be said to represent an attempt to "repoliticize" environmental issues, while travelling across scales and multiple alliances. It is true that in the United States (the birthplace of a self-conscious EJ movement in the 1980s), cooperation with and perhaps co-option by the state appears to have domesticated the movement. But the roots spread far into more violent environments overseas, to the global frontiers of the social metabolism (both in terms of resource extraction and waste dumping). Rather than be viewed as movements of militant particularism or simply focused on identity politics, we argue that global EJ holds the potential for more mature analysis of actual power relations and inequalities within society that may succeed in incorporating disparate struggles of minority and marginalized communities under a common master frame.

Bellamy Foster already noted in 2002 (p. 40) that "The struggle for material welfare among the great mass of the population, which was once understood mainly in material terms, is increasingly taking on a wider, more holistic environmental context. Hence, it is the struggle for environmental justice – the struggle over the interrelationship of race, class, gender and imperial oppression and the degradation of the environment – that is likely to be the defining feature of the twenty-first century."

We agree here with Bellamy Foster except that we believe that the environmentalism of the dispossessed is indeed motivated by material objectives – Inglehart's "post-materialist" interpretation does not apply to struggles for environmental justice. The gains and losses of the use of the environment are often unjustly distributed not only as regards other species or future generations of humans but also among humans living today. There are therefore many local movements expressing their grievances over such environmental injustices. Several groups have been producing inventories of ecological distribution conflicts (by country or by theme), such as OCMAL in Latin America on mining conflicts, or in Brazil Fiocruz and the EJ movement (Porto de Souza et al. 2012). Our own contribution at the ICTA-UAB has been to build up the EJ Atlas on ecological distribution conflicts with many outside collaborators. Although its coverage is still geographically and thematically uneven, on reaching 1700 conflicts by January 2016 we can begin to trace patterns in the dynamics of such conflicts.

Social mobilizations over resource extraction, environmental degradation, or waste disposal are not only about the distribution of environmental benefits and costs (expressed in monetary or non-monetary valuation languages); they are also about participation in decision-making and recognition of group identities (Schlosberg 2007; Urkidi and Walter 2011; Walker 2012; Sikor and Newell 2014). EJ research encompasses issues of exclusion (2001) but also of the potential new leadership of environmental movements by different social actors. E.g. in the environmentalism of the poor, as in EJ movements in general, it is crucial to recognize the contribution women make in poor communities both rural and urban (Agarwal 2001). Going beyond case studies, researchers now generate statistics on ecological distribution conflicts (Pérez Rincón 2014; Latorre et al. 2015; Özkaynak et al. 2015b; Temper et al. 2015) made possible by the EJ Atlas.

This article has highlighted some of the initial results from the Global Atlas of Environmental Justice. The EJ Atlas provides empirical material for a research agenda that contributes to understanding how inequalities are shaped through socio-metabolic transformations in the economy and how they are contested, and to what outcomes. Further documentation and analysis via a statistical political ecology holds significant promise for extending both the praxis and theory of environmental justice and geographical scholarship.

EJOs are interested in mapping ecological distribution conflicts to show not only injustices but also the instances of resistance to land and water grabbing, pollution from oil extraction, mining or waste disposal, uncertain threats from technologies like pesticide spraying or nuclear energy. The EJ Atlas collects many successes in stopping projects. The global movement for environmental justice is formed not only by these many local foci of resistance but also by intermediary rural or urban-based organizations which have developed their own vocabulary and slogans and put forward interlinked claims at several scales.

## Notes

The authors would like to thank all the EJ Atlas contributors and collaborators and a special thanks to Daniela Del Bene, the EJatlas coordinator, for her invaluable contribution to this work, as well as Arnim Scheidel for elaboration of the graphs. This work is based on the research supported by the Transformations to Sustainability Programme, which is coordinated by the International Social Science Council and funded by the Swedish International Development Cooperation Agency (Sida), and implemented in partnership with the National Research Foundation of South Africa (Grant Number TKN150317115354 ). The Transformations to ustainability Programme represents a contribution to Future Earth.

1  Strikes around the world www.laborbooks.com/Item/strikewrld.
2  http://xn-drittes-europisches-forum-xec.de/charta-von-tunis/charter-of-tunis/

## References

Acosta, A. 2011. "Extractivism and neo-extractivism: Two faces of the same execration." In *Beyond the Development*. Various authors. Quito: Rosa Luxemburg Foundation, pp. 61–86. www.tni.org/files/download/beyonddevelopment_complete.pdf.

Acselrad, H. 2010. "The 'Environmentalization' of Social Struggles – the Environmental Justice." *Movement in Brazil Estudos Avançados* 24 (68): 103–119.

Agarwal, A. and Narain, S. 1991. *Global Warming in an Unequal World: A Case of Environmental Colonialism*. New Delhi: Centre for Science and Environment.

Agarwal, B. 2001. "Participatory Exclusions, Community Forests and Gender: An Analysis for South Asia and a Conceptual Framework." *World Development* 29 (10): 1623–1648.

Agarwal, Bina. 1992. "The Gender and Environment Debate: Lessons from India." *Feminist Studies* 18 (1), Spring: 119–158.

Agyeman, Julian. 2005. "Alternatives for Community and Environment: Where Justice and Sustainability Meet." *Environment: Science and Policy for Sustainable Development* 47 (6): 10–23.

Barca, S. 2012. "On Working-Class Environmentalism: An Historical and Transnational Overview." *Interface: A Journal for and about Social Movements* 4 (2): 61–80.

Bullard, R. D. 1990. *Dumping in Dixie: Race, Class, and Environmental Quality*. Boulder, CO: Westview Press.

Carrere, R. and Lohman, L. 1996. *Pulping the South: Industrial Tree Plantation and the World Paper Economy*. London: Zed Books.

Castells, M. 1997. *The Information Age*, 3 vols. Oxford: Blackwell, 996, 98.

Castree, Noel. 2004. "Differential Geographies: Place, Indigenous Rights and 'Local' Resources." *Political Geography*, 23 (2), 133–167.

Conde, M. 2014. "Activism Mobilising Science." *Ecological Economics* 105: 67–77. doi:10.1016/j.ecolecon.2014.05.012.

D'Alisa, G., Burgalassi, D., Healy, H., and Walter, M. 2010. Conflict in Campania: Waste Emergency or Crisis of Democracy. *Ecological Economics* 70 (2): 239–249.

Demaria, Federico and Schindler, Seth. 2015. "Contesting Urban Metabolism: Struggles Over Waste-to-Energy in Delhi, India." *Antipode* 48 (2): 293–313.

Di Chiro, Giovanna. 2008. "Living Environmentalisms: Coalition Politics, Social Reproduction, and Environmental Justice." *Environmental Politics* 17 (2): 276–298.

Escobar, A. 2008. *Territories of Difference: Place, Movements, Life, Redes*. Durham: Duke University Press.

Fischer-Kowalski, F. and Haberl, H. 2015. "Social metabolism: A metrics for biophysical growth and degrowth, chapter 5." In J. Martinez-Alier and R. Muradian, eds. *Handbook of Ecological Economics*. Cheltenham: Edward Elgar.

Fischer-Kowalski, F. and Haberl, H. eds. 2007. *Socioecological Transitions and Global Change: Trajectories of Social Metabolism and Land Use*. Cheltenham: Edward Elgar Publishing Limited.

Foster, J. B. 2002. *Ecology Against Capitalism*. New York: Monthly Review Press.

Fraser, N. 1996. "Social Justice in the Age of Identity Politics: Redistribution, Recognition and Participation," The Tanner Lectures on Human Values, Stanford University, 30 April–2 May.

Fraser, N. 1999. *Adding Insult to Injury: Social Justice and the Politics of Recognition*, ed. Kevin Olson. London: Verso.

Gadgil, Madhav and Guha, Ramachandra. 1993. *This Fissured Land: An Ecological History of India*. 8, 4. New Delhi: Oxford UP.

Gamson, W. 1990. *The Strategy of Social Protest*, 2nd ed. Belmont, CA: Wadsworth Press.

Gonzalez de Molina, Manuel, Antonio Herrera, Antonio Ortega Santos, and David Soto. 2009. "Peasant Protest as Environmental Protest: Some Cases from the 18th to the 20th Century." *Global Environment* 4: 48–77.

Gottlieb, R. 2009. "Where We Live, Work, Play . . . and Eat: Expanding the Environmental Justice Agenda." *Environmental Justice* 2: 7–8.

GRAIN. 2008. "Seized! The 2008 Land Grab for Food and Financial Security." *Briefing*, October.

Greyl, Lucie, Healy, Hali, Leonardi, Emanuele, and Temper, Leah. 2012. "Stop That Train! Ideological Conflict and the TAV." *Economics and Policy of Energy and the Environment.* www.francoangeli.it/Riviste/Scheda_Rivista.aspx?IDarticolo=46542.

Haas, W., Krausmann, F., Wiedenhofer, D., and Heinz, M. 2015. "How Circular is the Global Economy? An Assessment of Material Flows, Waste Production, and Recycling in the European Union and the World in 2005." *Journal of Industrial Ecology*, 19 (5): 765–777.

Harvey, David. 1996. *Justice, Nature, and the Geography of Difference*. Cambridge, MA: Blackwell Publishers.

IUCN. 2007. Environmental Justice and Rural Communities, Studies from India and Nepal. http://cmsdata.iucn.org/downloads/iucn_environmental_justice.pdf. Accessed 15 September 2014.

Kapp, K. W. 1950. *Social Costs of Business Enterprise*. London: Asia Publishing House.

Keck, M. and Sikkin, K. 1998. *Activists Beyond Borders: Advocacy Networks in International Politics*. Ithaca, NY: Cornell University Press.

Kumar, Kundan. 2014. "The Sacred Mountain: Confronting Global Capital at Niyamgiri." *Geoforum* 54, July: 196–206. doi:10.1016/j.geoforum.2013.11.008.

Latorre, S., Farrell, K., and Martinez-Alier, J. 2015. "The Commodification of Nature and Socio-Environmental Resistance in Ecuador: An Inventory of Accumulation by Dispossession Cases, 1980–2013." *Ecological Economics* 116: 58–69.

Leff, Enrique. 2012. "Political Ecology: A Latin American Perspective." *Encyclopedia of Life Support Systems (EOLSS)[www.Eolss.Net].* http://dtserv3.compsy.uni-jena.de/__c1257c0d004f39a4.nsf/0/C3ACECACC9DD7B5CC1257C0E005BDF3A/$FILE/Leff,%20Enrique_Political%20Ecology%20in%20Latin%20America_eolss.pdf.

Lerner, S. 2010. *Sacrifice Zones: The Front Lines of Toxic Chemical Exposure in the United States* (preface by Phil Brown). Cambridge, MA: MIT Press.

Levien, Michael. 2012. "The land question: special economic zones and the political economy of dispossession in India." *Journal of Peasant Studies*, 39 (3-4), 933–969.

Levien, Michael. 2013. "Regimes of Dispossession: From Steel Towns to Special Economic Zones." *Development and Change* 44 (2): 381–407.

Lora-Wainright, Anna. 2013. *Fighting for Breath: Living Morally and Dying of Cancer in a Chinese Village*. Honolulu: University of Hawai Press.

Martinez-Alier, J. 1995. "Distributional Issues in Ecological Economics." *Review of Social Economy* 53: 511–528.

Martinez-Alier, J. 2002. *The Environmentalism of the Poor: A Study of Ecological Conflicts and Valuation*. Cheltenham: Edward Elgar.

Martinez-Alier, J. 2011. "The EROI of Agriculture and Its Use by the via Campesina." *Journal of Peasant Studies* 38 (1): 145–160.

Martinez-Alier, J., Anguelovski, I., Bond, P., Del Bene, D., Demaria, F., Gerber, J. F., Greyl, L., Haas, W., Healy, H., Marín-Burgos, V., Ojo, G., Firpo Porto, M., Rijnhout, L., Rodríguez-Labajos, B., Spangenberg, J., Temper, L., Warlenius, R., and Yánez, I. 2014. "Between Activism and Science: Grassroots Concepts for Sustainability Coined by Environmental Justice Organizations." *Journal of Political Ecology* 21: 19–60.

Martinez-Alier, J. and O'Connor, M. 1996. "Economic and ecological distribution conflicts." In R. Costanza, O. Segura and J. Martinez-Alier eds. Washington, DC: Island Press, pp. 153–184.

Martinez-Alier, J. and Temper, Leah. 2007. "Oil Politics from the South." *Economic and Political Weeekly* 42 (50), December 15–21: 16–19.

Martinez-Alier, J., Temper, L., Del Bene, D., Scheidel, A. 2016. "Is there a global environmental justice movement?" *J Peasant Stud*, 43: 731–755. http://dx.doi.org/10.1080/03066150.2016.1141198#.V1P9FfkrI2w.

McAdam, D. 1982. *Structural Continuities in Protest Activity: The Legacy of Sixties Activism.* Paper presented at the Annual Meeting of the American Sociological Association (San Francisco, CA, September 5–9, 1982).

McAdam, D. and Snow, D. A. 2009. *Readings on Social Movements: Origins, Dynamics and Outcomes*, 2nd edition. Oxford: Oxford University Press.

McMichael, Philip. 2010. *Contesting Development: Critical Struggles for Social Change.* New York: Routledge.

Moore, J. W. 2000. "Sugar and the Expansion of the Early Modern World-Economy: Commodity Frontiers, Ecological Transformation, and Industrialization." *Review: A Journal of the Fernand Braudel Center* 23 (3): 409–433.

Munda, G., Paruccini, M., and Rossi, G. 1998. "Multicriteria evaluation methods in renewable resource management: the case of integrated water management under drought conditions." In Beinat, E. and Nijkamp, P., eds., *Multicriteria evaluation in land-use management: methodologies and case studies.* Kluwer: Dordrecht, pp. 79–94.

Neumann, Roderick P. 2002. "Nature-State Territory: Toward a Critical Theorization of Conservation Enclosures." In R. Peets and M. Watts, eds., *Liberation Ecologies: Environment, Development and Social Movements.* New York: Routledge. pp. 195–217.

Newman, M. K., Lucas, A., LaDuke, W., Berila, B., Di Chiro, G., Gaard, G., Hogan, K., Kaalund, V., Plevin, A., Prindeville, D. M., and Sze, J. 2004. *New Perspectives on Environmental Justice: Gender, Sexuality, and Activism.* New Brunswick, NJ: Rutgers University Press.

O'Connor, James. 1988. Capitalism, Nature, Socialism a Theoretical Introduction. www.tandfonline.com/doi/abs/10.1080/10455758809358356.

O'Connor, Martin. 1993. "On the Misadventures of Capitalist Nature." *Capitalism Nature Socialism* 4 (3): 7–40. doi:10.1080/10455759309358553.

Ostrom, E. 1990. *Governing the Commons: The Evolution of Institutions for Collective Action.* Cambridge: Cambridge University Press.

Özkaynak, B., Aydın, C. I., Ertör-Akyazı, P., and Ertör, I. 2015a. "The Gezi Park Resistance from an Environmental Justice and Social Metabolism Perspective." *Capitalism, Nature, Socialism* 26 (1): 96–114.

Özkaynak, B., Rodriguez-Labajos, B., Aydın, C. I., Yanez, I., and Garibay, C. 2015b. "Towards Environmental Justice Success in Mining Conflicts: An Empirical Investigation." *EJOLT Report* 14: 96.

Pérez Rincón, M. A. 2014. "Conflictos ambientales en Colombia: inventario, caracterización y análisis." In L. J. Garay ed., *Minería en Colombia: control público, memoria y justicia socio-ecológica, movimientos sociales y posconflicto.* Bogotá: Contraloría General de la República, pp. 253–325.

Porto de Souza, M. F. 2012. "Movements and the Network of Environmental Justice in Brazil." *Environmental Justice* 5 (2): 100–104.

Porto de Souza, M. F., Pacheco, T., and Leroy, J. P. eds. 2013. *Injustiça ambiental e saúde no Brasil. O mapa de conflitos.* Río de Janeiro: Fiocruz.

Reitan, Ruth. 2007. *Global Activism.* New York: Routledge.

Routledge, Paul. 2003. "Convergence Space: Process Geographies of Grassroots Globalization Networks." *Transactions of the Institute of British Geographers* 28 (3): 333–349.

Sachs, W. 1995. "Global Ecology and the Shadow of Development." In George Sessions, ed., *Deep Ecology for the 21st Century*, pp. 417–27.

Schlosberg, D. 2007. *Defining Environmental Justice: Theories, Movements and Nature.* Oxford: Oxford University Press.

Sharp, G. 1973. *The Politics of Nonviolent Action*, 3 vols. Boston: Porter Sargent.

Sikor, T. and Newell, P. 2014. "Globalizing Environmental Justice?" *Geoforum* 54: 151–157.

Snow, David A. and Benford, Robert D. 1988. "Ideology, Frame Resonance, and Participant Mobilization." *International Social Movement Research* 1 (1): 197–217.

Soule, Sarah. 1997. "The Student Divestment Movement in the United States and Tactical Diffusion: The Shantytown Protest." *Social Forces* 75: 855–883.

Svampa, Maristella. 2013. "«Consenso de Los Commodities» y Lenguajes de Valoración en América Latina." *Nueva Sociedad* 244: 30–46.

Swyngedouw, E. 2010. "Impossible sustainability and the post-political condition." In M. Cerrata, ed., *Making Strategies in Spatial Planning.* Netherlands: Springer, pp. 185–205.

Tarrow, Sydney. 1998. *Power in Movement: Social Movements and Contentious Politics*, 2nd ed. Cambridge: Cambridge University Press.

Temper, L. 2014. *Environmentalism of the dispossessed: Mapping ecologies of resistance.* Doctoral dissertation. Barcelona: Universitat Autonoma de Barcelona.

Temper, L., del Bene, D., and Martinez-Alier, J. 2015. "Mapping the Frontiers and Front Lines of Global Environmental Justice: The EJ Atlas." *Journal of Political Ecology* 22: 256.

Temper, Leah and Martinez-Alier, Joan. 2013. "The God of the Mountain and Godavarman: Net Present Value, Indigenous Territorial Rights and Sacredness in a Bauxite Mining Conflict in India." *Ecological Economics* 96, December: 79–87. doi:10.1016/j.ecolecon.2013.09.011.

Temper, L., Yánez, I., Sharife, K., Ojo, G., Martinez-Alier, J., CANA, Combes, M., Cornelissen, K., Lerkelund, H., Louw, M., Martínez, E., Minnaar, J., Molina, P., Murcia, D., Oriola, T., Osuoka, A., Pérez, M. M., Roa Avendaño, T., Urkidi, L., Valdés, M., Wadzah, N., and Wykes, S. 2013. *Towards a Post-Oil Civilization: Yasunization and Other Initiatives to Leave Fossil Fuels in the Soil* (Barcelona: EJOLT Report No. 6).

Upton, Caroline. 2014. "The New Politics of Pastoralism: Identity, Justice and Global Activism." *Geoforum* 54, July: 207–216.

Urkidi, L. and Walter, M. 2011. "Dimensions of Environmental Justice in Anti-Gold Mining Movements in Latin America." *Geoforum* 42 (6): 683–695.

van der Velden, J. H. A. 2007. *Strikes Around the World, 1968–2005: Case-Studies of 15 Countries.* Amsterdam: Amsterdam University Press.

Walker, G. 2012. *Environmental Justice: Concepts, Evidence and Politics.* London: Routledge.

Walter, M., and Urkidi, L. 2015. "Community Mining Consultations in Latin America (2002–2012): The Contested Emergence of a Hybrid Institution for Participation." *Geoforum.* http://dx.doi.org/10.1016/j.geoforum.2015.09.007.

Žižek, Slavoj. 1992. *Looking Awry: An Introduction to Jacques Lacan through Popular Culture.* Cambridge, MA: MIT Press.

# 3 Red–green alliance-building against Durban's port-petrochemical complex expansion

*Patrick Bond*

## Introduction: overaccumulated merchant capital

Two processes are now underway, responsible for uprooting existing urban processes in many of the world's port cities, in the process amplifying the socio-ecological metabolism of capitalism. First, there is the intensified role of the city as an export platform, and second, rising contradictions associated with global over-production and the subsequent decline in shipping. These processes became more obvious since 2008, when many port cities appeared extremely over-extended. Trade crashed dramatically during the second half of that year, and commodity prices fell further. In many cities with major ports, there were social uprisings. While very few of these were centered on the direct issue of export orientation, the indirect causes of socio-political unrest can be traced, to some extent, to the perceived need to make cities more friendly to export-oriented – and increasingly unpatriotic – capital.

Dating to the liberation of the country from apartheid in 1994, the democratic South Africa's *Urban Development Strategy* states the neoliberal, export-oriented agenda clearly: 'Seen through the prism of the global economy, our urban areas are single economic units that either rise, or stagnate and fall together. . . . South Africa's cities are more than ever strategic sites in a transnationalized production system' (Ministry of Reconstruction and Development, 1994–95). But to be a 'strategic site' in an exceptionally competitive milieu requires the reconfiguration of port cities, according to Kim Moody (2014):

> Port extensions and the huge 'back of the port' logistics centers are gobbling up land and communities, often moving further and further inland. This in return requires new transport 'corridors.' It isn't just merchant capital because these relate to manufacturing production supply chains as well and, of course, commodities export. Pollution is massive.

But in the wake of the commodity super-cycle's rise and fall, port cities' reliance upon the maritime sector, tourism, and commodity exports has severe dangers, as the globalized economy begins what may become known as a 1930s-style 'deglobalization' era. *The Economist* argued in October 2013 in its cover story, entitled 'The Gated Globe',

> Globalization has clearly paused. A simple measure of trade intensity, world exports as a share of world GDP, rose steadily from 1986 to 2008 but has been flat since. Global capital flows, which in 2007 topped $11 trillion, amounted to barely a third of that figure last year. Cross-border direct investment is also well down on its 2007 peak . . . hidden protectionism is flourishing, often under the guise of export promotion or industrial policy.
>
> (*The Economist*, 2013)

The pause button will no doubt be lifted. Yet in what was otherwise a celebration of global flows, the consulting firm McKinsey Global Institute also acknowledged that a peak had been reached in 2007 with $29.3 trillion in flows – 52% of world GDP – which then sunk in relative terms over the next five years, to just 36%: 'This reflects the correction from the global credit bubble and deleveraging of the financial system. Financial flows have changed direction, too, with outflows from emerging markets rising from 7 percent of the global total in 1990 to 38 percent in 2012' (MicKinsey Global Institute, 2014). Beginning in May 2013, investors roiled South Africa and four other major emerging markets when the US Federal Reserve's Quantitative Easing began to be phased out ('tapered'). As a result of slightly higher US interest rates, outflows meant that four of the five BRICS – South Africa, India, Brazil, and Russia (which suffered again from financial sanctions imposed after its Crimea invasion) – experienced substantial currency crashes that, in turn, would limit their capacity to import.

Because of the economic turmoil affecting the BRICS, Indonesia, Turkey and similar sites, it is wise to recall the United Nations warning, that the world's financial markets aim to shift 'high-risk activities from more to less strictly regulated environments,' especially sites where massive state-subsidized and guaranteed infrastructure projects are envisaged (United Nations, 2013). In these sites, both borrower and lender are facing intense levels of desperation: to sink excess funds into mega-projects on behalf of multinational capital. The decline (1900–2002), rise (2002–11) and crash (2011-present) of commodity prices reflects this desperation, and also helps explain why ports are facing such intense competition, with fewer surpluses to draw upon for the sake of financing expansion. From 1982, the Third World Debt Crisis compelled commodity-producing economies to lower currency values and raise exports to pay off debt. The Bretton Woods Institutions and other banks restructured these economies into neoliberal export platforms.

With persistent oversupply, until 2002 there was a distinct downturn in world commodity prices, but a turning point in 2002 reflected a new critical mass in East Asian (especially Chinese) imports of raw materials. This led to a massive price spike that withstood the 2008–09 crash and ultimately peaked in 2011. Since then the prices of nearly every major mineral and fossil fuel has crashed, often by more than half. With slowing demand from China, the overall result contributed to a decline in world trade, not only dramatically in the 2008–2009 Great Recession, but in the period from mid-2011 to the present as global overproduction trends resurfaced.

Also since 2012, there has been a major decline in annual foreign direct investment at world scale, with the peak of $1.56 trillion reached in 2011, followed by a drop to $1.40 trillion in 2012 and to $1.23 trillion in 2014 (United Nations Conference on Trade and Development, 2015). The increase in US Federal Reserve interest rates in December 2015 is slowing real-economy activity even further, and one indication of the latter is the glut in corporate savings that follows a steady recent decline in corporate investment that in turn follows the decline in the rate of profit.

One specific victim of this stagnation is shipping. The mid-2008 peak for pricing transport of a typical container reflected the intense metabolism of commodity trading at the time, falling by more than 90% within six months. Even though after the 2009 recovery, commodity prices resumed their rise, the Baltic Dry Index of shipping prices never rose to even a third of their peak, and by 2016 sunk to a 30-year low. So while to carry a container from Shanghai to the US East Coast in March 2015 cost $2500, that price fell to $1500 by June and less than $400 by January 2016. At the same time, there was a dramatic rise in the capacity of 'post-Panamax' ships – carrying more than 5000 containers (so named because of the limits of the size that fit through the Panama Canal before 2016) – to the point that ships with more than 15, 000 containers were flooding the market. Such ships were so robotized that they had only 13 crew.

The question that many shipping observers in Latin America, Africa, and Asia were forced to ask by 2016, was whether their own capacity expansion had also gone too far. Would crashing commodity prices, rising US interest rates, ongoing European stagnation, worsening financial volatility and emerging market slumps (especially in the three most vulnerable BRICS: Brazil, Russia and South Africa) together doom shipping growth and thus the new port developments? And what, then, would that structural combination 'from above' imply for urban politics 'from below'?

## The Durban port-petrochemical expansion

South Africa's biggest single location-specific investment project ($25 billion – the cost estimated prior to what could become a typical 50%–300% price escalation) is the proposed eight-fold expansion of South Durban's port-petrochemical complex over the next three decades. The doubling of the petroleum pipeline capacity from Durban to Johannesburg recently cost $2.3 billion alone. The notorious refineries owned by BP, Shell and the Malaysian firm Engen present major health threats to residential areas. These neighborhoods have been occupied by black South Africans for generations – the 'Indian' areas of Merebank and Clairwood and 'colored' Wentworth – but have become very slightly desegregated since the end of apartheid, mainly through the influx of low-income black 'African' shackdwellers.[1] The potential to desegregate Durban was great in 1994, given large tracts of land that became redundant by deindustrialization, and the need for densification. But by all accounts, practically no progress was made.

Jobs for South Durban's vast unemployed labor reserve are desperately needed, and government's (myopic) national planners claim the expansion of world shipping, from the Panamax 5000-container ships to super post-Panamax ships more than three times larger, will raise annual container traffic from 2.5 million to 20 million units processed annually in Durban by 2040. However, local residents' organizations – united as the South Durban Community Environmental Alliance (SDCEA) – offer multiple overlapping critiques of this project, including the flawed participatory process; the destruction of small-scale farming and long-standing communities (with tens of thousands of expected displacements, major ecological problems in the estuarine bay, climate change causes and effects, and irrational economics fuelled by overly generous state subsidies but still resulting in an unaffordable harbor).

The framing of the campaign is of great importance not simply because the state and allied businesses falsely promise tens of thousands of 'jobs' (in an increasingly capital-intensive sector) but because an alternative vision is being established by SDCEA based on an ecologically-sensitive, labor-intensive economic and social strategy for the South Durban Basin. To achieve victory will require a major shift in the balance of forces, one which campaigners argue can be enhanced by financial sanctions against the project and its parastatal corporate sponsor, Transnet. This is a site-specific project but one with more general lessons for grassroots contestation of industrial mal-development.

Global contradictions are often amplified at lower scales, especially when intensified metabolisms of capitalist commerce and energy threaten widespread displacement, pollution, and community unrest. The 'spatial fix' to overaccumulation crisis is witnessed in the ongoing restructuring of world shipping, while externalities such as greenhouse gas emissions represent 'accumulation by dispossession,' as capital takes further control of non-capitalist territories, consistent with theories of imperialism and crisis displacement pioneered by Rosa Luxemburg (Luxemburg, 1968).

To illustrate with a detailed South African case study sometimes termed Africa's 'armpit' (for its noxious smell), the expansion of the Durban port and petrochemical complex is the main site-specific 'Strategic Investment Project' within the national government's 2012 National Development Plan. South Durban is the second highest-priority mega-project of the Presidential Infrastructure Coordinating Commission (after a coal railroad expansion) (National Planning Commission, 2012). Raising the vast funds required will be the most critical challenge, given SDCEA's willingness to begin a financial sanctions campaign against the project. The first phase of the work, costing approximately $4 billion, was pre-funded by the government and allied financiers so as to bring more oil from Durban to Johannesburg and shore up the Durban port's main existing quays. Major contestations ahead are over the much greater needs entailed in a new 'dig-out port' to be built on the site of the city's old airport as well as a logistics park and massive roads and rail lines.

## Transnet's investment strategy

But funding is already being lined up. In March 2013, during the Durban summit of the heads of state of Brazil, Russia, India, China, and SA (BRICS), a Chinese bank lent $5 billion to Transnet. This was mainly for the purpose of extending rail infrastructure further into the northern and eastern coal fields for subsequent coal exports mainly to India and China. But the funds also provided resources for the purchase of locomotives (mainly from Chinese producers, mainly for the Waterberg-Richards Bay coal route) and for Durban's harbor expansion, since such funding is essentially fungible. In addition to increasing the speed and magnitude of freight to the world's largest coal export terminal, at Richards Bay, Transnet has also been planning a fully-privatized port management model for the Durban Dig-Out Port.

Durban is also now a site of offshore oil prospecting by ExxonMobil, not far from the point where Africa's largest refinery complex stands in hyper-toxic South Durban. There, near-universal community opposition has emerged against Transnet's plans, including on grounds of climate damage. Transnet's Environmental Impact Assessment (EIA) consultants made a contentious statement in 2013 – that larger ships in the new port will allegedly result in lower emissions per container carried – because they failed to consider the alternative of not increasing shipping by the extreme eight-fold multiple.

Aside from the doubling of the width of a petroleum pipeline to Johannesburg, the first set of projects will result in a dramatic increase in existing port capacity, in order that 5000+ container 'post-Panamax' ships can be accommodated in the current harbor (stages 1–3). Originally, the dig-out port at the old airport site was to be excavated in 2016, with an anticipated first berthing in 2020 (stage 4), but in November 2015 Transnet announced an indefinite postponement due to adequate existing capacity. The final growth of the existing port will include an extensive dig-out of the area currently under Transnet railroad siding property (stages 5–6).

The helter-skelter growth of container traffic prior to 2008 reflected the liberalization of transport in the early 1990s, and with it, the move of freight to road-based trucking. That left large amounts of Transnet rail-related land mostly unused. The latter stages of the project are in close proximity to the predominantly Indian areas of Isipingo and Merebank in the south and Clairwood in the north, as well as the African township of Umlazi and the colored Wentworth area. The Clairwood area is most immediately threatened by Stages 1–3 port expansion, as trucking companies invade the residential space to stack containers.

Transnet's most critical challenge will be finding the money for an estimated $25 billion worth of other mega-projects , especially given the scale of the project and how many aspects are being contested. The Chinese bank loan apparently comes without conditions (and with terms not publicly disclosed), and subsequently, there were also several bond offerings of several hundred million dollars, including in the London markets in November 2013 where Transnet paid an enormous premium on its Rand-denominated bonds: 9.5%. But the longer-term threat to South Durban and other communities is that the BRICS New Development Bank launched in July 2015 will seek projects like this one, as exemplars of export-oriented infrastructure.

In July 2013, a high-profile meeting of the Durban Transport Forum heard Transnet's port expansion director Marc Descoins update his team's planning: 'The fatal flaws analysis yielded many risks but no show-stoppers' (Creamer's Engineering News, 2013). Descoins had not, at that time, factored in resident and labor opposition to the mega-project, its vast environmental implications, or rising disgust about construction-driven White Elephants. Tracing several of the problems with the port-petrochemicalexpansion in South Durban sheds light on the interconnections between social and environmental grievances, as well as a growing debate about SA's vulnerability to the world economy.

## The doubling of oil pipeline capacity

Transnet's Durban-Johannesburg oil pipeline construction project lasted from 2007–14. The mega-project, known as the 'new multi-product pipeline', cost $2.34 billion, a dramatic cost escalation in part because the pipeline was diverted hundreds of kilometers from the traditional route west along the N3 highway. That route ran through mostly-white Durban suburbs (Mariannhill, Hillcrest, Shongweni and Camperdown), and now the pipeline moves double the pre-existing oil volume through (mostly-black) South Durban, Umbumbulu and other former KwaZulu bantustan areas.[2]

According to Durban's leading environmental journalist, Tony Carnie, 'The $600 million petrol, diesel and jet fuel pipeline will replace the existing Durban-to-Johannesburg pipeline which was built in 1965. The existing pipeline is believed to have rust defects and cannot cope with the future demand in fuel growth in Gauteng (Carnie, 2008).' By moving the project southwards before turning west, the cost estimate rose by more than 50%. But there were many other cost increases, with the total reaching $2.34 billion by 2013, in part because of apparent construction company collusion on tendering by one of the main pipeline construction companies, Group Five Civil Engineering (Venter, 2013).

In his own 2012 review of the cost overruns, without considering construction company collusion, Public Enterprises Minister Malusi Gigaba uncovered 'systemic failings that compromised the intended outcomes' and he admitted that his project managers 'lacked sufficient capacity and depth of experience for the client overview of a mega-project of this complexity especially related to "analysis of risks". Nor were EIAs or water and wetland permits 'pursued with sufficient foresight and vigour' (Gigaba, 2012). Well before this became public knowledge (Group Five only stepped forward to confess its role in industry collusion in 2009), SDCEA offered several critiques of the pipeline, including the racially-biased routing; inadequate public participation; dubious motivations for the pipeline; government's failure to prevent, detect or manage pipeline leaks; and climate change (SDCEA, 2008).

According to SDCEA, the race and class bias were crucial reasons to reject Transnet's rerouting strategy, because 'The pipeline threatens people with potentially severe environmental safety and health problems (well known to refinery victims in South Durban), *in a manner that is discriminatory along class and racial lines.*' The local ecology itself was already saturated with toxins, SDCEA alleged in 2008:

> Durban Bay, in which the harbor is situated, is struggling to cope with the pollution loads from harbor and associated activities, contaminated riverine and storm-water inflows. The expansion will require further removal of aspects of the Bay's ecosystem, which will in turn further reduce the assimilative capacity of this threatened and fragile estuary. There have been major incidents affecting the harbor, including the September 2007 fire at Island View Storage. Reducing the amount of hazardous material being stored, handled, and transported in the harbor is a crucial first step to reducing the risk to people living, traveling, and working in the area. Yet the pipeline proposal will do the opposite. The routing of the pipeline south, directly through low-income black residential areas instead of through areas including farming lands owned by wealthy white South Africans, is suspiciously reminiscent of the environmental racism we in South Durban have become familiar with . . . The leaks that have occurred in existing petroleum pipelines have been devastating to South Durban, including the 1.3 million liters that spilled from Sapref lines in 2001, that were not detected until residents complained. According to present practices, only a leak of more than 1 percent will be detected. Incidents leading to a loss of product which is not detectable by the system may continue to pollute the soil and groundwater for a long time. During this period, many people, fauna and flora may be affected by the consequences of the pollution and not understand the cause until it is too late. In this case, the costs will not be borne by the polluter, as our legal framework requires.[3]

Many of the same complaints arose again four years later, in mid-2012, when the next stage of the port-petrochemical complex reached fruition: the proposal for a new dig-out port and expansion of the old port. The most heart-felt of the critiques levelled was against displacement because, for many Indian and African residents of South Durban, their earlier neighbors during apartheid were moved to South Durban from Cato Manor, a well-located residential area. Displacement was central to apartheid's racial segregation strategy. Now the same appeared imminent, though this time for class reasons.

## Displacement and the trucking threat

SDCEA, the Wentworth Development Forum and Merebank Residents Association and the Clairwood Residents and Ratepayers Association are justifiably convinced that the port-petrochemical project will generate not just traffic chaos, but residential displacement on a substantial scale. From the north, the old harbor's expansion creep will displace residents by the thousands from the culture-rich, 150 year old Indian and African community of Clairwood. That area's African shackdwellers and long-time Indian residents are already under threat from reckless trucking companies, who are beneficiaries of the rezoning – or simply failure to enforce existing zoning – that facilitates Back-of-Ports creep.

In the process of liberalized zoning and lack of residential area zoning enforcement by the municipality, ten Clairwood and nearby Bluff suburb residents were killed in the decade 2003–13 by truck accidents. Mostly carrying freight, these drivers killed 70 people in the course of 7000 accidents in Durban in 2012 alone. The worst single case occurred in September 2013, when 24 people were killed by a runaway freight truck on a mountain range within Durban city limits: the Field's Hill section of the alternative (non-tolled) highway from Johannesburg.

That tragic accident was revealing, for one of the world's three largest shipping companies, Evergreen, hired a local informal truck company which allegedly instructed its driver to avoid tolls to save $4. Police cracked down after the accident and found several of the company's trucks operating under unsafe conditions. The one that hit two commuter taxis was driven by an unqualified, underpaid immigrant driver; the truck's brakes failed on one of the steepest highways in the country. A few weeks later, government proposed restricting that particular hill to only 5 tonne trucks, banning 16 tonne trucks. But the broader problem of rising accidents was not addressed.

## Local ecological degradation

Opposition from local communities will grow even more intense once the largest part of the port expansion begins. The proposed dig-out port is where the old airport stood, on the southern border of Merebank. To dig a 1.5 kilometer length of soil 20 meters deep is dangerous, given how many toxic chemicals have come to rest there over the decades. Even Descoins conceded, 'We have to look at contamination issues. Hydrocarbons have been pumped around this area for decades and we know there have been some leaks.' That soil, water, and air pollution will exacerbate the five-year dust cover under which the dig-out port's construction will suffocate Merebank and Wentworth, the mainly Indian and colored communities of South Durban. These neighborhoods are already coated with regular oil-related sulfur and soot showers from the oil-refining complex, as witnessed in their world-leading asthma rates.

In addition to damage to human health, BirdLife SA observed that, since Durban has one of just three estuarine bays in SA, its 'ecosystem services' value of goods and services is vast: as a heat sink and carbon sink, for biodiversity, as a fish nursery, for waste disposal, and for storm protection. Moreover, the Bonn Convention's protections for bird migration should make estuaries and wetlands, such as South Durban's, immune from more cementing. In May 2013, Gigaba dismissed the worries over 'frogs and chameleons' (Gedye, 2013). In contrast, the ecological damage implied in this stage of Transnet's expansion was so extreme that the Department of Environmental Affairs rejected the first version of the EIA in October 2013 (Abadar, 2013), which described the impacts of the build-out of berths 203–205 – then able to handle ships of no more than 12 meters depth – so as to accommodate super-post-Panamax ships of 15,000 containers or more.

One of the two reasons was Transnet's failure to do more than 'monitor' the damage caused to the major sandbank in the middle of the estuarine bay, which hosts so many reproductive processes for fish and birdlife (Abadar, 2013). As SA's leading maritime journalist Terry Hutson remarked at the time:

> In Durban there is little likelihood of any big growth in volumes in the near future. A few years ago, the port went backwards in the number of containers it handled, dropping something like 200, 000 TEU in a year and there has been little growth since . . . So the questions remain: Does Durban need the deeper berths and aren't the bigger ships premature?
>
> (Hutson, 2014)

## Global ecological implications and local climate adaptation

The other reason Transnet suffered an early rejection of its EIA was due to the most important environmental problem of all, climate change. The firm's consultants (from Nemai and the Science Council) simply did not consider the impact of rising sea levels or extreme storms (Transnet, 2012). As oceans warm up, cyclones and hurricanes intensify, with resulting sea-level rise. 'The volume of Arctic sea ice has been reduced by 75 percent in just 30 years,' reported the world's most respected climate scientist, James Hansen in 2012: 'There is a danger that the ice sheets will begin to collapse and we could get several meters of rising sea levels in one year' (Cornell University, 2012). At that rate, big parts of central Durban would sink, along with other cities where coastal sprawl has left millions in low-lying danger: Mumbai (2.8 million inhabitants exposed as seawaters rise), Shanghai (2.4 million), Miami (2 million), Alexandria (1.3 million) and Tokyo (1.1 million).

Durban has suffered early indications of extreme weather events and associated damage. In March 2007, in one storm exacerbated by unusual tidal activity akin to a tsunami, Durban's main municipal official reported 'wave run-up heights' which 'peaked at 10.57 meters above Mean Sea Level.' The bulk of the beach sand was washed away along the coast and nearly a billion dollars' worth of coast infrastructure was destroyed. In June 2008, a storm submerged much of the South Durban Basin's main valley, cutting off the Bluff and Wentworth from the main access highway. In November 2011, the day before the United Nations Framework Convention on Climate Change (COP17) summit began in Durban, a rainstorm wreaked such havoc that a dozen people died when their poorly-constructed, publicly-funded houses collapsed on them. In August 2012, the same Durban port berths (203–205) proposed for expansion were severely damaged during heavy winds which bumped a ship up against cranes, resulting in a two week-long closure, and a few miles south, the Engen oil refinery was largely submerged by flooding.

Just as important, what of the mitigation challenge associated with the port-petrochemical complex? According to the Academy of Science of SA's 2011 book, *Durban: Towards a Low Carbon City*, 'The transport sector is pivotal to the transition to a low carbon city . . . The top priority was identified as the need to reduce the vehicle kilometers travelled in the road freight sector as this provided the greatest opportunity to simultaneously reduce emissions of GreenHouse Gases and traditional air pollutants' (Academy of Science of SA, 2011). The port-petrochemical expansion will do the opposite, in part because for decades, Transnet sabotaged its own rail freight capacity, allowing road trucking of container traffic to surge from 20% to 80%.

Yet in addressing the obviously adverse ecological implications of their project, Transnet hired Nemai Consulting, an EIA specialist with no apparent climate consciousness. They in turn hired a sub-contractor, an official of the SA Council for Scientific and Industrial Research, whose 2011 report, 'Modelling of potential environmental change in the port marine environment', also completely ignored climate change. Follow-up with officials of Nemai in 2012 generated this reply: 'The project will decrease the ship waiting and turnaround times which will have a lower carbon impact.' The consultants did not factor in the dynamic aspects of the shipping system, meaning that if there is an increase in efficiency by reducing the ships' offshore wait, the result is to speed up the system as a whole, thus *increasing* carbon impact (Bond, 2012–13).

The same carefree, denialist attitude to climate was evident in the doubling of oil pipeline capacity from Durban to Johannesburg. According to a SDCEA EIA critique (ignored by officials),

> The proposed pipeline will make a vast contribution to the climate crisis, yet the EIA only speaks in two areas, very briefly, of this problem. The Draft Scoping Report notes that the current Durban International Airport site is within the 1:100 year flood plain, and that the Island View site is 'potentially affected by sea level rise in the future as a result of climate change.' The Scoping Report promises to consider this in the future EIA. In addition, the Draft Scoping Report summary notes in 'TABLE 5–1: Summary of legal requirements that apply to the project and the EIA process' that the Kyoto Protocol is relevant, as it 'Commits a country to quantified emissions limitations and reductions.'
>
> In the first instance, SDCEA does not believe the Draft Scoping Report has begun to grapple properly with location of the pipeline along the South Coast. As our appendix of photographs of 2007–08 storm damage shows, even concrete structures came under severe attack from the elements and were found wanting, as a result of locations in low-lying coastal areas, including the Bluff, Wentworth and Merebank, through which the new pipeline will run. Other areas of Amanzimtoti and the South Coast were demolished in June 2008.

The Draft Scoping Report treats these dangers casually, in spite of the record of public infrastructural decay noted above, in which a variety of pipeline maintenance crises have arisen, causing enormous ecological despoilation. Second, the rise of $CO_2$ emissions that will be facilitated by the pipeline is immense, and is only referred to in the Draft Scoping Report as a potential legal problem, with no details provided. Since Minister of Environment and Tourism Marthinus van Schalkwyk has committed South Africa to substantive emissions cuts which will be formalized at the 2009 Copenhagen Conference of Parties to the Kyoto Protocol, a huge effort by all state agencies, including Transnet, will be required to reduce emissions in all areas. The proposed pipeline does the opposite, just as South Africa enters the 21st century with emissions that are 42 percent of the entire African continent's output, and 20 times higher per unit of per capita GDP than even the USA's emissions.

(SDCEA, 2008)

Whether pointing out emissions-reductions promises made in Copenhagen or in the 2011 Durban and 2015 Paris UN climate summits, it proved impossible to shame South African officials for climate denialism. In his February 2016 budget speech, Finance Minister Pravin Gordhan (2016) on the one hand proudly observed how in Paris "South Africa's response to the global climate change challenge has been prepared" but three sentences later he bragged, "work has begun on a new gas terminal and oil and ship repair facilities at Durban."

## Economic irrationality

Ironically, in spite of all the socio-economic controversies, financing for the port-petrochemical project may ultimately be threatened most by the project's inefficiency and lack of economic feasibility. The argument in favor of the port is mainly that jobs will be created and SA will have world-class infrastructure for export-led growth. But rising capital intensity at Transnet along with trade-related deindustrialization may result in fewer manufactured exports as well as net employment loss. This has been the norm since 1994 when democracy also ushered in economic liberalization after SA joined the World Trade Organization. Subsequent port expansion and Transnet restructuring did not create new jobs, but destroyed employment.

The project only makes financial sense if South Africa's economic development mentality is locked into national boundaries established in Berlin during the colonial 'Scramble for Africa' in 1885, the point at which borders were determined by white men representing imperial interests. As the region's main port-rail link to the largest market, Gauteng – and from there to the rest of the subcontinent – Durban is facing stiff competition from Maputo in Mozambique for shipments to Johannesburg, because it is a more direct, shorter and much less mountainous journey. In addition, there is general container-handling competition from other ports along the coast attempting to set up regional freight hubs and export processing zones, including a vast state-subsidized complex, Coega, in the Eastern Cape near Port Elizabeth (Bond, 2002).

As it stands, Durban's costs of processing freight are the highest in the world, at $1080 per container, or $400,000 per typical ship. What port advocates have not been able to do is explain how an additional $25 billion in investments (no doubt much more what with recent trends tripling original estimates) will cut operating and maintenance costs to competitive levels. Repaying the principle, interest on the capital, and all the additional costs will force much higher container-handling charges, leaving the real prospect of another white elephant. In Durban, similar projects that were anticipated to earn profits – such as the airport, convention center and marine entertainment complex – all have needed multi-million dollar annual taxpayer bailouts.

## An alternative strategy

Is an alternative to this flawed economic development strategy possible? A very different Strategic Investment Project would recognize the urgent need to detox South Durban and reboot the local economy towards more labor-intensive, low-polluting industry, and add much more public transport, renewable energy, organic agriculture not reliant upon pesticides, a 'zero-waste' philosophy, and a new ethos of consumption. The South Durban activists and the national Million Climate Jobs campaign want society to adopt this approach, but they remain on a collision course with Transnet, its financiers, the Treasury and Presidential Infrastructure Coordinating Commission, as well as the municipality. Unlike the Medupi campaign from February to April 2010, there is far more time for mobilization of advocacy pressure to halt Transnet's access to external financing, and hence the project itself.

In October 2012, at a Presidential Infrastructure Investment Conference in Johannesburg, Deputy Public Works Minister Jeremy Cronin confessed what was patently obvious in the neo-colonial SA economy: 'Too much of our development has been plantation to port, mine to port.' Instead, Cronin argued, South Africa needs 'social infrastructure, such as water, hospitals, schools, and housing, in order to prevent the kind of protests witnessed recently in the mining sector (CityPress, 2012).' Cronin's influence notwithstanding, this rhetoric is probably just a case of 'talk-left, invest-right': in mega-projects like Medupi and South Durban's port sprawl, against the interests of people and planet, and instead on behalf of corporate profits. In these respects, there was more continuity than change in the pre-1994 and post-1994 eras. For many years, such mega-projects have dominated corporate investment, and these have always entailed very generous state-supported subsidies, usually associated with mining (Free State Goldfields), smelters (Alusaf, Columbus), airports and ports (Richards Bay, Saldanha, Coega), mega-dams (Gariep, Lesotho), coal-fired power plants and other energy projects (Mossgas, Sasol oil-from-coal) and special projects (sports stadiums and the Gautrain).

There remains a formidable lobby for fossil fuel–based infrastructure investment in SA, ranging from mining houses to the construction industry. The elite mandate is to 'mine more and faster and ship what we mine cheaper and faster', as *Business Day* editor Peter Bruce ordained just as Gordhan was finalizing his $100 billion infrastructure budget in February 2012 (Bruce, 2012).

Thanks to this philosophy, South Africa's national and local ecological problems have become far worse, according to the government's 2006 Environmental Outlook research report, which noted 'a general decline in the state of the environment (South African Department of Environment, 2007).' By 2012, the country's 'Environmental Performance Index' ranking slipped to 5th worst of 133 countries surveyed by Columbia and Yale University researchers (Environmental Performance Index, 2015) For example, Gauteng, the country's main megalopolis, experienced water scarcity and water table pollution. When the first two Lesotho mega-dams were built during the late 1990s with World Bank financing, there were not only destructive environmental consequences downriver, but the extremely costly cross-catchment water transfer to Johannesburg raised water prices, thus, deterring consumption by poor people in low-income townships and generating world-class water protests.

With this level of degradation, it is no surprise that there is such intense labor, social and environmentalist resistance. The 2012–15 World Economic Forum *Global Competitiveness Reports* placed SA in the world-leading position for adverse employee-employer relations out of the 140 countries surveyed (World Economic Forum, 2012). And thousands of protests are recorded by police each year; in 2012–13, for example, the minister of police reported on '1, 882 violent public protests, (SAPA, 2013)' a number that rose above 2,200 in 2014–15.

But local protests rarely coagulate to threaten national power structures, aside from unusual moments such as the October 2015 student protests against high fee increases which led to three national targets on subsequent days and hence the state's $150 million tuition concession to the activists. But all attempts to change South Africa's carbon-intensive, export-oriented economic policy have failed, thus far. One harbinger of the coming conflict was in January 2014 when in parliament, SDCEA was prevented from testifying about the port-petrochemical complex during hearings on a fast-track Infrastructure Development Bill which passed a few weeks later, and which will reduce to a maximum of one year the approval processes for EIAs and other permits. As a result, if the project does not suffer more delays due to the overarching world capitalist stagnation of shipping, the only obvious pressure point will be for SDCEA to attack Transnet's financing.

What is at stake in South Durban, as in so many other similar sites of micropolitical-ecological struggle, is whether common sense prevails over profits, and the only determinant of that common sense appears to be the fusion of social justice and environmental advocacy, in what we can term a red–green coalition. That advocacy is typically aimed at swinging the balance of power in the favor of the former (common sense), by reducing the latter (profits), perhaps through non-violent civil disobedience of the sort pioneered in KwaZulu-Natal (in Newcastle, not far from Durban) in 1913 by Mahatma Gandhi; i.e., of the sort international anti-apartheid activists used to assist in ending apartheid. The most powerful weapon was financial sanctions. And whether the World Bank and other international lenders – including China and the coming BRICS New Development Bank – can be compelled to avoid new Transnet financing, is a matter of organizing prowess.

## Conclusion: activist narratives aiming to connect the dots

South Durban's experience so far corresponds to more general conclusions about community contestations of industrial activity as a result of global-local rescaling processes sometimes termed '*glocalization*. In the face of the widespread yet elusive power of transnational corporations, civil society nonetheless continually pressures companies to reduce environmental and social impacts from their activities, ' as Leah Horowitz explains:

> Protestors may use direct action, such as violent attacks, or discursive action, including court battles as well as attempts to tarnish the companies' reputations, which are increasingly important in a globalized world. All these costs contribute to 'the internalization of externalities.' Beyond direct costs to corporations, these actions influence the financial sector as investors realize that companies pass financial and reputational risks on to the institutions that support them, and that a company's management of environmental and social issues may provide an indication of its ability to tackle other management problems. These concerns have prompted investors to screen potential funding recipients, through mechanisms such as the FTSE4Good Index Series, and have inspired powerful funding agencies such as the World Bank to impose directives upon clients
>
> (Horowitz, 2002).

Aside from the top-down threats of capitalist irrationality, the greatest risk to Durban's proposed port-petrochemical complex expansion is the repertoire of mandatory tools in any activist's toolbox: popular education, democratic decision-making, mass-based organization, linkages of people across interest areas leading to new alliances, unity of purpose, an ability to transcend divisions, powerful analysis, fluidity and pragmatism combined with a profound commitment to eco-social justice principles, and effective strategies and tactics. There is not sufficient space to do more than reveal some of the discourses being developed in 2011–14 in South Durban by SDCEA activists and their allies. One risk that Transnet and major oil companies – even ExxonMobil – face is that the critical narrative catches on in the broader society, and affects the way we think about infrastructure priorities. The timing is propitious, because for at least two decades, South Africa has witnessed what are probably the most prolific protests in the world dedicated to improved 'service delivery' – i.e. demonstrations against lack of (or excessively expensive) water and sanitation, electricity, housing, clinics, schools, roads and the like). These have occurred in South Durban, but as ever, the challenge is linking people's immediate concerns to wider matters, i.e. to connect the dots between local and global and back again, and between economic, social and ecological matters.

SDCEA's activists were motivated by a variety of minor victories against polluting industries. In two cases, substantial landfills that were used as toxic dumps by unethical waste companies were shut down. SDCEA leaders of those campaigns, Bobby Peek and Desmond D'Sa, were successful in 1996 (Umlazi) and 2012 (Chatsworth), respectfully, and in each case they won the Goldman Environmental Prize for Africa two years later as a result. SDCEA recorded other victories, notably against the Engen and Sapref refineries which are collectively the largest refinery zone in Africa. Because of SDCEA lobbying, they both installed $SO_2$ scrubbers so South Durban is not nearly as thick with airborne pollution and the sickly-sweet smells of chemical emissions.

SDCEA's own strength ebbs and flows, as does any civil society institution fighting injustices where the adverse balance of forces is so glaring. In an earlier stage of opposition to the port-petrochemical expansion, in 2004–05, SDCEA gathered thousands of residents to halt a major link road planned from the city's main southern freeway to the port. In 2006 SDCEA began campaigning against the doubling of the oil pipeline capacity and its rerouting through South Durban. In 2008, SDCEA used the EIA to challenge the climate implications of a major project for the first time. But at that stage, neither protests nor allegations (quite valid) of environmental racism nor EIA interventions slowed Transnet; Gigaba openly admitted the roughshod way Transnet treated such contestation led to numerous problems in the pipeline's implementation.

In 2011, Durban municipal City Manager Mike Sutcliffe – perhaps the city's most controversial leader in history – drew up a secret plan, estimated to cost the equivalent of \$25 billion, for the entire South Durban Basin. The plan reflected many decades of official ambition to re-engineer the basin, in the wake of the 1940s-60s attacks on black residents which turned South Durban communities into racial enclaves. Racial settlement patterns existed nearly entirely engrained into the second decade of democracy, with the exception of Clairwood's desegregation by shack settlers as urban blighting began in the 1990s. Sutcliffe's master plan was only unveiled to the public in mid-2012 at which point a half-dozen community meetings called by the city under the rubric of public participation were taken over by SDCEA activists, led by D'Sa. A near unanimous sentiment was expressed in meeting after meeting: close down the event and refuse to have it declared a form of tick-off participation. The main planner, consultant Graham Muller, was repeatedly frustrated.

The narrative in the August 2012 pamphlet, 'ACT NOW! EXPANDING PORT, POLLUTION AND FREIGHT THREATEN SOUTH DURBAN' is worthy of even brief consideration because, like a poster for a March 2014 SDCEA protest at Durban's City Hall, it helps reveal activist attempts to link issues and constituencies. The first of eight SDCEA critiques in the pamphlet was that 'We need one planning process. The municipality refuses to discuss the port expansion projects, which are spear-headed by Transnet.' The city's strategy was to join Transnet in fragmenting the long 2014–2040 process of approval, construction, and operation so that the vast implications for the entire project are not collected in any single moment of opposition. In reply, SDCEA demanded 'a *single participation process* with all spheres of government, developers, and communities to chart a sustainable and common way forward. Otherwise we will be arguing one puzzle piece at a time and will never change the overall picture.'

The second critique was 'Cost vs. Benefit . . . Proponents boast 130,000 permanent jobs will be created – is this accurate? If correct this means a high capital investment of $190,000/job created. What other ways could this money be invested to create sustainable livelihoods without the terrible social and environmental impacts? Are the full costs – including community destruction, adverse health effects, and our greater contribution to climate change – being considered?' Activists suspected the jobs calculation was far out of touch with reality given, as noted earlier, that even the largest container ships are designed to have crew numbering less than two dozen (13 in the case of Walmart's 15 500-TEU China-California shuttle).

The third critique also questioned the planners' understanding of global shipping demand: 'Is the expansion justified? Transnet are arguing expansion based on projections for the growth in container handling. At an 8% growth rate their projections show that a capacity of only 12 million containers will be needed by 2040 – yet they are building capacity for 20 million. Is this growth rate attainable given competition from other ports, growing resource constraints, carbon taxes on shipping, and global economic collapse?' Activists pointed out that harbor efficiency was appalling and that Durban's notorious status of world's highest-cost port would not be changed by adding $25 billion in capital costs given high interest rates affecting repayment of loans plus high operating and maintenance costs.

The fourth critique was that 'Increased containers mean increased impacts, 'and that this would translate into 8x the traffic, pollution and noise . . . There will also be an increase in Port related illegal activity including smuggling, drug trafficking, prostitution and shebeens' (informal pubs).

The fifth was of the 'wrong fossil fuel development model. Port expansion will serve increased imports of consumer goods (60% of container cargo are imports to Gauteng), expansion of petro-chemical industries, fuel storage, and the automotive industry (Toyota). This does not take into account dwindling resources, especially oil, and the need to stop climate change.'

The sixth was the environmental risk: 'In addition to increasing climate change, port expansion will increase large water areas within the south Durban flood plain while removing the last natural wetlands. Toxic industry is also expanding in the basin. This increases the potential for flooding and hazardous chemical spills as extreme weather events increase.' Moreover, 'the Bay's estuarine ecosystem has been compromised to the point that it has lost resilience . . . The Bay provides a critical breeding ground for reef associated and migratory marine fish. 132 species of birds are found here and 62 species of endangered, migratory birds rest and feed here.' The sandbank's destruction in the first phase would wreck any remaining chance of restoring the harbor's ecological integrity.

The seventh was the resulting 'Community upheaval . . . Clairwood is earmarked for rezoning to logistics with some light industry. Six thousand plus people will be forced to relocate through market pressure, and with no active community present will inevitably result in the degeneration of historic cultural sites in the area. The port expansion requires 878 hectares of land for containers!'

The eighth critique was to ask, 'Freight – rail or road? The documents make reference to rail and interchange nodes. However, the documents refer to 'freight routes' which on some plans are shown as rail but more recently as roads.' Just over a year later, on the Field's Hill slope through the main mountain pass towards Durban, 24 people were killed by a runaway truck carrying a container belonging to Taiwanese-based shipping behemoth Evergreen. It was being freighted from Johannesburg by a small Durban truck transport agency, which skimped on paying toll fees (staying on the main highway with its more gradual slope would have cost $4 more), hired as a driver a low-paid Swazi national with an illegitimate license, and failed to have its faulty brakes repaired before the fatal trip. The SDCEA 'truck off' protest of 500 residents on the freight area's main throughway (Solomon Mahlangu Drive) in March 2012 had forewarned of this kind of risk, given that there were 7000 accidents in Durban in 2010 involving trucks, leaving more than 70 fatalities. In Clairwood alone, trucking companies invading the residential area with illegally zoned truck yards, and accidents there and on nearby Bluff roads had killed nine residents in the prior five years. The Clairwood community leader who opposed trucks the most vigorously, Ahmed Osman, was assassinated in April 2009, shot dead on his front porch in one of many unsolved crimes involving the deaths of Durban activists.

In spite of such dangers (D'Sa himself was a target of a night-time firebombing in his working-class flat in December 2007), the rhythm of street protest is also revealing. As the municipality and Transnet began public consultations in 2012, SDCEA activists were able to use the mass meetings as rallying points. For example, in September 2012, Clairwood's established Indian residents most immediately threatened by the existing harbor's expansion invited Finance Minister Gordhan – who 30 years earlier was a community organizer against apartheid housing in those very streets – to make a presentation defending Transnet and the city. He attempted to do so, using the standard neoliberal narrative of international competition, and specifically the threat that Maputo would get ahead in port traffic to Johannesburg (itself a reasonable proposition given that it is a shorter route without the Durban-Johannesburg mountainous terrain to cross).

Tellingly, however, Gordhan also hinted that a divide-and-conquer strategy lay ahead against SDCEA activists, because Clairwood is also a site of several thousand black African shackdwellers barely surviving in informal settlements, backyard slums, and even large tents. Fires regularly ravage these residents' shacks, destroying their belongings and often injuring (and even occasionally killing) people, including one night-time blaze that wrecked a double-yard settlement of 500 shacks in mid-2013. The mainly middle-class audience of traditional homeowners of Indian ethnic origin were reminded by Gordhan that the ANC's ability to mobilize in a relatively desegregated Clairwood could haunt a coming political showdown, in which those with the most to lose were Indians in Clairwood and Merebank, followed by those in the mainly colored area of Wentworth (which suffers the most pollution) and the traditionally white Bluff area.

Still, three months later, in December 2012, several hundred people heeded SDCEA's call to block the back port entrance, leaving a 3-kilometer-long queue of trucks. Protests slowed in 2013 as the port EIA process and other high-profile debates with Transnet and municipal politicians took priority. But by March 2014, when SDCEA held a march to City Hall of 800 residents, new issues and constituencies were added to the coalition, including farmers on the old airport land who are to be displaced as the Dug-Out Port is built, and subsistence fisherfolk whose access to the existing harbor was contested from the time of the 9/11 bombings – thus generating US paranoia over port security – until in 2013 they were permitted back into their traditional fishing area. The challenge for connecting dots and adding issue areas would arise in subsequent years, as the Umlazi Unemployed People's Movement (UPM) joined the anti-port coalition, for their ambition is to have the old airport land turned into low-income housing and labor-intensive industrial cooperatives. There is also potential for the country's largest trade union, the National Union of Metalworkers of South Africa (Numsa), to concretize its ambitions of a united front linking workers, residents, environmentalists, women, and youth. If Numsa succeeds in taking over the organization and representation of Durban port workers – as they were doing down the coast at the Coega container terminal – and evoking genuine eco-socialist politics, if the UPM leads land invasions at the airport before the digging is due to begin, and if Clairwood shackdwellers and nearby worker-hostel residents in Umbilo and Jacobs are fully organized, then the threat of racial divisions would fade.

However, it must be conceded, finally, that SDCEA remained weak when it came to an alternative approach to the South Durban Basin's development. As SDCEA's 2012 pamphlet reported, 'We must urgently invest in a post-fossil fuel development path including renewable technologies and resilience to climate impacts. Are we giving up our land, environment and community to facilitate imports feeding rampant consumerism?' That stark choice lay ahead not only for SDCEA, South Durban residents and the broader city – but for the country and world as a whole. With the capitalist 'development model' representing by far the greatest risk to the continuation of a decent life on a climate-constrained planet, and with inequality and political degradation out of control in South Africa and across the globe, then the showdown over South Durban's future would, in microcosm, signal whether disparate red and green forces can find unity in opposition, and use that unity to plan a future based on less risky ways of arranging economy, society and nature.

## Afterword

In mid-2016, as this book was going to press, the combination of global capitalist crisis (especially shipping overcapacity) and local resistance combined to postpone Durban's dig-out port. But according to a Transnet official, the country's single largest site-specific mega-project 'has been programmed and will not be abandoned. It is just a matter of timing. The view is that construction of phase one should begin by 2030, once the deepening of the pier one berth in the port and other port projects get underway' (Baillache, 2016). Instead of assuming a 6.5 percent annual growth in containers, Transnet would plan based on only a 3.5 percent growth estimate, a figure also likely to be far too optimistic if the long-term stagnation continued. The announcement was welcomed by SDCEA and its main NGO ally, groundWork (2016). It was:

> A result of SDCEA's organised resistance over many years . . . this is an important victory for SDCEA and the communities it represents, as it means retention of the community space as a residential zone, and no displacement of residents and workers such as the old Durban airport farmers.

That new breathing space is vital. But the main challenge in understanding South Durban, as in so many other sites where capital is in conflict with communities and environments (and especially when the conflicts relate to climate change), is to assess structure and struggle in a more balanced way. As commodity prices crashed and shipping capital overaccumulated in this critical period, it was natural that activists engaged in such permanent class and social struggles were bound to overestimate their role and likewise that capitalist planners were bound to under-estimate their mistakes, as they believe in the perpetual prosperity of a system that in reality generates such crises and resistances in the same breath.

## Notes

1  In South African terminology, the African, Indian and Colored people have been considered 'Black' in relation to the need to fuse their interests against the historic white apartheid project, though after 1994 when democracy was won, the breakdown of the cross-racial alliances has often been a painful feature of life in Durban and elsewhere, and in South Durban in 2015, the eruption of widespread working-class xenophobia against immigrants from the African continent was just one indication of the intensity of social division.
2  SDCEA suggested: 'Refurbishing the existing pipeline in an incremental manner (instead of doubling capacity), as maintenance is required, replacing the sections with a larger pipeline, using the existing route and servitudes, and installing additional pump stations, as and when required. Accelerating the upgrade of railways and public transport in Gauteng, so as to get more people and product off the roads to minimize transport-related congestion, fuel burning, emissions and associated health effects, by establishing urban transport networks to enable safe and affordable rail transport, linked to park and ride centers with connections to bus and taxi routes.'
3  On the climate, according to SDCEA, 'the rise of $CO_2$ emissions that will be facilitated by the pipeline is immense, and is only referred to in the Draft Scoping Report as a potential legal problem, with no details provided.'

## References

Abadar, I. (2013) Rejection of the final environmental impact assessment report for the proposed deepening, lengthening and widening of berths 203 to 205 at pier 2, container terminal, port of Durban, KwaZulu-Natal province, *Department of Environmental Affairs, Pretoria*, 2 October.

Academy of Science of SA (2011) Towards a low carbon city: Focus on Durban (www.assaf. org.za/2011/08/durban-on-a-pathway-towards-a-low-carbon-city/) Accessed 12 December 2015.

Baillache, E. (2016) Dig-out port part of much larger project, SouthCoast Sun, 28 July (http://southcoastsun.co.za/81499/dig-out-port-part-of-much-larger-project/) Accessed 26 August 2016.

Bond, P. (2002) *Unsustainable South Africa*, Merlin Press, London.

Bond, P. (2012–13) Correspondence with the Nemai consulting company, *Durban*, May 2012–November 2013.

Bruce, P. (2012) Thick end of the wedge, *Business Day*, 13 February.

Carnie, T. (2008) New route for R6bn fuel pipeline, *The Mercury*, 9 May.

CityPress (2012) Infrastructure roll out to cost R844 million (www.citypress.co.za/business/ infrastructure-roll-out-to-cost-r844bn-20121019/) Accessed 12 December 2015.

Cornell University (2012) We have a planetary emergency: Hansen, leading NASA climate scientist, urges unions to act (www.ilr.cornell.edu/news/GLIJamesHansen_102312.html) Accessed 12 December 2015.

Creamer's Engineering News (2013) Prefeasibility work starts on Durban Dig Out Port (www.engineeringnews.co.za/print-version/prefeasibility-work-starts-on-durban-dig-out-port-2013-07-05) Accessed 12 December 2015.

Gedye, L. (2013) South Durban's battle royal, *City Press*, 28 April.

Gigaba, M. (2012) *Where the Transnet Pipeline Project Went Wrong*, Statement by Public Enterprises Minister Malusi Gigaba, Pretoria.

groundWork (2016) Durban Port expansion squashed, Pietermaritzburg, 25 August (www. groundwork.org.za/archives/2016/news%2020160825%20-%20Durban%20Port%20 expansion%20squashed.php) Accessed 26 August 2016.

Horowitz, L. (2002) *Power, Profit, Protest: Grassroots Resistance to Industry in the Global North*, Capitalism Nature Socialism, *23(3)* 20–34.

Hutson, T. (2014) Berth-deepening is in the dock, *The Mercury*, 22 January.

Luxemburg, R. (1968) *The Accumulation of Capital*, Monthly Review Press, New York.

Mckinsey Global Institute (2014) *Global Flows in a Digital Age*, New York: McKinsey Global Institute.

Ministry of Reconstruction and Development (1994–95) *Urban Infrastructure Investment Framework*, Pretoria: Ministry of Reconstruction and Development, 17–41.

Moody, K. (2014) Personal Correspondence to author by email, London, 15 November 2014.

National Planning Commission (2012) National development plan (www.info.gov.za/ view/DownloadFileAction?id=172296) Accessed 12 December 2015.

SAPA (2013) Cops handled 12 399 protests, *IOL News*, 19 September.

South African Department of Environment (2007) State of the environment report (www. environment.co.za/environmental-laws-and-legislation-in-south-africa/the-state-of-the-environment-report-2006-brief.html) Accessed 12 December 2015.

South Durban Community Environmental Alliance (2008) Comments on the transnet multi product pipeline proposal, *Durban*, 7 July.

Transnet (2012) Environmental Impact Asssessment, Johannesburg, (http://berth203to 205expansioneia.co.za/documents/DraftScopingReport/Berth%20203-205%20 Final%20Scoping%20report%20review%20-%2025%20May%202012.pdf) Accessed 14 October 2016.

United Nations (2013) *World Economic Situation and Prospects*, Department of Economic and Social Affairs, New York.

United Nations Conference on Trade and Development (2015) World Investment Report, Geneva: United Nations Conference on Trade and Development.

Venter, I. (2013) Construction industry must deal with 'great anger' over collusion, says Upton. (www.engineeringnews.co.za/article/construction-industry-must-deal-with-great-anger-over-collusion-says-upton-2013-08-12) Accessed 12 December 2015.

World Economic Forum (2012) Global Competitiveness Report 2012–2013 (www.weforum.org/reports/global-competitiveness-report-2012–2013) Accessed 12 December 2015.

# 4 Indigenous by association

Legitimation and grassroots engagements with multinational mining in New Caledonia

*Leah S. Horowitz*

## Introduction: the importance of being legitimate

Legitimacy is the degree to which an entity, or its actions, are generally perceived or assumed to be "desirable, proper, or appropriate within some socially constructed system of norms, values, beliefs, and definitions" (Suchman 1995, 574). Legitimacy in the eyes of citizens is important for governments to achieve, as it reduces the likelihood of protest (Booth and Seligson 2005). Additionally, legitimacy may be sought by firms, particularly multinational corporations (MNCs), as well as by non-governmental organizations (NGOs). For all these entities, legitimacy is a resource that may lead to perceptions of the institution as having greater value, significance, dependability, and trustworthiness (Suchman 1995), hence encouraging public support in both cognitive and material terms (Palazzo and Scherer 2006). Conversely, a lack of legitimacy may increase the organization's vulnerability to accusations that can result in a loss of influence. For corporations, this can also lead to negative financial impacts (Meyer and Rowan 1977), as protestors destroy equipment, take the company to court, or organize boycotts, or as host country governments, viewing such social unease as evidence that an MNC does not have a 'social license to operate', increase regulations or barriers to entry (Oetzel and Doh 2009). Meanwhile, reputational concerns – in which legitimacy plays a necessary, albeit not always sufficient, role (Doh et al. 2010) – have prompted investors to screen potential funding recipients and have inspired powerful funding agencies such as the World Bank to impose directives upon clients (Szablowski 2002). Such financial repercussions are the key driver of corporations' attempts to achieve legitimacy, rather than any moral sense of "intrinsic social responsibility" (Scherer and Palazzo 2007, 1100).

Society has debated industry's social role ever since the Industrial Revolution, but pressure has increasingly intensified as citizens have become more aware of industry's impacts and able to mobilize against them, with support from transnational networks, facilitated by the Internet age (Castells 1996; Keck and Sikkink 1998). In a globalized "world society without a world state" (Palazzo and Scherer 2006, 78), social movements, or "[g]overnance beyond the nation-state" (Steffek 2003, 250), make companies' international profiles ever more important.

As power slips from "hollowing-out" nation-states (Jessop 1993), and moves toward both supra-national and local scales through a process labeled "glocalization"

(Swyngedouw 2000), simply following the law is no longer adequate evidence of legitimacy (Bendell 2000). Instead, an institution may need to engage actively in legitimation, the process of justifying its worthiness and thus its "right" to pursue the operations necessary for its continued existence (Maurer 1971, 361). By the 1970s, corporations had begun responding to the "crisis of legitimacy" they faced (Maurer 1971, 362) through the legitimation strategies of 'Corporate Social Responsibility': policies and procedures that (at least appear to) go beyond legal requirements to protect, or mitigate damage to, the human and non-human contexts within which they operate. As financial and reputational costs of ignoring opponents began to outweigh costs of addressing them (see Humphreys 2000), corporations saw a 'business case' for 'good' corporate citizenship (Zadek 2001). However, achieving this may become a "constraint" on the organization's behavior (Dowling and Pfeffer 1975, 126), necessitating continual adaptations of its procedures to keep pace with evolving social values, and/or costly public relations campaigns to sway public opinion, while limiting its range of available responses to potential issues (Oliver 1991). Therefore, the degree to which an organization requires social or political support, often due to its visibility or the scope of its activities, correlates with the extent of its legitimation efforts (Dowling and Pfeffer 1975). Not surprisingly, corporations may only make such efforts in response to direct pressure from powerful groups (Palazzo and Scherer 2006), when societal expectations are clear and widespread (Oliver 1991), the costs of capitulating to these demands are not prohibitively high, and/or firms see competitive advantage to doing so (Spar and La Mure 2003).

Clearly, legitimation processes may involve countering attacks from opponents who desire to halt the organization's activities; however, those opponents' legitimacy may in turn be vulnerable to challenge. Thus, debates about legitimacy may be manifestations of underlying power struggles. Through a study of resistance to a multinational mining project in New Caledonia, this chapter examines struggles over power in the form of struggles over legitimacy. One common strategy for achieving legitimacy is association with an entity already widely accepted as possessing it, such as an indigenous group. As this study shows, such legitimacy, or what I call 'indigenous legitimacy by association', may be a contested resource that is wrestled away from other groups in power struggles around industrial development.

## Legitimacy and how to get it

Legitimacy is particularly difficult to achieve for organizations that operate in multiple regions of the planet. In a complex, globalizing world, there are "no broadly accepted normative standards" (Palazzo and Scherer 2006, 77). Instead, MNCs face an increasingly multi-faceted array of contradictory legal requirements and social norms in the varied institutional and cultural environments within which they operate (Doh and Guay 2006; Habermas 2001). Meanwhile, they inevitably face increased suspicion due to being "foreign" (Kostova, Roth, and Dacin 2008). Moreover, MNCs may experience "legitimacy spillovers" – either positive or negative – as stakeholders at one site learn of a subsidiary's actions at another location, or even make predictions based on experiences with other organizations within that industry or from the same home country (Kostova and Zaheer 1999).

When striving for legitimation, institutions may change their activities to conform to social values through "substantive" changes in practices, even if these concern only highly visible but non-essential elements of operations. Perhaps more commonly, they aim for the cost-effective option of creating a merely "symbolic" appearance of conformity with social norms and expectations, such as by publicly espousing ideals without putting them into practice, concealing information, strategically framing decisions, finding excuses, or offering apologies (Ashforth and Gibbs 1990). When discovered, however, such attempts to engineer rather than earn legitimacy can backfire and result in public outrage.

Rather than attempting to satisfy an ever-growing diversity of demands or assuage increasingly varied anxieties through their own actions, whether substantive or symbolic, institutions may 'free-ride' on others' legitimacy by associating themselves with "other generally accepted legitimate objectives, institutions, or individuals" (Pfeffer and Salancik 1978, 196). For instance, corporations, as well as politicians and NGOs, all use arguments at least putatively based in science, building on perceptions of science as objective and trustworthy (e.g. Horowitz 2010), although they cherry-pick the findings, and the researchers, who best suit their particular agendas (Sarewitz 2004). However, scientific legitimacy has lost much traction as public trust in science and scientists has dwindled over the past 30 years, largely due to this very politicization of science (Gauchat 2012). Alternatively, political leaders may attempt to establish their moral legitimacy through association with religious figures and institutions (e.g. Kent 2006), or by referencing ideals of "traditional authority" (Weber 1978 [1968], 215). Following in the footsteps of colonial powers, post-colonial governments may try to cement their own legitimacy by forging strong ties to customary authority structures (e.g. Horowitz 1998). Corporations, in turn, may try to associate themselves with, or even co-opt, respected political or other leaders (Dowling and Pfeffer 1975). They may also seek alliances with celebrities (Ashforth and Gibbs 1990), or NGOs.

NGOs occupy an ambiguous position vis-à-vis legitimation, due to their complex relationships with corporations, governments, and international financial institutions (IFIs). The 1980s and 1990s saw a boom in NGOs, many of which originated with the intention to challenge the legitimacy of unfettered profit making and successfully drew attention to its negative social and environmental repercussions. Generally, NGOs themselves benefit from a high degree of legitimacy, due to growing popular distrust of governments and big business (Gray, Bebbington, and Collison 2006) and a concomitant view of NGOs as "guardians of civil society" (Chandoke 2002, 43). In the 1980s, the 'Washington Consensus' emerged as a "transnational policy paradigm" that promoted free markets and delegitimized governments' role in providing social services (Babb 2013); NGOs stepped in to fill the void, reinforcing their social role. Later, however, opposition to neoliberal austerity measures spread, and governments distanced themselves from the Consensus as harming their own "popularity and legitimacy"

(Soederberg 2004, 171). The World Bank and IMF switched from excluding NGOs to engaging them to help effectuate a "kinder, gentler" neoliberalism (Plehwe and Walpen 2006, 45), although in reality this constituted an attempt to "relegitimise" the fundamental goal of market-led development (Carroll 2010, 3). As IFIs involved NGOs in policy formulation and project implementation, some NGOs found themselves legitimating their former adversaries (Chandoke 2002). NGOs may confer moral 'legitimacy by association' on corporations, too, by publicly endorsing them. However, this process may result in "NGO capture" (Rodgers 2000, 41) whereby, due to a transfer of financial or other resources from the IFI or corporation to the NGO, the latter's goals become compromised and it may be accused of having been "seduced into a corporate lotus-eating bliss" (Gray, Bebbington, and Collison 2006, 328). Even when the NGO allies with a company in good faith, the latter may fail to "fulfill the social mission of the relationship" (Oetzel and Doh 2009, 114), thus harming the NGO's reputation. On the other hand, NGOs that challenge corporations' legitimacy may see their own legitimacy questioned via the argument that they are "largely self-appointed 'dogooders' who are not accountable to anyone other than themselves" (Naidoo 2004, 16).

Attacked from both sides, NGOs may need to reestablish their own legitimacy in the public eye, not least because reputations help determine donor funds. Just as corporations seek to achieve 'legitimacy by association' with NGOs, NGOs may attempt to associate themselves with other groups already perceived as legitimate. International NGOs, for instance, may partner with communities, local NGOs, or grassroots organizations (GROs), in order to improve their local legitimacy and convince outside observers that their approaches are suited to local conditions (Teegen 2003). However, they need to choose their affiliations carefully, as relationships with certain activist groups, such as those who resort to violence, may actually reduce an NGO's legitimacy (Baur and Palazzo 2011).

Meanwhile, GROs themselves may struggle to establish and/or maintain their own legitimacy, in the eyes of the international community, the government agencies they are lobbying, and the community on whose behalf they claim to perform this advocacy. While an outside observer might assume that the GROs must necessarily, by virtue of the 'grassroots' nature of the organization, represent local communities, communities are in fact heterogeneous and not all local residents may share the GRO's goals, particularly when they depend economically on the industrial activity that the GRO is targeting (see Perreault, this volume).

A notable subcategory of local communities is indigenous groups. Although there are various definitions of 'indigenous' and many disagreements over who may claim that status, one of the most cited definitions was provided by a United Nations (UN) Special Rapporteur in the 1980s (Martínez Cobo 1986):

> Indigenous communities, peoples and nations are those which, having a historical continuity with pre-invasion and pre-colonial societies that developed on their territories, consider themselves distinct from other sectors of the societies now prevailing on those territories, or parts of them. They form

at present non-dominant sectors of society and are determined to preserve, develop and transmit to future generations their ancestral territories, and their ethnic identity, as the basis of their continued existence as peoples, in accordance with their own cultural patterns, social institutions and legal system.

Since that time, indigenous peoples have received much attention from international bodies such as the International Labour Organization (1989), the UN (2008), and various national governments. Indeed, indigenous groups have "great moral claims on nation-states and on international society," due to prior or ongoing "inhumane, unequal, and exclusionary treatment" (Merlan 2009, 304). As awareness of these injustices has grown, an indigenous identity now holds great political and moral legitimacy on an international scale (Karlsson 2003). Thus, the international community's recognition of an NGO's alignment with indigenous people's interests is an important source of legitimation, which may then attract donor funds to the NGO and/or provide it with a voice in international forums. In turn, the NGO may be able to provide the indigenous community with money, scientific knowledge, and contacts. At the same time, positive interactions with indigenous communities are very important for corporations too; for instance, "constructive relationships between mining and metals companies and Indigenous Peoples" are a requirement for member companies of the International Council on Mining and Metals (ICMM 2013, 1). These sets of relationships, between indigenous communities and corporations, and between these communities and the NGOs and/or GROs targeting these corporations, may be incompatible. Through a study of disputes over mining in New Caledonia, this chapter explores what happens when stakeholders with very different agendas struggle over the ability to claim indigenous legitimacy by association.

## New Caledonia

New Caledonia is a particularly appropriate site for exploring struggles over indigenous legitimacy within grassroots engagements with industry. This Pacific island nation, the size of New Jersey, is a biodiversity "hotspot" with exceptionally high numbers of endemic species that are severely threatened, especially by mining activity (Kier et al. 2009; Richer de Forges and Pascal 2008). Mined since 1874, New Caledonia currently hosts over 30 active mine sites (DIMENC 2012), some locally-based and others run by MNCs. This mining prompts concern from a multitude of stakeholders, rural and urban, indigenous and non-indigenous (Horowitz 2008a).

Administered by France since 1853, at first serving as a penal colony, New Caledonia is a Melanesian archipelago with a population of approximately 246,000, comprised of several ethnic groups, primarily Melanesians known as Kanak (40%), and people of European ancestry (29%) who include descendants of nineteenth-century deportees as well as recent immigrants from the 'metropole' (Rivoilan and Broustet 2011). In Kanak societies, the first clans to settle in an area have customary (although not legal) rights to determine land use at that site, and they occupy the highest social position, with other clans hierarchically ranked in order of arrival (Bensa and Rivierre 1982). In the pre-colonial era, the chief, appointed by first-occupant clans, had no substantive authority but enjoyed "respectful brotherly affection" (Leenhardt 1937, 149). However, this position acquired greater significance after 1898, when colonial administrators created "lesser chiefs", responsible for a village, and "high chiefs", with authority over several villages, often distributing these titles themselves (Naepels 1998). These chiefs received new powers over land along with authorization to punish their subjects (Merle 1996). In 1947, administrators created village-level Councils of Elders. Later, the 1998 Nouméa Accords institutionalized eight Customary Regions, each with its own Customary Council. Each region selects two members of the Customary Senate, which has an advisory role on matters concerning Kanak identity. Clearly, colonial and post-colonial governance systems radically altered customary authority structures. Even in their mutated and convoluted contemporary forms, however, positions of customary authority command a high degree of respect from every corner of Kanak society.

The 1980s witnessed anti-colonialist uprisings, known as the "Events", which ended with the 1988 Matignon Accord (Henningham 1992). A decade later, the Nouméa Accords promised a gradual devolution of administrative authority to the territory, recategorized as a "sui generis collectivity" in 1999, although still a French possession. Meanwhile, New Caledonia was divided into northern, southern, and islands provinces. Many regulatory responsibilities were decentralized; for instance, the power to draft mining regulations was transferred to New Caledonia, with the provinces responsible for enforcing them (paragraph 3.2.5 of the Nouméa Accords).

Grande Terre, the main island, is estimated to possess nearly 25% of the world's nickel reserves (Mining Journal 1999) and is the second largest producer of ferronickel and fifth greatest source of nickel ore (Lyday 2006). In addition to an existing pyrometallurgical refinery, two more are in progress, colloquially called the northern and southern refineries (see Horowitz 2004). The 'Southern Refinery' project, officially Vale Nouvelle-Calédonie (known until 2008 as Goro Nickel), is located at the southern tip of Grande Terre (Figure 4.1). Inco, a Canadian MNC, purchased mining rights to the Goro site in 1992, and in 1999 completed a pilot refinery which, due to the ore's low mineral content, uses hydrometallurgical technology. This procedure, never before implemented in New Caledonia, uses acid under pressure to leach nickel and cobalt from the ore, with effluent discharged into the sea. In 2006 Inco was purchased by CVRD, a Brazilian MNC, world leader in iron ore production and the second largest producer of nickel. In 2007, CVRD changed its name to Vale. Operations are continuing to ramp up, despite delays caused by acid leaks in 2009, 2010, 2012, and 2014, and the effluent diffuser's rupture in 2013 (Pitoiset 2014).

In the early 2000s, local residents began to express increasing concerns about New Caledonia's threatened ecosystems. A multitude of GROs formed and splintered, mostly led by urban-based expatriates or Caledonians of European ancestry.

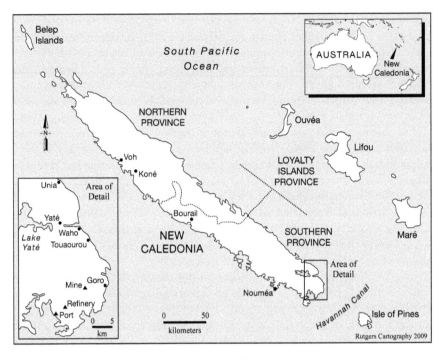

*Figure 4.1* New Caledonia and the Southern Refinery area.

These GROs took a range of approaches to the Goro Nickel project, with some choosing not to engage with this issue, others seeking to influence the company to ensure the best possible environmental performance, and others opposing its existence entirely. The latter, most extreme environmental GROs, worked most closely with Rhéébù Nùù, a group led entirely by Kanak that was formed specifically to focus on Goro Nickel. While not entirely opposed to the mining project, Rhéébù Nùù had concerns about its potential environmental impacts, particularly on the marine resources upon which the local population depends for subsistence and livelihood. They were also concerned that Kanak would not benefit adequately from employment with the project, as evidenced by the company's bringing workers from the Philippines for the construction phase. Believing that local residents needed to keep an "eye" on the project, they named the group Rhéébù Nùù, "eye of the country" in the indigenous language, Numèè. For six years, its leaders initiated a series of actions including the distribution of pamphlets denouncing Inco's activities, the holding of public meetings at local villages, open letters sent to political leaders, legal action in the courts, and blockades of the construction site which turned into violent encounters with armed police. Rhéébù Nùù also worked closely with another organization, the Indigenous Committee for Natural Resource Management (CAUGERN), created in 2005.

Having conducted fieldwork in New Caledonia since 1998, I began studying the Southern Refinery project in 2006. Between 2006 and 2012 I conducted face-to-face semi-structured interviews with over 120 stakeholders, including residents of villages near the mine site, leaders and members of grassroots organizations, representatives of international non-governmental organizations (NGOs), government officials, and mining company representatives. Additionally, I conducted telephone interviews with NGO and grassroots leaders, lawyers, researchers, and mining company officials, based in Australia, Canada, France and New Caledonia. All translations from French are mine. I use pseudonyms for all interviewees.

## The 'chain' of legitimacy by association

The various stakeholders' attempts to achieve legitimacy by association may be conceptualized as a 'chain', whereby (metaphorically) 'latching on' to another group already perceived as legitimate can confer some legitimacy onto one's own group, which can then confer legitimacy onto another organization. In New Caledonia, the original source of legitimation, perceived both locally and internationally as imbued with legitimacy, were the customary authorities. The legitimacy they possessed stood in sharp contrast to the government's lack of legitimacy.

In the eyes of many Southern Province residents in 2006, the state (Metropolitan France), as well as the collectivity and provincial levels of government, all provided inadequate environmental and social protections and were at best negligent and misguided, at worst corrupt and violent. According to these villagers, the government was unwilling to perform its duties vis-à-vis the mining project's negative impacts, and thus was guilty of allowing Inco to display a lack of respect for local people's rights and to fail to consider the environment. Part of this negligence was due to a lack of protective legislation, making New Caledonia an "ideal place" for Inco to conduct business (Roger, pers. comm. July 31, 2006). Several villagers expressed the belief that such a polluting refinery would not be built in a "civilized country" or anywhere that European or international norms were applicable, or where an adequate legislative framework was in place. Local residents saw this lacuna as a sign of feebleness on the part of the government: "This [environmentally irresponsible mining] is not done in Europe, why is it being done here? It's not done in Canada. They're doing it here because here the government is too weak" (Thomas, pers. comm. August 8, 2006). Others accused the government, or individual leaders within it, of accepting bribes from Inco or having personal interests in the mining venture. Indeed, the President of the Southern Province from 2004–2009, Philippe Gomès, was indicted in 2012 for illegal conflict of interest after Goro Nickel granted his air conditioner company a million-euro contract in 2005–2006, although he successfully appealed this decision a few months later (Matthieu 2012). Worst of all, though, in their view, had been the government's use of force against its own people. In April 2006, a blockade organized by Rhéébù Nùù turned violent with the destruction of approximately $13 million of equipment and encounters with armed police in which four gendarmes were injured and a protestor's vehicle was fired upon.

Ultimately, 36 protestors were arrested and work was partially suspended at the site for over two weeks. In the villagers' analysis, the government had called upon the armed forces to protect the MNC.

While elected officials from pro-independence parties were supposed to represent the interests of the Kanak, many community members had been disappointed by them as well. One village resident expressed dismay that, as he saw it, Kanak leaders had "turned their backs on us" (Léopold, pers. comm. July 28, 2006). He declared that these politicians, too, were "corrupt", thinking only of money, and couldn't be counted on. Others noted that the only time they saw their representatives was at the approach of elections, when candidates visited villages in an attempt to garner votes, and that they never made efforts to consult communities before making decisions. As one local resident insisted, "we no longer trust anyone in political parties" (Nicolas, pers. comm. August 2, 2006).

In contrast, despite the vast alterations of customary authority systems occasioned by the colonial period, respect for customary authorities – whether they have inherited or been elected or appointed to these positions – constitutes a crucial component of contemporary Kanak cultural-political identity. Throughout New Caledonia, Kanak tend to judge the legitimacy of any endeavor according to whether it has been initiated, and/or supported, by customary authorities (Horowitz 2008b). Here, local residents put their faith in a revitalization of customary authority as the true representative of the interests of the Kanak people. As one person explained, "I think we have to reassert the value of the customary structure. Because when we saw for politics, there's a free-fall there. [ . . . ] Whereas let's give back to our chieftainships the power to express themselves" (Céléstine, pers. comm. July 14, 2006).

Meanwhile, the Kanak possessed great political and moral legitimacy on an international scale by virtue of being an indigenous people. Notably, the UN (2007) lists New Caledonia as one of the "16 Non-Self-Governing Territories" on its "decolonization list" of nations that should become autonomous. Thus, both customary legitimacy (Kanak people's sense that a project has support from customary authorities) and indigenous legitimacy (the international community's acceptance of a project or group as representative of Kanak interests) are important stakes in a project of any scope in New Caledonia. Both may be achieved through demonstrations of customary authorities' approval.

### The chain's first link: Rhéébù Nùù secures indigenous legitimacy

Not surprisingly, from their inception both mining company and protest group attempted to garner the support of customary authorities. In the 1990s, before beginning work on the pilot refinery, Inco representatives performed a customary ceremony with local chiefs and customary land owners in an official show of respect. However, they relied heavily on a few individual ties. Over the years, they built a close relationship with the chief of Goro, the village closest to the mine site, spurring resentment from others who contested his clan's claims to authority over local lands. When the chiefs of Goro and Unia, the most populated local village, both died in 2004, the mining company was left without a close ally among local residents. In the midst of intra-village tensions between supporters and opponents of the mining project, no new chiefs were appointed for several years.

At first, Rhéébù Nùù was more successful in publicly winning customary authorities' support for its activities and reinforcing its own legitimacy through this association. In its narrative, the chiefs of Goro and Unia had initiated the group's creation. Somewhat ironically, the chiefs had chosen as Rhéébù Nùù's main leader a man named Gabriel, a charismatic figure who had recently ended a political career but was from a clan low on the local customary hierarchy. As members of 'recently-arrived' clans, Gabriel and his co-leader had no authority over land-use issues, except as spokespersons for landowner clans. After the chiefs died, then, Rhéébù Nùù continued to position itself – in fact, defined its very identity – as representing the customary authorities of the far south of New Caledonia. Rather than, like Inco, relying on close ties to a few individuals, they had forged a broader base of legitimacy by involving as large a number of customary authorities as possible in the very foundation of the group. At Rhéébù Nùù's inception, its leaders had strategically invited customary authorities from the entire archipelago to participate in ceremonies, if not in actual decision-making processes. On July 12, 2002, the newly-formed protest group erected a *bois tabou* – a large pole, carved with human faces and animals in a traditional style – on a nearby mountain where ancestral spirits were known to reside. Long strips of printed cloth were then tied around the pole. This was a version, writ large, of a practice used throughout New Caledonia to signal a conflict over resources (Naepels 1998). Gabriel invited all the high chiefs of the Djubea Kapone customary region where the mining project is based, and nearly all participated (Mapou 2003). Customary authorities and other local residents expressed confidence that Rhéébù Nùù was fighting for the interests of the Kanak people (see Horowitz 2009). One local resident noted that Rhéébù Nùù was not like NGOs based in Nouméa because it followed customary protocols and worked with customary authorities. He insisted that Rhéébù Nùù was "the work of the elder," Goro's late chief, who had given the group its name (Lucien, pers. comm. August 12, 2006). Rhéébù Nùù's president agreed, adding, "that's where our strength lies" (Maurice, pers. comm. August 14, 2006). Others recalled that the chiefs of Goro and Unia had kept the best interests of their people in mind and had therefore created the protest group in order to defend them against a large, powerful multinational.

This customary legitimacy at the local level translated into indigenous legitimacy at the international scale. Like the Maasai described by Hodgson (2002, 1095), Kanak leaders learned to reframe their concerns "in the terms of the indigenous rights movement" and thus "gained greater visibility, increased legitimacy, and enormous resources". Some of these resources took the shape of support from a wide range of NGOs and GROs around the world. Rhéébù Nùù leaders communicated with these groups via e-mail and visited them overseas (their tickets purchased with NGO funds) or welcomed them to New Caledonia where they jointly met with mining company officials. They shared experiences and ideas with other indigenous groups in Australia, Canada and French Guiana, and kept the world informed of their plight via a website in English and French, designed and maintained by a bilingual expatriate volunteer. Their supporters included scientists and lawyers both overseas and at home, who – owing to their interest in environmental and/or human rights issues – worked for a pittance that was raised through village-scale fundraising activities such as bingos and t-shirt sales. In summary, both the company and the protest group organized customary ceremonies and attempted to secure the support of customary authorities in order to affirm their own legitimacy, but Rhéébù Nùù did so far more successfully.

## The second link: local grassroots groups ally themselves with Rhéébù Nùù

Because of the political and moral legitimacy the indigenous people possessed, local non-indigenous environmentalist GRO leaders recognized the strategic necessity of working with them: "We will never be able to do it seriously, if we don't have the Kanak with us" (Marcel, pers. comm. 14 July 2006), as "we will never have the legitimacy that they have [ . . . ] in the eyes of the international collectivity" (Marcel, pers. comm. 15 July 2006). As one activist noted bitterly, members of non-indigenous ethnicities do not have the same "lip service" paid to them by the United Nations and other international agencies (Christophe, pers. comm. 22 July 2009). Instead, "former colonists" – as the descendants of deportees and other settlers are viewed – have to "take responsibility" for their ancestors' destruction of Kanak lands (Marcel, pers. comm. 15 July 2006). Clearly, the GROs needed the Kanak on their side. In 2001, two environmentalists took two influential Kanak to Inco's headquarters in Canada, where they confronted Inco officials and met with representatives of an environmental and social justice NGO (who had provided the flights) as well as with Innu and Inuit who had faced a similar project on their lands. The GRO leaders were pleased that their Kanak colleagues engaged fully with the situation, challenging Inco officials to explain why they had not asked permission of the customary landowners before beginning their activities and why they persisted in neglecting indigenous people's rights when that approach had failed elsewhere. Upon return to New Caledonia, the Kanak leaders put together a "solid dossier" and met with local customary authorities to plan how to address the "aggression" facing them. The GRO leaders believed that this awareness-raising resulted in the creation of Rhéébù Nùù (pers. comm. 22 July 2009).

The environmentalists thus viewed Rhéébù Nùù as necessarily possessing indigenous legitimacy in the international eye, by virtue of its membership being entirely Kanak. The non-indigenous GROs' role, in this view, was to make the Kanak aware of the power of their social position as indigenous people. When I remarked to one environmentalist that at the time of my previous fieldwork, in 2001, the Kanak had not seemed to make much use of international rights-based discourses, he agreed that over the subsequent five years, with his help, they had begun to discover the power of a discourse of "recognition of the basic rights of indigenous people" (Arthur, pers. comm. 10 June 2006). He felt that he had "started a process" in 2000 by talking with influential Kanak and making speeches in local villages, and then "pushed" the Kanak to take action (pers. comm. 22 March 2006). Others similarly saw the indigenous people's increasing "awareness of their legitimacy" as a "victory" for the environmentalists (Marcel, pers. comm. 15 July 2006), as their own struggle against the mining project was thus legitimated. Meanwhile, GRO leaders felt that the relationship was mutually beneficial; their work was "complementary" to that of Rhéébù Nùù (Marcel, pers. comm. 14 July 2006), as they possessed "a certain expertise" (Stéphane, pers. comm. 24 June 2006), including "technical" and "scientific" information. One described their role as that of "supplier" as, behind the scenes, they could "provide Rhéébù Nùù with the necessary environmental facts" which the indigenous group would "have its militants apply" by making demands of the provincial government or the mining company (André, pers. comm. 23 June 2006). While this GRO leader was proud that his organization was "close" to the "customary authorities" and boasted that while "we recognize their legitimacy, they recognize the work that we do" (pers. comm. 29 August 2006), another admitted that the environmentalists were, in some sense, "manipulators", albeit with Kanak "complicity" (Marcel, pers. comm. July 15, 2006).

Indeed, Marcel "reproached" himself for having been responsible for "pushing" the Kanak to resist the mining project (pers. comm. 15 July 2006), which had resulted in the April 2006 violence described earlier. The environmentalists attempted to distance themselves from this violence, at least outwardly. As one emphasized, "We don't always agree. [ . . . ] Rhéébù Nùù acts as it sees fit to act on the ground, and there, of course, we can't intervene." However, he lamented with some frustration that "our way is [ . . . ] done on paper, in front of tribunals, and that's been going on since. . . . Some GROs, they've been here for 25 years and nothing has come of it" (André, pers. comm. 23 June 2006). Secretly, therefore, the GRO leaders were pleased that the indigenous group had "done an excellent job" of creating an "electroshock" that got their point across; one environmentalist recognized that "in their position, that's exactly what I would have done" (Marcel pers. comm. 15 July 2006). This social position was not shared by the non-indigenous environmentalists, who had supported Rhéébù Nùù discretely by supplying provisions to the protestors camped along the road to the mine site, yet did not feel that they were able to participate overtly in such actions. They could not "play a game like that", which "risked harming the quality of our actions" as the GROs' image would be damaged if they were viewed as violent extremists themselves (Marcel, pers. comm. 15 July 2006).

The environmentalists were therefore content to allow the indigenous group, with its political and moral legitimacy in the eyes of the international community, to be the public face of their protest, positioning themselves instead as its 'supporters', as long as Rhéébù Nùù maintained the identity and desires assigned to it by the GROs. Behind the scenes, however, the environmentalists attempted to present themselves as 'spokespersons' for the protest group, and indeed for all Kanak institutions. For instance, in 2006 one environmentalist sent the provincial government a document insisting that his GRO "supports the Rhéébù Nùù

Committee in its demands concerning Goro Nickel's chemical refinery." Meanwhile, though, the document characterized Rhéébù Nùù – and indeed all Kanak groups – as simply sharing his GRO's criticisms, insisting that the government should "comply with our remarks, our conditions and our demands which are also those of CAUGERN and the Customary Senate". In this approach, Rhéébù Nùù became part mask, part marionette, providing a politically legitimate public image from behind which, and partly through which, the environmentalists could directly or indirectly carry out their work. However, they also attempted to distance themselves from the activists' violence, an association with which can threaten the legitimacy of NGOs and GROs (see Baur and Palazzo 2011).

Six weeks after the episode of April 2006 described earlier, Rhéébù Nùù, company representatives, non-indigenous environmental groups, and government officials sat down for a series of closed-door Round Table discussions organized by the Southern Province. Eventually, the government excluded the environmentalists and then found itself excluded as the discussions evolved into talks between representatives of the mining company (now Vale, which had purchased Inco) and of the Kanak community. Ultimately, in September 2008, four Rhéébù Nùù leaders, 25 customary authorities and two company representatives signed a "Pact for Sustainable Development of the Far South [of New Caledonia]" (hereafter 'the Pact'). The mining company committed to creating a Corporate Foundation to fund local development initiatives and a "Consultative Customary Environmental Committee" (CCCE), to recruiting and training local "environmental technicians", and to reforesting other companies' long-abandoned mine sites, without addressing any of the environmental impacts from the Vale project itself. In exchange, Rhéébù Nùù members committed to "assert their point of view not through violent or illegal actions, but by dialogue" (Vale Inco, Conseil Coutumier de l'Aire Drubéa Kapume, and Comité Rhéébù Nùù 2008). One grassroots leader labeled this a "deal with the devil" (Jean-Philippe, pers. comm. 31 August 2009), and many environmentalists refused to talk with the indigenous group's leaders, viewing them as having manipulated the situation to their own monetary advantage. However, they overlooked the cultural complexities occurring behind the scenes. Crucially, they had taken Rhéébù Nùù's indigenous legitimacy for granted, forgetting that although the group was comprised of Kanak, it based its own customary legitimacy, and ultimately its indigenous legitimacy in the international eye, on its association with customary authorities. Ironically, then, Rhéébù Nùù's indigenous legitimacy was vulnerable, contingent upon its relationship with the customary authorities, a relationship which could be – and, as the next section will show, indeed was – severed by the MNC which then captured this indigenous legitimacy for itself.

## Breaking the chain: Vale captures indigenous legitimacy

By mid-2006, customary authorities' support for Rhéébù Nùù was eroding. They began to express mixed feelings about the protest group, viewing it not as the activist arm addressing their concerns but as an independent and increasingly unruly entity. Without the chiefs of Goro and Unia, who had passed away in 2004, as figureheads, Rhéébù Nùù's customary legitimacy became less clear, and customary authorities began to complain that it no longer respected them: "At first we started off well, but today they say they speak in the name of customary authorities, but the customary authorities haven't given them leave to speak" (Dominique, pers. comm. 10 July 2006).

In part, this dissatisfaction stemmed from the violence which Rhéébù Nùù members, acting independently, had begun to perform against not only the company but also fellow villagers – sometimes the deceased chiefs' families – who did not support their protest activities. Explaining why he had never joined Rhéébù Nùù, one customary authority voted "yes to their demands, no to their methods" (Guy, pers. comm. 14 September 2010). In addition to disagreements about means, Rhéébù Nùù members and customary authorities did not always agree on the ends they were trying to achieve. Rhéébù Nùù had been created with the explicit aim of keeping an 'eye' on the project's potential impacts, but not shutting it down entirely. After the chiefs had passed away, however, the group's youth had become more assertive, sometimes taking action in the group's name but without its leaders' authorization. Having heard stories of the anti-colonialist "Events" of the 1980s in which their elders had engaged, these young activists often used the same term to reference Rhéébù Nùù's struggles against the company, which was comprised – as the colonial administration had been – of wealthy white foreigners. Camping together on the village outskirts, these young people found a sense of Kanak identity in rebelling against a foreign institution, and many desired to shut down the project altogether. Their attitude and passion contrasted sharply with the customary authorities' more conservative view that employment with the mining project would be in the best interest of the next generation. Although Rhéébù Nùù leaders continued to insist that their aims were "not to destroy the project but to defend the environment and our rights to our natural heritage" (Comité Rhéébù Nùù 2008, 3), customary authorities began to complain that through its aggressive actions, the group was sending mixed messages; its goals were "not stated clearly" (Dominique, pers. comm. 10 July 2006).

Feeling increasingly uncomfortable with their relationship to the protest group, several customary authorities expressed resentment at becoming pawns in Rhéébù Nùù's game, as it attempted to claim a customary legitimacy which its main leaders lacked: "On the hierarchical scale they are the lowest. [ . . . ] They aren't customary authorities but they always use the customary authorities" (Jean-Claude, pers. comm. 20 July 2011). With no customary claims to local lands, Rhéébù Nùù's leaders needed to "provide some weight [ . . . ]. That's why they always bring elders [customary authorities] with them [ . . . ] to support them" (Loïc, pers. comm. 26 July 2011). However, the main leader, Gabriel, had kept all power for himself: "He said we have to include the customary authorities; as soon as he did, he asked to be president" (Loïc, pers. comm. 26 July 2011). Thus, customary authorities felt that Rhéébù Nùù was using them for their legitimacy in the interest of its own agenda, rather than representing them. Meanwhile, Vale was doing its best to position Rhéébù Nùù as a fringe element that represented neither customary authorities nor the general population (Horowitz 2012).

The series of talks that the Southern Province initiated in the wake of the April 2006 events did not bring Vale and Rhéébù Nùù any closer to a resolution, even with the 2007 intervention of an international NGO specializing in mediation. In early 2008, the company began laying the pipeline that would dump effluent into the marine environment, sparking fresh protests and blockades. In the midst of this turmoil, Rhéébù Nùù was swept into office at the municipal level, reinforcing many customary authorities' perception of the group as "political", not "customary", and therefore not authorized to "speak on behalf of the chiefs" (Félix, pers. comm. 11 August 2010). However, the protest group vehemently denied that it had become a political party and continued to base its identity in customary legitimacy; a 2008 brochure proclaimed, "Rhéébù Nùù is the word [mouthpiece] of the chieftainships, the clans, and the indigenous Kanak of the South!"

At this point, Vale flew in a legal specialist from Brazil as the new lead negotiator. He took a different tactical approach, the distinguishing feature of which, and the basis of its 'legitimacy', was that it was more 'inclusive'. Criticizing previous strategies that had "focused on talking to those who were most able to disrupt operations" (Benke 2010), the negotiator realized that exclusive engagement with the main source of trouble had allowed Rhéébù Nùù to exert pressure on Vale. In attempting to achieve efficiency, the company had not seen a need to negotiate with other, less troublesome, community sectors. However, instead of the failed strategies of countering protestors with force or addressing their demands directly, Vale could counterbalance and undermine their influence by capturing the deeply-held cultural ideal of customary legitimacy. To do this, it needed to broaden its engagement strategy, including not the entire community, as many women and young people sympathized with the protest group, but the sector most sympathetic to the project: customary authorities, who were also, of course, at the top of the social hierarchy.

Against Rhéébù Nùù's claim to have been initiated by local chiefs, in the negotiator's version the group had been "created by the municipal council" and thus had no basis in – in fact had excluded – "traditional structures of representation and leadership". In contrast, in reaching out to customary authorities, he was following culturally correct protocols by understanding "the customary leadership structures and interests" and engaging directly "with all legitimate customary representatives of all tribes related to the project" (Benke 2010). Thus, beyond taking the focus off Rhéébù Nùù, the company began working to undercut the group's claims to customary/indigenous legitimacy and instead establish Vale's own claims to that powerful resource. Customary authorities' increasing disillusionment with the protest group, detailed earlier, provided just that opportunity. The tripartite negotiations that ensued effectively marginalized Rhéébù Nùù; if the group was, as it claimed, representing the customary authorities, the presence of the latter at the table rendered the protestors redundant, and silenced them.

Sidelined at the negotiation table, Rhéébù Nùù's voice had no outlet but through their lawyer, who co-drafted the Pact. This lawyer, however, inadvertently strengthened Vale's capture of customary legitimacy. Drawing upon his specialization in indigenous rights, he took literally Rhéébù Nùù's continued insistence that their sole purpose was as an arm of the customary authorities and interpreted the group's demands as being primarily for "recognition of the indigenous people" (pers. comm. 22 September 2009), prioritizing recognition over their environmental and economic concerns and severing their ties to former allies such as urban-based environmentalists and government agencies. He drafted a long 'preamble' (about a third of the document), which described the customary authorities' "demands to see recognized the legitimate place of he who originates from the history of this land" and their ultimately successful "search for an agreement that would take into account each actor's legitimacy" (Vale Inco, Conseil Coutumier de l'Aire Drubéa Kapume, and Comité Rhéébù Nùù 2008). He later expressed satisfaction that Vale had "understood [ . . . ] that it was necessary to recognize the place of the first people, and so not to consider them as subjects, as pawns, but rather as partners" (pers. comm. 22 September 2009). He thus failed to recognize that both protest group and mining company were using the customary authorities precisely as pawns, for the legitimacy they represented.

Meanwhile, protest group leaders were becoming anxious about their dwindling support among local villagers, many of whom disapproved of the group's violent tactics and/or were impatient to enjoy the promised employment, despite continued environmental anxieties. If Rhéébù Nùù could at least engineer an agreement and convince customary authorities to sign it, the group would regain "a little respect" from local residents (Loïc, pers. comm. 26 July 2011). Paradoxically, though, as customary authorities' support for the mining project became highlighted through their engagement in the Pact negotiation process, Vale finally captured customary legitimacy, wresting it away from Rhéébù Nùù and thus delegitimizing the protestors, repositioning them as subordinates within their socio-cultural hierarchy. While some customary authorities were content with this situation, others worried that they had been coopted and continued to express anxieties about environmental impacts and disappointment with the limited economic benefits offered.

In capturing customary legitimacy, Vale also captured indigenous legitimacy from the international perspective. Ironically, to maintain his group's indigenous legitimacy in the eyes of the international community, Rhéébù Nùù's main leader found himself needing to team up with the MNC. At a UN workshop, Gabriel joined Rhéébù Nùù's lawyer and Vale's negotiator in presenting a "case study from New Caledonia," lauded by the UN as an exemplary process that had led to a "mutually acceptable result" (OHCHR 2009, 5). Two years later, the UN Special Rapporteur on the Rights of Indigenous Peoples also praised the Pact, which ensured "Kanak oversight of the environmental impact of the project" and provided economic benefits through an "innovative mechanism", the Corporate Foundation (Anaya 2011, 11). In stepping between Rhéébù Nùù and the customary authorities, Vale had severed the protest group's link to customary/indigenous legitimacy, and thus also that of the non-indigenous environmentalists who had claimed indigenous legitimacy through their relationship to Rhéébù Nùù (Horowitz 2015). As that chain was dissolved, a new one was formed in which Vale was the institution that successfully claimed legitimacy by association through its ties to customary authorities and in which, ironically, the Kanak protestors were forced to demonstrate their own indigenous legitimacy via their relationship to Vale.

## Conclusion

This chapter has built on understandings of ways that both corporations and NGOs attempt to legitimate themselves through association with other entities already perceived as legitimate. It has used a study of conflicts over a multinational mining project in New Caledonia to examine what happens when 'indigenous legitimacy by association' becomes the object of struggle among stakeholder groups with competing agendas. For Kanak, respect for customary authority is a deeply ingrained cultural norm and also constitutes a crucial aspect of Kanak cultural and political identity. Therefore, within Kanak societies, customary authorities' endorsement is necessary for a project or group to be viewed as legitimate. At first, Rhéébù Nùù, an indigenous protest group that targeted the mining project, achieved both 'customary legitimacy' vis-à-vis fellow Kanak, through association with customary authorities, and, concomitantly, 'indigenous legitimacy' in the international eye. This legitimacy provided them with important sources of support within local communities and from urban-based GROs and international NGOs. It also became an asset to which others attempted to hitch themselves through alliance, or that they tried to wrest away for themselves; in either case, processes of legitimation through association with Rhéébù Nùù involved some manipulation in the interest of the others' agendas, just as the indigenous activists had attempted to use the customary authorities for the legitimacy they represented. Urban-based, grassroots environmentalists sought to associate themselves with Rhéébù Nùù's indigenous legitimacy through alliance with this group, presenting themselves as sharing common goals. Meanwhile, the mining company was trying to capture this indigenous legitimacy through association not with Rhéébù Nùù, with whom they had failed to reach agreement over the past six years, but with the customary authorities that the protest group claimed to represent, a claim on which Rhéébù Nùù based its own legitimacy. Ultimately, the company successfully captured indigenous legitimacy and undermined Rhéébù Nùù's identity as representatives of the customary authorities. In order to maintain its own indigenous legitimacy, Rhéébù Nùù was left with little choice but, along with the customary authorities and mining company, to sign a 'Pact' that, incidentally, excluded the non-indigenous environmentalists along with all other Kanak community members.

Thus, this study shows that struggles over power may manifest themselves as struggles over legitimacy. All legitimacy is relational; like beauty, it is in the eye of the beholder, the product of social norms, cultural understandings, and political identities. Indigenous legitimacy, a powerful resource within grassroots environmental engagements, derives much of its power from a contemporary recognition of the long global history of mistreatment of indigenous peoples. As this chapter shows, other stakeholders who do not share this history may nonetheless try to benefit from the legitimacy it creates by associating themselves with indigenous groups, which inevitably involves some attempt at manipulation. Meanwhile, indigenous legitimacy by association is not fixed but continually remade through shifting social relations and struggled over through contingent, dynamic processes of (de)legitimation involving multiple stakeholder groups who attempt to harness this legitimacy to competing agendas.

## References

Anaya J. (2011) "Report of the Special Rapporteur on the rights of indigenous peoples on the situation of Kanak people in New Caledonia, France." United Nations General Assembly, A/HRC/18/35/Add.6, 23 November 2011.

Ashforth B. E., and Gibbs B. W. (1990) "The double-edge of organizational legitimation" *Organization Science, 1* 177–94.

Babb S. (2013) "The Washington Consensus as transnational policy paradigm: Its origins, trajectory and likely successor" *Review of International Political Economy, 20* 268–97.

Baur D., and Palazzo G. (2011) "The moral legitimacy of NGOs as partners of corporations" *Business Ethics Quarterly, 21* 579–604.

Bendell J. (2000) "Introduction: Working with stakeholder pressure for sustainable development" in Bendell J ed, *Terms for endearment: Business, NGOs and sustainable development* Greenleaf, Sheffield 14–30.

Benke R. (2010) "Perspective: Interview with BASESwiki, December 17, 2010". Retrieved from: http://baseswiki.org/en/Vale_New_Caledonia,_Negotiation_of_a_Sustainable_Develop ment_Pact_with_Local_Stakeholders,_Canada_2008, Accessed March 10, 2011.

Bensa A., and Rivierre J. C. (1982) *Les Chemins de l'alliance : L'organisation sociale et ses représentations en Nouvelle-Calédonie (Région de Touho – Aire linguistique cèmuhî)* SELAF, Paris.

Booth J. A., and Seligson M. A. (2005) "Political legitimacy and participation in Costa Rica: Evidence of arena shopping" *Political Research Quarterly, 58* 537–50.

Carroll T. (2010) *Delusions of development: The World Bank and the post-Washington Consensus in Southeast Asia* Palgrave-MacMillan, London.

Castells M. (1996) *The rise of the network society* Blackwell Publishers, Cambridge, MA.

Chandoke N. (2002) "The limits of global civil society" in Glasius M, Kaldor M and Anheier H eds, *Global civil society* Oxford University Press, Oxford 35–53.

Comité Rhéébù Nùù. (2008) "Véé e gué – véé rèè yè – djii djarù – 2008." Nouméa, Rhéébù Nùù.

DIMENC (Direction de l'Industrie des Mines et de l'Énergie). (2012) "Les sites d'activité du nickel en Nouvelle-Calédonie 2012". Retrieved from: www.dimenc.gouv.nc/portal/ page/portal/dimenc/mines_carrieres/mines, Accessed April 7, 2013.

Doh J. P., and Guay T. R. (2006) "Corporate social responsibility, public policy, and NGO activism in Europe and the United States: An institutional-stakeholder perspective" *Journal of Management Studies, 43* 47–73.

Doh J. P., Howton S. D., Howton S. W., and Siegel D. S. (2010) "Does the market respond to an endorsement of social responsibility? The role of institutions, information, and legitimacy" *Journal of Management, 36* 1461–85.

Dowling J., and Pfeffer J. (1975) "Organizational legitimacy: Social values and organizational behavior" *The Pacific Sociological Review, 18* 122–36.

Gauchat G. (2012) "Politicization of science in the public sphere: A study of public trust in the United States, 1974 to 2010" *American Sociological Review, 77* 167–87.

Gray R., Bebbington J., and Collison D. (2006) "NGOs, civil society and accountability: Making the people accountable to capital" *Accounting, Auditing & Accountability, 19* 319–48.

Habermas J. (2001) *The postnational constellation: Political essays* MIT Press, Cambridge, MA.

Henningham S. (1992) "Nickel and politics in New Caledonia" in Henningham S and May R J eds, *Resources, development and politics in the Pacific Islands* Crawford House Press, Bathurst, Australia 64–78.

Hodgson D. L. (2002) "Precarious alliances: The cultural politics and structural predicaments of the indigenous rights movement in Tanzania" *American Anthropologist, 104* 1086–97.

Horowitz L. S. (1998) "Integrating indigenous resource management with wildlife conservation: A case study of Batang Ai National Park, Sarawak, Malaysia" *Human Ecology, 26* 371–403.

———. (2004) "Toward a viable independence? The Koniambo Project and the political economy of mining in New Caledonia" *The Contemporary Pacific, 16* 287–319.

———. (2008a) "Destroying God's creation or using what He provided? Cultural models of a mining project in New Caledonia" *Human Organization, 67* 292–306.

———. (2008b) "It's up to the clan to protect: Cultural heritage and the micropolitical ecology of conservation in New Caledonia" *The Social Science Journal, 45* 258–78.

———. (2009) "Environmental violence and crises of legitimacy in New Caledonia" *Political Geography, 28* 248–58.

———. (2010) "Twenty years is yesterday: Science, multinational mining, and the political ecology of trust in New Caledonia" *Geoforum, 41* 617–26.

———. (2012) "Translation alignment: Actor-network theory, resistance, and the power dynamics of alliance in New Caledonia" *Antipode, 44* 806–27.

———. (2015) "Culturally articulated neoliberalization: Corporate social responsibility and the capture of indigenous legitimacy in New Caledonia." *Transactions of the Institute of British Geographers* 40(1): 88–101.

Humphreys D. (2000) "A business perspective on community relations in mining" *Resources Policy, 26* 127–31.

ICMM (International Council on Mining and Metals). (2013) "Indigenous peoples and mining: Position statement" ICMM, London (www.icmm.com/publications/pdfs/5433.pdf). Accessed 25 August 2016.

ILO (International Labour Organization). (1989) "Convention concerning indigenous and tribal peoples in independent countries (No. 169)" ILO, Geneva (www.ilo.org/dyn/normlex/en/f?p=normlexpub:12100:0::no::p12100_instrument_id:312314). Accessed 25 August 2016.

Jessop B. (1993) "Towards a Schumpeterian workfare state? Preliminary remarks on post-fordist political economy" *Studies in Political Economy, 40* 7–39.

Karlsson B. G. (2003) "Anthropology and the 'indigenous slot': Claims to and debates about indigenous peoples' status in India" *Critique of Anthropology, 23* 403–23.

Keck M. E., and Sikkink K. (1998) *Activists beyond borders: Advocacy networks in international politics* Cornell University Press, Ithaca, NY.

Kent A. (2006) "Reconfiguring security: Buddhism and moral legitimacy in Cambodia" *Security Dialogue, 37* 343–61.

Kier G., Kreft H., Lee T. M., Jetz W., Ibisch P. L., Nowicki C., Mutke J., and Barthlott W. (2009) "A global assessment of endemism and species richness across island and mainland regions" *Proceedings of the National Academy of Sciences of the United States of America*, 106 9322–27.

Kostova T., Roth K., and Dacin M. T. (2008) "Institutional theory in the study of multinational corporations: A critique and new directions" *Academy of Management Review*, 33 994–1006.

Kostova T., and Zaheer S. (1999) "Organizational legitimacy under conditions of complexity: The case of the multinational enterprise" *The Academy of Management Review*, 24 64–81.

Leenhardt M. (1937) *Gens de la grande terre* Gallimard, Paris.

Lyday T. Q. (2006) "The mineral industry of New Caledonia" in USGS (US Geological Survey) ed, *US Geological Survey Minerals Yearbook* US Geological Survey, Reston, VA 17.1–17.2.

Mapou R. (2003) "La Parole de l'autochtone Kanak du Sud et de ses chefferies." Nouméa, Rhéébù Nùù.

Martínez Cobo J. (1986) "Study of the problem of discrimination against indigenous populations: UN Doc. E/CN.4/Sub.2/1986/7 and Add. 1–4." United Nations, New York.

Matthieu. (2012) "L'affaire des climatiseurs de Goro: le député Philippe Gomes peut souffler . . ." *Calédosphere*, December 4.

Maurer J. G. (1971) "Legitimation, social responsibility, and regulation" in Maurer J G ed, *Readings in organization theory: Open-system approaches* Random House, New York 361–63.

Merlan F. (2009) "Indigeneity: Global and local" *Current Anthropology*, 50 303–33.

Merle I. (1996) "Le régime de l'indigénat et l'impot de capitation en Nouvelle-Calédonie. De la force et du droit: le genèse d'une législation d'exception ou les principes fondateurs d'un ordre colonial" in Saussol A and Zitomersky J eds, *Colonies, territoires, sociétés: L'Enjeu français* L'Harmattan, Paris 223–42.

Meyer J. W., and Rowan B. (1977) "Institutionalized organizations: Formal structure as myth and ceremony" *American Journal of Sociology*, 83 340–63.

*Mining Journal.* (1999) "Inco's new PAL: October 29, 1999", *333* 340.

Naepels M. (1998) *Histoires de terres kanakes* Belin, Paris.

Naidoo K. (2004) "The end of blind faith? Civil society and the challenge of accountability, legitimacy and transparency" *Accountability Forum*, 2 14–25.

Oetzel J., and Doh J. P. (2009) "MNEs and development: A review and reconceptualization" *Journal of World Business*, 44 108–20.

OHCHR (Office of the United Nations High Commissioner for Human Rights). (2009) "International Workshop on Natural Resource Companies, Indigenous Peoples and Human Rights: Setting a Framework for Consultation, Benefit-Sharing and Dispute Resolution: Unpublished report." Geneva, Office of the United Nations High Commissioner for Human Rights.

Oliver C. (1991) "Strategic responses to institutional processes" *Academy of Management Review*, 16 145–79.

Palazzo G., and Scherer A. G. (2006) "Corporate legitimacy as deliberation: A communicative framework" *Journal of Business Ethics*, 66 71–88.

Pfeffer J., and Salancik G. R. (1978) *The external control of organizations: A resource dependence perspective* Harper & Row, New York.

Pitoiset A. (2014) "Nouvelle Calédonie: un nouvel arrêt qui tombe mal pour l'usine Vale" *Les Échos*, May 8.

Plehwe D., and Walpen B. (2006) "Between network and complex organization: The making of neoliberal knowledge and hegemony" in Plehwe D, Walpen B and Neunhöffer G eds, *Neoliberal hegemony: A global critique* Routledge, London and New York 27–50.

Richer de Forges B., and Pascal M. (2008) "La Nouvelle-Calédonie, un « point chaud » de la biodiversité mondiale gravement menacé par l'exploitation minière" *Journal de la Société des Océanistes, 126–127 95–112.*

Rivoilan P., and Broustet D. (2011) "Recensement de la population 2009" *Synthèse, Institut de la Statistique et des Études Économiques Nouvelle-Calédonie, 19 1–4.*

Rodgers C. (2000) "Making it legit: New ways of generating corporate legitimacy in a globalising world" in Bendell J ed, *Terms for endearment: Business, NGOs and sustainable development* Greenleaf, Sheffield 40–48.

Sarewitz D. (2004) "How science makes environmental controversies worse" *Environmental Science & Policy, 7 385–403.*

Scherer A. G., and Palazzo G. (2007) "Toward a political conception of corporate responsibility: Business and society seen from a Habermasian perspective" *Academy of Management Review, 32 1096–120.*

Soederberg S. (2004) *The politics of the new international financial architecture: Reimposing neoliberal domination in the global South* Zed Books, London.

Spar D. L., and La Mure L. T. (2003) "The power of activism: Assessing the impact of NGOs on global business" *California Management Review, 45 78.*

Steffek J. (2003) "The legitimation of international governance: A discourse approach" *European Journal of International Relations, 9 249–75.*

Suchman M. C. (1995) "Managing legitimacy: Strategic and institutional approaches" *The Academy of Management Review, 20 571–610.*

Swyngedouw E. (2000) "The Marxian alternative: Historical-geographical materialism and the political economy of capitalism" in Sheppard E and Barnes T J eds, *A companion to economic geography* Blackwell, Oxford 41–59.

Szablowski D. (2002) "Mining, displacement and the World Bank: A case analysis of Compania Minera Antamina's operations in Peru" *Journal of Business Ethics, 39 247–73.*

Teegen H. (2003) "Business-government-NGO bargaining in international, multilateral Clean Development Mechanism projects in the wake of Kyoto" in Doh J P and Teegen H eds, *Globalization and NGOs: Transforming business, government, and society* Praeger, Westport, CT 107–28.

UN (United Nations). (2007) "Decolonization United Nations success story, albeit unfinished one, Deputy Secretary-General tells special committee". Retrieved from: www.un.org/News/Press/docs/2007/gacol3151.doc.htm, Accessed August 30, 2009.

United Nations. (2008) "Declaration on the rights of indigenous peoples." United Nations, New York.

Vale Inco, Conseil Coutumier de l'Aire Drubéa Kapume, and Comité Rhéébù Nùù. (2008) "Pacte pour un développement durable du Grand Sud." Vale Inco Nouvelle-Calédonie, Nouméa.

Weber M. (1978 [1968]) *Economy and society: An outline of interpretive sociology* University of California Press, Berkeley.

Zadek S. (2001) *The civil corporation: The new economy of corporate citizenship* Earthscan, London.

# Part II
# Relationships

# 5 Governing from the ground up?

Translocal networks and the
ambiguous politics of
environmental justice in Bolivia

*Tom Perreault*

## Introduction

In October 2009, Bolivian President Evo Morales declared the Huanuni River valley, in the Andean department of Oruro, to be in a state of environmental emergency. For nearly 100 years, the Huanuni mine, currently operated by the state mining corporation COMIBOL (Corporación Minera de Bolivia), has emitted untreated mining waste directly into the Huanuni River. The president's decree (Decreto Supremo, or Presidential Decree, number 0335, hereafter DS 0335), mandated environmental remediation projects at the mine site and in affected communities downstream. This marks the first time in Bolivian history that this declaration – normally reserved for 'natural' disasters such as floods, droughts or mudslides – has been invoked in a case of anthropogenic environmental degradation. Morales' declaration signals a potentially important shift in the Bolivian government's approach to mining, which historically has been permitted to operate with little oversight and scant regard for social and environmental impacts. A growing body of scientific evidence, however, has merely confirmed what local residents have long known: that levels of pollution in the river (as well as in Lake Uru Uru, into which it flows) are dangerously high, with profoundly negative implications for the lives and livelihoods of people living downstream.

Morales' declaration was slow in coming. It was only after years of mobilization by residents of rural communities and urban neighborhoods that the president released the decree. Ultimately, he was persuaded by growing pressure, including a march from the city of Oruro to the capital La Paz, organized by the Oruro-based grassroots environmental justice network, the Coordinator for the Defense of the Desaguadero Basin and Lakes Uru Uru and Poopó (Coordinadora en Defensa de las Cuencas del Río Desaguadero y Lagos Uru Uru y Poopó, CORIDUP). CORIDUP represents some 80 communities throughout the greater Lake Poopó watershed, as well as neighborhood groups within the city of Oruro. Having received legal recognition in 2006 (following several years of organizing), CORIDUP is the first sustained community-based mobilization in response to the effects of mining activity in the region. Previous protest movements, from individual communities or focused on singular events, failed to gain traction and were easily ignored, coopted, or repressed by the pro-mining local state or by miners themselves.

This chapter examines CORDIUP's organizing efforts, which led to the release of DS 0335 in 2009, and its work in facilitating remediation and acting as a liaison between affected communities, state agencies, and COMIBOL. As such, this chapter is in part the story of CORIDUP's success: grassroots mobilization forced the government to enact policy aimed at fixing environmental damage and compensating affected residents. However, this chapter also probes what lay behind and beyond this apparent success. As a 'grassroots' organization, CORIDUP is at once rooted in the rural communities and urban neighborhoods whose interests it represents, and embedded in translocal networks that stretch far beyond the Huanuni valley. Moreover, CORIDUP enjoys only tenuous support among its member communities, while many local residents are resigned to living with extreme pollution and have been largely *de*-mobilized by years of hardship and official neglect. The next section of the chapter discusses the historical context of mining in Oruro. This is followed by a discussion of the mobilizing efforts that led to CORIDUP's establishment, and its activities leading up to, and in the years since, the release of DS 0335. The chapter ends by considering the multi-scalar, networked relations through which CORIDUP has been able to organize and the structural limitations to efforts on the part of social movement activists to alter the state's extractive agenda.

## Mining and its discontents

Since the 1990s, policy reforms of various sorts – ranging from neoliberal to nationalist – have combined with waves of domestic and foreign investment to intensify mining, oil and gas extraction throughout Latin America. The processes of investment, policy reform, and environmental transformation associated with resource extraction in Latin America are by now well documented (see, inter alia, Bebbington 2012a, b; Bebbington and Bury 2013; Perreault 2014; Urteaga 2011a). Of more direct interest to this chapter are the forms of social mobilization to which extraction gives rise. As Bebbington et al. (2008b) note, people mobilize politically in response to resource extraction both as a defense of livelihoods and in order to contest what Habermas (1987) referred to as the colonization of the 'lifeworld' – the quotidian sphere of practice and social relations through which people come to understand and give meaning to the world around them. As Bebbington et al. (2008b: 2890) suggest, "[S]ocial mobilization can be understood as a response to the threats that particular forms of economic development present, or are perceived as presenting, to the security and integrity of livelihoods and to the ability of a population in a given territory to control what it views as its own resources." In this sense, collective actions in response to extractive activities – as with collective action in other social, economic and political spheres – can be understood simultaneously in material and symbolic terms (cf. Escobar et al. 1998). Rural peoples defend actual or perceived threats to the material resources they need for social reproduction – water for drinking and irrigation, land for growing crops and grazing animals, etc. – even as they struggle to maintain some measure of social autonomy and cultural continuity

(Budds and Hinojosa 2012; Bury 2008). Certainly, such threats to livelihood and lifeworld are present in the Huanuni valley, where residents' lives are profoundly shaped by acute mining contamination and extreme poverty (López et al. 2010). These are two key axes through which social relations of domination and subordination are experienced in a region where indigenous and *campesino* (peasant) peoples – who are the majority of the rural Andean population – are commonly viewed as inferior to miners and urban professionals, who hold considerably higher economic and socio-political status, and who at times denigrate indigenous and campesino peoples as a hindrance to national development; a sentiment prevalent even in the Bolivia of indigenous president Evo Morales (cf. Bebbington 2012b).

But whereas struggles against what Harvey (2003) has termed 'accumulation by dispossession' have surely become a major feature of collective action (Bebbington et al. 2008a), not all forms of mobilization easily map onto this category. On the Bolivian altiplano, as in many parts of the central Andes, where the history of mining dates to the pre-Hispanic era and livelihoods often integrate smallholder agriculture with periodic work in the mining industry (giving rise to regionally-, culturally-, and economically-defined 'agro-minero' communities; see Urteaga 2011b), social mobilization rarely takes the form of anti-mining protests. Rather, where mobilization occurs in relation to mining on the altiplano it most often revolves around calls for greater control over mining operations on the part of local communities (CEDIB 2012) or miners themselves (Marston and Perreault, forthcoming). Anti-neoliberal mobilization and associated calls for greater national control over natural resources have similarly animated social movement protests in recent years (Perreault 2006). While embracing contests over livelihood and the defense of lifeworlds, struggles over resource nationalism extend further, into the realms of formal politics and contests over the very meanings of development and its relationship to national identity (Farthing and Kohl 2013; Perreault 2013b). These struggles are further developed in the following section, in which I consider the historical, social, and environmental importance of mining in Bolivia.

## Histories and geographies of mining in Oruro

During the Colonial period, Oruro's mining economy was overshadowed by that of Potosí to the south, with its enormous silver deposits. When world silver markets crashed in the late nineteenth century, activity shifted to Oruro and northern Potosí, whose mountains are rich in tin (Madrid et al. 2002; Nash 1993), and for a time during the mid-twentieth century, Bolivia was one of the world's leading exporters of that mineral. In the first decades of the twentieth century, the Huanuni, Uncía, Catavi and Siglo XX mines, controlled by a small cadre of mining elites, represented the center of gravity of the Bolivian economy. Following years of violent repression, miners played a central role in the 1952 Social Revolution, as they formed the vanguard of the revolutionary forces that defeated the sclerotic and corrupt military government, and swept into power the National Revolutionary Movement (MNR) and its exiled leader, Víctor Paz Estenssoro. The MNR government, which briefly shared power with Bolivia's main labor union, the Workers' Central of Bolivia (COB), nationalized the mines and created the state mining company, COMIBOL (Dunkerley 1984). It is perhaps ironic that it was not only the MNR, but Paz Estenssoro himself, in his fourth and final (non-consecutive) term as president, who implemented the first wave of neoliberal measures in the mid-1980s, closing the state-run mines and largely dismantling COMIBOL. The sudden loss of over 20,000 jobs in mining, and thousands more in ancillary employment, devastated the region. As a consequence, many ex-miners and their families moved to the urban centers of La Paz, El Alto and Cochabamba, while many others moved to the tropical Chapare region of Cochabamba department to grow coca for the booming cocaine trade. Many of those who remained, along with others who moved into the region in the wake of the mine closures, joined mining cooperatives, operating at the margins of the formal economy, with no environmental oversight or labor protections (Francescone and Díaz 2013; Michard 2008; Moeller 2002).

The neoliberal reforms of the 1980s and '90s restructured the conditions for mine ownership, labor and rent distribution. Foreign investment in Bolivia's mining sector slowly increased during this period, as part of a broader international mining boom (Bebbington 2009; Bridge 2004; Kaup 2013). With the election of Evo Morales and his Movement to Socialism (MAS) party in 2005, the sector has again undergone an important shift. Following the May 2006 nationalization of hydrocarbons (Kaup 2010), Morales reconstituted COMIBOL, giving it a much larger role in managing national mining production – even if it is still a shadow of what it was from the 1950s through the 1970s. COMIBOL's reorganization was sparked by a fratricidal confrontation at the Huanuni tin mine between miners employed by COMIBOL and those organized into mining cooperatives. The conflict erupted in October 2006, and resulted in 17 deaths and over 100 injuries (Howard and Dangl 2006). With its reconstitution, COMIBOL absorbed over 4500 *cooperativista* miners (increasing the mine's workforce nearly ten-fold). The mine's massive expansion both enabled and necessitated a dramatic increase in production (López 2011; López et al. 2010).

With this expansion, the Huanuni tin mine is the region's single largest source of mine-related water and soil contamination. In its nearly 100 years of operation, it has never had an adequate retention facility for containing mining waste, and instead has dumped untreated water and waste material directly into the Huanuni River, which flows through (or adjacent to) dozens of indigenous-campesino communities downstream on its way to Lakes Uru Uru and Poopó. Pollution has grown steadily in recent decades, with the adoption of the chemical intensive sink-and-float system of processing ore (Nash 1993). As a large, state-owned tin mine employing thousands of miners, however, Huanuni is exceptional in many respects. Whereas COMIBOL miners account for about 6% of Bolivia's mining workforce, mining cooperatives, with about 115,000 miners, account for roughly 88% of the sector's total labor force. Similarly, COMIBOL accounts for just 6% of total mining production by value, while the remaining 94% of mining production is divided almost evenly between cooperatives and privately held mines (Achtenberg 2014). Indeed, as important as it is, Huanuni is the sole state-owned mine in the immediate region, and is flanked by cooperatives and privately held mines, most of which extract silver, lead, zinc and tin in complex.

Numerous scientific studies have documented the region's devastating legacy of environmental degradation, mostly in the form of acute water and soil contamination (see, for instance, García-Guinea and Harffy 1998; López 2011; López et al. 2010; PPO 1996). In addition to the direct release of chemicals and contaminated water into the environment, acidic drainage from mine tailings leach heavy metals and lowers the pH of soils and surface waters. Quintanilla and García (2009) identified heavy metals such as mercury, lead, arsenic, cadmium, iron, copper and zinc in rivers throughout the Lake Poopó watershed (which includes the Huanuni valley) – in all cases exceeding levels permissible under international standards and Bolivian law (see also López et al 2010; Montoya et al. 2010; Perreault 2013a). There is little doubt, then, that centuries of mining have left a toxic legacy in Oruro. How this legacy is experienced by the residents of the region, and how they mobilize to confront it, is the focus of the rest of this chapter.

### Environmental suffering in Oruro

The indigenous-campesino[1] residents of Oruro's Huanuni valley and Desaguadero basin are among the most impoverished in Bolivia, with some 46.3% of the population living in what the United Nations Development Program characterized as 'extreme poverty' (as compared to 32.7% for Bolivia as a whole, and 12.6% in Latin America). The city of Oruro itself has relatively low rates of extreme poverty (at 33%), but outside the capital, every municipality in the department has an extreme poverty rate over 70% (UPADE 2010). This high altitude region (the city of Oruro is located at an elevation of 3700m) is characterized by a cold and semi-arid climate, and in many areas its soils are highly saline – one of the world's largest salt pans, the Salar de Uyuni, is located south of Oruro. In this challenging environment, rural residents have long engaged in semi-subsistence agriculture, typically growing potatoes, fava beans, and quinoa, along with a mix of vegetables (including onions, carrots, and turnips) where conditions permit. Residents also raise cattle, sheep and sometimes llamas for meat and market, and sell milk, yogurt and fresh cheese for local consumption. The inherent difficulties of agricultural production in this region have only been exacerbated by mine-related water and soil contamination. Discouraged by the lack of economic opportunities and the difficulty of rural life, many residents leave their communities for urban centers such as Oruro, La Paz, Cochabamba, Buenos Aires or, increasingly, São Paulo.

The environmental impacts of mining are experienced in a myriad of ways by those living downstream and downwind. In Oruro's southern neighborhoods, which abut the tailings and processing facilities of the Baremsa metallurgy plant and lay just downhill from the Itos mine, residents breathe the dust that blows off the slag heaps during the dry season (April-October), while during the rainy season (November-March), acid runoff drains downstream, polluting water and soil. In the communities of Intimarca and Mallku Kocha,[2] downstream from COMIBOL's Huanuni mine, sediments laden with heavy metals, salts and chemical toxins are deposited at the mouth of the river, adjacent to agricultural fields and pasture. Urban residents complain that air pollution from the metallurgy facilities, while residents of rural communities suffer from respiratory and skin ailments, and have watched their crops wither and their livestock die. Stories of deformed calves and lambs (or aborted, deformed fetuses) are commonplace (Perreault 2013a).

Profound environmental degradation frames peoples' everyday conversations, and provides a touchstone by which people come to understand their lives. CORIDUP president Félix Laime expressed it this way: "When I was a boy, the area had lots of vegetation, it produced potato, quinoa, *chuño* [a form of dried potato and a staple of the altiplano diet]; campesinos didn't need to buy more than a few vegetables to live. These days they have to buy everything because the land doesn't produce anything" (quoted in Forno and Pauwels 2009: 20). Similarly, Don Braulio, an indigenous authority from Intimarca, explained his personal experience this way,

> Regarding the impact of the mines, Intimarca is a complete trash dump. The water is now totally saline. Before, when I was still a child, we had wells that were good, good. Now, in comparison, no. Before, we made cheese, we had 20 or 30 cows, but now no. There aren't any. The forage, with the contamination, the totora (reeds) that the cows eat, they don't give any nutrition. There's no milk, they die. This is coming from Huanuni. It's contaminating everything . . . The water itself is totally contaminated with it. It's ruining us. The grasslands used to be, ahhh, so good, so tall. But now there's not one left. There's nothing. It looks like a salt pan (*salar*). When it rains, this water from the salt pan, it's not drinkable, it's not good for anything . . . With the pollution we have to carry water from (the town of) Machacamarca to the countryside to drink and cook. Before, we used to get water from a well, but not anymore. When we drink this water now we get sick.
>
> (author interview, 30 May 2011)

Similarly, Don Gerardo, one of CORUDUP's founding members (and an official with the departmental government at the time of our interview), described his community, Mallku Kocha, which is among the most acutely contaminated by mining waste. The deposition of sediments laden with heavy metals has made agriculture in the community all but impossible:

> Look, this place used to be an orchard [*vergel*], filled with totora (reeds), this whole place. All this area that is now (barren) plain, really used to be an orchard. The rivers that are now clogged with sediment, that you've seen

yourself, were deep rivers. I used to see fish, no problem, it was crystal clear. There were duck eggs [a locally important source of food] and eggs of other birds too – I used to go gather them in quantity. There were cattle. I had my boat – there was so much water that I had to travel by boat . . . Look, all these lands that really used to produce, have all been converted into desert. And it's advancing more and more.

(author interview, 20 May 2011)

The pictures painted by Don Braulio, Don Gerardo and Félix Laime draw on images and experiences common in such descriptions, and which I heard repeatedly during in my conversations with local residents: crystalline waters, wetlands full of totora reeds, plentiful fish and waterfowl, bountiful agricultural production. I do not doubt that there is truth in these representations, and it is certainly the case that mining contamination has resulted in profound environmental and social transformation (López et al. 2010; Perreault 2013a). However, one must interpret such reminiscences with care. Given the long history of mining in the region, environmental conditions within recent memory are unlikely to have been as idyllic as these men describe. Moreover, the communities these men speak of, which are among the most contaminated by mining activity, were also subject to the forced labor and racialized subjugation of the hacienda system until its abolishment in 1953. But as Javier Auyero and Débora Swistun (2009) have pointed out in their exploration of environmental suffering in a Buenos Aires shantytown, statements about the past are never *only* about the past, and are always also reflections on the present. Such reminiscences, then, serve to measure peoples' current reality, by holding it up for comparison to an idealized history, and in so doing help shape collective memories of a vanished past and a shared understanding of a degraded present. As with processes of social mobilization elsewhere in in the Andes (c.f. Farthing and Kohl 2013; Himley 2014), this shared understanding plays a vital role in CORIDUP's organizing processes, as I discuss in the next section.

## Mining and mobilization: environmental justice organizing in Oruro

In contrast to its neighbor Peru, Bolivia has seen relatively little organized opposition to mining. Given widespread concern over (and mobilization around) mining in its northern neighbor, together with the obvious negative social and environmental effects of mining practices in Bolivia (López et al. 2010; Perreault 2013a), and the pivotal political role played by Bolivia's social movements in recent decades (García Linera et al. 2004; Gustafson 2010), one might expect to find a well-organized populace mobilized in opposition to mining projects – especially those of transnational firms. In fact, such mobilization is notable primarily by its absence. There are various ways to explain this situation. Perhaps the most fundamental explanation has to do with basic location: whereas many of Peru's large-scale mining projects are open pit operations located in agrarian regions and which provide few employment opportunities for local residents, in Bolivia, most mining occurs on the altiplano, and many residents find some level of employment in the mining industry as cooperativistas or temporary laborers. With the region's long mining history, many current residents are descended from populations who moved into the region (voluntarily or otherwise) to work in the mines, or whose labor produced foodstuffs and other goods consumed in mining centers. Many residents have few economic alternatives and many engage in mining activity of various sorts, during some point in their lives. This is particularly true for men, for whom many more opportunities exist in the mining sector (and for whom the dangerous and physically demanding work is often seen as a rite of passage), although some women still work as *pailliris*, sorting crushed mine tailing to recover trace amounts of silver, tin and zinc ore (see Nash 1993; Robins 2011).

Another factor affecting the lack of broad-based, grassroots mobilization against mining in Bolivia is the size and breadth of the mining workforce. Mining cooperatives, which include the vast majority of actual miners in the country, operate similarly to traditional mining firms, and in most cases are less egalitarian than their name would suggest (Achtenberg 2014). The unique structure of Bolivia's mining labor force means that tens of thousands of cooperativista miners, working for hundreds of cooperatives, are distributed throughout dozens of mining centers in Potosí, Oruro, and La Paz departments. While some cooperativistas are single men from outside the region, many are local residents who had formerly worked for the state mining firm, COMIBOL. Cooperativistas represent a highly organized and politically influential sector of the altiplano's population (Michard 2008). The broad spatial distribution of cooperativista miners, combined with their well-known political militancy and capacity for occasional violence (Francescone and Díaz 2013; Howard and Dangl 2006), make it particularly difficult for community residents, indigenous-campesino organizations or environmentalists to mobilize around mining issues, let alone oppose mining itself. The combination of these factors makes it all the more surprising that CORIDUP has managed to sustain its organizing efforts for nearly a decade, in the face of pervasive apathy, steady opposition, and occasional hostility from politicians, miners, and the broader population.

### CORIDUP's mobilizing efforts

CORIDUP operates out of a non-descript office at the back of a compound in Oruro's working-class southern neighborhood. On its door is a simple paper sign in plain lettering, "Espacio de Justicia Ambiental" (Space of Environmental Justice). CORIDUP defines itself as an environmental justice organization – one of only a small handful of such organizations in Bolivia – and is primarily concerned with the social and environmental impacts of Oruro's mining waste. In its official history, it describes its mission this way: "As an organization (CORIDUP), we want to reach those who still do not think of future generations, who are cloistered beneath an economistic vision; we ask them to leave their haphazard economistic paradigms or models and join the collective struggle to defend our mother earth, who gives us life, who houses and feeds us, and in this way achieve environmental justice" (CORIDUP n.d.). In what follows, I discuss CORIDUP's campaigns and its relations with the people it represents. In doing so, I write about CORIDUP as a singular entity. It is not, of course, and in fact it represents some 80 rural communities and urban neighborhoods. But it also produces reports and makes presentations at public meetings as an organization, and its members elect leaders to represent the group's views. The internal complexity of the group is somewhat obscured by this singular representation (cf. Wolford 2010), but my goal is to examine CORIDUP as an organization, in the context of its interactions with other actors: indigenous-peasant communities, government officials, NGOs, researchers and activists. My own interactions with CORIDUP form part of these entanglements. These interactions began in 2009, and I have returned most years since, including for a six-month period in 2011, when I conducted field research in the Huanuni valley, in collaboration with CORIDUP and the Centro de Ecología y Pueblos Andinos (Center for Ecology and Andean Peoples, CEPA), a small Bolivian NGO, which provides guidance and material support, including office space, to CORIDUP. This field research consisted of 45 in-depth, semi-structured interviews with community residents, CORIDUP activists, administrators of the Huanuni mine company and representatives of various municipal, departmental and national-level government agencies. In addition, I spoke with university researchers and functionaries from an array of NGOs and international development agencies active in Oruro. I also surveyed a total of 125 households in 14 communities in the Hunauni river valley, and conducted chemical analysis of soil and water samples taken along a transect in the Huanuni valley.

As an organization, CORIDUP is decidedly male and middle aged. Of the seven or eight people who regularly populate the office and who are most involved in planning and implementing the group's work, only one is a woman. Often the youngest person in the room, her role is typically confined to administrative and behind-the-scenes labor. Other women serve on CORIDUP's elected 11-person directorate, but are less active with the organization on a day-to-day basis. CORIDUP is also decidedly working class. The active members come from indigenous-campesino communities and low-income urban neighborhoods in and around the city of Oruro, all of which are affected by mining waste. These are not bourgeois environmentalists to be sure, but nor do CORIDUP's activists conform neatly to Martínez Alier's conception of the environmentalism of the poor (Martínez Alier 2003), whose concerns are circumscribed by their immediate material needs. Rather, in their statements and their activism, CORIDUP's members express a primary concern for environmental justice and, more broadly, for environmental conditions that have markedly deteriorated in recent decades.

CORIDUP held its first meeting for communities affected by mine-related pollution in 2006, in the town of Machacamarca. An old hacienda center and railway station, Machacamarca serves as the administrative center of the *municipio* (similar to a county) of the same name. But the group's activists trace their mobilization to 2000, and an oil pipeline rupture that spilled thousands of liters of crude oil into the Desaguadero river northwest of the city of Oruro (Montoya et al. 2002). The spill contaminated drinking and irrigation water for communities downstream, and inspired a mobilizing effort on the part of local community members to force the national government and the Transredes Corporation, which operated the pipeline, to remediate the damage and compensate residents of affected communities. It soon became apparent, however, that those most capable of mobilizing and pressuring government officials to take action – and therefore, those who captured the greatest share of the limited compensation funds – were the few communities with irrigation systems. Peasant irrigators were already well organized into local associations, with connections to extensive regional and national networks of water users, NGOs, government ministries and international aid agencies (Perreault 2005, 2008). In making claims for environmental remediation and financial compensation, irrigators and their communities were able to draw on their previous experience of mobilization, as well as their local organizational structures and the broader networks of which they were a part.

CORIDUP activists explain that the spill had the effect of heightening their awareness both of environmental issues and the need for effective organizing. As Don Gerardo put it,

> Before the oil spill, here no one knew about environmental issues, in spite of the Environmental Law. Thanks to this oil spill, practically all the people . . . began to make demands of [the pipeline operator] Transredes, in the sector of the oil spill . . . And after that, we practically woke up to the importance of environmental issues, for our *Pachamama* [Earth Mother]. And after the problems of the oil spill were ended . . . [it was clear that] this was not the only kind of pollution, we also realized that there were other forms of pollution. Inti Raymi [mine], sometimes Huanuni [mine], mining cooperatives, artisanal mines, private mines, even wastewater here in the city of Oruro, acid mine drainage from San José [mine], etcetera, etcetera
>
> (author interview, 20 May 2011).

In this telling, the 2000 oil spill provides a defining moment and key discursive reference point that sparked awareness both of environmental issues and of the need for collective action in order to advance community members' claims for government and corporate compensation. It is also worth noting that 2000 was the year of the Cochabamba 'water war,' the iconic mass protest against the privatization of that city's drinking water and sewerage service (Olivera 2004; Peredo et al. 2004). The water war, in turn, was a key moment in a roughly five-year process of social struggle against the traditional political elites and their neoliberal economic programs, which culminated in the forced resignation of two presidents and the election of current president Evo Morales (Gutiérrez Aguilar 2014; Hylton and Thomson 2007). Thus, CORIDUP's organizational process took place in the context of growing social mobilization and widespread discontent with the country's existing political economic order.

The lack of action on the part of state agencies and the campesino federation is in part a result of mining's economic and political hegemony in Oruro and Potosí. A common refrain in these departments is that mining is the backbone of the Bolivian economy. Surely this was once true, particularly on the altiplano (Nash 1993), but mining was long ago eclipsed economically by hydrocarbons as Bolivia's primary source of revenue. Mining remains locally important in Oruro and Potosí, however, where cooperativistas represent an economically and politically influential sector of the population. Mining's hegemonic status also has deep historical roots. Miners played a crucial role in overthrowing the Bolivian military in the 1952 Social Revolution (Dunkerley 2007), and monuments to the revolutionary miner abound in cities and mine centers in the region. This storied history has helped forge strong class solidarity between miners and campesinos, as reflected in the close alignment between Oruro's campesino federation (Unitary Syndicalist Federation of Peasant Workers of Oruro, FSUTCO) and the miners' unions (the Bolivian Federation of Mine Workers, FSTMB, and the National Federation of Mining Cooperatives, FENCOMIN), which have poor relations with CORIDUP and CEPA. Although the campesino federation has an environmental commission, it has done little to address environmental concerns in campesino communities. As Ernesto, one of the CORIDUP leaders explained to me, in his slow, measured tone,

> within the structure of the campesino federation for example, there are secretaries: a secretary general, a secretary of environment – this secretary of environment had the responsibility of taking measures to make sure that the communities affected by pollution would be helped. But nevertheless it isn't enough, no? Those *compañeros* who assume those positions were closely related with the mine operators, and so of course they weren't going to do anything. So, what are the affected communities to do? Well, organize, to present demands.
>
> (author interview, 29 July 2013)

Ernesto's statement points to social tensions that shape CORIDUP's organizing strategies, and serve to circumscribe its demands. Because CORIDUP (like Cochabamba's irrigators movement, and the indigenous organizations CIDOB and CONAMAQ; see Perreault 2005, 2008; Perreault and Green 2013), is not part of Bolivia's syndicalist organizational structure (which involves campesino federations, along with unions for factory workers, teachers, medical workers and others), it is criticized by these organizations as being a 'parallel' group. It therefore struggles for legitimacy as a social movement, which complicates its efforts at broad-based organizing. CORIDUP must also temper its demands in the face of opposition, and occasional open hostility, from the miners' unions. Miners' unions have accused CORIDUP of seeking to close the mines and portray the group as a direct threat to miners' livelihoods and, by extension, the economic wellbeing of Oruro as a whole. Partly as a result of this hostility, CORIDUP takes pains to assert that it is not opposed to mining itself, but rather asks only that mining firms engage in 'responsible mining' and operate according to the practices established under the 1992 Environmental Law. As Don Gerardo told me,

> It is true for example that Oruro is a mining department, we are not opposed to mining – it sustains the department. We're not saying that they should close the mines. But they should – *we are in the 21st century* – they should work according to the law, without polluting. If they use water, it should also be suitable for irrigation [downstream from mine operation]. This is what we are demanding.
>
> (author interview, 20 May 2011; emphasis in original statement)

Two years later, Ernesto asserted,

> We as an organization ask that the mine operators comply with the Environmental Law, and the mine operators don't like it. They manipulate the miners, no? The businessmen say, 'CORIDUP wants to close the mine because they say we don't comply with environmental law.' Well, then the miners mobilize, saying they don't recognize us [as a valid organization] and that they only recognize the campesino federation, because they know the campesino federation won't do anything. They'll continue working irresponsibly.
>
> (author interview, 29 July 2013)

CORIDUP activists are acutely aware of the hostility their actions elicit from mine operators and their allies, and know that outright opposition to mining is a politically untenable (and potentially dangerous) position. Thus, CORIDUP frames its message in legal terms, such that reference to the 1992 Environmental Law is a recurring trope in its rhetoric. Bolivia's 1992 Environmental Law (Law no. 1333, *Ley de Medio Ambiente*) is a touchstone of CORIDUP's discursive framing of mining waste. The law is widely seen as progressive and strong – despite the fact that it was promulgated by the widely reviled and now exiled neoliberal president Gonzalo Sánchez de Lozada – and it is referenced repeatedly in CORIDUP documents, presentations and everyday speech. In this way, CORIDUP is careful to moderate its positions, and avoid being seen as too radical. It frames its demands in legal and technical, rather than overtly political terms. This might be understood as an inverse 'antipolitics machine,' in which CORIDUP's legalistic discourse serves to 'render technical' the highly uneven power relations and institutional arrangements that result in the region's acute environmental degradation (cf. Ferguson 1994; Li 2007). Whereas Ferguson, Li and others have examined the ways that development discourse serves to depoliticize policies and practices that upend lifeways, and to insert state power ever more deeply into the lives of marginalized citizens, CORIDUP skillfully deploys a legal discourse to point to the lack of state action in implementing environmental laws. Its critique of mining operations is framed discursively in technical terms, as violations of the 1992 Environmental Law, and therefore in need of redress on legal grounds. Such a discourse is evidence of the disciplining effect of mining's hegemony in Bolivia: the measured discourse of CORIDUP members positions the group squarely within the bounds of what are politically and socially acceptable demands, even as it reinforces their identity as responsible environmental citizens (cf. Agrawal 2005; Li 2007). Moreover, while its activists may individually criticize the cooperativistas in private conversations, CORIDUP as an organization studiously avoids confrontation with mining cooperatives, and concentrates its efforts on private firms (both transnational and Bolivian) and the state mining corporation COMIBOL. This position is evident in its organizing efforts in the Huanuni valley, discussed next.

## Multi-scalar entanglements

CORIDUP is a membership organization, meaning that it works with, and through, community and neighborhood organizations that voluntarily associate with it – what Horowitz (2011, 2012) and others characterize as a grassroots organization (GRO), in order to differentiate it from more professionalized and better established non-governmental organizations (NGO). Thus, its relationships with its base organizations is a crucial component of its mobilizing efforts, and provide it a measure of political legitimacy when interacting with government officials and other social movement organizations. In using the admittedly problematic term of 'community,' I am referring to spatially- and demographically-defined corporate communities of Quechua-speaking indigenous-campesino peoples, who are the descendants of former laborers (*pongos*) tied in racialized servitude to agricultural estates under the highly exploitative hacienda system. With Bolivia's 1953 agrarian reform, the hacienda system was abolished, and the lands of each hacienda divided among the *pongos* who worked it. Contemporary communities in the Huanuni valley thus represent former hacienda lands, and most current residents are either former *pongo* laborers or their children or grandchildren. Each such community has a legally recognized association to which all members belong by inheritance (rather than location). My intention here is not to romanticize the notion of indigenous-campesino community, or to erase their internal differences (see Creed 2006a, b). Rather, it is to acknowledge the fact that, as an organization, CORIDUP interacts with community associations, as well as NGOs, government agencies, the state mining firm, and other entities.

CORIDUP's relationship with its member communities is fraught with ambiguity. The group mediates relations between community residents and the various government officials, COMIBOL representatives, NGO functionaries, and researchers (both Bolivian and foreign) working in the region and involved in the decree. From the perspective of community residents, CORIDUP is often seen as just one more group among many working in the region – if it is recognized at all. For example, of the 125 Huanuni valley households I surveyed in 2011, 42 (34%) told me they had never heard of CORIDUP, and of the 66% who were familiar with the group, few respondents had a good understanding of its mission or achievements. Most saw it as yet one more outsider organization, largely indistinguishable from the NGOs, bilateral aid agencies, and state entities that have worked in the region from time to time. CORIDUP's achievements – even the passage of the decree itself – are easily forgotten, as evidenced by the many community members who told me that CORDUP had not done anything for them.

For their part, CORIDUP activists perceive the demands on them as twofold. As one of the group's activists told me in 2010 (at that time, nearly a year after the passage of DS 0335), they feel pressure from community members to act on their behalf and force government action. At the same time, however, this activist expressed feeling pressure from government officials (particularly within the Vice Ministry of Environment, which was charged with coordinating projects related to the decree), who wanted communities to be patient with the complicated process. In the view of this activist, CORIDUP acts as a spokesperson (*portavoz*) for the communities, but must also represent the views of the ministries coordinating the decree (cf. Dietrich 2011).

CORIDUP activists interact with other sets of actors as well, on whom they are dependent for funding and guidance. The organization's offices are located within a building owned by the Bolivian NGO, CEPA (www.cepaoruro.org), which in turn is funded in part by the Belgian NGO CATAPA (Technical Academic Committee for Assistance in Environmental Issues), a volunteer organization that provides funding and technical assistance to environmental and social service organizations in Bolivia, Peru and Guatemala (www.catapa.be). As a consequence of its involvement with CEPA and CATAPA, CORIDUP coordinates regularly with volunteers, researchers and journalists from Europe and North America. These include highly trained technical consultants from Belgium, whose expenses are paid by CATAPA, and who work with CORIDUP for months at a time, as well as researchers (such as myself), whose projects entail occasional interaction and volunteer work, sometimes over a period of several years. This also includes an array of short-term volunteers, students, journalists and NGO functionaries. CEPA has strong connections with the Catholic Church, by way of the Oblate brothers (to which its founder belongs), and receives support from the Bolivian environmental NGO LIDEMA (Environmental Defense League), which in turn receives funding from an array of northern environmental NGOs (www.lidema. org.bo). Nothing about these arrangements is unusual. Rather, they are typical of the extensive transnational, networked relations through which southern NGOs, indigenous organizations, peasant associations and social movements commonly operate (Bebbington and Kothari 2006; Perreault 2003). Indeed, it would be extraordinary if CORIDUP were *not* linked into such networks. But it bears considering that these international networks serve at once to provide CORIDUP with national and international legitimacy and prestige, and to distance it from some residents of its member communities, who have accused the group of neglecting its base and enriching themselves on what is commonly perceived as international largesse. Many residents have deep suspicions of CORIDUP's connections with state officials and foreign funders and activists, and have grown both weary and wary of intrusive outsiders (researchers included, it must be said), who come to study the region's problems. Thus, the very entanglements that allow CORIDUP to function (through funding, logistical support, technical assistance, and personal relationships) also serve to diminish its standing in the eyes of some residents of its member communities. As a result, CORIDUP enjoys only tenuous support among the communities it represents, while many local residents are resigned to living with extreme pollution and have been largely *de*-mobilized by years of hardship and official neglect. Migration out of the region is widespread, particularly among the young.

### The campaign for a presidential decree of environmental emergency

Of CORIDUP's various campaigns, arguably the most successful has been its effort to force government action to remediate mining contamination in the Huanuni valley, which resulted in Evo Morales' 2009 Presidential Decree 0335. Such an outcome was never likely. Not only is the decree's 'environmental emergency' designation normally reserved for 'natural' disasters such as landslides, floods and droughts, but the economic and political influence of mining in Oruro meant that any effort to curb the industry's practices would meet with stiff resistance locally. Knowing how difficult it would be to force government action, CORIDUP pressed its demands carefully. Following a series of site inspections and community-based meetings, in October 2007 the group organized a series of inter-institutional workshops (*mesas de trabajo*), involving central and departmental government officials, COMIBOL, and affected communities. Within a year, however, the optimism that accompanied the workshops had worn off, as it became apparent that the various state agencies in attendance had either little intention or capacity (or both) to take meaningful action. Working with sympathetic officials within the Ministries of Rural Development, and Environment and Water, the group coordinated a second round of workshops, held in June 2009. The objective of this second meeting was to give new impetus to the commitments made two years earlier, and to more clearly define the responsibilities of the various institutions involved. Of the many demands proposed in the workshops, the only one that was tangibly realized was DS 0335.

As part of this process, CORIDUP activists held meetings in affected communities in order to determine priorities for remediation and compensation. Working with researchers in Oruro, they then produced a legal and scientific study of the affected region to detail the social, economic and environmental problems associated with mine contamination. CORIDUP presented this study, together with the results of community-based consultations, to the departmental government, which formally declared a state of environmental emergency in the Huanuni River watershed. Thus, with resolutions at the municipal level (via community-level meetings) and through the departmental government, the path was cleared for the decree to be elevated to the Vice Ministry of Civil Defense (at the level of the central government), which is responsible for emergency declarations. Progress was slow, however, and by October 2009 CORIDUP activists had decided to increase pressure on governmental officials. As recounted in CORIDUP's own account of the events, "As is public knowledge . . . owing to the stubbornness of our politicians it was necessary to undertake a march from the city of Oruro to the city of La Paz, as a signal of pressure so that our demands would be listened to, and only in this way was the release of Presidential Decree 0335 achieved . . ." (CORIDUP n.d.: 11).

The marchers were met in the Aymara city of El Alto, perched on the altiplano above the capital La Paz, by Vice Minister of Environment Juan Pablo Ramos, who announced that President Morales had released DS 0335. Public spectacles such as marches, hunger strikes, road blockades, and mass protest are not only commonplace, but are an expected and essential part of Bolivian politics, without which government officials rarely take notice of community demands (Goldstein 2004). As Ramos told me, "In Bolivia it is accepted that part of democracy is social mobilization. So, if the mobilization is consistent, solid, and the demand is perceived as important, it has effect. In this case, [DS 0335] was approved because there was political will, but also because the march to La Paz pressured the President to approve it" (author interview, 10 June 2011). When Ramos met the marchers in El Alto to announce the Presidential Decree, they must surely have been satisfied at what seemed like the culmination of years of hard work. In fact, the decree's passage was only an early step in a much longer organizing process. Indeed, much work lay ahead.

Following the announcement of the decree, CORIDUP embarked on a series of community-based meetings to communicate its terms and educate (*socializer*) residents of affected communities of their rights under the decree and the need for collective action to maintain pressure on government agencies. I attended several of these meetings in 2010 and 2011, and witnessed the sense of impatience with the slow pace of government action. CORIDUP activists worked hard to explain the details of the decree and urged patience and persistence on the part of community members. As activists explained repeatedly, the decree is complicated, and involves six areas of action, coordinated through six different vice-ministries in five different ministries, focused in four different municipios.[3] Moreover, no specific funding from the central government was provided for carrying out the various projects mandated by the decree. Coordination was noticeably lacking, and local officials expressed their confusion and frustration at the demands placed on them. By September 2012, CORIDUP had grown frustrated by the lack of progress toward implementing the decree, and convened a meeting in the offices of Oruro's departmental government, in order to bring together representatives of the various ministries involved. Although government representatives reported progress for each line of action, these did not translate into visible, on-the-ground action. Consequently, residents of the Huanuni valley expressed frustration and cynicism, as often with CORIDUP as with government ministries and COMIBOL.

Many residents of the Huanuni valley express skepticism that conditions will ever change, and have grown cynical in the face of seemingly endless meetings and announcements that bring no tangible improvement in their condition. As a result, many communities are largely de-mobilized, and have resigned themselves to living with contamination, and to the hopeful waiting that comes diminished expectations (Auyero and Swistun 2009). Many residents are also conflicted about mining itself and its role in their lives. This was evident in a discussion I had with Doña Lucila, in the courtyard of her home in the community of Chuspa. Like many others, Doña Lucila told me that the Huanuni Mining Company has never done any remediation projects in Chuspa, nor have any of the residents received compensation for the damage done to their lands and water, let alone for the disruption caused to their families and way of life. She also insisted that there is no solution (*remedio*) to the problem of mining contamination. The problem is too great, she said, and the government really cannot do anything about it. When I asked her if there is a solution to the pollution problem, she replied, "I don't believe so. It's contaminated, contaminated. The wind continues to blow dust (from mine tailings), and the acid drainage (copajira) continues. There's no solution." She then said something I did not expect. In spite of all the pollution and official neglect, she said that Oruro could not survive without mining. She commented that the social welfare payments (*bonos*) funded by mining royalties are important because they have improved life for many people. Doña Lucila's statement captures a sense of resignation that I heard many times in my conversations with people in the Huanuni valley. Many residents and local activists acknowledge the daunting scale of the pollution problem, and the fact that the local environment, and the lives it once supported, have been irreparably altered. But Doña Lucila also expressed a sense of tension within Bolivia's extractive economy, and the benefits – however meager – they provide to the country's poor. The hegemony of the mining economy is such that even those who pay its heaviest price see little alternative but to support it.

These tensions are pervasive in the Huanuni valley, where there is little appetite left for meetings and marches. Conditions have remained largely unchanged in the years since the decree's release, as the government has failed to commit any funding to remediation efforts and has shown little commitment to seeing it through. Meanwhile, CORIDUP continues to mobilize, though with decreasing intensity and greater frustration than in 2009. By mid-2011, CORIDUP representatives were spending considerably less time in the communities than it was in the year following the release of DS 0335 and instead spent more time in meetings with state officials and NGO representatives in La Paz or the city of Oruro. Indeed, by all appearances they seemed to relish these contacts, and spoke often of the meetings they attended, and their growing national reputation. By contrast, they seemed comparatively less interested in continuing their work in community organizing, and were reluctant to attend community meetings, even when organized by officials from the municipios involved in DS 0335. In spite of several invitations, no one from CORIDUP was present at one such meeting I attended, called by officials from the municipio of Machacamarca (within the Huanuni valley) in May 2011, and only two members were present at a follow-up meeting involving the same officials. In subsequent conversations with me, CORIDUP activists dismissed the importance of these meetings, stating that in the past, the mayor and other top officials of Machacamarca had not attended meeting in the municipio. While perhaps understandable in these terms, CORIDUP's declining involvement in Machacamarca is notable, given that the group is generally well regarded by municipal officials and has much to offer in terms of skills, contacts and resources to the impoverished and understaffed municipal government. Meanwhile, CORIDUP was central in the establishment in 2012 of a national-level organization of communities affected by mining, CONAM-PROMA (Coordinadora Nacional de Afectados por la Minería y Protección del Medio Ambiente, National Coordinator of Communities Affected by Mining and Protection of the Environment). CONAMPROMA's first elected president was Félix Laime, who at the time was also president of CORIDUP. This helped deepen CORIDUP's relations with regional- and national-level environmental organizations in Bolivia, even as their connections with base communities appeared to be fraying.

## Discussion and conclusion

This chapter has examined processes of grassroots mobilization in relation to mining contamination on the Bolivian Altiplano. Activism of this sort assumes authority to speak on behalf of affected populations. Indeed, CORIDUP activists come from rural communities and urban neighborhoods impacted by the acid runoff, toxic sediments and caustic dust that emanates from mine centers upstream and upwind. These are local residents who know viscerally the environmental, social and health effects of mining waste – emphatically not urban elites. But while CORIDUP may reasonably be considered a 'grassroots' organization, it is embedded in translocal networks that stretch far beyond the Huanuni valley, and include Bolivian and European NGOs, volunteers and researchers, and frequent interactions with government officials in Oruro and La Paz. This has placed CORIDUP in an ambiguous position relative to the communities it represents, and as many residents told me, they now view it as just another organization working in the impoverished and polluted region. In this sense, then, CORIDUP activists are at once local and extra-local; both of the communities and outside them. Thus, with Horowitz (2012), I would caution against any facile 'insider/outsider' understanding of community organizing in the Huanuni valley. Indeed, CORIDUP's ambiguous positioning relative to its member communities actually provides the group a measure of legitimacy. As Brother Humberto, the founder and director of CEPA explained to me, CORIDUP plays a crucial role as intermediary between the communities of the Huanuni valley and the various state institutions and mining firms involved in DS 0335. According to this view, the communities need CORIDUP to convey their demands to the state and mining firms, even as the state agencies and mining firms need CORIDUP to communicate with the communities on their behalf. Much of CORDUP's representativeness, then, is derived from this intermediary position, as it is viewed as a legitimate actor both from 'above,' by the state and mining firms, and 'below,' by its member communities (cf. Dietrich 2011). Grassroots legitimacy, in this sense, is relational and contingent, embedded within shifting and extensive networks that link actors operating across multiple spatial scales (see Horowitz, this volume).

The release of DS 0335, declaring an environmental emergency in the Huanuni valley, was a signal victory for CORIDUP. Not only does it represent the first time in Bolivian history that this declaration has been used for anthropogenic contamination, but it marks one of the very few tangible achievements of community-based efforts toward remediating acute mining waste and compensating affected populations. But the decree also exposed the limits to such mobilization in the fact of mining's economic and political hegemony. One such limitation stems from the hostility of mining cooperatives toward CORIDUP's organizing efforts, and to any attempt to place limits on mining activities, including the implementation of environmental controls or remediation measures. Well-organized and highly militant cooperativista miners have emerged as key political allies of Evo Morales, and played a central role in the formulation of the revised 2014 Mining Law (Achtenberg 2014; Marston and Perreault, forthcoming). In Bolivia, where mining has figured so centrally into understandings of the nation, struggles over resource control and national identity have fused, leaving little room for mobilization against mining activities. As a consequence, CORIDUP must tread carefully, always moderating its discourse. Broad-based anti-extraction positions similar to those in other Latin American countries are simply untenable in Oruro, where mining enjoys political, economic and cultural hegemony, and where thousands of rural residents are considered agro-mineros, integrating mine work with smallholder agriculture. Resource extraction remains crucial to the Bolivian economy, providing the bulk of foreign exchange revenue and funding cash transfer programs designed to assist the country's poor (Kohl and Farthing 2012). Even those whose lives have been most affected by mining see no viable alterative. This reality, as much as the daunting scale of Bolivia's accumulated mining waste, presents a fundamental challenge to any effort to reverse Bolivia's dependence on resource extraction.

## Acknowledgements

My thanks to my *compañeros* and *compañeras* with CORIDUP and CEPA for their patience and support, and especially to Don Román Mamani and Hermano Gilberto Pauwels, without whose support this work would not have been possible. This research was supported by a Fulbright Hays Faculty Research Fellowship, the Geography Department of Syracuse University, and various grants internal to the Maxwell School of Syracuse University. Special thanks to Leah Horowitz for her detailed comments on an earlier draft of this chapter. Thanks as always to Meredith for her patience and understanding. This chapter is dedicated to the memory of my friend Ben Kohl, who keeps teaching me about Bolivia. *Jallalla Ben.*

## Notes

1 Residents of this region are indigenous (Quechua or Aymara) in ethnicity and campesino (peasant) in socio-economic class.
2 I have adopted pseudonyms for all indigenous-campesino communities and for all interviewees, except for government officials whose positions are well known and a matter of public record. All quotes were transcribed and translated from the Spanish by the author.

3  The six areas of action are: (1) mitigation, treatment and environmental control, to be implemented by the Ministry of Mining and Metallurgy; (2) environmental conservation, to be implemented by the Vice-Ministry of Water Resources and Irrigation (Ministry of Environment and Water); (3) drinking water and sanitation, implemented by the Vice-Ministry of Drinking Water and Sanitation (Ministry of Environment and Water); (4) environmental education, implemented by the Ministry of Education; (5) environmental health, implemented by the Ministry of Health and Sports; and (6) impact management, implemented by the Vice-Ministry of Civil Defense (Ministry of Defense). The six lines of action are to be coordinated by the Vice-Ministry of Environment (Ministry of Environment and Water).

# References

Achtenberg E. (2014) Conflict over new Bolivian mining law highlights mining sector contradictions. *North American Congress on Latin America* (https://nacla.org/blog/2014/5/9/conflict-over-new-bolivian-law-highlights-mining-sector-contradictions 9 July 2014).

Agrawal A. (2005) *Environmentality: Technologies of Government and the Making of Subjects.* Duke University Press, Durham.

Auyero J. and Swistun D. (2009) *Flammable: Environmental Suffering in an Argentine Shantytown.* Oxford University Press, New York.

Bebbington A. (2009) "The new extraction: Rewriting the political ecology of the Andes?" *NACLA Report on the Americas* 42(5) 12–20.

Bebbington A. (2012a) *Social Conflict, Economic Development and Extractive Industry: Evidence from South America.* Routledge, London.

Bebbington A. (2012b) "Underground political ecologies: The second annual lecture of the Cultural and Political Ecology Specialty Group of the Association of American Geographers" *Geoforum* 43 1152–1162.

Bebbington A. and Bury, J. eds. (2013) *Subterranean Struggles: New Dynamics of Mining, Oil, and Gas in Latin America.* University of Texas Press, Austin.

Bebbington A., Hinojosa L., Humphreys Bebbington D., Burneo M.L., and Warnaars X. (2008a) "Contentions and ambiguity: Mining and the possibilities of development" *Development and Change* 39(6) 965–992.

Bebbington A., Humphreys Bebbington D., Bury J., Muñoz J.P., and Scurrah M. (2008b) "Mining and social movements: Struggles over livelihood and rural territorial development in the Andes" *World Development* 36(12) 2888–2905.

Bebbington A. and Kothari U. (2006) "Transnational development networks" *Environment and Planning A* 38 849–866.

Bridge G. (2004) "Mapping the bonanza: Geographies of mining investment in an era of neoliberal reform" *The Professional Geographer* 56(3) 406–421.

Budds J. and Hinojosa L. (2012) "Restructuring and rescaling water governance in mining contexts: The co-production of waterscapes in Peru" *Water Alternatives* 5(1) 119–137.

Bury J. (2008) "Transnational corporations and livelihood transformations in the Peruvian Andes: An actor-oriented political ecology" *Human Organization* 67(3) 307–321.

CEDIB (2012) *Dossier de Prensa: Minería, Tierra y Territorio – Mallku Khota.* Centro de Documentación e Información Bolivia (CEDIB), Cochabamba, Bolivia.

CORIDUP (n.d.) *CORIDUP busca justicia ambiental. Unpublished manuscript, Coordinadora en Defensa de las Cuencas del Río Desaguadero, Lagos Uru y Poopó (CORIDUP).* Oruro, Bolivia.

Creed G.W. (2006a) "Community as modern pastoral" in Creed G.W. ed, *The Seductions of Community: Emancipatinos, Oppressions, Quandries*. School of American Research Press, Santa Fe 23–48.

Creed G.W. (2006b) "Reconsidering community" in Creed G.W. ed, *The Seductions of Community: Emancipatinos, Oppressions, Quandries*. School of American Research Press, Santa Fe 3–22.

Dietrich A.S. (2011) "Coercive harmony, deep capture and environmental justice in Puerto Rico" *Development and Change* 42(6) 1441–1463.

Dunkerley J. (1984) *Rebellion in the Veins: Political Struggle in Bolivia, 1952–1982*. Verso, London.

Dunkerley J. (2007) "The origins of the Bolivian revolution of 1952: Some reflections" in Dunkerley J. ed, *Bolivia: Revolution and the Power of History in the Present*. Institute for the Study of the Americas, London 214–254.

Escobar A., Dagnino E., and Álvarez S.E. eds. (1998) *Cultures of Politics, Politics of Cultures: Re-Visioning Latin American Social Movements*. Westview, Boulder.

Farthing L. and Kohl B. (2013) "Mobilizing memory: Bolivia's enduring social movements" *Social Movement Studies* 12(4) 361–376.

Ferguson J. (1994) *The Antipolitics Machine: Development, Depoliticization, and Bureaucratic Power in Lesotho*. University of Minnesota Press, Minneapolis.

Forno E. and Pauwels G. (2009) "Contaminación ambiental y actores sociales en Bolivia: Un balance de la situación" *Tinkazos: Revista Boliviana de Ciencias Sociales* 27(12) 9–32.

Francescone, K. and Díaz, V. (2013) "Cooperativas mineras: Entre socios, patrones y peones" *PetroPress* 30(January–February) 32–41.

García-Guinea J. and Harffy M. (1998) "Bolivian mining pollution: Past, present and future" *Ambio* 27(3) 251–253.

García Linera A., Chávez M., and Monje P.C. (2004) *Sociología de los Movimientos Sociales en Bolivia: Estructuras de Movilización, Repertorios Culturales y Acción Política*. Oxfam/Diakonia, La Paz.

Goldstein D. (2004) *The Spectacular City: Violence and Performance in Urban Bolivia*. Duke University Press, Durham.

Gustafson B. (2010) "When states act like movements: Dismantling local power and seating sovereignty in post-neoliberal Bolivia" *Latin American Perspectives* 37(4) 48–66.

Gutiérrez Aguilar R. (2014) *Rhythms of the Pachakuti: Indigenous Uprisings and State Power in Bolivia*. Duke University Press, Durham.

Habermas J. (1987) *The Theory of Communicative Action (Volume 2): System and Lifeworld*. Polity Press, Cambridge.

Harvey D. (2003) *The New Imperialism*. Oxford, London.

Himley M. (2014) "Mining and history: Mobilizing the past in struggles over mineral extraction in Peru" *Geographical Review* 104(2) 174–191.

Horowitz L. (2011) "Interpreting industry's impacts: Micropolitical ecologies of divergent community responses" *Development and Change* 42(6) 1379–1391.

Horowitz L. (2012) "Power, profit, protest: Grassroots resistance to industry in the global north" *Capitalism, Nature, Socialism* 23(3) 20–34.

Howard A. and Dangl B. (2006) Tin war in Bolivia: Conflict between miners leaves 17 dead. *Upside Down World*, 20 September (http://upsidedownworld.org/main 3 December 2012).

Hylton F. and Thomson S. (2007) *Revolutionary Horizons: Past and Present in Bolivian Politics*. Verso, London.

Kaup B. (2010) "A neoliberal nationalization? The path dependent constraints and socio-material obstacles to natural gas led development in Bolivia" *Latin American Perspectives* 37(3) 123–138.

Kaup B. (2013) *Market Justice: Political Economic Struggle in Bolivia*. Cambridge University Press, Cambridge.

Kohl B. and Farthing L. (2012) "Material constraints to popular imaginaries: The extractive economy and resource nationalism in Bolivia" *Political Geography* 31(4) 225–235.

Li T.M. (2007) *The Will to Improve: Governmentality, Development and the Practice of Politics*. Duke University Press, Durham.

López, E. (2011) "Bolivia: Agua y minería en tiempos de cambio" in Urteaga P. ed, *Agua e Industrias Extractivas: Cambios y Continuidades en los Andes*. Instituto de Estudios Peruanos, Lima 61–88.

López E., Cuenca A., Lafuente S., Madrid E., y Molina P. (2010) *El Costo Ecológico de la Política Minera en Huanuni y Bolíviar*. PIEB, La Paz.

Madrid E., Guzmán N., Mamani E., Medrano D., and Nuñez R. (2002) *Minería y Comunidades Campesinas ¿Coexistencia o Conflicto?* PIEB, La Paz.

Marston, A. and T. Perreault (forthcoming) Consent, coercion and *cooperativismo*: Mining and environmental governance in Bolivia, *Environment and Planning A*.

Martínez Alier J. (2003) *The Environmentalism of the Poor: A Study of Ecological Conflicts and Valuation*. Edward Elgar Publishing, London.

Michard J. (2008) *Cooperativas Mineras en Bolivia: Formas de Organización, Producción y Comercialización*. CEDIB, Cochabamba.

Moeller H. (2002) *Dinamitas y Contaminantes: Cooperativas Mineras y su Incidencia en la Problemática Ambiental*. PIEB, La Paz.

Montoya J.C., Amusquivar J., Flores A., Mollo A., and Sánchez P. (2002) *Efectos Ambientales y Socioeconómicos por el Derrame de Petróleo en el Río Desaguadero*. PIEB, La Paz.

Montoya J.C., Amusquivar J., Guzmán G., Quispe D., Blanco R., and Mollo N. (2010) *Thuska Uma: Tratamiento de Aguas Ácidas con Fines de Riego*. PIEB, La Paz.

Nash J. (1993) *We Eat the Mines and the Mines Eat Us: Dependency and Exploitation in the Bolivian Tin Mines*. Columbia University Press, New York.

Olivera O. (2004) *¡Cochabamba! Water War in Bolivia*. South End Press, Cambridge, MA.

Peredo C., Crespo C., and Fernández O. (2004) *Los Regantes de Cochabamba en la Guerra del Agua*. CESU/UMSS, Cochabamba.

Perreault T. (2003) "Changing places: Transnational networks, ethnic politics, and community development in the Ecuadorian Amazon" *Political Geography* 22(1) 61–88.

Perreault T. (2005) "State restructuring and the scale politics of rural water governance in Bolivia" *Environment and Planning A* 37 263–284.

Perreault T. (2006) "From the *Guerra del Agua* to the *Guerra del Gas*: Resource governance, neoliberalism, and popular protest in Bolivia" *Antipode* 38(1) 150–172.

Perreault T. (2008) "Custom and contradiction: Rural water governance and the politics of *usos y costubmres* in Bolivia's irrigators' movement" *Annals of the Association of American Geographers* 98(4) 834–854.

Perreault T. (2013a) "Dispossession by accumulation? Mining, water and the nature of enclosure on the Bolivian Altiplano" *Antipode* 45(5) 1050–1069.

Perreault T. (2013b) "Nature and nation: The territorial logics of hydrocarbon governance in Bolivia" in Bebbington A., Bury J., and Young K. eds, *Subterranean Struggles: New Geographies of Extractive Industries in Latin America*. University of Texas Press, Austin 67–90.

Perreault T. ed. (2014) *Minería, Agua y Justicia Social en los Andes: Experiencias Comparativas de Perú y Bolivia.* PIEB, La Paz.

Perreault T. and Green B. (2013) "Reworking the spaces of indigeneity: The Bolivian ayllu and lowland autonomy movements compared" *Environment and Planning D: Society and Space* 31 43–60.

PPO (1996) *Documento Final: Plan de Gestió´n Ambiental. Plan Piloto Oruro* Ministerio de Desarrollo Sostenible y medio Ambiente, Secretar´ıa Nacional de Minería, and Swedish Geological AB: La Paz.

Quintanilla J. and García M.E. (2009) "Manejo de recursos hídricos-hidroquímica de la Cuenca de los lagos Poopó y Uru Uru" in Crespo Alvizuri P. ed, *La química de la Cuenca del Poopó.* DIPGIS – Instituto de Investigaciones Químicas, UMSS, La Paz 117–143.

Robins N.A. (2011) *Mercury, Mining and Empire: The Human and Ecological Cost of Colonial Silver Mining in the Andes.* Indiana University Press, Bloomington.

UPADE (2010) Human development in the department of Oruro. *Unidad de Análisis de Políticas Sociales y Económicas (UPADE) and United Nations Development Program* (www.udape.gob.bo/portales_html/ODM/Documentos/Boletines/Bol_2010_04_Eng.pdf 25 March 2011).

Urteaga P. (2011a) *Agua e Industrias Extractivas: Cambios y Continuidades en los Andes.* Instituto de Estudios Peruanos, Lima.

Urteaga P. (2011b) "Agua e industrias extractivas: Cambios y continuidades en los Andes" in Urteaga P. ed, *Agua e Industrias Extractivas: Cambios y Continuidades en los Andes.* Instituto de Estudios Peruanos, Lima 19–58.

Wolford W. (2010) *This Land is Ours Now: Social Meaning and the Meaning of Land in Brazil.* Duke University Press, Durham.

# 6 Between sacrifice and compensation

## Collective action and the aftermath of oil disaster in Esmeraldas, Ecuador

*Gabriela Valdivia*

## Introduction

On the north entrance to the city of Esmeraldas, in northwest Ecuador, used to be a three-part mural with the message "*Don't contaminate your home, don't contaminate your future*" (Figure 6.1). Painted in July 2012 by Magni Lajones Araujo, an Esmeraldeño artist and teacher, the mural was a resident's view of everyday environmental pollution in Esmeraldas: smoke from the local state-owned refinery (the largest and most important in Ecuador), the haziness of traffic pollution, deforested landscapes, and abundant garbage and human waste on land and rivers. In the foreground stands an Afro-descendent man, facing forward with tears rolling down his face. In the background, the emblematic green rolling hills that bound the west side of the city, also in a blurred, smoky form. And flowing from behind the man is the Esmeraldas River, which flanks the east side of the city, its waters transporting oil and garbage. In between the man and the hills is a blue bus transporting the tiny silhouettes of refinery workers, and the simple outline of a grey refinery spewing grey-colored fumes from a tall chimney into the blue sky. The sharp, black outline of the silhouettes and bus stand out against the weeping man and the hills, as if independent of the hazy Esmeraldas. On the front of the bus reads the word "boss." In early February 2014, in the midst of local elections, the mural was completely painted over with campaign slogans for regional elections.

While the erasure of the mural is an ephemeral moment in the political life of the city, it is also a statement on the entanglements of the oil economy with everyday struggles. It might be tempting to interpret the degraded environmental quality portrayed in the mural as a "normal" consequence (externality) of an oil-enabled "good life:" a mode of living based on the generalized, mass-consumption of oil and oil derivatives (Huber 2013). Obscured in this recognition are questions about the distribution of life and death in petro-capitalist economies: who bears the costs of this greater good, through what mechanisms and technologies of government, and according to whose values? These questions are fundamental to understanding how refinery cities like Esmeraldas become "sacrifice zones" (Lerner 2010) of oil-enabled life: communities who bear the industrial burdens of oil-capitalism in the name of a greater good.

*Figure 6.1* "Don't contaminate your home, don't contaminate your future," by Magni Lajones Araujo. The mural won first prize in a 2012 competition organized by the Frente de Artistas Populares de Esmeraldas, a collective of artists dedicated to the promotion of the arts in the city.

The Esmeraldas refinery, built in 1977, sits at the end of a 500-km pipeline that brings oil from the Amazon to the Esmeraldas seaport. It is the final node in a complex of nation-building that promised to bring economic growth and development via sovereignty over oil resources (Galarza Zavala 1972). Along the lines of "if you build it, it will come," the Ecuadorian state framed the refinery as an engine of modernization in Esmeraldas, a space imagined as underused/empty though it was home to a significant Afro-Ecuadorian population reliant on patronage networks and small-scale economies, and which had historically resisted the centralized colonial and then republic governments. The new roads that connected the refinery to the national transportation network fueled a rapid urbanization. Since the 1980s, rural settlers have occupied the buffer zone of the refinery, some settling right against the fence that demarcates the end of refinery property, even as these were zoned for industrial use. Without formal land titles, the new settlers were pushed out and their houses torn down, but they continued to return. Most don't have land titles but can claim de facto residence. Through patronage networks that linked them to the municipal government, they lobbied for incorporation and for access to basic urban services in exchange for their political votes. Those who organized and used their patronage networks secured paved roads, electricity, and garbage collection.

Today, the industrial buffer zone surrounding the refinery has residential blocks with cement homes, paved roads, schools, and health centers; active neighbor associations; and a diverse informal economy. Neighbors often complain of skin rashes and respiratory ailments. Some link these ailments to the presence of the refinery, which they say is "killing them slowly." Others blame the poor quality of water, sewage, and garbage collection services, a reminder of the historical lack of public services in the city (UNEP 2006). During the rainy season, sewage systems spill waste onto streets and dirt roads turn into rivers of mud. Unpaved roads limit emergency and security vehicles access to neighborhoods, which according to residents, leads to high levels of criminality. The mural demanded an ethical response to these experiences of petro-sacrifice in Esmeraldas: how the harms that accompany modernization matter to those who live in this exceptional space of pollution, where people wait for the bus, hang out, and carry on with their lives.

Moral responses to pollution often take the form of grassroots mobilization and collective action, where individuals *think and act together* to pressure local governments to intervene in the structures of burden distribution. Collective action demands a response to the afflictions experienced, such as chronic and terminal illnesses, congenital conditions (intellectual and physical), low environmental quality (e.g., smog, taste of water), poor access to basic urban resources and services (e.g., paved roads, water and sewage systems), devalued land and property, etc. (Auyero and Swistun 2009; Little 2014). These burdens, harms, and/or lack of access to resources, are often an effect of historical inequalities rather than simply "discrimination" (Pulido 2000). Governmental response to collective action often includes some combination of reparation, compensation, and mitigation to redress these situations but not necessarily to change the historical inequalities that shape them (Checker 2005; Horowitz 2012; Lerner 2010). In some cases, collective action can be successful, triggering changes in how industry operates and increasing regulatory oversight (Cole and Foster 2001). In others, uneven power relations with state and industry actors can demobilize collective action (McGurty 2007; Zebrowski 2014).

This chapter examines one of the best-known collective action responses against oil pollution in Esmeraldas, which emerged after a devastating fire on February 26, 1998, when somewhere between 8,000–16,000 gallons of gasoline and crude oil leaked into the Teaone River, a black water river that snakes throughout the southern portion of the city. A day before the disaster, neighbors telephoned refinery personnel to report a stronger-than-usual smell of gasoline. Some report their calls were received but ignored, others that the telephone rang without answer. The strong smell came from gasoline leaking from a pipeline fractured due to stress from a landslide provoked by heavy rains. The gasoline pooled into a ditch below and mixed with water that eventually fed into the Teaone River. At around 10:00pm on February 26, a spark lit up the mix, turning it into a fire that rolled through the living quarters of oil refinery personnel and moved through the water and sewage systems, first into neighboring homes and then into ditches that fed into the Teaone River. Approximately 60 homes on the river banks were consumed in the fire, killing over 100 people.

Stories about this fire are etched in popular memory.[1] Gas cylinders in the kitchens of private homes exploded with deafening booms, which witnesses described as feeling in the middle of a war zone. Along the Teaone River, the treetops burned. People threw themselves into the river, thinking it was a safer space. The fire was finally controlled around six in the morning, the following day. The ground was covered with stains of fuel and large portion of the terrain appeared blackened months after the event. A pungent stench could be perceived for weeks. People didn't know where to go for shelter. Residents could not drink the water, or turn on their stoves. Schools closed. Some people left, vowing to never return. Others, equally scarred, stayed; they didn't have anywhere else to go.

Individually or through neighborhood associations, people sued the national oil company, Petroecuador, for negligence and delayed emergency response. One by one these demands were dismissed, however. Sometimes settlements were reached outside of court through patronage networks and/or coercion. In other cases neighborhood representatives gave up with the belief that they were "too small, too powerless." Yet others did not receive any compensation at all, as they were illegally settled in the affected areas and had no legal standing as propertied subjects. By 2000, only one of the 15 neighborhoods seeking justice remained firm in its demands, La Propicia Uno, a neighborhood that settled at the meeting of the Teaone and Esmeraldas Rivers. La Propicia Uno was a recently incorporated urban parish of the city and legally inscribed as an entity with rights. Through the neighborhood organization, the *Comité Delfina Torres Viuda de Concha* (Comité), neighbors used existing legal frameworks to seek redress for injured and contaminated bodies, loss of life and loved ones; and alienation from livelihoods and rootedness (Derecho Ecuador 2003).

This collective action framing secured the support of a local lawyer who handled the case pro bono, and of well-known environmental organizations like Ecuador's Acción Ecológica, who chaperoned and guided the terms of denunciation and reparation outlined in the lawsuit. In 2002 La Propicia Uno was granted a multi-million compensation and mitigation package to be executed by Petroecuador between 2003 and 2004. By 2006, however, only a portion of the sentence had been carried out and there was no grassroots mobilization to demand its completion. Why and how did collective action unravel?

This chapter examines the challenges to collective action in La Propicia Uno that the compensation process revealed. I first outline the emergence of collective action and its interruption in La Propicia Uno. Then, I turn to participant observation and interviews conducted between 2012 and 2014 and archival analysis of community documents, newspapers, and legal documents to bring ethnographic detail to how individuals think and feel about, and take action on loss and compensation. To get a fuller picture of collective action in La Propicia Uno, I interviewed non-governmental advocates of the neighborhood; Petroecuador community relations representatives; and municipal government representatives. I conclude with a discussion on the need for more open understanding of how scholars and allies recognize and practice advocacy.

## Collective action in Esmeraldas

Soon after the 1998 fire, residents of affected neighborhoods came together to demand a response from state authorities. Backed by Ecuadorian organizations involved in the high-profile case of Amazonian peoples against Texaco's oil legacy, Esmeraldeño residents organized to present a united front.[2] But their case was different; they were not indigenous peoples living in a protected area, and they did not have claims to ancestral rights. They also were unfamiliar with how to stake claims – *reclamos* – against the industrial complex. This is not to say that Esmeraldeños did not have organizational experience. Residents of Esmeraldas are experienced in forming *comités barriales* (neighborhood committees and associations) to demand labor opportunities and access to urban resources (e.g., land, water, urban public works). Many had experience in syndical organization through involvement with the banana boom that lasted until the 1950s (Moncada 2002). And political parties have entrenched patronage networks in Esmeraldas, which articulate political interests and local demands for basic services and urban benefits (Jacome and Martines Fissau 1977). But the 1998 fire needed a different sort of activism and reflection, one centered on the reparation and compensation for environmental damages incurred to the space they had just begun to settle. The racialized space in which they lived demanded that they re-think and re-articulate their struggle, often framed as an Afro-Ecuadorian rural migrant experience, with urban environmental affliction.

La Propicia Uno leaders framed their collective action as *"la lucha del pueblo"* (the people's fight), a position they claim characterized the struggles of a broader constituency for a better life. To them, Petroecuador had neglected implementing appropriate security measures that guaranteed their safety and they demanded the company improve the quality of their urban spaces via compensation and mitigation packages. The point was not to question the order of rule or their status as an afflicted people, but to improve their urban experience within already existing relations of power.

Collective action took local and transnational forms. Residents wrote letters to Petroecuador, talked with the press, and contacted local government representatives to demand a response. Seeing their case ignored and rejected by the local courts, they expanded the geography of their collective action (Palma and Alvarez 2005). Along with Amazonian peoples, Esmeraldeños toured with organizations sympathetic to indigenous environmental rights in Western Europe, to exceed "the problem" of place-boundedness and of fragmentation which "capitalism . . . can feed upon" (Harvey 1989: 313). Nationally, they marched alongside indigenous peoples demanding the recognition of their rights to a dignified life.[3] Supported by their own monetary collections and by allies, men, women, and youth from La Propicia Uno marched the streets of Quito and occupied the offices of the Ministry of the Environment and the Ministry of Well Being. They occupied key transportation routes in Esmeraldas and at one point cemented one of the waste disposal pipes of the refinery stating that it "has to stop dumping on others and needs to start dealing with its own waste once and for all." Doing so, they forged connections between petro-capitalist accumulation and personal narratives about how, when, and why harmful things happened. Disasters are *re*-cognized through these traveling personal stories; absorbed into other discourses, affective attachments, and practices to become lived memories of collective action (e.g., Auyero and Swistum 2009; Fortun 2001; Kosek 2006; Povinelli 2011).

On October 29, 2002, after several setbacks at the local courts, the Supreme Court Justice in Quito sentenced Petroecuador to pay $USD 11 million in compensation and mitigation projects to La Propicia Uno.[4] "We made history; this is the first time in Latin America that a lawsuit is won against an oil company," stated the president of the Comité, Patricio Reyes (Toro 2004). The settlement was unprecedented indeed, prompting local newspapers to refer to La Propicia Uno as "the world's richest neighborhood" (Diario Hoy 2004). Residents placed high hopes on the funds, expecting that these would address the abandonment that characterized this neighborhood prior to the fire (no access to paved roads, electricity, and water, sanitation, and health services). Hundreds of residents from other neighborhoods moved to La Propicia Uno in hopes of capturing some of the benefits.

### Collective action, interrupted

Collective action was led by the Comité, a board of men and women who together represented the neighborhood's demands for more dignified living environments. But misinformation on the terms and the timeline of Petroecuador's response translated into feelings of doubt, to the point that the legitimacy of the board was questioned by both the community and government actors. Comité members sued each other constantly between 2002 and 2011, forcing some to leave in fear of the escalation of accusations and death threats. Advocates such as the Municipality of Esmeraldas and the Vicariate of Esmeraldas first intervened to try to smooth out internal conflict (Toro 2004). By 2006, they decided to "step aside" in response to the difficulties experienced by the board. Seeing the unraveling of the Comité, Petroecuador decided to halt the completion of the sentence until neighborhood consensus was achieved.

Collective action was interrupted in two interrelated ways. The first concerns how La Propicia Uno is conceptualized as a political agent. Collective action is often attributed to a thinking and acting "agent of livability," the community who defends the urban environment in order to secure livelihoods (Evans 2002). Taking livability into their own hands, communities put pressure on local government representatives, secure advocates, and fight devaluation and oppression. Communities engage in collective action through established social and political assets, such as shared longevity of residence, common cultural ties, and associational life. Collective action also can emerge once a common end seems like a feasible possibility (Evans 2002).

La Propicia Uno is not a homogeneous agent, however. Located on the floodplains of the Teaone and Esmeraldas Rivers and separated by hilly terrain from the city, it is a space of continuous settlement. In the 1950s it was a hacienda bequeathed to its workers. People from all over Esmeraldas moved to La Propicia Uno, seeking to escape economic depression in rural areas. By the mid-1990s, it consisted of 18 square blocks with limited and non-existent basic urban services for close to 300 families (over 1,500 people). Some came to avoid the chaos of the city; others to come closer to it. Some self-identify as mestizo, others as mulatto, and others as black. Some have lived in La Propicia Uno for decades, others are recent settlers. Some are professionals with nine-to-five white-collar jobs, others are unemployed and underemployed. And some are affiliated with political parties with deep patronage networks, while others are indifferent to these.

Collective action interruption also must be understood in relation to diversity in common existence. Individuals experience life not according to singular social categories of difference and ordering (e.g., race, gender, ethnicity and class) but through their interdependence and interlocking with governmental power (Mollett and Faria 2013; Nightingale 2011). This intersectionality is key to recognizing challenges to how individuals think and act collectively. Collective action presumes a common consciousness of oppression, injustice, and devaluation perpetrated against a subaltern group or groups (Roberts and Jesudason 2013; Soni-Sinha 2013). Communities that act together, like La Propicia Uno, are assumed to have a certain homogeneity of interests and politics, or at least the capacity to build one in the face of a common experience of devaluation. In this regard, dominant models of "emancipatory agency" presume that members of a collective (e.g., women, people of color, workers) have a common understanding of freedom, will, and intentionality that becomes a moral compass of action.

The trouble with assuming the agency of the collective is twofold. First, dominant understandings of collective action rest on the liberal belief that all human beings not only have an innate desire for freedom (we all seek to assert our autonomy when allowed to do so), but that groups with common experiences of subjection share an understanding of what constitutes such freedom. Second, in dominant frames of collective action, agency is recognized as acts that challenge oppressive social norms. Those who uphold oppressive norms, and those who challenge freedom as emancipation from the constraints of subjugation, are at best seen as apolitical or suffering from false consciousness, and at worst, as dangerous to emancipatory action (Bautista 2008; Mahmood 2011).

In La Propicia Uno, while demanding compensation from Petroecuador was a united, collective strategy to achieve freedom from abandonment, actually securing compensation changed how the community acted. It did so in three interrelated ways. First, once the lawsuit was settled, other sorts of agency, bracketed within collective action, became more visible, giving the sense of internal disorganization. How to manage compensation disbursement to benefit individual interests and desires became more important than achieving collective freedom from contamination and devaluation. As money circulated in the form of public works contracts, questions arose about how individuals should think and act together: How will the funds be held and distributed? Who will have the power to decide and influence how the money is used? How will I fare? How can I secure my position? Answers to these questions were framed in relation to the interests of individuals and not always along the lines of the *pueblo*, the imagined collective.

Second, compensation strengthened social norms and behaviors that limited the emancipatory capacities of collective action. While La Propicia Uno's successful case was unprecedented, the governmental response they demanded was not. La Propicia Uno demanded urban infrastructural improvements to compensate for environmental suffering, demands not always directly related to the fire. According to a former Comité president in 2013, public works "made sense" as a compensation package – victims were familiar with patron-client relations to secure basic urban needs. Collective action, thus, was not an interruption of the status quo; victims demanding goods to recognize their suffering consented to the norms that perpetuate their subjugation. As he explained, "in our minds, this is what the people wanted and needed." Petroecuador and other governmental entities coordinated and executed the urban services demanded, with limited participation by the affected neighbors, as had already been the case through established patron-client relations. The demand for *and* the execution of compensation and mitigation reproduced existing power interdependencies.

Finally, the suspension of compensation in 2006 fueled *agotamiento*, the gradual material and spiritual exhaustion of the Comité's relationship with the broader community. Activists in Chiapas, Mexico refer to the process of wearing out activism as a "*guerra de agotamiento*" (a war of exhaustion) (Pérez Sales, Santiago and Alvarez 2002). Unlike overt, sensational violence, exhaustion stems from the moral and psychological wasting endured under conditions of "slow violence" (Nixon 2011), suffering that is attritional but discounted because it is perceived as deadly only in long temporal scales. *Agotamiento* is more than abandonment, it is the antonym of endurance that signals the end of strength and persistence (Povinelli 2011). *Agotamiento* in La Propicia Uno names the dismantling of collective action through governmental inaction (and silence) that precludes people from seeing a goal at hand, make ends meet, access basic services, or flourish in healthy environments.

## The political aftermath of the fire

This section offers a closer look at how individuals make sense of the challenges of collective action after the 1998 fire. Each moment showcases how the ability to think and act together is not 'natural' to communities but exists within relations of power that strengthen and throw into question collective action.

### Private archivists: remembering the people's fight

> The women's organization led some of the best fights . . . they were the ones who got the corrupt people out of local ministries . . . In June 2006, they occupied the offices of the Ministry of Well-Being in Esmeraldas . . . our committee had sent numerous letters to point out how outsiders and corrupt state officials were infiltrating our neighborhood, but our demands were ignored. The women went to the office . . . three hundred people stood outside and didn't let the director enter the building. Some women took off their clothes and occupied the space until the director gave up and walked away. A number of officials were later removed.
>
> (Interview with former president of La Propicia Uno neighborhood association, 2013)

Baring female bodies to visibilize social demands in patriarchal societies, as the quote earlier suggests, effectively disrupted the status quo of everyday business in Esmeraldas, and brought the spotlight to the continued oppression experienced by members of La Propicia Uno. Men and women who remembered this moment of resistance laughed in solidarity as they recalled it, treasuring their "victory" as evidence that this is a fight worth fighting for. Like the occupation of government offices in both Esmeraldas and Quito, the defacement and intervention in refinery installations, marches and road blocks, and the intense media campaign on local newspapers and radio stations (Palma and Alvarez 2005) were strategies to not lose sight of the ties between private and collective interests. A resident of La Propicia Uno put this point in perspective in 2013 when describing her own experience with the people's struggle:

> [women] are the ones who stay home, we look after our children and family . . . we understand basic needs. So we are the ones who have the consciousness. If my son becomes ill and I don't know how to cure him, and if there is a medicine that I can't buy. This is our call to the fight, to confront the state if necessary.

There are also less public but equally powerful ways of sedimenting the memory of collective action. Some of the women who blocked the doors of the Ministry also relied on careful documentation to build a neighborhood body of evidence. Such is the case of Fernanda (a pseudonym), a former resident of La Propicia Uno. Fernanda grew up in the city of Esmeraldas, where she lived with her parents until she met her partner. In 1994, they moved to La Propicia Uno, where a family member sold them a small plot of land to start a family of their own. Fernanda knew about La Propicia Uno since her childhood; one of her aunts settled there in the 1980s and Fernanda spent many weekends in this peaceful quiet place to get away from the busy city center.

Fernanda sees herself as a "behind-the-scenes" activist who collects, categorizes, and archives information on the aftermath of the fire. In a third-floor bedroom of an unfinished house facing the Esmeraldas River, she covered a table and bed with hundreds of newspaper clippings, copies of official memos, photos, and environmental reports. In this blending of private and public domains, she carefully poured over the evidence, calling out loudly dates and titles to introduce their meaning:

> *La Hora* [newspaper], Sunday May 19, multiple spills. Title: 'They Search for Those Responsible for Contamination' . . . 2010, title, 'Uncontrollable Spill' – this came after the process we led, we need to be attentive to these things. Even President Correa made observations about the need to redress those that are contaminated . . . November 5, 2010: 'President Correa Offers his Apologies for the Contamination Generated by the Refinery.' Another one, no date: 'Esmeraldas is Scared of Contamination.' This one: Neighborhood Implores for the Control of Contamination' – the water is contaminated. In this one, it says: 'The Provincial Government is Interested in Cleaning up the Teaone River' – but they have never done it. This one: *El Universo* [newspaper], 'A Minimal Attempt to Regenerate the Teaone,' Sunday 27, 2007.

This moment of cataloguing and naming captures the challenges of keeping alive the memory of a community who thinks and acts together. Earlier that morning, Fernanda had engaged in a failed expedition. We had darted across the streets of downtown Esmeraldas, into the offices of the Ministry of Social and Economic Inclusion. She quickly inquired about some papers, waited for about 20 minutes to receive a response, and left for another government building, the Ministry of Urban Development and Housing. Here, the documents that she was looking for were not available either. She was asked to wait. Outside the building, she confided that she was trying to track down the documents that verified the legal establishment of the Comité. The teller in the first office could not locate them anywhere – most likely a "typical" *traspapeleo* (misfiling), Fernanda was told. This was no minor clerical error. Fernanda understood the dangers of a *transpapeleo*. She was in the midst of demanding that the most recently elected Comité in 2010 be legally recognized, a demand that had been countered by residents "with other interests" who had not been elected to be committee members. Without these documents, explained Fernanda, people from other neighborhoods – "people who do not belong here" – have run for elections and bought votes to win (*La Hora* 2010). Outside parties gained entry into the neighborhood by illegally securing property titles, others by discrediting the neighborhood's political leadership. Some residents, another Comité member claimed, traded "the people's fight" for their personal benefit. Fernanda needed to have her facts backed: how many members are registered in the neighborhood, the status of their membership, the composition of the previous committee, and whose votes were counted in the latest election. As of this June 2013 morning, the facts were missing. In the state offices that Fernanda visited, there was no record that the Comité, legally constituted in 1996, had ever existed.

And so we ended up in Fernanda's house that afternoon, facing the boxes of privately-stored evidence that would counter the *transpapeleo* of the official state archive. As one of the Comité's founding members, she kept legal copies of all documents related to its political life. When La Propicia Uno was incorporated as an urban parish in 1996, it had small dirt paths that would flood into muddy rivers with the winter rains. Its main entrance flooded regularly and neighbors used canoes to travel from their homes to the main road during the rainy months. People depended on the nearby rivers for food, water, the extraction of sand, and household maintenance (e.g., bathing, washing clothes, cooking). The "only thing happening," explained Fernanda, was the neighborhood struggle for the rights to basic urban services, such as electricity, water, sewage, and road infrastructure. With the 1998 fire, instead of lobbying local governments for the right to a dignified urban life, they turned to suing Petroecuador for disaster compensation to meet their urban needs.

Sitting next to Fernanda, I thought about her careful archival practice. How each note was cradled as a memory of "the people's fight" – "this is when we thought about the identity cards for witnesses of reparation," "this is when we went to the press to denounce contamination damages," and "this is how we made sure things were accomplished, *correctly*" – gave away the political commitments embodied in her gendered performance of the caring archivist. As a survivor of the 1998 fire, she diligently clips newspaper announcements and notifications of its echoes. Her archive is not a mere repository; it is evidence of collective action. Her urgency is not that people will forget the fire but that the ethos of community unity will be forgotten.

At the heart of enduring the misfilings is the USD $5 million or so left of the settlement. Fernanda's private efforts to keep the memory of the fight alive are a way of thinking and acting collectively when there seems to be no end to the wait for compensation. Time, as Auyero and Swistun (2009) remind us, is the locus of conflict but also of acquiescence. Residents of La Propicia Uno saw the compensation response as recognition of their fight for a more livable urban space – an ethical response to their suffering. Its interruption is an extension of the wait for a common end. In such sorts of waiting, people continue to endure environmental suffering and substandard living conditions. Anxieties over the achievement of a common end under exhausting circumstances were evident during a short walk through La Propicia Uno. With another neighbor, we walked through a narrow dirt path that ends at a large cement block that was supposed to be a basketball court. Two poles with hoops stood at the ends. The surrounding area was taken over by regrowth. In contrast to the more central and visible areas of the neighborhood, with its paved streets and lights, this back part of the neighborhood was muddy and in disarray. This space had been imagined as common space for safe entertainment. Fernanda pointed to the compensation waiting to happen, 11 years after the sentence was dictated: the area for spectators, volleyball court and children play area, the lights for evening games, and the nets. She pointed to the missing promenade and contention wall, where she and neighbors had imagined themselves strolling along the waters of the Teaone River. These were the urban projects of the "good life" they envisioned with the lawsuit funds. She tapped the dirt path with her foot, wondering about the lack of sewage systems and how intestinal diseases still ravage young children.

This brief glimpse into Fernanda's story allows us to better understand the distance between collective and personal freedoms. Fernanda worries about how compensation has alienated her knowledge of the fight, and how others are throwing into question her efforts. Moreover, she cannot live in La Propicia Uno anymore; she has been accused of corruption and her life threatened if she returns. Without de facto residence, she cannot vote for or run for a position in the Comité; she cannot have a say in the disbursement of the compensation funds. The urgency of her private archives is to maintain the emancipatory ties of collective and personal alive so that they don't become misplaced.

While Fernanda experiences exhaustion of her fight through alienation, the case of former president of La Propicia Uno, Jose Luis Guevara, examined next, illustrates the extremes of *agotamiento*.

### The memo wars: the exhaustion of the people's fight

My arm twisted in a tight embrace with Fernanda's arm. The thin, Afro-descendant man walking ahead of us held a small metal bar in his hand. He slowly swung it from side to side as he guided us across the courtyard of the Esmeraldas rehabilitation facility for men, enough to signal to the nearby inmates that we were ready to confront the risks associated with entering this space. He was our bodyguard on this 2013 visitation day. At the end of the courtyard, Jose Luis Guevera, a picture of exhaustion, waited for us in a small church. Fernanda unceremoniously gave our bodyguard a small plastic bag with a home-cooked meal to pay for his services. "This is for you," she said – and we were escorted inside the church. Inmates and family members met in this "safe space" to reconnect and update each other about the outside world. Two other members of La Propicia Uno were already there.

Fernanda suggested visiting Jose Luis to hear "the true story about what happened after the fire."[5] Jose Luis was elected president of the Comité in 2000 and again in 2002, when the lawsuit was won. He describes his struggle to keep the Comité alive as the "fight to recover the dignity of the community." His narrative anchored around experiences of dispossession and marginality among poor, Afro-descendant Ecuadorians. Leader of La Propicia Uno for close to 15 years, he talked about how after the lawsuit was settled, the neighborhood felt more like home than ever before: neighbors bonded over their common tragedy, acts of civil disobedience, and Petroecuador's compensation package. Their unity was the people's power and they vowed to use the funds to invest in urban livability. The potential for change also attracted families from other parts of town. From the approximately 1,450 residents (about 250 families) in 1998, the community tripled in size by 2006.

Few residents understood how the process of compensation allocation worked, however. While some imagined the distribution of set amounts per neighbor, the legal system had put a tight leash on the conditions of disbursement. According to Supreme Court records (Derecho Ecuador 2003), the funds could not be cashed in by individuals but only disbursed through material improvements that would benefit the community as a whole, which was legally represented by the Comité. The Comité and its allies drafted a list of priority public works infrastructure – water sewage and treatment of wastewaters, storm-water drainage, rock-fill to stabilize riverbanks, and concrete retaining walls among the top five priorities – but they had little direct influence on how these would be carried out, when, and by whom. The Comité was not able to decide or distribute funds either, but had to contract Petroecuador and governmental institutions (such as the municipality and public works ministries) to carry out the improvements. In other words, the funds remained under the control of the state at all times.

According to Jose Luis, between 2002 and 2006, Petroecuador hired several contractors to carry out numerous projects among the listed priorities, from asphalt to cobble-stone paving to a new school and maternity ward, to sidewalks. But how these projects were allocated also tells a story of dispossession. According to the law, if a public agency hires private firms for contracts above $USD 120,000, the process must be carried out through public solicitation and a period of competition, where contractors spell out their proposed work and cost. Any project below this amount can be allocated directly, without entering the public competition. During the first four years of the settlement, Petroecuador hired several contractors at under $USD 120,000 per project. This turned the process of compensation into a chaotic theater of compensation: infrastructure was put in place one block at a time, sometimes by different contractors.

Neighbors drew on collective action to demand greater transparency from Petroecuador. They used their social capital to raise funds through food sales, bingos, and community raffles to train themselves as "human rights overseers." They drew on their allies to coordinate professionalization workshops through which to train in *veedurias* (oversight practices) and purchased identity cards and uniforms they could wear while "out in the field" overseeing the implementation of compensation. They took pictures, wrote reports, asked questions from workers and contractors – information that would then be archived and catalogued.

Meanwhile, neighbors and friends saw Jose Luis go to Europe and South Africa to meet with environmental and human rights organizations, and to Quito, where he spent several weeks meeting with environmental organizations and other allies. These frequent travels were seen as suspicious and reinforced ambiguity and jealousy. In 2003, a board member removed Jose Luis from his charge while he was out of the country. In June 2006, Jose Luis was elected president again, receiving more than 60% of the votes, though he was the only candidate. Residents displeased with his re-election vowed to dispute the results. According to a neighbor, he was "too authoritarian," and "the USD $11 million [were] not . . . [his] inheritance . . . but the result of the people's struggle" (*La Hora* 2006b). While Jose Luis saw himself taking an authoritative position in order to underscore the urgency of the people's fight (the people cannot, *should not* wait), other community members saw his actions as overstepping the axiom of thinking and acting together as a collective. At stake was the reproduction of internal political subordination of those who wait versus those who reap the benefits of authoritarian decisions (Auyero 2012). To interrupt Jose Luis's authority, in July 2006, another Comité election took place (unbeknownst to Jose Luis), where a different leadership board was elected. The rationale for the second election was that there were "undefined irregularities" in the conduct of the previously elected board (*La Hora* 2006a).

The national context was key to the resolution of the divided leadership. 2006 was a year of magnified political contestations in Ecuador: social movements had forced the nation's president out and a new formulation of identity politics, focused on the recognition of indigenous and Afro-Ecuadorian collective rights, was being constituted (Becker 2011). The neighborhood's conflicted leadership matched this moment of political upheaval. Between July and December 2006, a prime electoral campaign time in Ecuador, over a dozen memos circulated between Jose Luis, the Ministry of Social and Economic Inclusion, the governor, the Ombudsman office of Esmeraldas, and the Prefect's office, regarding the contested legitimacy of the two elected boards. The memos convey the sense of a community divided by political affiliations. Highlighting the intersectional subalternity of La Propicia Uno, the memos framed the problem as one of routine racialized discrimination against Afro-Ecuadorians and obstacles to the emancipation of the "provincial mentality of the poor" in Esmeraldas.

Complicating this intersectional positioning was the fact that the second Comité elected was publicly affiliated with a political party different from the national leading party. Using the system of official memos to communicate with state institutions and representatives, Jose Luis wrote to the Ombdusman Office in Quito and to the ViceMinister and Minister of Well-Being in Quito, using the language of multiculturalism and collective rights of Afro-descendent peoples to decry how regional offices in Esmeraldas, affiliated with the opposition's political party, violate the right of Afro-descendants to freely elect their leaders through legal, democratic processes. Freedom of collective action among subaltern peoples, the memos emphasized, is limited by electoral battles among dominant political parties. As Jose Luis had hoped, the state institutions in Quito followed up with an investigation of ethical conduct and reprimanded provincial representatives for their "unethical" and "undisciplined" behavior, according to a July 7, 2006 memo sent by then Vice Minister of Well-Being in Quito, Nicolas Narajo. The memo wars led to the destitution of the provincial director of the Ministry of Well-Being and with the restitution of Jose Luis's leadership in the Comité.

Jose Luis's story offers insights into the conditions of the exhaustion of collective action. Conflict can destroy mobilization. Funds turn allies into competitors scrambling for control and attract others who can co-opt the work of grassroots leaders. Internal struggles not only plague social change, they exhaust it. Jose Luis talked about how divisions grew within the community as a result of external political battles, through threats and fears that introduced doubts and disillusionment. People also worried about their ability to keep up the fight. Collective action demands continuous presence: to defend community takes away time and resources to provide for individual family needs. Collective action is expensive: mobilizing people, writing memos, going to governmental offices is financially and materiality taxing. Jose Luis's own precarious situation as an imprisoned leader is exemplary of this exhaustion. In jail, he worries about his personal safety and does not know when he will be trialed. His alienation from the "people's fight" has no timeline. He cannot access resources or contribute to daily needs of his family, but must rely on the time and strength of others. With the alienation of the original Comité and the gradual exhaustion of activists such as Jose Luis, collective action is shifting, breaking into new organizations that might not share the same normative positions as those who won the lawsuit in 2002.

### Advocacy: misrecognizing the people's fight

> We asked ourselves, who are we and what do we want . . . because to us Esmeraldeños, they say: you are an "endless cauldron of sport stars," "the capital of salsa," "lazy blacks," "the best beaches on earth."
>
> (Estupinan 2005: 140)

> Our problem is that we have told ourselves that we are black . . . We are like a Bob Marley song . . . The Esmeraldeño waits to act: Emancipate ourselves from mental slavery; None but ourselves can free our minds.
>
> (Interview with representative of the
> Municipality of Esmeraldas, 2013)

Collective action in La Propicia Uno would not have been as successful without the aid of multiple advocates, from the Municipality of Esmeraldas, to various state institutions, to faith-based and environmental non-governmental organizations. One of the take-home messages from interviews with these advocates is that community members were not prepared to handle the hefty amount of money that came with the Petroecuador sentence. As a non-governmental representative who accompanied La Propicia Uno in solidarity with their cause explained in 2013:

> The problem starts at the beginning: they give USD $11 million to poor, marginalized peoples to do infrastructure works for the benefit of the neighborhood. But they don't give them the resources to manage, oversee, or be part of the process. These are people with limited financial means and training. Many times [our organization] covered their travels, hired consultants, and so on to make things work but very little changed. And then I realized: perhaps I am contributing to the problem – I am making the illness last longer. That is when I decided to step aside and let them forge their own path.

And in 2012, an environmental non-governmental ally commented on the intersectional limitations of the compensation package and how these fuel inaction:

> We conducted an assessment of the compensation process along with the citizen's oversight committee around 2006. We found a breach in the process of completing the sentence in both the compensation and mitigation points. But that is where it ended . . . we accompanied the community to the Ombudsman's Office and it was a mess. Both elected boards were there, and they contradicted each other. The Petroecuador representative said he was willing to work with them but that they first had to decide who was in charge. And he left it there . . . And with that, [Petroecuador] washed the sentence off its hands.

Key to these observations is that collectively challenging oppression, before and after the sentence, was necessary to the successful completion of the sentence. Collective action made the lawsuit possible and *veedurías* made sure that Petroecuador was acting in the best interest of La Propicia Uno. Advocates also point to the importance of what appears as *disorganization* from within. Their descriptions of "what actually happened" in La Propicia Uno illustrate how disorganization is seen as the result of a sort of insufficiency to counter oppression. For some, the division of leadership stems from the underdevelopment of collective political consciousness to the point that individuals see their own socioeconomic interest as the main scale of action while losing faith in a common understanding of freedom from oppression. For another ally, dis-organization resulted from "third worldism": being available to the commoditization of political thought via patriarchal systems of government, where individuals are transformed into subjects of power and educated in solutions thought and developed by others. And for yet another ally, disorganization emerges from subaltern intersectionality: it is born out of the historical devaluation of life according to social position, so that generations of material poverty – poverty of food, clothing, exclusion, alienation – become a political mode of being that makes individuals docile to clientelar relationships. The assumption in these advocate positions is that neighbors have lost their way; as moral subjects suffering from oppression, they should desire freedom from extenuating circumstances, to appropriate resistance as a normative emancipatory sentiment. This is the advocate's vision of "the people's fight." To not desire the progressive politics they advocate is misguided. But therein lies the problem: the sort of freedom that advocates imagine neighbors should desire is the freedom they imagine is best for Esmeraldeños. Perhaps, as Saba Mahmood (2011) suggests, emancipation is not normative to agency but a naturalization of a progressive politics that assumes exploited and marginalized subjects are not authentic when they don't act as desired. Advocates too are situated within historically specific power relations, and their intended and unintended actions influence what is perceived as good and possible (Fortun 2001).

Refinery community relations representatives offer a complementary perspective on advocacy for "the people's fight." In our interviews in August 2012, refinery community relations representatives situated themselves as Esmeraldeños who have experienced devalued urban spaces and are familiar with local patron-client relations: "Before coming to work here, I thought the same way that all Esmeraldeños think: that the refinery is the solution to most problems, long and short-term ones . . . Today, I continue to believe this." These refinery representatives thus do not see themselves as different from other Esmeraldeños; they understand the needs and are familiar with the frustrations expressed by community members. But their positionality as employees of the refinery also distances them from this collective subjectivity. The daily tasks of the refinery's liaison is to listen to the demands of leaders of the hundreds of unincorporated neighborhoods and to produce a distance between refinery and neighbors through the negotiation of favors, from personal requests for jobs, to donations for seasonal festivities and construction materials, to traffic lights and stop signs. Often times these patron-client requests are granted, as long as they are not "unsurmountable" and forge ties with surrounding communities.[6]

Being the liaison in these exchanges of unequal power is taxing, reflected a social relations representative: "when you enter the sphere of social projects, you have to be involved in things that have *nothing to do* [my emphasis] with your work. You keep track of what people want. You get involved in people's problems. Your mind is weighed down with the worries of others." While Petroecuador representatives might qualify neighborhood demands as unrelated to the *actual* work of the refinery, it is evident that the shadow social services they mediate are fundamental to the work of petro-capitalism in Esmeraldas. They are based on and reproduce social norms of subjection based on the understanding that Esmeraldeños recognize that the refinery is a powerful neighbor and that they are predisposed to seeking dependencies with the refinery. In the early 2000s, for example, with the proposed expansion of oil extraction activities and the building of a new heavy-crude pipeline, the refinery invested in the provision of water and sewage systems, schools, and health services, which appeased some of the collective action developing in Esmeraldas at the time. Maintaining the status quo, i.e., meeting needs through patron-client relations, is a state response to "the people's fight" that has *everything to do* with refinery operations.

## Conclusions

This chapter was inspired by a question that haunted my visits to Esmeraldas: in a place so ravaged by oil pollution, where is collective action? While most Esmeraldeños freely talk about the 1998 fire as a marker of the city's modern history, few know exactly what happened to La Propicia Uno's unique trajectory of resistance. Some people mentioned truncated futures: the people of La Propicia Uno "were entangled with corruption and lost their way." Or, "They are still fighting, but they have reached a dead end." Others were more upfront about their involvement with the neighborhood's future. For example, a municipal representative confided that he bought a house in La Propicia Uno in the hopes that he too could benefit from the settlement, but in his experience, the Comité is "too tightly knit." He bought the house from a "desperate *mulata*" – who in his assessment could do nothing with the house. In a telling example of his class and gender privilege, he shared how he fixed the front of the house so that it looks inhabited, but he mostly lives in another neighborhood. He volunteered to take me on a "toxic tour" of the neighborhood so that I could see the poor conditions in which people live. We visited the maternity ward and the day nursery as examples of how the Petroecuador funds had been invested. He failed to say that these projects were not directly handled by Petroecuador but by the Vicariate of Esmeraldas, whom the Comité lobbied to enter as a neutral guarantor to avoid the impasse of frozen funds. He attends the neighborhood meetings religiously, and even "starts some fires," in hopes that like-minded neighbors will loosen the tight grip on the Comité and "do something" with the paralyzed funds.

The ethnographic moments described dissect these simplistic, essentializing interpretations of environmental struggles in zones of petro-sacrifice, and illustrate the intersectional natures of power/knowledge relations in La Propicia Uno. Each narrative illustrates collective action in process, whether from the intimate spaces of the private archive, or from the spaces of the men's prison, an ironically "safe space" for alternative Comité meetings. Attention to advocacy reflections shows how the sociality of disaster compensation and mitigation works towards normalizing zones of sacrifice in the context of petro-capitalist societies. All three moments highlight the double work of compensation. On the one hand it served as the recognition of social justice: La Propicia Uno was awarded monetary compensation, not only for fire damages but also for a longer historical abandonment that became morally evident as a result of the fire. Residents desired compensation as a way to improve urban livability. On the other hand, compensation served as a mechanism of misrecognition and interruption. It condoned social discrimination, as it didn't address the conditions under which environmental suffering persists among vulnerable peoples who co-exist with the oil complex, and it bracketed the very conditions through which it became a viable response to environmental suffering demands: long-standing patron-client relations. Petroecuador's inaction following the sentence makes evident how the state's obligation to respond to oil-related suffering is not guaranteed. According to observers, it is this lack of obligation towards those affected that fuels the emancipatory poverty of compensation projects. Residents are objects of improvement and not subjects of their own histories. The focus turns to how they become angry and confused, or mystified, and away from how the very process of compensation structures these frames of inaction.

As advocates and refinery personnel suggest, it is not difficult to see why compensation demands took the form that they did. The 1998 fire, through its violence and devaluation, not only reinforced a habit of patron-client relations already in place but also substantiated its continuous relevance. It is tempting to gloss over the agencies within collective action that seem to counter the emancipatory project of environmental justice in La Propicia Uno, as misguided, colonized, or "third worldism." They are not easily explained as building progressive politics. Yet misrecognizing them as false or uninformed is a way to erase them. These agencies evidence a sense of practiced adaptation to the conditions of exhaustion and endurance, though we might not always be capable of understanding them as such within our own discursive projects of collective action.

## Acknowledgements

This research was supported by the National Science Foundation (NSF) Award 1259049. The Institute for the Arts and Humanities (IAH) at UNC supported the camaraderie necessary to write and think about life with oil in Ecuador. This research would not have been possible without the friendship, insight and activism of Marcela Benavides, Kati Alvarez, Janeth Cando, Andrea Castillo, Yarita Giler, Hector Lañón, Paola Lastre, and Carlos Erazo. In Esmeraldas, I thank those who shared their life stories of petroleum-related struggle and their contagious passion for social justice and change. All errors of interpretation remain mine.

## Notes

1  See the video documentary "*La Bomba de Tiempo*" (The Time Bomb), available at: www.youtube.com/watch?v=T2AOoW9OGYY
2  See the reporting blog by Acción Ecológica (www.accionecologica.org/petroleo/casos-legales/texaco) for careful documentation of the case of Amazonian peoples in Ecuador against oil-afflictions. For English language syntheses of the case, see Barrett (2014), Sawyer (2004) and Valdivia (2007).
3  The fifth indigenous uprising took place in January 2001 against free trade treaties with the United States and European countries and the neoliberalization of the national economy. The uprising led to the overthrow of then president Jamil Mahuad.
4  La Propicia Uno initially sued the refinery for USD $35 million.
5  Jose Luis is accused of killing a neighbor, which he claims was in self-defense. He and his family have received death threats and warnings from many of his neighbors in the past.
6  This pattern changed after 2010, during the second Correa administration.

# References

Auyero, J. (2012) *Patients of the state: The politics of waiting in Argentina*, Durham, Duke University Press.

Auyero, J. and Swistun, D.A. (2009) *Flammable: Environmental suffering in an Argentine shantytown*, New York, Oxford University Press.

Barrett, P. (2014) *Law of the jungle: The $19 billion legal battle over oil in the rain forest and the lawyer who'd stop at nothing to win*, New York, Crown Publishers.

Bautista, J. (2008) "The meta-theory of piety: Reflections on the work of Saba Mahmood." *Contemporary Islam 2*, 75–83.

Becker, M. (2011) *Pachakutik: Indigenous movements and electoral politics in Ecuador*, Lanham, MD, Rowman & Littlefield Publishers.

Checker, M. (2005) *Polluted promises: Environmental racism and the search for justice in a southern town*, New York, New York University Press.

Cole, L.W. and Foster, S.R. (2001) *From the ground up: Environmental racism and the rise of the environmental justice movement*, New York, New York University Press.

Derecho Ecuador. (2003) "Official Registry, March 19 2003." *Revista Judicial Derecho Ecuador* (www.derechoecuador.com/productos/producto/catalogo/registros-oficiales/2003/marzo/code/17765/registro-oficial-19-de-marzo-del-2003#anchor443352). Accessed August 24, 2014.

Diario Hoy. (2004) "El barrio más rico del mundo está en Esmeraldas." November 6, *Diario Hoy*, Esmeraldas (www.hoy.com.ec/noticias-ecuador/el-barrio-mas-rico-del-mundo-esta-en-esmeraldas-191033.html). Accessed June 25, 2013.

Estupinan, E. (2005) "La crisis ambiental en Esmeraldas y la intervencion de los actores locales." In: Hanekamp, E. and Ponce, J., *Quien Conspira Contra el Ambiente?*, Quito, Abya Yala, 99–104.

Evans, P.B. (2002) *Livable cities?: Urban struggles for livelihood and sustainability*, Berkeley, University of California Press.

Fortun, K. (2001) *Advocacy after Bhopal: Environmentalism, disaster, new global orders*, Chicago, University of Chicago Press.

Galarza Zavala, J. (1972) *El festín del petróleo*, Quito, Ediciones Soltierra.

Harvey, D. (1989) *The condition of postmodernity: An enquiry into the origins of cultural change*, Cambridge, Blackwell, 1990.

Horowitz, L. (2012) "Power, profit, protest: Grassroots resistance to industry in the Global North." *Capitalism Nature Socialism 23*, 20–34.

Huber, M.T. (2013) *Lifeblood: Oil, freedom, and the forces of capital /c Matthew T. Huber*, Minneapolis, University of Minnesota Press.

Jacome, N. and Martines Fissau, V. (1977) "La formacion del estrato popular de Esmeraldas en el contexto del desarrollo provincial." *Revista Ciencias Sociales 3*, 89–143.

Kosek, J. (2006) *Understories: the political life of forests in northern New Mexico*. Durham: Duke University Press.

La Hora. (2006a) "Caso Propicia está politizado." July 6, *La Hora*, Esmeraldas (http://lahora.com.ec/index.php/noticias/show/449309/-1/%E2%80%98Caso_Propicia_est%C3%A1_politizado%E2%80%99.html#.V78nBU0wi70). Accessed August 24, 2016.

———. (2006b) "Impugnaran elecciones en barrio La Propicia 1." June 12, *La Hora*, Esmeraldas (http://lahora.com.ec/index.php/noticias/show/439761/-1/Impugnar%C3%A1n_elecciones_en_barrio_La_Propicia_1.html#.V78m3k0wi70). Accessed August 24, 2016.

———. (2010) "No terminan problemas en La Propicia 1." December 21, *La Hora*, Esmeraldas (http://lahora.com.ec/index.php/noticias/show/1101066357/-1/No_terminan_problemas_en_La_Propicia_1.html#.V78mh00wi70). Accessed August 24, 2016.

Lerner, S. (2010) *Sacrifice zones: The front lines of toxic chemical exposure in the United States*, Cambridge, MIT Press.

Little, P.C. (2014) *Toxic town: IBM, pollution, and industrial risks*, New York, New York University Press.

Mahmood, S. (2011) *Politics of piety: The Islamic revival and the feminist subject*, Princeton, Princeton University Press.

McGurty, E.M. (2007) *Transforming environmentalism: Warren County, PCBs, and the origins of environmental justice*, New Brunswick, Rutgers University Press.

Mollett, S. and Faria, C. (2013) "Messing with gender in feminist political ecology." *Geoforum* 45, 116–125.

Moncada, J. (2002) *Esmeraldas una joya sin pulir*, Quito, Ediciones la Tierra.

Nightingale, A.J. (2011) "Bounding difference: Intersectionality and the material production of gender, caste, class and environment in Nepal." *Geoforum* 42, 153–162.

Nixon, R. (2011) *Slow violence and the environmentalism of the poor*. Cambridge: Harvard University Press.

Palma, E. and Alvarez, S. (2005) "Comentarios a la ponencia de Ernesto Estupinan." In: Hanekamp, E. and Ponce, J., *Quien Conspira Contra el Ambiente?*, Quito, Abya Yala, 137–144.

Pérez Sales, P, Santiago, C, Alvarez R (2002) "Ahora apuestan al cansacio: Chiapas, fundamentos psicológicos de una guerra contemporánea" Mexico City: Grupo de Acción Comunitaria y Centro de Derechos Humanos Miguel Agustín Pro Juárez.

Povinelli, E.A. (2011) *Economies of abandonment: Social belonging and endurance in late liberalism*, Durham, Duke University Press.

Pulido, L. (2000) "Rethinking environmental racism: White privilege and urban development in Southern California." *Annals of the Association of American Geographers* 90, 12–40.

Roberts, D. and Jesudason, S. (2013) "Movement intersectionality." *Du Bois Review: Social Science Research on Race* 10, 313–328.

Sawyer, S. (2004) *Crude chronicles: Indigenous politics, multinational oil, and neoliberalism in Ecuador*, Durham, NC, Duke University Press.

Soni-Sinha, U. (2013) "Intersectionality, subjectivity, collectivity and the union: A study of the 'locked-out' hotel workers in Toronto." *Organization* 20, 775–793.

Toro, M. (2004) "La Propicia quiere cambiar tras ganar indemnización." *El Universo*, February 9 (www.eluniverso.com/2004/02/09/0001/12/EA43A878BBD74D3CA371B9A8F4101FFD.html). Accessed August 24, 2016.

United Nations Environment Programme (UNEP) (2006) *GEO Esmeraldas : perspectivas del medio ambiente urbano*, Ecuador: FUDAMYF.

Valdivia, G. (2007) "The 'Amazonian trial of the century': Indigenous identities, transnational networks, and petroleum in Ecuador." *Alternatives: Global, Local, Political* 32, 41–72.

Zebrowski, E. (2014) *Hydrocarbon hucksters: Lessons from Louisiana on oil, politics, and environmental justice*, Jackson, University Press of Mississippi.

# 7 From contested cotton to the ban on brinjal

India's shifting risk narratives in opposition to genetically engineered agriculture

*Julia Freeman, Terre Satterfield*
*and Milind Kandlikar*

## Introduction

Debates over the risks and benefits of genetically engineered (GE) crops have had important implications for their use in India. The promotion of GE crops as a tool for farmers resembles classic development initiatives, with proponents, including the government of India, steadfast in their confidence for a (bio)technological solution for marginal producers facing declining yields, growing costs of production, and 'onrushing' conditions of poverty (Jansen and Gupta, 2009). The country also has a vibrant history of public debate over its agricultural and economic development led by a robust civil society critiquing those initiatives that promise to improve the environment and living conditions of the poor. This chapter looks to India's English language oppositional narratives regarding GE agriculture – as gauged by interviews with civil society groups, their own publications, and media coverage – to examine how the GE controversy in that country has evolved and why. Our analysis extends from the commercialization of GE crops, contrasting the approval of GE cotton in 2002 and its current widespread use, against the more recent moratorium for GE brinjal (or, eggplant) in 2010. The disparity in these cases provides a useful vantage point by which to assess anti-GE risk narratives in public debate. We look to social theory regarding risk and narrative in order to interpret civil society's stance against India's GE crops and regulatory regime.

Within the social studies of risk, there are important differences distinguishing GE crops from prior agricultural interventions. Beck (1992) has postulated that novel risks are transforming the experience of hazards in social life and are integral to transitioning industrial(izing) societies into 'risk societies'. These risks tend to erode scientific authority due to high levels of uncertainty or debate around technical questions, and can underscore the paramount role of trust in shaping risk acceptability (Lupton, 1999). Beck's category of new and qualitatively unique risks that are perceived to threaten irrevocable damage to life on earth (Wilkinson, 2001) can arguably be applied to genetically engineered agriculture, given the socio-political anxiety and regulatory challenges it has raised, and the global scope of the technology's reach (Beck, 1995). Indeed the perception of risk continues to linger around GE crops despite systematic reviews of research arguing the technology is safe for people and the environment alike (Klümper and Qaim, 2014; Nicolia et al., 2014). The risk society thesis has been applied most fully and investigated most thoroughly in Europe and North America (Beck, 1992; Beck, 2009). However Beck (2006; 2009) also anticipates a variety of reflexive responses to global risks including in less-industrialized societies. In this chapter we propose that India is undergoing a *risk transition* that aligns with its transitioning economy, and that as a result those groups contesting the rise of GE in India would do so in ways distinct from what has been observed in Northern post-industrial societies.

There is growing interest in how the risks and benefits of GE crops are playing out in the developing world (Aerni, 2002; Curtis et al., 2004). To the extent that risk theorizing about the developing world is being undertaken, lower-income countries have been characterized as undergoing a risk transition whereby these countries juggle what might be termed 'traditional risks' involving threats to physical wellbeing stemming from inadequate food, shelter or health care (e.g. from exposure to diseases like malaria, or indoor air pollution from cooking stoves) (Smith, 2001; Smith and Ezzati, 2005). However, these pressing concerns do not relieve lower-income countries from other 'late modern risks' stemming from nuclear or biotechnologies, for example, that may be more delayed, diffuse, or technically uncertain (Jewitt and Baker, 2011). Beck describes reflexive modernization as a central feature of transition, including processes of 1) risk externalization (whereby regulators and governments become targets of widespread blame or subject to the complaint that they have failed to protect 'the public'), and 2) individualization (where citizens skeptical of expert systems are 'thrown back upon themselves' with little certainty and greater individual responsibility in managing these risks) (2009: 54). Nevertheless, we recognize that lower-income countries are not transitioning through these risks in a uniform way, but rather in response to different situational and structural factors. Factors may range from what crops and genetic traits are involved, whether or not the products were developed domestically, the state-level investment in biotechnology, farmer incentives for the uptake or rejection of GE, and the NGO presence and/or media stance regarding the technology. Thus, China has widely adopted nationally developed Bt cotton (Pray et al., 2002), while Thailand has rejected transgenic papaya (Davidson, 2008). Given such diversity, the chapter addresses the question of how we might begin to systematically track and characterize the nature of risk debates in the developing world, thereby better understanding the dynamics of social and policy transitions, and responses to emerging risk, therein. One promising means for examining this question is by tracking anti-GE risk narratives – produced by civil society groups, in this case – in order to see how they may resemble or differ from those being produced by countries more conventionally labeled 'risk societies'.

Narrative analysis calls attention to the wide range of types of, and conditions for, risk knowledge and it challenges researchers to work against the imposition of their own analytical frames (Henwood et al., 2010: 18). Following Henwood, Pidgeon, Parkhill and Simmons, we consider variable articulations of risk to be 'reflexive meaning-making' (2010: 17) and we are especially interested in how anti-GE narratives in India have changed, as civil society actors endeavor to find an audience in a noisy democracy undergoing risk transition. The narrative-based approach places this work within qualitative and interpretive traditions of risk research by investigating the 'contextually embedded, morally committed, value laden and affectively charged stories' about risk (Henwood et al., 2010: 6). Looking to the specific and shifting forms these risk narratives have taken in India since the commercialization of Bt cotton in 2002, we ask: how might these anti-GE risk narratives resemble or differ from those of the risk societies? We find that while there are varying ways that India's opponents of GE crops articulate risk through particular narratives, it is the distinct pattern of movement, the ebb and flow of the risk narratives themselves, that is most telling.

The data for this paper are drawn from two primary sources: interviews with civil society members, including NGOs and other public figures critical of agricultural GE; and the close reading of NGO publications, website postings, films, and articles covering aspects of the controversy from key Indian sources (*The Hindu, Times of India,* and *Economic Times* newspapers alongside the periodical *Economic and Political Weekly*). Interviews were conducted between 2008 and 2009 in New Delhi, Hyderabad and Bangalore, three cities housing important figures and groups contributing to the debate. Representatives from five significant NGOs working on GE issues participated in the study. Among them, two groups work primarily on regional issues, while there are two national-level NGOs, and the last has international affiliation. Additionally, two staff members of an organic cotton farmers' association, along with two public figures (vocal and well-published experts on the subject) were interviewed. The identities of these nine participants are concealed by pseudonyms (which sometimes obscure the speaker's gender) given that some preferred to remain confidential and the set of interviewees is small. Interviews were approximately one hour and focused on the regulation and biosafety of GE crops and participants' work as it related to agricultural GE in India. It is worth noting that though many of the various organizations occasionally work together, this does not mean they share a uniform assessment of GE agriculture. Rather, our findings reveal an 'orchestra of positions' (Visvanathan and Parmar, 2002) ranging from a critical regard for the technology's potential to a fundamental opposition to GE farming. Media reports and civil society gray literature complement the interview data by providing historical perspective and mapping when anti-GE risk narratives are deployed or rescinded. They also demonstrate the extent to which civil society networks have been involved at all levels of the debate, from opinion pieces in the press, to holding rural NGO-based community discussions, to launching large-scale demonstrations in urban settings. Documents include technical reports describing how agricultural GE works, along with its risks, as well as studies evaluating actual outputs of early Bt cotton published by civil society groups (Qayum and Sakkhari, 2005). Others describe the limitations of

GE farming, and provide assistance with alternative models of agricultural production, often emphasizing organic or non-pesticidal management (Kuruganti and Ramanjaneyulu, 2008).

In what follows, we characterize India's anti-GE narrative shifts and explain the pattern that has emerged as an ongoing effort by civil society groups to find their audience and raise their concerns. We identify three overarching themes across the risk narratives: social justice, agronomic integrity, and health risks. Our characterization of the movement of these dominant narrative groups ultimately informs not only our understanding of the changing conditions of the GE risk debates; it also questions a stages-logic that would cast risk transition in overly linear or 'progressive developmentalist' terms. We expect a modestly sized and comparatively affluent group of urban and internationally focused NGOs to share these late modern, global risk concerns. However, we also want to afford primacy to India's large agrarian population, and recognize that civil society led debates are not necessarily well connected to the priorities and problems faced by this population. The chapter concludes that the current invocations of risk resonate best with India's urban and educated upper middle-class consumers, bearing strategic successes as a result, but this targeted mobilization is leaving India's rural and agrarian poor largely outside the debate.

## Resistance movements: shifting anti-GE risk narratives

### Social justice narratives prior to GE commercialization

Before the commercialization of India's first GE crop in 2002, the national agricultural GE debate focused on the arrival of multinational corporations and their potential impact on India's farming population; emerging from the anti-globalization movement sustained by civil society networks and farmer's organizations during the 1990s. The Indian government had positioned itself on the frontier of biotechnology development early on, establishing a National Department of Biotechnology in 1986 (Ramaswami and Pray, 2007). Meanwhile, civil society actors called attention to potential exploitation of farmers by big biotechnology companies, arguing that the technology would ensnare farmers with ever more expensive agricultural products requiring ever increasingly high inputs (Shiva et al., 1999).

Monsanto – the well-known multinational biotechnology and agri-chemical company – partnered with the Indian seed company Mahyco (Maharashtra Hybrid Seeds Company) and together (as MMB) were an early applicant for the commercial release of India's first genetically engineered crops. By 1998, the multinational was being targeted by anti-GE activism and Monsanto's pre-existing reputation as a company with questionable business practices meant that incorrect assertions about its dissemination of sterile 'Terminator' seeds nevertheless seemed feasible (Herring, 2005). Concomitantly, alarming rates of suicide deaths among indebted farmers in several parts of India became symbolically incorporated into larger concerns around a globalizing agriculture industry operating in tension with local interests (Shiva and Jafri, 2002). Indeed, these tragic reports have recently been reincorporated into anti-GE risk narratives, as we will see next.

Early resistance to GE crops challenged the corporation from a number of vantage points, including a 'Monsanto Quit India' campaign that linked its presence as a foreign influence to India's history of forging national independence (Shiva, 1998). Similarly, farmers of the *Karnataka Rajya Ryota Sangha* (Karnataka State Farmers' Association) and other farmers' organizations launched 'Operation Cremate Monsanto', burning trial Bt cotton crops in Karnataka's Raichur and Bellary districts arguing they were illegal and that farmers involved had not been adequately informed that the crops were GE (Scoones, 2005). Critiques invoking the class of risks we classify as based on principles of social justice focus largely on how the technology impacts small farmers and their right to circulate seed. Monsanto's role in the development of agricultural GE in India, and the potential dependence of marginal producers on a globalizing corporate seed industry are also within the narratives. They signal civil society's concern with what they see as alarming directions for the country's agricultural development more generally.

Bt cotton, as India's imminent inaugural GE crop, was replete with the aforementioned concerns. (Bt cotton contains genetic material from the soil bacterium *bacillus thuringiensis* to lend the hybrid plant an increased capacity to resist *lepidopteran* pests). Social justice was at issue again when the Government of India responded to cotton-farmer advocacy regarding the price of GE seed by introducing 'economic viability' (measured as the cost of seed, anticipated demand for the product, and amount of land expected to be used in cultivation) as a component of the National biosafety assessment guidelines (Gupta, 2000). This meant any proposed GE crop must actively benefit farmers, rather than merely presenting a limited hazard. This comprised a significant extension of international agreements around biosafety. Similarly, Delhi passed its remarkable Protection of Plant Varieties and Farmers' Rights Act (PPVFR) in 2001 (Brahmi et al., 2004) despite a global impetus to harmonize national law around intellectual property (Herdt, 2006). The PPVFR explicitly identifies *farmers' rights* and protects their proprietary claims to circulate seeds in a traditional manner, which is an important move for an agrarian country like India where the 'grower/ breeder distinction' is less meaningful, as many farmers are major suppliers of seed and develop their own varieties (Seshia, 2002). GE seed helped blur this grower/breeder distinction further when farmers were found planting unregulated Bt cottonseed in Gujarat in 2001. While the Government sought to shut down its circulation, many farmers managed to backcross the hybrid with their own seed before it was banned (Herring, 2007). The event provided a new hook for civil society networks to draw forward agronomic risks and regulators were left open to significant reproach as their capacity to ensure the biosafety of GE crops was questioned. For their part, Gujarati farmers and politicians were emboldened to demand the immediate approval of the Bt cotton. The government responded by moving Mahyco-Monsanto's Bt cotton application through its final stages of regulatory approval, releasing three 'Bollgard' hybrids as legitimate options for farmers looking for GE seed (Scoones, 2006).

Social justice was soon displaced by agronomic risk. Five interviewees explained that at this time, state-level enthusiasm for GE seed channeled farmers toward a risky technology by presupposing a lack of other viable options. They described how GE became cast as the only means to avoid a chemical treadmill of increasing pesticide usage, while alternative agricultural methods, such as integrated pest management, were absent from the state-level conversation entirely. As Dr. Iyer, a well-regarded scientist and NGO representative said with notable dismay, '*regulation should be about assessing the best alternatives – right now it's about the worst ones!*' (Pers. Comm., 05–12–2009) At the same time, civil society actors found themselves unable to rework their own justice and inequity claims with the evidence of resourceful farmers who had caught industry, government and civil society alike off guard by risking the use of stealth Bt seed, and arguing forcefully for the approval of Bt cotton. After commercialization, farmers cultivated Bt cotton widely. The 'area under cotton cultivation in the country has gone up from 24000 ha in 2002 to 8.4 million ha at present' (Lok Sabha Secretariat, Government of India, 2012: 28). This tension between farmers' actions and civil society's concerns helps account for the recession of the social justice narrative that dominated the risk debates up to this point, by framing farmers as victims of MNCs, or questioning GE's benefits.

Farmers were recast as active agents, albeit misled into choosing a technology that often failed, and civil society groups invoked farmers' vulnerability while working on their behalf. Devinder Sharma noted that 'most farmers in the Asia-Pacific region are poor and *cannot afford risk*, particularly since no effective crop insurance mechanisms are yet in place . . . these poor farmers are being deliberately pushed into a trap' (emphasis added, Sharma, 2004, n.p.). Civil society actors also described farmers being coerced by unscrupulous and false marketing campaigns, and have reported the employment of dancing girls, the use of dishonest advertisements, and pressure tactics to sell GE seed (Greenpeace India, 2005). As Dr. Barad, an influential scientist and NGO representative, reported in an interview, farmers are

> shown videos of Gods and mythology and Ram and Guru Nanak and everything under the sun and Superman. And they're bombarded with these videos and the farmer is not making a decision on the basis of the seed, he's making a decision on the basis of the Ramayan, you know? So it's very – it's stealth marketing.
>
> (Pers. Comm., Delhi, 03–31–2009)

Corporate aggressiveness and a shaky regulatory regime have left opponents unconvinced of the safety and usefulness of the technology; however, subsequent events would bring agronomic concerns to the forefront of the debate. Meanwhile, these social justice narratives bore essentially 'local' arguments about the anticipated dependency of traditional Indian farming systems upon new GE seed. Locals, however, did not always take up these arguments. Consequently, from 2002 onwards more globally typical risk narratives about agronomic or consumer impacts of GE crops are effectively called to the fore of India's debate with remarkable success.

### Agronomic integrity and civil society skepticism

The commercialization of three MMB Bt cotton varieties in 2002 signaled in particular the rise of agronomic risks in the debate. It was no longer sufficient to warn farmers of the disadvantages of GE seed; attention shifted to critiques of Bt cotton's performance, and skepticism regarding its benefits. Within these new narratives, debates about crop yields and ecological impacts became central to evaluating and discursively marking the technology as risky. In the years that immediately followed the discovery of the regulatory failure manifest in Gujarat's stealth seeds, there was considerable confusion over distinguishing legal from unauthorized seed, or even seed that genuinely contained the Bt trait from spurious hybrids that were falsely advertised as GE. Bt cotton's introduction to India was unsatisfactory to critics, given both the rush to provide a 'legitimately regulated' seed, and the experimentation underway with unregulated varieties (Sahai, 2002).

From 2002 onwards, one of the most enduring challenges made against GE crops, and MMB cotton hybrids in particular, involved their agronomic viability and conflicting reports about the seeds' yield performance. Critics familiar with cotton production pointed out that the MMB hybrids were not particularly strong performers in terms of their boll size or crop yield (Sahai, 2002). Improved resistance to bollworm would not dramatically improve an otherwise poor hybrid (Sahai and Rahman, 2003). Civil society actors argued that hype over the technology was actually masking the weak performance of the early Bt cottons (GRAIN, 2007) and that the crop was 'failing' outright in certain locations (RFSTE, 2002). Questions about the efficacy of Bt cotton have simmered for years (Sahai, 2005) and Herring has shown the longevity of the Bt crop failure dispute maintains a usefulness as part of an international GE debate even if it is no longer 'sustainable scientifically' (2009). Still, across various industrializing countries with variable growing conditions, the performance and significance of GE crops has proven to be 'highly variable, socio-economically differentiated and contingent on a range of agronomic, socio-economic and institutional factors,' and thus resistant to over-generalizations, be they critical or favorable in tone (Glover, 2010: 482).

PV Satheesh, Director of the Deccan Development Society, writes of meeting a farmer whose Bt cotton crop has failed but who will continue planting it because Chinese farmers were doing well with the crop (Satheesh, 2003). Among interview participants, most articulated the lack of state-level interest in alternative agricultural development and limited options for farmers as leading to the widespread uptake of Bt cotton. We don't mean to imply, however, that as social justice concerns retreated and agronomic risks were advanced (supported by the troubled commercialization of Bt cotton), that the focus on farmers' rights fully vanished from the risk narratives employed by civil society. When interviewees were asked how they account for the widespread use of Bt cotton (by 2010 some 6.3 million of India's cotton farmers were growing Bt seeds) (James, 2010) some argued that seed sellers were only stocking Bt cotton hybrids, thereby abolishing any choice for farmers to select non-Bt options. Many interviewees considered farmers to be simply making the best of the constricted options available to them. Mr. Khurmi, a local level civil society actor, replied, '*It's difficult to say that Bt is what farmers wanted. I think farmers in India were at the stage where they had nothing to lose*' (Pers. Comm., 04–13–2009). He laments a lack of alternatives even as his own work provides assistance with alternative modes of agricultural production.

Proponents of Bt cotton claimed that farmers would save money by buying fewer pesticides and losing less of their crop to pests (Bennett et al., 2005). However, opponents pointed out that high-tech seeds also came at a higher price and that increased costs and unstable yields rendered Bt cotton an un-economical choice for farmers (Sahai and Rahman, 2003). Greenpeace India demanded compensation for farmers for crop failures, the withdrawal of Bt seed from the market, and for the government of Andhra Pradesh to 'blacklist' Monsanto and 'disallow it from deluding farmers with its propaganda' (Special Correspondent, 2003). Other NGOs pointed to a lack of 'accountability mechanisms for such uneven performance' (Ramanjaneyulu and Kuruganti, 2006). The Andhra Pradesh government ordered Mahyco-Monsanto to reduce their seed prices, and ultimately won a contempt petition before India's Monopolies and Restrictive Trade Practices Commission (MRTPC) against MMB for failing to comply (Venkatesan, 2006). However, regulatory concerns, first linked to stealth and spurious seed, and then again by their price and purported crop 'failures', remained consistently at the foreground of agricultural GE opposition in India. They have in fact been used to highlight each of the risk narratives at some point or another. Meanwhile, data on the economics of Bt began to enter the debate, challenging the aforementioned claims and demonstrating increases in yield and farmer income (Bennett et al., 2005; Pray et al., 2005). Shah, on the other hand, challenges the very notion of framing our understanding of Bt technology in the blunt terms of its 'success' or 'failure' as far too limited. He argues that, in Gujarat at least, the growing use of Bt cottonseed is best understood in terms of its place within historical (Green Revolution) agrarian practices, and the cultural performance of technology (Shah, 2008). This call for context is one echoed in our own effort to characterize the transitioning and shifting risks in the country's GE debates by looking to specific events, regulatory structures, key actors, and environmental conditions wherein the seeds are planted.

Media reports also began to emerge from Warangal and surrounding districts describing 1800 sheep dying from grazing in Bt cotton fields (Sadeque, 2008). Later refuted by academic research (Herring, 2009), the sheep stories nevertheless continue to circulate, and assessments of livestock grazing in Bt field remain contested (Lok Sabha Secretariat, Government of India, 2012: 71). Concomitantly, as farmers increasingly adopted Bt cotton so too did civil society increase their work articulating the potential risks associated with farmers' exposure to GE plants and seed. In one report, produced by members of the People's Health

Movement 'Jan Swasthya Abhiyan' and other environmental activists, health effects ranging from mild to severe skin, respiratory and eye allergies were investigated; and the report called for further research into the causes of symptoms and preventative measures (Gupta et al., 2005). Still, the focus on health risks was not productively brought forward until a subsequent shift in risk narratives focused on consumer consumption a few years later.

By the mid-2000's the GE debate in India had become increasingly marked by what Herring has called a 'deep disjuncture' between the concerns and arguments raised by the opponents of GE, and the actions of the farmers 'they claim to represent' (2008). The incongruity between anti-GE narratives and many farmers' instrumental economic concerns came into sharp relief. Civil society positioned India's cotton farmers as succumbing to an ineffective, high-risk, GE-seed industry as the area of land covered by GE crops in India continued to grow (to 10.6 million hectares in 2011) (ISAAA, 2011). They also championed farmers as the rightful producers and distributors of biosafe cottonseed and other crops (Shiva, 2012) (despite farmers' widely reported disregard of biosafety protocols for planting Bt cotton). An important example of this is the lack of refugium being planted around Bt cotton fields. A small package (50 grams) of conventional cotton is included with the 400 grams of Bt cotton used to plant an acre of land, in order to plant a barrier around the field that protects against the development of bollworm resistance to the Bt toxin. The reasons for the rejection of refugium practices by farmers are manifold and not well studied but include: confusion regarding the practice, economic efficiency strategies, and concerns regarding the quality of refuge seeds (Freeman, 2012: 168–9). The first instance of resistance to pink bollworm was reported in 2010 (Jebarai, 2010).

Over the course of the early 2000's, GE opposition was also playing out in the courts, where civil society groups sought the impartiality they found lacking in regulatory processes. In facing a request to ban GE field trials, the Supreme Court concluded that in fact, 'such technical matters can hardly be the subject of judicial review. The Court has no expertise to determine such as issue, which, besides being a scientific question, would have very serious and far-reaching consequences' (Aruna Rodrigues & Ors vs Union of India & Ors, Supreme Court of India, 2012). This formal acknowledgement of the limits of its technical competence may suggest the apex Court is responsive to the anti-GE risk narratives in circulation. In light of numerous interventions, including court-ordered GE moratoriums, the appointment of new members to the GEAC, and ongoing monitoring, such limitations certainly have not impeded the Supreme Court from maintaining an important role in the unfolding of the GE debate in India (Freeman et al., 2011).

### Health risks and the rise of the consumer

Ultimately, the chaffing of civil society's social justice and agronomic risk narratives against the realities of farmers' priorities in Bt cotton production helped to spur a re-orientation of resistance toward the risks of food crops in the commercialization pipeline, and Bt brinjal in particular, as discussed in the following section.

This most recent period reflects a disappearance of cotton farmers as the focus of anti-GE narratives and examines the growing concern instead with the risks presented to India's consumers via Bt brinjal (eggplant). Brinjal, known as a 'poor person's food', is widely grown by marginal farmers on very small plots of land (one estimate maintains that an average resource poor farmer cultivates 0.4 hectares of brinjal) (Choudhary and Gaur, 2009). Yet the crop is equally known as the 'King of Vegetables', consumed widely, and esteemed for nutritional and ayurvedic qualities (ISAAA, N.d). India is the second largest producer of the crop worldwide (Choudhary and Gaur, 2009) and despite its popularity among marginal farmers, brinjal can require significant inputs, particularly in terms of insecticides to fend off its most problematic pest, the fruit and shoot borer.

Through a 'public-private partnership', Mahyco and a number of Indian Agricultural Universities developed Bt brinjal hybrids using Monsanto's Cry 1Ac gene (the same as used in Bt cotton). Seven of these were approved by regulators for outdoor multi-site trials in 2004 (Choudhary and Gaur, 2009). However, in 2006 public interest litigation brought about by Aruna Rodrigues, PV Satheesh and Rajiv Barua led to a complete ban on all GE trials, including Bt brinjal, for one year (Sharma, 2009). Public interest litigation involves writ petitions sent to the Supreme Court as a means to advocate on behalf of disenfranchised citizens in the name of the public good. These agricultural GE litigations turned out to be important fora for civil society to intervene in the regulatory process. When the ban was lifted in 2007, the Supreme Court appointed two prominent, senior scientists, M.S. Swaminathan and P.M. Bhargava, as special invitees for all GEAC meetings at which fresh approvals were to be considered (Legal Correspondent, 2008). Thereafter, regulators allowed large-scale outdoor research and the generation of new biosafety data by the Indian Institute of Vegetable Research (Choudhary and Gaur, 2009). On 14 October 2009, the GEAC recommended the release of Bt brinjal for commercialization (Shah, 2011), based on the experts' report, but the next day the Ministry of Environment and Forests overrode the decision. Responding to vocal opposition from civil society, the minister at the time, Jairam Ramesh indicated he would first conduct a series of consultations with stakeholders in January and February of 2010, prior to any final approval for the crop's release (Staff Reporter, 2010).

Ramesh visited seven cities around the country in brinjal producing areas and important biotech centers. The meetings were conducted in the local language as well as Hindi and English, with 250 representatives or more made up of all stakeholders (farmers, scientists, agricultural experts, farmers organizations, consumer groups, citizen forums, NGOs, government officials, media, seed suppliers, traders, doctors, lawyers and others) invited to each consultation (Ramesh, 2010: 2). More than 8,000 participants attended the highly charged meetings, and oppositional voices dominated. Ramesh's consequent decision to implement a moratorium on Bt brinjal showcased both the strength of opposition networks and Ramesh's desire for maintaining transparency in India's GE risk management (Chowdhury and Srivastava, 2010).

Bt brinjal may be promoted in similar terms as Bt cotton (namely, that resistance to pests increases yields for farmers and that fewer applications of insecticides lessens environmental impacts) (Choudhary and Gaur, 2009), but the terms through which Bt brinjal is being successfully resisted are notably different. Oddly, the Bt cotton experience seems to have had little influence in shaping public reception to Bt brinjal. After the GEAC approved Bt brinjal for commercial release in 2009 risk narratives regarding the crop focused on human health risks and questions of consumer choice. For example, concern that the regulatory regime does not require adequate testing for health effects of consuming Bt brinjal over the long term (Pers. Comm., Dr. Chatterjee 04–20–2009). Calls soon arose for a more precautionary approach to regulation and release (Staff Reporter, 2010). As health risks continue to be brought forward, occasional overlaps with agronomic imperatives have been noted. In particular, since India is the country of origin for brinjal there is concern that crop biodiversity will be jeopardized if GE hybrids are widely grown (Lok Sabha Secretariat, Government of India, 2012: 155).

As part of this cautionary stance, interview participants Mr. Penna, an NGO representative and Dr. Chatterjee, scientist and commentator, articulated the importance of, and challenges to, protecting consumer choice by labeling GE foods. Both felt that labeling of Bt brinjal was highly impractical given that brinjal comes from myriad sources and remains largely unpackaged in market environments (Pers. Comm, Mr. Penna 04–30–2009 and Dr. Chatterjee 04–20–2009). However, others have suggested that labels are crucial to providing consumers with the information to make informed choices (see http://cseindia.org/content/bt-brinjal-why-we-should-not-make-a-mash-it). Indeed, the importance and unfeasibility of labeling has been a strategic point of critique employed by Greenpeace to halt the release of Bt brinjal (Shelton, 2010: 413). In 2012 the Ministry of Consumer Affairs, Food and Public Distribution announced that packaged foods containing genetically modified food would indeed be labeled as 'GM' (Nandi, 2012a). Remarkably, rather than celebrating the development, Greenpeace lamented that most of India's foods are unpackaged and therefore remain unlabeled. Given that Bt cotton is the only authorized GE crop being grown in India (and cottonseed oil is only occasionally used to fry foods), the initiative addresses imported foods that might contain GE ingredients such as Round Up Ready soy or Bt corn. This may be of interest to urban elites buying packaged foods but the majority of consumers will be both unaffected and oddly excluded from the move, begging the question: what other, more explicitly pro-poor or progressive agricultural development initiatives are passed over in favor of labeling?

Online organizing and documentary filmmaking (e.g. Bhardwaj, 2007) have become prominent modes of English language anti-GE campaigning in India. 'The Coalition for a GM Free India' formed in 2006 and serves as an umbrella for member groups from 15 states working on anti-GE and alternative agricultural development initiatives (Kurunganti and Ramjaneyulu, 2008). Their website, 'GM India Info' (http://indiagminfo.org/) along with others such as the 'I Am No Lab Rat' site (www.iamnolabrat.com/) serve as compendiums of oppositional research, news reports, and as public outreach tools. The Coalition appears to work primarily as a loose nexus for those organizations (from community development groups or organic farming initiatives, to larger anti-GE campaigners like Gene Campaign and Greenpeace). They inform allies of stakeholder consultations and draw on regional support as needed for campaigning through village councils and farmer's meetings, political rallies and local newspapers. The risks of Bt brinjal have also been dramatically conveyed through a film released in 2009 titled 'Poison on the Platter', likening the release of GE food crops to the nuclear attacks that ended World War II (Bhatt and Kanchan, 2009). Objects that enter the body are, as Douglas (1984) has shown, treated with a heightened regard and this quality of special risk – of bodily hazard – coupled with a framing of brinjal as an Indian crop with considerable heritage, have proven to be particularly potent.

Concurrently, advocacy regarding the anticipated benefits of Bt brinjal was muted and diffuse. The crop does not appear to rally farmers as a cohesive population of 'brinjal producers' as they tend to be among the most marginal farmers, growing many other kinds of vegetables, and negotiating a widely varying set of livelihood strategies. There is also less pressure upon state governments to advocate on behalf of this dispersed population than was sometimes the case for Bt cotton growers (Herring, 2007). The approval of Bt cotton was similarly halting until farmers jumpstarted authorization by first resorting to unregulated seed, and then subverting the government's attempt to withdraw the GE seed by backcrossing the stealth seeds with their own. Indeed, Bt brinjal is in the commercialization pipeline in neighboring countries such as Bangladesh and the Philippines, and Indian regulators are concerned that, as with cotton, similar informal seed dissemination may ultimately take place (Mohan, 2010).

### Agronomic crisis and revisiting the social justice narratives after GE commercialization

While direct activism regarding farmers' rights has largely waned since 2002, at various points concern for those Devinder Sharma has dubbed the so-called 'hapless farmers' (2004) was revisited after the commercialization of GE crops. Widespread suicide deaths of indebted marginal farmers across India captured national and international attention over these years, and some civil society groups sought to link GE technology and farmer tragedy (Shiva and Jalees, 2006). The ten-year anniversary of Bt cotton's release saw a particular effort to reinforce the association (Kuruganti, 2012; Nandi, 2012b). Academic reports demonstrate that Bt cotton is not the cause, nor even 'a necessary condition' for India's farmer suicides (Gruère and Sengupta, 2011: 333). A recent study looking at the commercialization period finds that farmer suicides decrease with increasing farm size and yield, but increase with the area under Bt cotton cultivation (Gutierrez et al., 2015: 11). Yet the farmer suicides signal a profound and complex agrarian crisis felt across a range of conditions and crops, prior to the use of GE seed. When a 2012 report from the Parliamentary Standing Committee on Agriculture drew explicit links between the suicides and Bt cotton failures (Lok Sabha Secretariat, Government of India, 2012: 151), the force of this risk narrative became clear, even as researchers have shown the highest numbers of suicide deaths to have taken place four years prior to the commercialization of the GE seed (Gruère and Sengupta, 2011; Stone, 2013: 70). Bt cotton farmers remain the poster children for rural economies with poor access to credit, cycles of indebtedness, and tremendous vulnerability in the face of erratic weather conditions and problems with pests. India's scientific community has defended the technology from such accusations of culpability (N.A, 2008), but the crisis, particularly in the region of Vidarbha, Maharashtra has caught the public imagination and media's attention (satirized in the 2010 film Peepli Live [Khan et al., 2010]) and ultimately highlights the widening gulf between rural and urban India.

## Contested science, elusive biosafety, and the conditions of transitioning risk

Anti-GE activism has seen consumer choice advocacy brush up against farmers' rights, as different risk narratives are jostled to best represent the aspirations of these groups within the country's agricultural development. Central to this is a remarkable clash between distinct 'social justices', highlighting the range of Indian publics, including farmers who would grow GE crops, and urban consumers encouraged to avoid them. There is a cutting irony in the current predominance of claims around the importance of choice for urban consumers, in that this stance would also actively deny the choice of marginal producers interested in access to GE seed.

India's anti-GE movement has come to share certain features with others around the world and exhibits characteristics anticipated by social theory. The most prominent of these involve articulations regarding the political nature of regulation, concern regarding scientific uncertainties about genetic engineering, contention about socio-political control of the technology, and the importance of trust in the negotiation of these concerns (Fukuda-Parr, 2007). As Beck (2009) also suggests, under circumstances where science is contested regarding the nature of a risk, the public's trust in risk managers becomes increasingly relied upon, and not surprisingly when trust is low 'the remaining options are precaution or avoidance' (Boholm, 2003). Thus, India's civil society has worked hard at encouraging a national precautionary stance by highlighting what they deem to be inadequate scientific assurance of the biosafety of GE crops. They have challenged the regulatory regime (through legal challenges and political campaigns) and have symbolically marked GE as affectively negative through the use of hyperbolic film and witty web campaigns aimed at India's urban consumers.

Our interviews also highlighted the importance of uncertainty in civil society risk narratives, typically stating that there is still much to learn about genetics and the science of recombinant DNA. Ms. Varman, who works with an NGO based in rural India, described the uncertainty surrounding the use of the Bt gene as follows:

> As a gene, it can't act alone, but will with other genes . . . [and] we don't know how the other genes are affecting that particular gene. It might make

a new disease, or an allergic response that is completely new. So, all these things have to be studied.

(Pers. Comm., 04–28–2009)

Dr. Chatterjee – as a scientist and commentator – on the other hand, was particularly concerned with a lack of long-term data yet available regarding the potential impacts of agricultural GE (Pers. Comm., 04–20–2009). In India as elsewhere (see Finucane and Holup, 2005), the rhetorical emphasis on uncertainty as a point of mobilization works at once to position scientists and regulators as hasty and illegitimately confident in their projects, while civil society members stand as sober purveyors of a safer science and more comprehensive regulatory requirements. It is not uncommon for NGOs in India to quite literally provide alternative scientific analyses of Bt cotton risks in technical reports (produced through citizen science or NGO supported research) used to lobby government or provide an alternative set of citable claims about the impacts of the technology (e.g. Qayum and Sakkhari, 2002). In doing so, civil society campaigns worked along lines anticipated by the risk society thesis. That is, we see at once an externalization of risk, whereby regulators are not trusted to gauge the threat of GE, and the process of individualization follows, as India's consumers are pressed with the responsibility of sorting out the GE debates.

Scientists and regulators cannot assure a risk-free biotechnology nor perhaps a system for ascertaining risk that would operate beyond reproach. If biosafety tests are conducted on goats ingesting Bt cotton stubble for two years, the question can easily become why not three years of testing? And why not conduct those tests on sheep as well? The criteria for establishing biosafety might be technically determined, but its credibility is politically hewn. So when the GEAC's expert panel authorized the release of Bt brinjal on the grounds that it was safe for Indian farmers and consumers (in scientific terms, according to national biosafety criteria) it was nevertheless ultimately found to be risky enough (in political terms) to warrant a moratorium.

Many farmers, however, have demonstrated a different risk calculus in facing the uncertainties presented by GE. There are of course a range of farmer perspectives and practices at work in India today, from the cultivation of desi varietals, to organics, to Bt crops. However, we suggest that farmers are generally positioned to be more 'experience-near' to many of the possible hazards presented by GE agriculture (e.g. reliance on new technology, unintended ecological effects, added expenses). As such, research suggests they are more likely to turn to coping strategies based on utility based maximization, and cost-benefit choices (Boholm, 2003). In this sense, farmers growing GE might well be productively considered a 'counterpublic' to the 'official public' of civil society speaking on behalf of the citizenry (Hess, 2011). As a counterpublic, farmers in Gujarat first organized along their community and political networks in order to advance the claim that regulated access to Bt cotton was in their interest. Moreover, as more farmers became familiar with Bt cotton and reports of its benefits began to circulate at the village level, the demand for this seed continued to increase. This point is in fact more complex, as evidence of faddism and deskilling have also been reported to be guiding farmers' seed choices around Bt cotton (Stone, 2007). Still, as the perception of the benefits of the seed increased, farmers' perceptions of the risks are expected to fall. And there have been years where the demand for Bt cotton has outstripped the country's capacity to supply GE cottonseed (Bhosale, 2011; N.A., 2011). The point is all the more pertinent in lesser income countries where the promise of extractible benefits may supersede concerns about risk and even trigger price escalations for seed due to high demand. Still, farmers – while a topic of much debate – infrequently contribute to the GE debate directly. More common is the fervent argument by others over questions of what would benefit farmers, spurring significant policy changes in India, including the protection of farmers' rights to freely exchange seed (through the PPVFR – which was also supported by farmer's associations) and the inclusion of economic viability data in regulatory biosafety criteria.

There are curious silences that become evident when contrasting India's case to affluent risk societies. Little attention, for example, has been afforded the question of how Bt cotton has affected pesticide use and exposure, particularly when pesticides and chemicals more broadly are key foci of risk contestation in Europe and the United States (e.g. Hirsch and Baxter, 2009). This calls for further consideration of the conditions under which societies undergoing a risk transition may become compelled to take up certain risky technologies over others, and what conditions might result in a push toward or away from GE crops. The irreversibility and uncontrollability of the technology were both important themes to emerge from our interviews, as was a pronounced skepticism of the trustworthiness of the biosafety regulatory system currently in place and the corporations involved. The contexts in which GE applications are employed are clearly important factors in how citizens assess risk, and Siegrist (2000: 195) has found that in fact people rarely 'reject biotechnology altogether'. Thus, medical biotechnologies are employed without remark, while Bt brinjal as a food crop (even if grown by disparate farmers under widely varying conditions) has garnered political traction in a way that even Bt cotton did not. On the other hand, Glover argues 'the idea of GM crop technology as an intrinsically pro-poor development success story has been sustained in academic, public and policy arenas . . .' (2012: 995), yielding another narrative that warrants critical investigation. We recognize that pro-GE narratives are as rich in meaning making and as steeped in contested claims-making as the anti-GE narratives considered here. Indeed, the significance of shifting risk narratives and targeted 'publics' is becoming clear, as GE debates rise and fall across the developing world.

## Conclusion

For decades now, India's civil society has been mobilizing around GE crops, no easy task in a country undergoing a risk transition where many publics contend with a spectrum of other hazards. Civil society has faced its own critics and become more reflexive; the most compelling of these critiques focus on the basis by which civil society continues to resist Bt cotton in the face of mounting evidence of its benefit to farmers (Stone, 2011). Certainly many Indian NGOs concerned with agricultural GE also actively encourage alternatives such as integrated pest management, organic cultivation, or localized seed banking practices. Such approaches might well focus less on targeting a particular tool for crop improvement (while condemning others), and could enrich their efforts by calling attention to the underlying and systemic problems in India's agricultural development (Stone, 2011). Civil society will also, however, continue to play an important role as monitors of an assertive industry (Kurmanath, 2011) and critics of a changing regulatory regime. The defense of both farmers' and consumers' rights remain essential.

This chapter reveals the vitality and transmutability of the risk transition, as the ongoing ebb and flow of anti-GE narratives traced in this chapter point to a civil society seeking its most propitious public. Initially, GE-opponents assumed more vulnerable citizens (e.g. farmers) were natural allies as has been the case for advocates of social welfare or equality more broadly. But instead, what risk debates in transitional states may do is reveal those who see themselves as still primarily concerned with traditional risks (too near to poverty, worried about basic living conditions or avoiding disease) and those who instead attend to late modern ones (GE for example). Specifically, employing the health-risk narrative and directing campaigns at urban consumers has lent civil society remarkable political traction, leading to a moratorium on Bt brinjal. This strategic success has its costs, however, and we question the extent to which India's much larger and myriad publics are effectively considered and included in this discussion. Most importantly, we remain concerned that India's marginal farmers may at once be those most impacted by shifting risk narratives and excluded from genuine participation in India's ongoing GE debates.

# References

Aerni, P. (2002) 'Stakeholder attitudes toward the risks and benefits of agricultural biotechnology in developing countries: A comparison between Mexico and the Philippines', *Risk Analysis*, 22(6): 1123–37.

Aruna Rodrigues & Ors vs Union of India & Ors, Supreme Court of India (2012) Author: S. Kumar Bench: S.H. Kapadia, A.K. Patnaik, Swatanter Kumar. Available at: http://indiankanoon.org/doc/17826198/?type=print

Beck, Ulrich (1992) *Risk society: Towards a new modernity* (M. Ritter, Trans.). London and Thousand Oaks: Sage.

——— (1995) *Ecological politics in an age of risk*. Cambridge: Polity Press.

——— (2006) 'Living in the world risk society', *Economy and Society*, 35(3): 329–45.

——— (2009) *World at risk*. Cambridge: Polity Press.

Bennett, R., Y. Ismael, U. Kambhampati and S. Morse (2005) 'Economic impact of genetically modified cotton in India', *AgBioForum*, 7(3): 96–100

Bhardwaj, Ajay (Producer & Director). (2007) *So Shall You Reap* [Motion Picture]. India: Mainstay Productions.

Bhatt, Mahesh (Producer) and Kanchan, Ajay (2009) 'Poison on the Platter' [Motion Picture], India: A CAC Production.

Bhosale, Jayashree (2011) 'Bt cotton seed shortage to shrink kharif acreage', *The Economic Times*, February 11. http://articles.economictimes.indiatimes.com/2011–02-11/news/28540448_1_bt-cotton-seeds-mahyco-monsanto-biotech-seedshortage (accessed 3 July 2012).

Boholm, Åsa (2003) 'The cultural nature of risk: Can there be an anthropology of uncertainty?', *Ethnos*, 68(2): 159–78.

Brahmi, P., S. Saxena, and B.S. Dhillon (2004) 'The protection of plant varieties and farmers' rights Act of India', *Current Science*, 86(3): 392–8.

Choudhary, B. and K. Gaur (2009) *Brief 38 the development and regulation of Bt Brinjal in India (Eggplant/Aubergine)*. Ithaca, NY: ISAAA, 1–102.

Chowdhury, N. and N. Srivastava (2010) 'Decision on Bt-Brinjal: Legal Issues', *Economic & Political Weekly*, 45(15): 18–22.

Curtis, Kynda R., Jill J. McCluskey, and Thomas I. Wahl (2004) 'Consumer acceptance of genetically modified food products in the developing world', AgBioForum, 7 (1&2): 70-75.

Davidson, S.N. (2008) 'Forbidden fruit: Transgenic papaya in Thailand', *Plant Physiology*, 147(2): 487–93.

Douglas, M. ([1966] 1984) *Purity and danger: An analysis of the concepts of pollution and taboo*. London: Ark.

Finucane, M.L. and J.L. Holup (2005) 'Psychosocial and cultural factors affecting the perceived risk of genetically modified food: An overview of the literature', *Social Science & Medicine*, 60(7): 1603–12.

Freeman, J., T. Satterfield, and M. Kandlikar (2011) 'Agricultural biotechnology and regulatory innovation in India', *Science and Public Policy*, 38(4): 319–31.

Freeman, Julia (2012) 'How do "imagined farmers" negotiate actual risks? Biosafety trade-offs in Bt cotton production in Andhra Pradesh, India', *Journal of Political Ecology*, 19(8–13): 162–73.

Fukuda-Parr, Saikiko (2007) 'Introduction: Genetically modified crops and national development priorities', in S. Fukuda-Parr (ed.), pp. 3–12, *The gene revolution: GM crops and unequal development*. London, UK: Earthscan.

Glover, Dominic (2010) 'Is Bt cotton a pro-poor technology? A review and critique of the empirical record', *Journal of Agrarian Change*, 10(4): 482–509.

——— (2012) 'Exploring the resilience of Bt cotton's pro-poor success story', *Development and Change*, 41(6): 955–81.

GRAIN (2007) 'Bt Cotton: The Facts behind the Hype', www.grain.org/article/entries/582-bt-cotton-the-facts-behind-thehype (accessed 15 September 2010).

Greenpeace India (2005) 'Marketing of Bt Cotton in India: Aggressive, Unscrupulous and False', 1–6. www.greenpeace.org/india/Global/india/report/2005/9/marketing-ofbt-cotton-in-indi.pdf (accessed 23 August 2012).

Gruère, G. and D. Sengupta (2011) 'Bt cotton and farmer suicides in India: An evidence-based assessment', *The Journal of Development Studies*, 47(2): 316–37.

Gupta, A. (2000) Governing biosafety in India: The relevance of the Cartagena Protocol. Belfer Center for Science and International Affairs, John F. Kennedy School of Government, Harvard University.

Gupta, A., A. Mandloi, and A. Nidhi (2005) 'Impact of Bt Cotton on Farmers' Health (in Barwani and Dhar District of Madhya Pradesh)'. Investigation Report in two parts. Part One www.lobbywatch.org/archive2.asp?arcid=6265 (accessed 16 September 2012);

Part Two www.lobbywatch.org/archive2.asp?arcid=6266 (accessed 16 September 2012).

Gutierrez, A.P., L. Ponti, H.R. Herren, J. Baumgartner, and P.E. Kenmore (2015) 'Deconstructing Indian cotton: Weather, yields and suicides', *Environmental Sciences Europe*, 27: 12.

Henwood, K., N. Pidgeon, K. Parkhill, and P. Simmons (2010) 'Researching Risk: Narrative, Biography, Subjectivity', Forum Qualitative Sozialforschung/Forum: Qualitative Social Research. www.qualitative-research.net/index.php/fqs/article/viewArticle/1438 (accessed 1 June 2012).

Herdt, R.W. (2006) 'Biotechnology in agriculture', *Annual Review of Environmental Resources*, 31: 265–95.

Herring, Ronald J. (2005) 'Miracle seeds, suicide seeds, and the poor', in R. Ray and M.K. Kazenstein (eds.), pp. 203–230, *Social movements in India: Poverty, power, and politics*. Oxford: Rowman and Littlefield.

——— (2007) 'Stealth seeds: Bioproperty, biosafety, biopolitics', *Journal of Development Studies*, 43(1): 130–57.

——— (2008) 'Opposition to transgenic technologies: Ideology, interests and collective action frames', *Nature Reviews Genetics*, 9(6): 458–63.

——— (2009) 'Persistent narratives: Why is the "failure of Bt cotton in India" story still with us?', *AgBioForum*, 12(1): 14–22.

Hess, D.J. (2011) 'To tell the truth: On scientific counterpublics', *Public Understanding of Science*, 20(5): 627–41.

Hirsch, R. and J. Baxter (2009) 'The look of the lawn: Pesticide policy preference and health-risk perception in context', *Environment and Planning C: Government & Policy*, 27(3): 468–90.

ISAAA, International Service for the Acquisition of Agri-Biotech Applications (2011) 'Brief 43-2011: Executive Summary–Global Status of Commercialized Biotech/GM Crops: 2011', www.isaaa.org/resources/publications/briefs/43/executivesummary/default.asp (accessed 15 May 2012).

——— (N.d.) 'Pocket K no. 35: Bt Brinjal in India', www.isaaa.org/resources/publications/pocketk/35/default.asp (accessed 30 November 2010).

James, Clive (2010) 'Global status of commercialized biotech/GM crops: 2010', *ISAAA Brief*, 42, 1–279.

Jansen, K. and A. Gupta (2009) 'Anticipating the future: "Biotechnology for the poor" as unrealized promise?,' *Futures*, 41(7): 436–45.

Jebarai, Priscilla (2010) 'Bt cotton ineffective against pest in parts of Gujarat, admits Monsanto', *The Hindu*, 6 March. www.thehindu.com/news/national/article183353.ece (accessed 10 June 2010).

Jewitt, S. and K. Baker (2011) 'Risk, wealth and agrarian change in India: Household-level hazards vs. late-modern global risks at different points along the risk transition', *Global Environmental Change*, 22(2): 547–557.

Khan, A., K. Rao (Producers), and A. Rizvi (Director) (2010) Peepli Live [Motion Picture]. India: Aamir Khan Productions.

Klümper, W. and M. Qaim (2014) 'A meta-analysis of the impacts of genetically modified crops', *PLoS One*, November 3, 9(11). doi:10.1371/journal.pone.0111629.

Kurmanath, K.V. (2011) 'Genetic engineering panel objects to Mahyco's weed trials in non-Bt cotton', *The Hindu Business Line*, February 9. www.thehindubusinessline.com/industry-and-economy/agri-biz/article1200450.ece (accessed 15 March 2011).

Kurunganti, Kavitha (2012) '10 Years of Bt Cotton–False Hype and Failed Promises Exposed', IndiaGMInfo. March 21. http://indiagminfo.org/?p=393 (accessed 23 March 2012).

Kuruganti, Kavitha and G.V. Ramanjaneyulu (2008) *Genetic engineering in Indian agriculture: An introductory handbook.* Secunderabad: Centre for Sustainable Agriculture.

Legal Correspondent (2008) 'PIL: Prohibit release of harmful GM seeds', *The Hindu*, 13 August. www.ddsindia.com/www/dds_news/The%20Hindu%20%20National%20%20PIL%20prohibit%20release%20of%20harmful%20GM%20seeds.htm (accessed 21 August 2009).

Lok Sabha Secretariat, Government of India (2012) 'Cultivation of Genetically Modified Food Crops – Prospects and Effects', Committee on Agriculture: 37th Report. August 9. New Delhi.

Lupton, Deborah (1999) *Risk.* London: Routledge.

Mohan, B. Krishna (2010) 'Bt brinjal from Bangladesh, Philippines might find its way to India', *Business Standard*, 12 February. www.business-standard.com/india/news/bt-brinjalbangladesh-philippines-might-find-its-way-to-india/12/42/385460/ (accessed 2 March 2010).

N.A., No Author (2008) 'Pro-GM scientists contest linking farmers' suicide to Bt cotton', The *Economic Times*, 28 March. http://articles.economictimes.indiatimes.com/2012–03–28/news/31249683_1_bt-cotton-moratorium-on-bt-brinjal-anti-gm (accessed 2 April 2012).

———— (2011) 'Shortage of Bt cotton seeds may hit 2011–12 production: ABLE', *Business Standard*, 15 February. http://business-standard.com/india/news/shortagebt-cotton-seeds-may-hit-2011–12-production-able/125831/on (accessed 3 July 2012).

Nandi, J. (2012a) '"GM" label on packaged food soon.' *Times of India*, 18 June, http://articles.timesofindia.indiatimes.com/2012–06–18/delhi/32297996_1_gm-food-bt-brinjal-food-debate (accessed 3 July 2012).

———— 2012b. 'The Bt show at 10', *Times of India*, 1 April, http://articles.timesofindia.indiatimes.com/2012–04–01/special-report/31269811_1_bt-cotton-bt-technology-bt-crop (accessed 2 April 2012).

Nicolia, A., A. Manzo, F. Veronesi, and D. Rosellini (2014) 'An overview of the last 10 years of genetically engineered crop safety research', *Critical Review of Biotechnology*, 34 (1): 77–88.

Pray, C.E., Huang, J., Hu, R., Rozelle, S. (2002) 'Five years of Bt cotton in China–the benefits continue', The *Plant Journal*, 31(4): 423–30.

Pray, C.E., P. Bengali, and B. Ramaswami (2005) 'The cost of biosafety regulations: The Indian experience', *Quarterly Journal of International Agriculture*, 44(3): 267–90.

Qayum, A. and K. Sakkhari (2002) 'Did Bt cotton save farmers in Warangal: A season long impact study of Bt cotton Kharif 2002 in Warangal District of Andhra Pradesh'. Hyderabad: Andhra Pradesh Coalition in Defence of Diversity and the Deccan Development Society: 26–54.

———— (2005) 'Bt cotton in Andhra Pradesh, A Three-year assessment: The first ever sustained independent scientific study on Bt cotton in India'. Hyderabad: Andhra Pradesh Coalition in Defence of Diversity, the Deccan Development Society, and the Permaculture Association of India.

Ramanjaneyulu, G.V. and K. Kuruganti (2006) 'Bt cotton in India: Sustainable pest management?', *Economic and Political Weekly*, sec. 41(7): 561.

Ramaswami, B. and C.E. Pray (2007) 'India: Confronting the challenge–the potential of genetically modified crops for the poor', in S. Fukuda-Parr (ed.), pp. 156–74, *The gene revolution: GM crops and unequal development.* London, UK: Earthscan.

Ramesh, Jairam (2010) 'Ministry on environment and forests decision on commercialization of Bt cotton', *The Hindu*, 9 February. www.thehindu.com/news/national/article 103839.ece (accessed 16 September 2010).

RFSTE (2002) 'Failure of Bt cotton in India', 26 September, www.biotech-info.net/bt_failure. html (accessed 24 March 2010).

Sadeque, Najma (2008) 'After a disastrous track record in 40 countries, Bt cotton is "welcomed" in Pakistan', *Financial Post*, 5 December. www.dailyfpost.com/archives/btcotton. htm (accessed 16 September 2010).

Sahai, S. and S. Rahman (2003) 'Performance of Bt cotton: Data from first commercial crop', *Economic and Political Weekly*, 38(30): 3139–41.

Sahai, Suman (2002) 'Bt cotton: Confusion prevails', *Economic and Political Weekly*, 35(21): 1973–74.

—————— (2005) 'The science of Bt cotton failure in India', *The Hindu*, 29 August. www. hindu.com/2005/08/29/stories/2005082906321100.htm (accessed 3 February 2011).

Satheesh, P.V. (2003) 'Finally I have seen Bt cotton', Seedling, GRAIN: January. www. grain.org/article/entries/353-finally-i-have-seen-bt-cotton (accessed 10 August 2010).

Scoones, Ian (2005) IDS Working paper 256 – Contentious politics, contentious knowledges: Mobilising against GM crops in India, South Africa and Brazil. Brighton, Sussex: Institute of Development Studies.

—————— (2006) *Science, agriculture and the politics of policy: The case of biotechnology in India.* Hyderabad: Orient Blackswan.

Seshia, S. (2002) 'Plant variety protection and farmers' rights: Law-making and cultivation of varietal control', *Economic and Political Weekly*, 37 (27): 2741–7.

Shah, E. (2008) 'What makes crop biotechnology find its roots? The technological culture of Bt cotton in Gujarat, India', *The European Journal of Development Research*, 20(3), 432–47.

—————— (2011) '"Science' in the Risk Politics of Bt Brinjal." Economic & Political Weekly. 46(31):31–37. www.epw.in/perspectives/science-risk-politics-bt-brinjal.html (accessed 3 July 2012).

Sharma, Ashok (2009) 'Supreme court vacates ban order on GM crop trials', *Financial Express*, 18 February. www.financialexpress.com/news/supreme-court-vacates-ban-order-on-gm-crops-trials/272520/ (accessed 20 January 2010).

Sharma, Devinder (2004) GM *food and hunger: A view from the South.* New Delhi: Forum for Biotechnology and Food Security.

Shelton, A.M. (2010) 'The long road to commercialization of Bt brinjal (eggplant) in India', *Crop Protection*, 29(5): 412–14.

Shiva, V., A. Emani, and A.H. Jafri (1999) 'Globalisation and threat to seed security: Case of transgenic cotton trials in India', *Economic and Political Weekly*, 34(10/11): 601–13.

Shiva, V. (1998) 'Monsanto, quit India', Campaign Letter, 12 November. http://caravan. squat.net/ICC-en/Krrs-en/Monquitin-en.htm#shiva (accessed 10 August 2010).

—————— (2012) 'The seed emergency', *Deccan Chronicle*, 13 January. www.deccanchronicle. com/columnists/vandana-shiva/seed-emergency (accessed 16 May 2012).

Shiva, V. and A.H. Jafri (2002) 'Seeds of suicide: The ecological and human costs of globalization of agriculture', in V. Shiva and G. Bedi (eds.), *Sustainable agriculture and food security*, pp. 169–184. New Delhi: Sage Publications India.

Shiva, V. and K. Jalees (2006) *Seeds of suicide: The ecological and human costs of seed monopolies and globalisation of agriculture.* New Delhi: Navdanya.

Siegrist, M. (2000) 'The influence of trust and perceptions of risks and benefits on the acceptance of gene technology', *Risk Analysis*, 20(2): 195–204.

Smith, K. (2001) 'The risk transition in developing countries', in J. Kasperson and R. Kasperson (eds.), *Global environmental risk*, pp. 148–172. Tokyo, Japan: United Nations University Press.

Smith, K.R. and M. Ezzati (2005) 'How environmental health risks change with development: The epidemiologic and environmental risk transitions revisited', *Annual Review of Environmental Resources*, 30: 291–333.

Special Correspondent (2003) 'Bt cotton farmers suffered losses, says Greenpeace', *The Hindu*, 17 April. www.hindu.com/2003/04/17/stories/2003041703430400.htm (accessed 16 September 2010).

Staff Reporter (2010) 'Without modification: A setback for GM in India', *The Economist*, 11 February. www.economist.com/node/15498385 (accessed 2 July 2012).

Stone, G.D. (2007) 'Agricultural deskilling and the spread of genetically modified cotton in Warangal', *Current Anthropology*, 48(1): 67–103.

——— (2011) 'Field versus farm in Warangal: Bt cotton, higher yields, and large questions', *World Development*, 39(3): 387–98.

——— (2013) 'A response to Herring and Rao', *Economic and Political Weekly*, August 17, 48(33): 70–2.

Venkatesan, J. (2006) 'A.P. files contempt petition before MRTPC against Monsanto', *The Hindu*, 27 June. www.hindu.com/2006/06/27/stories/2006062704310700.htm (accesssed 13 September 2010).

Visvanathan, S. and C. Parmar (2002) 'A biotechnology story: Notes from India', *Economic and Political Weekly*, 37(27): 2714–24.

Wilkinson, I. (2001) 'Social theories of risk perception: At once indispensable and insufficient', *Current Sociology*, 49(1): 1.

# Part III
# Internal dynamics

# 8 Contesting development

## Pastoralism, mining and environmental politics in Mongolia

*Caroline Upton*

## Introduction

In 2007, Tsetsegee Munkhbayar, a young Mongolian herder turned environmental activist, was awarded the prestigious and financially lucrative international Goldman Environmental Prize.[1] The Goldman website lauds its award recipients as nothing less than 'grassroots environmental heroes . . . [engaged in] sustained and significant efforts to protect and enhance the natural environment, often at great personal risk'. Munkhbayer's 'Green Nobel' was conferred for his work in resistance to mining-induced environmental degradation, promotion of citizen engagement and facilitation of state accountability, initially through the Onggi River Movement (ORM) and subsequently through the Mongolian Nature Protection Coalition (MNPC).

Six years later in September 2013, in what may appear a sharp reversal of fortune, Munkhbayer and colleagues were arrested outside Mongolia's parliament and branded 'terrorists', while protesting against the government's planned amendment of a key mining-related environmental law.[2] Munkhbayer and three fellow activists were subsequently each sentenced to some 21 years in prison.

At the time of writing these jail sentences had recently been reduced by an appeals court in Ulaanbaatar, following protests by the activists' families, civil society organisations, and international bodies such as Rivers Without Boundaries. The activists' own umbrella organisation, the United Movement of Mongolian Rivers and Lakes (UMMRL) also contested the initial sentences, not only on human rights grounds, but through explicit reference to 'land, water and terrestrial riches' as 'the riches of the people', and to traditional nomadic stewardship and culture (UMMRL 2014). In doing so they suggested a counterpoint to the mainstream industrial development visions typically associated with extractive economies, both in the specific case of Mongolia and beyond.

The aforementioned high-profile 'moments of contention' bring into view some key parameters of this ongoing struggle in Mongolia. What remains largely invisible, however, are explicit engagements with processes and temporality in the formation and dissolution of alliances amongst activists. Similarly obscured are the agency of non-human actors and their role in shaping trajectories of activism and possible futures (Dittmer 2014). Finally, the importance of the individual as a site of resistance, linked to contested concepts of environmental citizenship, demands attention (Mason 2014). This chapter seeks to address aspects of these lacunae. Specifically, it draws on contemporary geographical debates, with particular reference to 'mainstream' social movement theory and to notions of assemblage, commons and temporality, to interrogate grassroots activism in this case, wherein the issues at stake have direct resonance for multiple, comparable encounters between grassroots communities and industrial development worldwide. It argues that dynamism, impermance, individual performances of environmental citizenship and the agency of the 'more-than-human' taken together provide new and productive insights into the micropolitics of environmental activism.

## Geographies of protest and resistance

### Emergence: political opportunity structures

Social movement scholarship has long debated the role of political opportunity structures (POS) in shaping grassroots activism (Leach and Scoones 2007). POS-based analyses typically identify points of weakness, openings and resources of a political system as integral both to the emergence of resistance and its character, thus placing POS as key independent variables, premised on the rational responses of actors to new opportunities (Vrablikova 2014). However, recent widespread critiques of inherently structuralist, POS-based analyses point to contradictory indications over relationships between state structures and the emergence of activism; the marginalisation of ideology, culture and identity; and the neglect of local agency and motivations therein (Voss and Williams 2009).

### Enacting resistance: political process theory

Framing processes have assumed increasing importance in attempts to theorise activism. They also constitute explicit recognition of the agency of activists, within the wider approach of political process theory (PPT) (Rutland 2013). Attention to framing, the strategic creation/ emphasis of shared norms and understandings, thus re-orientates the predominantly structural explanations of POS-based scholarship towards temporalities, cultural factors and specificities, while acknowledging the agency of non-state actors (Rutland 2013). Nonetheless, greater attention to the processes through which common identities are shaped and enacted remains a priority (Leach and Scoones 2007). Emergent aspects of geographical scholarship around assemblage, commons and activist identities, enable just such new and challenging insights into the constantly renegotiated dynamics of grassroots mobilisations and engagements with industrial development.

### Assemblage, commons, and the environmental citizen

#### Assemblage

Assemblages, described as 'the coming together of various entities into a loose aggregate', and as provisional, 'heterogenous mixture(s) of constituent parts' (Davies

2012, 274; Dittmer 2014, 387), are characterised by impermanence, dynamism and 'relations of exteriority', by which components may simultaneously be part of and shaped, but not defined by, multiple assemblages (Anderson *et al.* 2012).[3] In the context of social movements, assemblage thinking challenges emphasis on nested scales, to stress relationality between components and the ways in which actors may simultaneously negotiate multiple spatialities (Davies 2012, 2013).

Furthermore, assemblages explicitly encompass both human and non-human actors. Blaser (2014, 49) highlights how attention to these 'always-emergent (heterogenous) assemblage(s) of humans and non-humans' unsettles understandings of agency and power relations and questions what a politics would look like that took the agency of the non-human seriously. Gibbs (2013) provides a partial answer. In tracing how land, people, climate, animals, and water in Australia co-constitute an assemblage, she emphasises both the agency of assemblages and the utility of assemblage thinking in reframing environmental policy.

One final, related point in this decentring of humans is the attendant unpredictability of outcomes. The inherent dynamism of assemblages, combined with the distribution of agency across human and non-human actors means that, to a greater extent than previously admitted, 'a range of contingent futures is always possible' Dittmer (2014, 388). Such perspectives call into question more structuralist approaches to social movements, whilst simultaneously emphasising the importance of temporality in considering and assessing activism and its 'lines of flight'; or the ways in which particular activist assemblages break down or are transformed (after Deleuze and Guattari (1987), cited in Dittmer 2014).

*Commons*

Contemporary thinking on commons has moved far beyond the land-based commons at the core of Hardin's 'tragedy' and Ostrom and others' subsequent critique/ refutation. Recent work on indigenous rights and community economies emphasises how communal rights may not only underpin systems of managing land, but also point to diverse forms of social organisation, ontologies, beliefs and values systems, often in conjunction with post/ non-capitalist politics and as focus for grassroots resistance.

Notions of commons and shared heritage may also extend to subsoil resources, and similarly reflect diverse ontologies which position extractive economies in particular ways and may give rise to mining-related activism, as emphasised in Bebbington's (2012) 'political ecologies of the subsoil'.

Commons thinking in its multiple senses has particular resonance in the Mongolian case, and in the current mobilisation around the extractive economy, as explored next, following a brief commentary on the third pertinent strand of contemporary thinking: environmental citizenship.

*(Becoming) the environmental citizen*

Recent work on the activist subject offers new directions in social movement scholarship through emphasis on the individual as well as the movement and it's wider (transnational) networks (Rutland 2013). Concepts of environmental citizenship emphasise how citizens are continuously (re)made, with differing enactments of citizenship (e.g. through activism and protest), underpinned by diverse, culturally specific and *personal* understandings of citizenship's nature, meanings and responsibilities (Hobson 2013; Mason 2014).

In summary, through a case study of contemporary mobilisations around mining-related activism in Mongolia, this chapter makes the argument that:

- Attention to assemblages provides productive insights into the emergence, and trajectories of grassroots social movements, building on but moving beyond structuralist POS and PPT approaches. Through assemblage-based emphasis on formation rather than form, 'thicker' accounts' of social movements and everyday politics are enabled, in the Mongolian case through highlighting how particular conjunctures of people, laws, events, knowledges, values produce *specific* actions at *specific* moments. Furthermore, recognition of spatialities as actively produced by and within the assemblage and extending from local pastures and commons, through to translocal linkages, emphasises both agency and temporality in grassroots resistance.
- Admission of the agency of non-human entities within assemblage thinking is important in explaining the nature and cultural specificities of activism. In Mongolia, cultural beliefs and values around land and nature have given rise to a form of cosmopolitics, linked to clear incentives for grassroots mobilisation (Sneath 2014). Beyond this, non-human entities continue to epitomise the concept of distributed agency, through shaping the form and practices of mobilisation. In the Mongolian example, 'performative and ritualised moments of commonality', integral to the repertoires of local grassroots movements, draw heavily on Buddhist and Shamanic heritages to garner and maintain support, whilst concepts of 'appropriate' relations with the non-human shape notions of responsibility for individual environmental citizens.
- Further emphasis on the individual environmental citizen/activist is a key aspect of analysis of social movement dynamics and trajectories. The making of environmental citizens emerges as one overarching and consistent goal of Mongolia's grassroots movements, within a wider context of fragmentation, dynamism, and impermanence. Diverse meanings and understandings of environmental citizenship also help to explain the different trajectories of Mongolia's River Movements (RMs) and their leaders.

These propositions are explored in what follows through first setting out some key aspects of the Mongolian context and mining-related assemblage. The chapter then proceeds to examine current activism around mining, through attention to POS/ PPT and assemblage-based accounts. The latter empirical sections draw on the author's primary data; specifically key informant interviews with RM leaders in Ulaanbaatar and with herder members and activists at sites in Omnogov *aimag* (province) in 2008; follow-up interviews with key informants from the Mongolian Nature Protection Civil Movement Coalition (MNPCM) in Ulaanbaatar in 2011 and 2013; and interviews with five key informants from MNPCM and UMMRL in 2014, to provide further critical insights. These latter sections also draw on media reports and the aforementioned organisations' published statements.

## Mongolian context: mapping out the assemblage

### History/context

Mongolia emerged from some 70 years of state socialism in the early 1990s. In the latter part of this Soviet period Mongolia's rural, herding population were compelled to become members of Soviet-inspired collectives (*negdel*). As waged employees, they tended state-owned, livestock herds on extensive state-owned pasturelands. However, despite discourses of Soviet-era modernity, elements of traditional land use and mobility were retained (Upton 2012). Historical analyses suggest little overt conflict or endogenous activism over land amongst Mongolian herders in Soviet and pre-soviet eras (Bawden 1968).

In post-decollectivisation Mongolia, mobile pastoralism remains a key livelihood strategy for over 30% of the population. International donor interventions have increasingly shaped practices and visions of national futures, not least in relation to land and the place of 'traditional' nomadic pastoralism therein. For example, negative discourses on nomadism and commons, often expressed in terms of the need for 'rational', productive use of land, were evident in the immediate aftermath of decollectivisation (Sneath 2001). An incipient 'Tragedy' was also posited in the 1990s in the context of an apparent breakdown of customary institutions, characterised by land-related conflicts. However, where present these conflicts were local, usually transitory events. The emergence of more overt, grassroots activism around pastureland in Mongolia has occurred much more recently, and primarily in the context of mining-related land alienation.

### Mining

Mapping of extensive copper, gold and fluorspar reserves, in conjunction with a favourable legislative framework for foreign investors (under the 1997 Minerals Law), prompted significant expansion of mining activities, with Mongolia recently branded 'a new mineral investment frontier' (MNMA 2007). Key companies include the British/Australian multinational giant Rio Tinto, leaders in the development of the major Oyu Tolgoi mine.

By 2006 Mongolia's minerals sector accounted for 17% GDP and 58% of export earnings, rising to 30% and more than 80% respectively by 2012 (World Bank 2006). Issues of alleged curtailment of herders' land rights, through mining-induced land degradation or physical exclusion from customary grazing areas, have emerged in conjunction with this booming minerals economy, as have wider concerns with 'resource nationalism'. The latter has become an urgent topic of debate, linked to government changes in foreign investment/ mining laws, associated economic uncertainty and protests both from mining companies and local constituents.

Mongolia also has a burgeoning informal mining sector. Recent estimates suggest some 100,000 people, including herders, participate in this activity (widely known as 'ninja' mining) (Byambajav 2014).

Thus, both informal miners and formal mining companies are key actors in contemporary assemblages, as are state policies/ policy-makers, international donors and local herders. Other key human components of the assemblage, namely the grassroots resistance movements, such as Munkhbayar's Onggi River Movement (ORM), their entanglements with mining companies, the state and international supporters are explored in further detail in the next section. First, however, it is necessary to consider the non- or more-than-human aspects of the mining assemblage.

### Land, nature and the more-than-human

A key strand of contemporary mining-related struggles in Mongolia is the concept of the land as commons and shared heritage. Mining resistance is further complicated by cultural concepts surrounding land and gold. High (2013, 754) emphasises that 'elected politicians are only some of the agents that appear on the political scene. . . . with politics not necessarily delimited to the human realm'. Central to re-emergent shamanic/ Buddhist beliefs and cultural norms around nature and environment (*baigal*) is the idea that landscapes are inhabited by spiritual entities (*gazaryn ezed*, 'lords of the land'), necessitating respectful, reciprocal relations with nature (Sneath, 2014, 461). *Baigal* does not, therefore, translate in the same way as Eurocentric understandings of nature and environment. Rather, it also includes 'animals, mountains, trees, grass, weather. . . . (etc.) . . . as active subjects which have their own ways of being that affect human beings, just as humans have ways of life that affect them' (Humphrey and Sneath 1999, 3, cited in Empson 2011, 87). In other words, they comprise a kind of 'sacred geography', wherein establishment of resource rights require favourable relations with local spiritual entities. (Empson 2011, 236).

Mining troubles these beliefs in a range of ways. 'Appropriate', respectful relations with nature have typically included prohibitions on disturbing or digging of the soil. A lama quoted in High (2013, 758) argued 'Mining is like having a thorn pressed into your hand. That's how much nature and the land hurt'. Non-human agency in this context may thus admit of gold, land and diverse spiritual entities. Evidence of the perceived agency of spiritual entities is apparent in the reported proliferation of demands on Buddhist lamas by miners and mining companies to enact rituals to appease these spirits. Sources cited in High (2013) suggest that as many as 80% of Ulaanbaatar-based mining companies commission these kinds of rituals.

Understanding of grassroots activism thus demands attention to an assemblage encompassing Mongolia's 'spiritually lively, animate environment', as well as to the shaman and Buddhist lamas, who effectively function as spiritual intermediaries (Cassidy 2012, 21).

## Emergence of resistance and POS-based accounts

The appearance of ORM in 2001 is arguably the first significant manifestation of grassroots mining resistance in modern Mongolia. Munkhbayar, the chair of the *sum* (district) council and a local herder, was integral to initiation of collective action (Beck *et al.* 2007). By 2006 ORM was one of 11 similar organisations, who together formed the Homeland and Water Protection Coalition of River Movements or the Mongolian Nature Protection Coalition (MNPC). The formation of the MNPC highlights futher expansion of concern beyond the restoration of local river basins to greater emphasis on issues of (pastureland) governance and citizens' rights, within the context of mining, including through more concerted attempts at political engagement. In 2008 the MNPC split, following alleged threats of violence against mining companies' property by a small number of movement members. These latter movements subsequently formed a new umbrella organisation, the United Movement of Mongolian Rivers and Lakes (UMMRL), with subsidiary groups such as Munkhbayar's 'Fire Nation' (*Gal Undestan*), being key actors in the September 2013 protests. Other former members went on to create the Mongolian Nature Protection Civil Movement Coalition (MNPCM), which espoused less overtly oppositional politics. Diverse tactics and 'lines of flight' are considered further next (see Assemblage/ Commons/ Environmental Citizenship).

A POS-based analysis suggests the periodic emergence and contraction of new opportunities for political influence which do not necessarily coincide with the emergence of ORM and subsequent movements. The 1992 Constitution established Mongolia as a multi-party democracy, with a reportedly 'rather liberal' legal context (Beck *et al.* 2007; CIVICUS 2005, 9). Nonetheless, recent critiques highlight high levels of corruption and the periodic predominance of single parties, especially the Mongolian Peoples Revolutionary Party (MPRP) in the political sphere; thus tending to close down political space and prospects for genuine democratic opposition (CIVICUS 2005; Transparency International 2013). In particular, the period 2000–2004, which coincided with the emergence of the ORM and a number of other River Movements (RMs), is highlighted as one of diminishing opportunity for widen citizen engagement and democracy, linked to the landslide victory of the MPRP in the 2000 elections (CIVICUS 2005; Mearns 2004; *pers. comm.*, River Movement members, 2008).

Events post 2004, marked by the founding of a number of further RMs and the formation of the Mongolian Nature Protection Coalition (MNPC) in 2006, fit more closely with POS-based analyses: political instability occasioned by the MPRP's loss of a clear majority in 2004 and subsequent resignation of the coalition government (2006) allegedly created space for citizens to voice their discontent, not only though the RMs, but in wider demands for state accountability and transparency (CIVICUS 2005; *pers. comm.* 2008). Subsequent proliferation of grassroots activists groups and networks following the MNPC split in 2008 could also be read in this way, although personal accounts of Movement activists as explored in the next section, reflect a far wider set of drivers, political/legal contexts and motivations. The state of emergency declared following post-election riots in July 2008 and widespread arrests of those protesting about foreign influence in the mining sector, also argue against such simplistic interpretations.

Thus, POS-based analyses retain some explanatory power, but are insufficient in isolation to explain the emergence or subsequent shapes of protest. Recent events suggest fragmentation in forms of protest and emergence of diverse groups and forms of activism with apparently little accompanying change in endogenous POS. These can be explained and theorised rather differently, both through PPT and especially assemblage framings.

## Performing resistance: networks, framings and PPT

One advance of PPT over POS theory is PPT's emphasis on social networks in facilitating the emergence and maintenance of resistance (Rutland 2013). For Mongolia's RMs, 'local homeland councils' (*nutagyn zovlol*) are important examples. These have become foci for expression of identity, fundraising and political lobbying (Sneath 2010). Typically situated in the capital, Ulaanbaatar, they seek to support their home *aimags* (regions) politically, financially and socially (Sneath 2010). Certain nascent RMs have been able to exploit these networks. As one RM leader explained 'When I went to visit . . . *aimag* for a relative's funeral, local people complained to me about mining activities. . . . As a member of an *aimag* support group in Ulaanbaatar, I went back and explained the situation. . . . (later) members of the Ulaanbatar-based group went back to the local area and held a meeting. . . . that's when this movement began. . . . ' (*pers. comm.*, 2008).

Networks and mutual learning between movements have also proved important within MNPC. As an ORM activist explained, 'we were the only example at the time for other movements.. people came and asked for our experience . . . of course other local people had strong views, but they didnt know how to establish and run this kind of movement' (*pers. comm*, 2008).

PPT also emphasises the importance of framing practices in mobilisation and maintenance of resistance. Recent representations of nomadism in Mongolia suggest a particular understanding of nature, care for and rights to land, increasingly linked with resurgent Buddhist and Shamanic beliefs.[4] Older herder informants in particular commented on traditional, spiritual attitudes towards nature, their eradication in the collective era and the implications for nature (*pers. comm.*, 2008). Such factors have resonance for framings and mobilising strategies employed by the ORM and its successor RMs in a number of ways.

One of the ORMs early publicity strategies, a walk along the length of the Onggi River in 2004, included not only local herders, but Buddhist lamas. As part of this 'ecology protest march', lamas officiated at a series of religious ceremonies at which prayers were offered for the 'preservation and protection of the Onggi ecosystem' (Beck *et al.* 2007, 7; *pers. comm.*, River Movement members 2008). In 2011, an event organised by the MNPCM (Mongolian Nature Protection Civil Movement Coalition) at Tsogt Chandmani mountain, Tov *aimag*, highlighted the importance of the site as a 'world watershed', threatened by uranium mining licenses. Through diverse means including performances drawing directly on Buddhist cosmologies, both the beauty and fragility of the site were emphasised, as part of a call to resistance. Given the recent re-emergence of Buddhism and Shamanism in post-Soviet Mongolia, these events, akin to 'performative and ritualised moments of commonality', are highly symbolic and strategically deployed not only as part of a rallying cry and public information exercise, but as a call to assertion of commonly-held local understandings of nature and conservation (Leach and Scoones 2007, 21).

ORM (Onggi River Movement) and MNPCM (Mongolian Nature Protection Civil Movement Coalition) have also successfully collated and deployed scientific/technical data in mobilisation of diverse constituents and in attempts to hold the government and mining companies to account. For example ORM employed independent consultants to provide scientific data on the impact of mining on the Onggi River system, enabling them to dispute others' 'expert' claims (Beck *et al.* 2007). These examples emphasise the politics of knowledge in initiating and sustaining activism, through activists' deployment not only of one, but often of multiple forms of expertise in order to strengthen claims and facilitate the widest possible engagement with local constituencies.

To summarise, in Mongolia post-Soviet reforms facilitated the emergence of new opportinuties, performances and spaces of activism, supported by emergent networks. However, POS and PPT-based analyses have only limited explanatory power. Assemblage-based analysis, to which I now turn, offers important innovations in this regard.

## Assemblage/commons/environmental citizenship

Some key aspects and components of the Mongolian mining assemblage have been sketched out earlier. Following recent work (Anderson *et al.* 2012; Gibbs 2013), the emphasis here is not only on individual actors within the assemblage but on their (shifting) relations of exteriority; the decentring of human agency and the temporality and dynamism of encounters and outcomes.

### *Water/land/commons*

Land and water resources in Mongolia have resonance and agency within the assemblage through materialities, spiritual and rights-based dimensions. The drying up of the Onggi River and Ulaan Lake and local pollution prompted the emergence of the ORM in 2001, irrespective of ostensible closure of POS. According to ORM activists:

> The source of the Onggi River is in U . . . sum (district). It usually runs over 400km to Ulaan Nuur (Red Lake). The ORM started after all the mining and issuing of licences began in the area and the environment started to be destroyed. . . . The Ulaan lake dried up completely and people had to move away.
>
> (pers. comm., 2008)

Leaders of other RMs gave similar accounts of the initial drivers for activism:

> Gold mining started in our area in the early 1990s.. but the companies didn't do any rehabilitation and then the T. . . . River, dried up. That was one of the main reasons we established the Movement [in 2005] . . .
>
> (pers. comm., 2008).

In this case, water exercises agency in its absence as well as presence. Such findings echo Gibb's (2013) work on water assemblages in Australia, wherein socially constructed as well as climate-induced water scarcity was part of a wider assemblage of human and non-human entities which together gave rise to displacement of indigenous populations. For Mongolia, climate also formed an important part of the emergent (anti) mining assemblage in early/ mid-2000s, as *dzud* (natural disasters) enhanced the negative effects of mining and drying up of rivers on herders' already precarious livelihoods (*pers. comm., River Movement members, 2008*).

For land, ideas of shared custodianship remain powerful (Upton 2012). This is despite well-documented and growing challenges to 'traditional' norms, occasioned by increasing pressure on pasture resources and new mechanisms of exclusion. Such 'traditional' perspectives are evident in herders' notions of rights and reciprocity in relation to neighbouring herders, and grounded in understandings of land as a shared heritage, linked to citizenship and the Mongolian Constitution. Land (as commons) thus forms another important component of the emergent Mongolian assemblage, on which mining may exert material effects through pasture degradation, severing of migration routes and, compromising access to winter pastures and shelters (*pers. comm., herding households, Omnogov aimag, 2008*). The mining/ commons nexus is further reflected in contested concepts of resource nationalism, and the ways in which this is variously resisted, enacted and deployed through legislation, by mining companies and by activist movements, as traced in the next section.

### Strategies/networks/environmental citizenship

Legislative changes are key to understanding recent events as part of an assemblage-based analysis. Specifically, parliament's intention to repeal/ weaken the Law with the Long Name (LLN), a key law designed to protect water resources from adverse impacts of mining, was the ostensible driver of the September 2013 protests and the subsequent imprisonment of Munkhbayar and colleagues. Although never implemented in full, this flagship law became pivotal to a series of dynamic rapid events as RM and other activists competed with mining companies to influence the government, amidst foreign companies' fears of an increasingly unfavourable investment climate, evidenced in plummeting economic growth and FDI.

Within this context the 2009 Law with the Long Name (LLN) underscores both the agency of RMs, being originally developed by UMMRL (United Movement of Mongolian Rivers and Lakes) in conjunction with parliament members, and the resonance of the environment and particularly water as actors within the wider assemblage. Following Slater (2013), it also highlights the law itself and its (varying degrees of) implementation as a collective practice of humans (policy-makers, UMMRL, mining companies) and non-humans (water, pasture, maps, pollutants etc.), both shaped by and provoking particular forms of activism. Following its adoption in 2009, and in the face of widespread protests from mining companies, the government initially failed to implement the LLN. This prompted new strategies of protest from UMMRL, from the performative, through legal to direct action strategies. A protest camp in Sukhbaatar Square in 2011, during which UMMRL activists symbolically fired arrows at parliament, epitomises the former, while reported firing of guns on mining equipment of companies allegedly operating in breach of LLN in 2010, the latter. Hunger strikes following detainment of key activists also became part of the repertoire. In 2011 UMRL brought a successful landmark case against the Mongolian government for its failure to implement LLN, leading to the first batch of mining licences being revoked under LLN in 2011/12.

Together with a law to suspend issuing of new licences (2010) and the revocation of over 100 existing licences (2013) as part of internal corruption investigations, Mongolia once more began to appear a hostile place for foreign investment (Els 2013). This prompted a renewed cycle of pressure from mining companies within the dynamic assemblage of human (including the newly elected Democratic Party from 2012) and non-human actors, including key laws such as the LLN, financial flows and a declining economy, ultimately facilitating the resurgence of economic over environmental concerns in the political sphere.

Events of September 2013, when UMMRL members and other activists gathered outside parliament to protest the proposed amendments to LLN may be seen as a culmination of the above 'lines of flight'. According to one UMMRL informant:

> no one was listening to us . . . we had to do this symbolic demonstration to attract attention. . . . we just planned to organise a peaceful strike . . . to tell people what was happening . . . and submit a petition to parliament members . . . we hoped that we could somehow keep this law (LLN).
> (pers. comm. 2014; UMMRL Statement, 2014)

The UMMRL statement issued in the aftermath of the sentencing further concurs that:

> 'the demonstration was planned as a symbolic action showing that the people not heard by authorities have been left with only one option . . . to hold rifles in their hands . . . there was no violence and no one was hurt . . . they were brought to the demonstration as a purely symbolic act . . .'
> (UMMRL Statement, 2014).

This statement was shaped by the wider contexts outlined earlier and informed by reports of increasing tensions between local communities and mining companies in the countryside. As an informant explained,

> Since the LLN was first approved, these conflicts were reduced. . . . then there was a rumour that the LLN would be changed. Because of this some

mining companies started (activities) again, ignoring the law . . . this was a very crucial situation for us.

(UMMRL Statement, 2014)

At stake, according to this analysis was not only water (quality), but a whole way of life:

> if we keep (clean) water and rivers we can keep our pasture and traditional nomadic way of life . . . by keeping this law we can keep pasture for our livelihood and through keeping the pasture we can keep our culture and tradition. . . .
> (pers. comm. UMMRL activist, 2014)

Reports of what actually happened on 16 September 2013 are conflicting. To summarise from published accounts, members of *Gal Undestan*, who were later arrested and sentenced, brought firearms and (inactive) grenades to the protest (Tolson 2014). Accounts further state that a shot was subsequently fired, although accidentally and with no injury or damage to persons or property (Goldman Prize 2013; Tolson 2014). Initial charges branded the group 'terrorists', accused of 'attempting to threaten the wellbeing of society and public order'. Published sources note the subsequent, significant reductions of these initial 21 year sentences to between 1 and 10 years. They are less forthcoming on the specific reasons for this reduction.[5]

Important for this analysis are the *evolution* of protest strategies in relation to changing contexts and relations with other stakeholders. Key aspects of these strategies have been outlined for ORM, MNPC and UMMRL, and have variously entailed performative, through legal to direct action strategies, in some instances deployed simultaneously, but with a growing tendency towards more overtly oppositional tactics by UMMRL. Also important are the *intersections* between changing strategies and splits within the RMs, which serve to emphasise the importance of dynamism and temporality in assemblage-based understandings of social movements. The development of a network of RMs from the original ORM to form the MNPC by 2006, although short-lived, was an important stage in the evolution of activism. It was marked not only by widening of scope of formerly essentially place-based concerns to wider notions of environmental governance and citizenship as previously noted, but new forms of political engagement (*pers. comm.*, River Movement activists, 2008).

The Asia Foundation Facilitated MultiStakeholder Forum on Responsible Mining (MSF) is a case in point here. The MSF emerged in 2006 in response to the conjunction of recent rapid growth in Mongolia's mining sector, emergent environmental concerns and potential loss of investor confidence associated with a new windfall profits tax (*pers. comm.*, River Movement activists, 2008). The notion of 'responsible mining' thus became central to and the ultimate goal of the MSF, in which mining companies, politicians, RMs and NGOs were brought together to attempt to resolve these challenges and tensions. Although previously enjoying some support from foreign donors, the links with the Asia Foundation and the MSF constitued a far more significant step change for RMs, not least as RM leaders became increasingly Ulaanbaatar-based, thus weakening links with countryside constituencies (*pers. comm.*, 2008; Byambajav 2014). In 2007 the 51 MSF members agreed a common definition of responsible mining, and a series of underlying principles, including responsibility for the safety of people and the environment. However, this apparent progress was not to be sustained. By 2008 the MNPC (Mongolian Nature Protection Coalition) had split. Critical points of departure included a 2008 press conference at which six of the RMs, including ORM, stated their intention to defend themselves and their livelihoods in the face of alleged intimidation from mining company guards (Simonov 2013). For these RMs, the doctrine of 'responsible mining' had increasingly little purchase in the face of continued expansions of mining activities, with attendant conflict and environmental degradation in some rural areas (*pers. comm.*, 2008; Byambajav 2014; Simonov 2013). The 2008 declaration led to a break with the Asia Foundation (and thus with the MSF) and with former MNPC colleagues, who rejected these more confrontational tactics, despite continuing to espouse shared goals (*pers. comm., River Movement members, 2013, 2014*).

This is more than an oft-repeated story of the co-option of a formerly radical grassroots movement. Here, despite shared recent histories, relations of exteriority within the assemblage acted differently on the different actors to produce increasing differentiation and divergence in strategies, if not in goals. As the original umbrella group MNPC (Mongolian Nature Protection Coalition) split into the more radical UMMRL (United Movement of Mongolian Rivers and Lakes) and the more mainstream MNPCM (Mongolian Nature Protection Civil Movement Coalition) groups, these different strategies then became further entrenched, in UMMRL's case through the development, enactment and defence of the LLN (Law with the Long Name). In MNPCM's case, the commitment to less confrontational tactics continues to be played out through strategies such as the development of 'Nature and Environment Legislative Scorecards' and 'Greenstar Reports', through which the public are informed about the voting record of MPs in relation to environmental issues, thus being designed to produce an informed electorate, and to develop norms of social responsibility and accountability (MNPCM 2009).

Thus pivotal moments such as the 2008 declarations have interacted with other components of the assemblage to sever some of the 'fleeting, contingent ties' that produced particular forms of collaboration and outcomes (Nicholls *et al.* 2013, 11). These divergent lines of flight have then become further embedded through new strategies and tactics, in turn forging new networks of support. For Munkhbayar, recent confrontational tactics and his subsequent arrest have drawn international bodies such as Rivers Without Boundaries more firmly into the assemblage, as they continue to protest the basis and duration of the jail terms. Perhaps more unexpectedly Munkhbayar's status as a Goldman Prize winner has not only garnered (carefully worded) support from the official awarding body itself, but seems to be bringing into being new networks between former prize winners (Rivers Without Boundaries 2014). For the MNPCM, networks have continued to develop around engagement with policy-makers for example through the recently revived Responsible Mining Initiative. Networks continue to touch and overlap, but divergent lines of flights, which can be traced back to particular events and contexts, look set to entrench divisions within a dynamic, evolving grassroots movement.

One intriguing aspect of commonality that remains, however, is the resonance of individual notions and performances of environmental citizenship. According to MNPCM, rights and responsibilities interrelate to produce a particular form of citizenship. Recent Greenstar Reports emphasise Mongolian citizens as the owners of a shared or common wealth, encompassing a wide array of mineral and natural resources as well as land. This endows them with rights in terms of decision-making about, as well as actual shares in, wealth. Mongolian citizens are not, however, to be merely passive recipients of revenues, but are urged to 'know, monitor, influence and charge with responsibility' mining practices and revenue allocations (MNPCM 2010). In this way, a particular sort of environmental citizen is brought into view: active and imbued with rights, but also responsibilities in relation to protection of the natural environment. Thus the notion of 'responsible mining' encompasses not only the responsibility of mining companies to protect and rehabilitate land and water, but the responsibility of citizens to hold them to account. The vision here is not the banning of mining *per se*, but the development and continued enactment of responsible mining wherein environmentally sensitive areas are avoided, mining-related impact is minimised, wealth is shared justly, and an engaged, active environmental citizenry discharge their responsibilities to the 'motherland' (*pers. comm.*, RM members, 2011, 2013).

UMMRL and Munkbayar also emphasise the shared heritage of Mongolians and extend powerful concepts of commons (in land) to natural resources more widely. The emphasis in their recent pronouncements is less on rights to shared wealth than on rights and responsibilties in relation to the environment. Following the sentencing in 2014, a statement from UMMRL demanded that 'in accordance with the Mongolian Constitution, the people of our homeland have a right to defend their native interests'. Further letters and complaints to the government and judiciary position the groups' actions in September 2013 in light of 'performing their civil duties and preventing threats to national security, human rights. . . . (and the) environment . . .' (*pers comm*, UMMRL member, 2014). In relation to the UN Declaration on Human Rights, the group further assert the right to protect the means of livelihoods and existence: they argue, 'If drinking water, animal pastures, hay fields and wintering places are not the very means of existence for nomadic pastoralists, what is?' Thus, perceived failures by the government to perform their duties as 'guardians of environmental resources', have, by this line of argument, necessitated a particular performance of environmental citizenship on the part of UMMRL/ Fire Nation members.

Thus it could be argued that one overarching and consistent goal of the ORM, the now defunct MNPC and its successors (UMMRL and MNPCM) is the making of environmental citizens, not least in relation to culturally powerful concepts of 'the motherland' as a shared/common heritage and responsibility. The nature of this citizenship is contested, dynamic, and imbued with personal interpretations and meanings. In adopting this perspective, both temporality and the individual, as important aspects of the scalar dimensions of social movements, are brought into view.

## Conclusion

Mining resistance movements and their activities have been portrayed in some quarters in the light of a direct confrontation between traditional nomadic heritage and livelihoods and the 'predatory capitalism (which has) invaded Mongolia . . .' in other words a 'clash of civilisations', with Mongolia itself viewed as 'under attack' (Snow 2011). In the wider context of grassroots engagement with industrial development beyond Mongolia, the stories of such encounters are rarely ones of simplistic, binary oppositions, but rather of complexity and change, as encounters/ engagements shift between the confrontational and adaptive at particular moments and under particular circumstances. In the Mongolian case, an assemblage-based analysis draws attention to shifting alliances and entanglements; between members within particular RMs, between the various RMs through the coalitions (MNPC, MNPCM, UMMRL) formed in the Movements' recent history; between RMs and other activists, both within Mongolia and beyond; and between RMs, donors and policy-makers. These 'fleeting and contingent ties' (Nicholls *et al.* 2013, 11) both produce and are produced by particular tactics and strategies, in turn linked to expansion and evolution in the goals of particular Movements. Thus importantly, and with respect to future thinking about grassroots resistance, assemblage thinking takes us away from a 'dualism of political domination and resistance. . . .' but rather requires us to 'think through how these processes are co-constituted in the process of "becoming"' (Davies 2013, 31). In this way, assemblage thinking moves beyond the more structuralist POS and PPT framings, which although providing some insight in this case, cannot capture the full range, complexity, and dynamism of these encounters.

The admission of non/ more-than-human actors in assemblage-based analyses further challenges the assumed predominance of human intentionality in shaping practices and outcomes. As highlighted in the earlier analysis, examination of land, water, spirits and spiritual beliefs, laws, gold, commons as part of contemporary mining assemblages begins to bring into focus their agency in co-constituting strategies, goals, and performances of resistance. Following Blaser (2014, 52), the non-human matters, in ways that go beyond their deployment merely as tools for mobilisation . . . or as 'metaphor(s) mobilised to save the environment from the ravages of industrialism . . .', although they undoubtedly remain powerful in this regard.

Inherent in these tensions and temporalities are notions of environmental citizenship and individual understandings of rights and responsibilities therein. These can be shown to produce and to justify particular strategies and performances on the part of Movement members, notably in relation to the events of September 2013, subsequent sentencing of Munkhbayar and colleagues and appeals against the duration and the basis of these sentences. Environmental citizenship, its performance and the *making* of environmental citizens, not least in relation to responsibility and to culturally powerful concepts of commons and the more-than-human, emerges as a shared concern and goal of otherwise apparently divergent actors, following the demise of the MNPC. Strategies and tactics of resultant organisations vary, and show a degree of path dependence, for example as non-human aspects of the assemblage such as the LLN become central points of reference for UMMRL, provoking new, diverse arrays of tactics. Nonetheless, networks continue to overlap around environmental citizenship as both a call to action and goal of RMs.

Underpinning the earlier discussion are the impacts that some mining and mining practices have had on the Mongolian environment, and beyond this on cultures and livelihoods, in the recent past. Nonetheless, stated goals of RM members are rarely the banning of mining *per se*, but its appropriate regulation, with due cognisance of cultural norms, non-human actors, herders' land rights, environmental protection, community voices in decision-making and citizens' rights as shared custodians of Mongolia's resources. In a recent article, Munkhbayar argued that, 'the traditional Mongolian perspective of loving nature and mother earth is being forgotten . . . as a people we are at a dead end. We must get ourselves away from the idea that economics is everything and that economics will save us' (Bloomberg News 2011). Inevitably, different visions of development futures are at stake here, promoted through competing and in some instances old discourses, which are finding new traction in these contemporary encounters. For example, the conflation of modernity with industrial development and typically with sedentarisation, in opposition to 'traditional' nomadism destined to be superseded by 'progress' has a long (and infamous) history in pastoralist societies. Echoes of such discourses are evident here, as are ideas of common lands as 'empty lands', ripe for development. They are also evident in the construction of Mongolia's rural spaces as resource frontiers, sources of wealth, inevitably to be incorporated into the global capitalist economy.

Grassroots movements thus currently stand at the conjunction of multiple discourses and as but one small part of a vibrant, dynamic mining assemblage. New trajectories and 'lines of flight' have emerged from recent events, but the decentring of human agency and relations of exteriority render outcomes highly uncertain. The notion of environmental citizenship and figure of the environmental citizen remain one point of relative stability, around which goals and future visions cohere.

At the time of writing in 2014, a government announcement had recently confirmed that the next stage of the giant Oyu Tolgoi development would go ahead in 2015. Munkhbayar and colleagues remained in prison, and the future of the LLN remained highly uncertain, with recent governmental amendments to some of its provisions having provoked hunger strikes amongst activists in Ulaanbaatar. Debates over 'responsible mining' continue.

### Notes

1 According to the Goldman website (www.goldmanprize.org/), the Goldman Prize constitutes the largest financial award in the world for grassroots environmentalists. It is widely referred to as the 'Green Nobel'.

2 The *Law to Prohibit Mineral Exploration and Mining Operations at Headwaters of Rivers, Protected Zones of Water Reservoirs and Forested Areas* (2009), widely known in Mongolia as the *Law with the Long Name* (LLN).

3 These definitions are offered in the full awareness that Assemblage thinking draws on a range of intellectual traditions, variously emphasising assemblage as concept, process, form, ethos.

4 Of course, this is only one set of framings. Other framings and discourses for example around conservation have highlighted alleged overgrazing and destructive practices of herders.

5 As the subject of ongoing appeals, the specific legal issues are not commented on further here.

# References

Anderson, B., Kearnes, M., McFarlane, C., and Swanton, D. (2012) "On assemblages and geography" *Dialogues in Human Geography*, 2 (2) 171–189.

Bawden, C. (1968) *The Modern History of Mongolia*. London: Weidenfield and Nichollson.

Bebbington, A. (2012) "Underground political ecologies: The second annual lecture of the cultural and political ecology speciality group of the association of American geographers" *Geoforum*, 43 (6) 1152–1162.

Beck, L., T. Mendel, T., and Thindwa, J. (2007) "The enabling environment for social accountability in Mongolia" Social Development Department, Sustainable Development Network, World Bank, Ulaanbaatar, Mongolia.

Blaser, M. (2014) "Ontology and indigeneity: On the political ontology of heterogenous assemblages" *Cultural Geographies*, 21 49–58.

Bloomberg News. (2011) Mineral-rich, people-poor Mongolia prepares for flood of money (www.bloomberg.com/news/articles/2011-07-21/mineral-rich-people-poor-mongolia-prepares-for-flood-of-money). Accessed May 5, 2014.

Byambajav, D. (2014) "The River Movements' struggle in Mongolia" *Social Movement Studies*. DOI: 10.1080/14742837.2013.877387 (www.tandfonline.com/doi/full/10.1080/14742837.2013.877387#.VB09rU10xjo).

Cassidy, R. (2012) "Lives with others: Climate change and human-animal relations" *Annual Review of Anthropology*, 41 21–36.

CIVICUS (World Alliance for Citizen Participation). (2005) "Civil society index country report: Mongolia" (www.civicus.org/new/media/CSI_Mongolia_Country_Report.pdf). Accessed 4 September 2014.

Davies, A. (2012) "Assemblage and social movements: Tibet support groups and the spatialities of political organisation" *Transactions of the Institute of British Geographers*, 37 273–286.

Davies, A. (2013) "Identity and the assemblages of protest: The spatial politics of the Royal Indian Navy Mutiny, 1946" *Geoforum*, 48 24–32.

Deleuze, G. and F. Guattari. (1987) *A Thousand Plateaus*. London: Continuum.

Dittmer, J. (2014) "Geopolitical assemblages and complexity" *Progress in Human Geography*, 38 (3) 385–401.

Els, F. (2013) "Mongolia gears up for the fight of its mining life" *Mining.com* (www.mining.com/Mongolia-gears-up-for-the-fight-of-its-mining-life-70319). Accessed 3 September 2014.

Empson, R. (2011) *Harnessing Fortune: Personhood, Memory and Place in Mongolia*. Oxford: Oxford University Press.

Gibbs, L. (2013) "Bottles, bores and boats: Agency of water assemblages in post/colonial inland Australia" *Environment and Planning A*, 45 467–484.

Goldman Prize. (2013) The Goldman Prize calls for a fair and transparent trial for Tsetsegee Munkhbayar (www.goldmanprize.org/blog/goldman-prize-calls-fair-and-transparent-trial-tsetsegee-munkhbayar). Accessed 6 June 2014.

High, M. (2013) "Cosmologies of freedom and Buddhist self-transformation in the Mongolian gold rush" *Journal of the Royal Anthropological Institute*, 19 753–770.

Hobson, K. (2013) "On the making of the environmental citizen" *Environmental Politics*, 22 (1) 56–72.

Humphrey, C. and Sneath, D. (1999) *The End of Nomadism? Society, State and the Environment in Inner Asia*. Durham: Duke University Press.

Leach, M. and Scoones, I. (2007) "Mobilising citizens: Social movements and the politics of knowledge" IDS Working Paper 276, IDS, Sussex.

Mason, K. (2014) "Becoming Citizen Green: Prefigurative politics, autonomous geographies, and hoping against hope" *Environmental Politics*, 23 (1) 140–158.

Mearns, R. (2004) "Decentralisation, rural livelihoods and pasture-land management in post-socialist Mongolia" *The European Journal of Development Research*, 16 (1) 133–152.

Mongolian Nature Protection Civil Movement Coalition (MNPCM). (2009) *Green Star: Mongolian Nature and Environment Legislative Scorecard: Fall 2008 and Spring 2009 Parliamentary Session*. Ulaanbaatar: Edo Publishing.

Mongolian Nature Protection Civil Movement Coalition (MNPCM). (2010) *Green Star: Mongolian Nature and Environment Legislative Scorecard: Fall 2009 and Spring 2010 Parliamentary Session*. Ulaanbaatar: Soyombo Printing.

Mongolia Nature Protection Coalition (MNPC). (2007) *Membership Directory*. Mongolia: MNPC, Ulaanbaatar.

Mongolian National Mining Association (MNMA). (2007) Mongolia's mining sector: Government policy (www.miningmongolia.mn). Accessed 27 May 2014.

Nicholls, W., Miller, B., and Beaumont, J. (2013) Introduction: Conceptualising the spatialities of social movements (http://dare.uva.nl/document/509947). Accessed 28 May 2014.

Rivers Without Boundaries. (2014) Sentence for Mongolian Goldman Prize Winner and other green activists reduced by 65 years (www.transrivers.org/2014/1257/). Accessed 5 May 2014.

Rutland, T. (2013) "Activists in the making: Urban movements, political processes and the creation of political subjects" *International Journal of Urban and Regional Research*, 37 (3) 989–1011.

Simonov, E. (2013) A short history of the law with the long name' rivers without boundaries (www.transrivers.org/documents/rivers-and-mining/the-short-history-of-the-law-with-long-name/). Accessed 20 June 2014.

Slater, L. (2013) "Wild rivers, wild ideas': Emerging political ecologies of Cape York Wild Rivers" *Environment and Planning A*, 31 763–778.

Sneath, D. (2001) "Notions of rights over land and the history of Mongolian pastoralism" *Inner Asia*, 3 41–59.

Sneath, D. (2010) "Political mobilisation and the construction of collective identity in Mongolia" *Central Asian Survey*, 29 (3) 251–267.

Sneath, D. (2014) "Nationalising civilisational resources: Sacred mountains and cosmopolitical ritual in Mongolia" *Asian Ethnicity*, 15 (4) 458–472.

Snow, K. (2011) Goldman prizewinner shoots up foreign mining firms in Mongolia: Western deceptions and the extinction of the nomads (www.consciousbeingalliance.com/2010/12/post-2). Accessed 10 February 2013.

Tolson, M. (2014) "Eco-warrior or eco-terrorist? Mongolia jails environmentalist for 21 years'" *Asian Correspondent* (http://asiancorrespondent.com/118997/mongolia-tsetsegee-munkhbayar-jail/). Accessed 2 February 2014.

Transparency International (2013) Mongolia (www.transparency.org/country#MNG). Accessed 5 May 2014.

United Movement of Mongolian Rivers and Lakes (UMMRL). (2014) Untitled statement (16 February 2014). Issued following arrest and sentencing of Munkhbayer and colleagues (www.transrivers.org/2014/1257/). Accessed 2 August 2014.

Upton, C. (2012) "Managing Mongolia's commons: Land reforms, social contexts and institutional change" *Society and Natural Resources*, 25 156–175.

Voss., K. and M. Williams. (2009) "The local in the global: Rethinking social movements in the new millennium". Working Paper Series, Institute for Research on Labour and Employment, UC Berkeley.

Vrablikova, K. (2014) "How context matters? Mobilization, political opportunity structures, and nonelectoral political participation in old and new democracies" *Comparative Political Studies*, 10 1–27.

World Bank. (2006) *Mongolia: A Review of Environmental and Social Impacts in the Mining Sector 2*. Washington: The World Bank.

# 9 Micropolitics in the Marcellus Shale

*Eleanor Andrews and James McCarthy*

I'm for responsible natural gas development . . . I think that, if people educate themselves a little bit about natural gas drilling, you've got ten percent that don't want it no matter what, you've got ten percent that want it no matter what – all they care about [is] the money – and you got eighty percent that's in the middle that's okay with it, as long as it's done safely.

(Pennsylvania landowner regarding Marcellus Shale development, 2011)

## Introduction

The "extractive frontier" has been the subject of much critical attention over the past decade. Scholars and activists broadly agree that the fossil fuel industry is making great efforts to extract fossil fuels from new sites and sources, often ones that had until recently been deemed inaccessible, because of technological challenges, political risks, costs, or a combination thereof (Bridge 2008; Bridge and Le Billon 2012). Many such sites and sources are for the moment described as "unconventional," including deep offshore sources of oil and gas, oil sands in Canada and Venezuela, and shale oil and gas, although of course the unconventional becomes the conventional all too quickly. Many observers have suggested that the expansion of this extractive frontier has brought with it greater risks for society, the environment, and for the industry itself in certain respects: as extraction moves into more challenging physical situations, costs increase and the risks of accidents and the difficulties of controlling them rise; as extraction moves into new locations, particularly in the global North, it becomes the subject of greater scrutiny and opposition by citizens and groups with more social power, particular legal rights, and often a greater willingness to consume fossil fuels than to live in the sites of their production.

A great deal of scholarly and political attention has thus focused on not only the expansion of this extractive frontier, but on the myriad forms of resistance it is provoking: everything from struggles over indigenous land rights, battles over pipelines, and statewide fracking bans to a newly invigorated and radicalized grassroots environmental movement focused on climate change (McKibben 2014; Skocpol 2013). Journalist, activist, and author Naomi Klein has called these struggles "Blockadia," arguing that they constitute an increasingly organized movement of resistance to not only the fossil fuel industry, but to the neoliberal capitalism that it powers (Klein 2014). While many academics are skeptical of Klein's focus on place-based activism and assertion of growing lateral connections among such efforts (see Huber 2015; Johnson 2015; Watts 2015), there is substantial agreement that the expansion of extraction is indeed leading to increasing mobilization and resistance.

While the recent focus on the extractive frontier and the wave of resistance to it may be new, the analytical framework underlying many of these studies is an old and familiar one: that mobile, often multinational, capital, especially in extractive industries, provokes resistance as it invests in, develops, and extracts materials and wealth from specific, usually rural, places is a thesis that animates many fields of scholarship and political analysis. Specifically, versions of that basic thesis have been central to the fields of rural sociology, rural geography, and political ecology, and the literatures on extractive regions/peripheries and the so-called "resource curse" that span those and other fields (Le Billon 2012). Conversely, scholars such as Gaventa (1982) have focused on the phenomenon of quiescence or consent, in which people seemingly accept the domination and exploitation of a place by an industry: Gaventa uses an effectively Gramscian analysis to explain how the coal industry used its massive control over multiple avenues and arenas of social life in a coal-mining region of Appalachia to de-politicize contested issues and maintain hegemony. Such analyses still begin, though, from the premise that resistance *ought* to be occurring: that it would be the logical response to the intense, localized social and environmental exploitation and degradation wrought by industry, and that it is the absence of resistance that must be explained. They are thus examining the flip side of the same basic thesis. In both scenarios, the fundamental presumed dynamic is that of opposition between the interests of industry and the people who live and work in the places of industrial development, with the question being whether people yield to industry's power or fight back, and if the latter, when, how, and to what effect.

By contrast, we focus in this chapter on a case that illustrates a less confrontational and perhaps less romantic dynamic: in many instances, grassroots actors in sites of industrial development welcome or at least assent to that development, and their political engagement turns far more on asserting control over the conditions under which it occurs and the distribution of the risks and benefits, than on finding ways to prevent or end it. Such scenarios can be found in the aforementioned literature: as Watts notes, many the indigenous activists in the Niger Delta portrayed by Klein as members of "Blockadia" actually "want more from oil, not less of it" (2014, 110). Horowitz (2011) and others have explored cases in which industrial development has led to sharply divergent agendas within communities, including the desire by some to retain industrial activity, if on contested terms. The multiplicity of responses to industrial development has led to an increased focus on what Horowitz (2008, 2011) terms "micropolitical ecology," or the examination of the reasons for and dynamics of such disparate reactions within given communities. In most such cases, the overall context is quite polarized. Our point, though, is that some forms of grassroots engagement with industrial development are far less confrontational than the overall context, and seek to contest the terms of industrial activity rather than the basic fact of it.

In this chapter, we explore in detail the responses of rural Pennsylvanians to the extraction of unconventional natural gas from the Marcellus Shale – a phenomenon very much a part of the extractive frontier discussed earlier. We briefly discuss some of the different ways in which residents responded to fracking (as it has become popularly known), and then focus on one critical response: the formation of landowner coalitions that collectively bargained with industry for better terms in leasing land for drilling. Drawing on intensive, semi-ethnographic fieldwork by the lead author, we argue that such coalitions emerged as both important actors in, and terrains of, environmental governance. On the one hand, to the extent that they acted as unified fronts in the negotiation of leases, and communicated with one another as part of an increasingly large and dense network, they shaped the broader dynamics of the Marcellus Shale boom, with effects well beyond the physical properties of their members. On the other hand, in a familiar pattern, most coalitions are internally heterogeneous and shot through with power dynamics, making them as much terrains of politics as unitary actors in them. Following from the latter point, we argue that an exploration of these politics within and between coalitions can be advanced by and contribute to an emerging "micropolitical ecology" (Horowitz 2011).

The chapter proceeds as follows. First, we briefly review the empirics of the Marcellus Shale natural gas boom, and then describe some of the wide range of political reactions it engendered. Second, we explore in detail one such response, the landowner coalitions, looking at their diversity, their effects, and their internal and external dynamics. Finally, we discuss how we might theorize their roles as forms of grassroots engagement with industrial development and continue to broaden our understanding of environmental governance and its hybrid institutions.

## The Marcellus Shale drilling boom and political responses

Shale is an unconventional source of natural gas, and differs from conventional sources in its methods of production and associated legal regimes, which shape the physical, legal, and economic dimensions of its development in particular ways. It is accessed through hydraulic fracturing (popularly known as "fracking"), whereby water, combined with sand and a small amount of chemical additives, is injected underground at high pressures to force open fissures in the shale, releasing gas (Department of Energy 2009). A typical well requires the injection of millions of gallons of water, a great deal of which returns to the surface contaminated with the added chemicals and dissolved minerals and must be disposed of (Lave and Lutz 2014). Unlike vertical drilling for conventional gas, horizontal drilling follows a geological stratum for thousands of feet underground. A single well can thereby access the shale layer and its gas across an extended area underground, typically in "units" of one square mile (640 acres), although this can vary. The ability to reach out laterally from one well means that fewer wells are needed to extract gas from a given area than in vertical drilling, but each well pad has a substantial footprint.

Companies must lease the mineral rights to 100% of the aboveground acres in a unit, which may belong to multiple landowners, or limit their drilling accordingly. The landowners then divide the royalties from gas produced in that unit, based on the percentage of the unit that they own. Horizontal drilling therefore requires consent across unbroken swaths of acreage. It bears noting that the US has a unique property regime wherein private landowners own the rights to the minerals and resources under their land, and may therefore sell or lease them. Without this private control of underground resources, the case we examine would have been entirely different. The mineral rights of a property can be sold to a different owner, creating a "split estate"; the rights, responsibilities, and returns of mineral rights owners and aboveground landowners may differ.

The Marcellus Shale formation lies 4000–8500 feet beneath New York, Ohio, Pennsylvania, and West Virginia, with its natural gas deposits described as potentially "a century's worth of reserves . . . in the shale under our feet" (Obama 2011). Estimates of its recoverable resources (methane gas) range from 84 to 141 trillion cubic feet (US Energy Information Administration 2012). Natural gas has been characterized as a "bridge fuel" to renewable energy, as it emits fewer greenhouse gases and byproducts when burned. Indeed, shale gas exploration in the Northeast was driven by the emerging role of natural gas in a putative nationwide transition to lower-carbon sources of energy, as well as rising natural gas prices and technological advances, namely high-volume, slickwater hydraulic fracturing and horizontal drilling (Department of Energy 2009; US Energy Information Administration 2012).

Extraction of natural gas from the Marcellus Shale by all accounts transformed the areas with the most activity. The first well was drilled in Pennsylvania in 2003, followed by approximately 8,400 unconventional wells through 2015 (Pennsylvania Department of Environmental Protection 2016). Drilling and infrastructure construction led to a massive increase in truck traffic on often marginal roads, while an influx of workers from other states quickly snapped up available rentals, established long-term residencies at hotels, and drove up local housing prices (Schafft 2014).

The extent of the drilling and the rapidity of its onset divided communities and kindled fierce debate over energy policy, environmental risks, and the distribution of costs and benefits. Pennsylvania has been home to oil and gas development in the past, yielding mixed effects on perceptions of the more recent shale gas drilling. On one hand, residents of areas with local histories of extraction had more knowledge of and comfort with drilling, but on the other, the legacies of environmental degradation and irresponsible coal mining made many in the broad region hesitant (Brasier et al. 2011). Many local landowners benefited, as companies leased their mineral rights for unprecedented payouts. But as the downsides of living in a landscape of energy production became increasingly apparent, a vocal opposition emerged, skeptical of drilling technologies largely new to the

Pennsylvania public. Some residents sought bans on drilling and a broad-based "fractivist" movement materialized in Pennsylvania and neighboring states.

Boosters emphasized the sheer amount of gas accessible and its potential effect on global energy markets, as well as the lesser carbon footprint of burning natural gas, with its potential role in a "broad portfolio of energy resources" (Howarth et al. 2011, 274). They likewise made optimistic predictions regarding the number of jobs in the natural gas industry (projecting 180,000 in Pennsylvania alone (Considine et al. 2011)), billions of dollars from leasing and royalty payments, infrastructure renewal, tax revenues, and a general revitalization of aging communities, all protected by increasingly sophisticated risk management technologies. Technological and scientific expertise were enlisted as authoritative. The industry and its allies pointed to the long history and safety record of hydraulic fracturing in other regions, and called for the input of scientific experts in any new regulation. In short, the major arguments for extracting natural gas from the Marcellus Shale were about economics, employment, and energy independence, with assurances about the low risk of environmental problems.

By contrast, activist and academic critics of the "fracking" boom raised a variety of concerns. They pointed to the relatively new nature of the relevant technologies of extraction, namely high-volume hydraulic fracturing and horizontal drilling, and the potential for carelessness and accidents in the rush to drill. Activists named environmental concerns such as the amount of water required for hydraulic fracturing, the farm and forest fragmentation from shale gas infrastructure's extensive footprint and spatial distribution, the potential for spills and air pollution, and the risk of water contamination through underground gas migration and aboveground spills. They furthermore pointed out the non-inclusion of hydraulic fracturing in several federal environmental regulations and the nondisclosure of toxic chemicals used as additives in hydraulic fracturing. Local citizens cited dangerous increases in truck traffic (for construction, water delivery and removal, and more), strains on public services, other nuisances and hazards, and their limited voice (Jacquet 2009). These concerns, dramatized in the documentary *Gasland* (Fox 2010), were central to a multi-state "fractivist" movement. In New York State, the pushback was successful: a moratorium of many years was followed by the announcement of an outright ban on drilling in 2014.

It is impossible to understand these developments without situating them in the legal and regulatory context in Pennsylvania. Formally, drilling for natural gas in the US is, by federal policy, regulated primarily at the state level. The injection of chemical-laden water into the ground and its production of toxic wastes would normally make it subject to the federal Safe Drinking Water Act, the Resource Conservation and Recovery Act, and the Comprehensive Environmental Response, Compensation, and Liability Act, but legislation passed in 2005 explicitly exempted the industry from those laws, while the US Environmental Protection Agency has chosen not to classify oil and gas wastewater as "hazardous material" (see Lave and Lutz 2014, 741). The federal government has delegated to the states primary responsibility for monitoring and enforcement of those federal standards that do apply.

Pennsylvania's state government, in turn, was highly sympathetic to the oil and gas industry during the boom, which began during the administration of Democrat Ed Rendell (who served as governor from 2003 to 2011) and peaked during the administration of Republican Tom Corbett (who served from 2011 to 2015). Both governors and many appointees in their administrations, including those in charge of the environmental oversight and enforcement agencies, had extensive financial and professional ties to the oil and gas industry (Galbraith 2013). During Rendell's administration, state funds were paid to private security contractors to monitor anti-fracking protesters (some of whom were consequently put on terrorist watch lists) (Andrews and McCarthy 2013). Corbett received $1.8 million in campaign contributions from the oil and gas industry while running for governor. Two months after taking office, he said in an address, "Let's make Pennsylvania the hub of this [drilling] boom. Just as the oil companies decided to headquarter in one of a dozen states with oil, let's make Pennsylvania the Texas of the natural gas boom" (Colbert 2011). Corbett quickly pushed through changes in state laws effectively prohibiting municipalities from banning or substantially regulating oil and gas drilling or associated activities (Galbraith 2013), and allowing doctors to access details regarding fracking chemicals in medical emergencies – but not to discuss them with their patients (Sheppard 2012). Corbett's administration likewise resisted popular support for a tax on gas production in the state (Colaneri 2014a); directed Department of Environmental Protection personnel not to take any restrictive action with respect to the fracking industry, including issuing fines for violations, without clearing it with the industry-friendly head of the Department (Galbraith 2013); and prohibited state Department of Health employees from speaking with residents who called concerning natural gas extraction (Colaneri 2014b). The Pennsylvania Democratic Party explicitly called Corbett's actions a "payoff" to the oil and gas industry in return for campaign contributions (Hopey 2011).

Many municipal governments, for their part, did attempt to pass local ordinances banning or severely limiting hydraulic fracturing for natural gas. Their efforts included a range of tactics: zoning ordinances that would ban drilling and other processes, regulation of associated hazards and nuisances (e.g., wastewater disposal, noise, light, and traffic), stringent bonding requirements, local moratoria, and symbolic resolutions that supported anti-drilling legislation in other areas. Some of these, such as Pittsburgh's ordinance of 2010, were forthright political statements, invoking the right to local self-government, advocating new rights for residents, and rejecting corporate personhood. At least 57 communities across the state adopted ordinances with "prohibitive limits" (Klaber 2011). These bans on drilling, however, stood in deliberate violation of Pennsylvania's Oil and Gas Act (1984), which expressly "preempts and supersedes the regulation of oil and gas wells." Given the state laws discussed earlier, the validity of these municipal bans was questionable, although challenges from industry yielded mixed results in the Pennsylvania courts. Municipal governments were generally held to have the authority to regulate but not ban otherwise legal activities within their borders, so many cases turned on whether strict regulations amounted to a de facto ban.

A critical backdrop for these struggles was the possibility of "forced pooling," a process broadly akin to eminent domain. In most oil and gas-producing states, if a certain majority percentage of the land in a unit is already leased for development, nonparticipating landowners can be compelled to allow drilling under their land, for the sake of efficiency. Pennsylvania does *not* have forced pooling provisions applicable to the Marcellus Shale, but several bills to institute it were drafted in the state legislature during the early years of the boom. The threat of forced pooling was thus a critical component of the context in which individual landowners and coalitions made decisions about leasing their lands.

## Landowner coalitions

Within this political landscape of debate and contestation, coalitions of landowners began to form primarily for the purpose of negotiating better lease terms with companies interested in drilling on lands owned by the members. Understanding the genesis and evolution of these coalitions demands a prior understanding of how oil and gas companies went about securing leases with private landowners.

Such companies attempt to secure leases for the lowest possible economic compensation and a minimum of environmental and other considerations, within the bounds of local, state, and federal regulations. In the early days of the boom, company representatives went door-to-door to negotiate with private landowners, who typically did not have much information or understanding about the value of their mineral rights (Liss 2011). The earliest leases in the Marcellus Shale stayed at or near the minimum royalty payment required by law (12.5%), and per-acre bonus payments, the other major economic component of a lease, remained small (between $5 and $100).

In response to the limited information and bargaining power available to most individual landowners in negotiations with companies, landowners across the Marcellus began to organize themselves into coalitions to negotiate collective agreements and secure more profitable and favorable leases. The conditions that paved the way for their rise were not new (e.g., the private holdings of mineral rights, fluctuating lease markets, an imbalance of information between the two sides of the negotiating table, etc.) and a few landowner groups had formed in response to exploration for oil and conventional gas in the 1980s. From 2005 onward, however, landowners began to organize themselves in much greater numbers, as the spatial extent of development, perceived costs, and potential benefits for landowners grew. By 2011, there were approximately 60 landowner coalitions in Pennsylvania.

### Research and methods

Between June and September of 2011, the lead author conducted semi-structured interviews with 39 key informants: mostly leaders and members of 15 Pennsylvania coalitions, and a few lawyers, consultants, and Penn State extension associates. Respondents were identified through online directories and snowball sampling. They represent the largest and most active coalitions. Interviews were recorded, transcribed, and analyzed through open coding and conventional content analysis, using Excel and NVivo qualitative analysis software. These extensive interviews were invaluable for understanding the origins and operations of landowner coalitions. Leaders described how they juggled the legalese of leases, the economics of lease markets, and educational outreach, while organizing members, managing costs, and sometimes responding to anti-drilling sentiment in their area. Members described their ongoing shale gas education and how they sought balance and control within coalitions. Primary documents were made available by participants or through public websites, including draft and final leases, coalition acreage maps, discussion forums, and coalition newsletters and emails.

### Findings

The first thing that stood out about the landowner coalitions was their diversity: in timelines, origins, objectives, size (number of members and extent of acreage), organization and leadership, leasing status (leased, unleased, or still negotiating), and the local legal and political context. The smallest were just a few hundred acres owned by a handful of neighbors; the largest one had more than 100,000 acres and 1300 members. Coalitions' distribution roughly matched the general outlines of the Marcellus Shale development, except that they were scarcer in the areas that were leased earliest, before they could be organized. Most coalitions were based in one township or county; the largest covered several counties. In some areas, one coalition dominated the negotiations between landowners and drilling companies; in others, coalitions coexisted and even competed. One coalition was a well-organized political force of over 1,300 people, managed by elected representatives who rotated on committees; another was made up of five neighbors who only stayed together long enough to secure a lease. A group near Pittsburgh was made up of wealthy landowners who took their time negotiating; most were dominated by members anxious not to let the economic opportunity pass by. Some made millions of dollars collectively, and others ended up unleased. Leaders brought diverse assets that they marshaled for recruitment and negotiations: Wall Street experience, a history of activism and organizing, expertise in geology and natural gas, extensive social networks (in the case of a schoolteacher who had taught across the county for most of her lifetime), good reputations, free time (often in retirement), bookkeeping skills, and facility with public speaking. In sum, in spite of generally similar functions, the groups exhibited a diversity of leadership, membership, and goals.

What coalitions took away from negotiations was just as varied as what they brought to the table. Their work was in principle quite similar: leaders volunteered time and expertise to negotiate agreements with natural gas drilling companies. But, in practice, lease outcomes varied enormously, in terms of monetary compensation, length of lease, extent of subsurface rights leased, and other elements. Payments on a per-acre basis ranged from $1,100 to $5,750, and royalties were between 18% and 20%, in some cases with additional payments for landowners who agreed to host the drill pad. Many clauses covered legal matters such as unit sizes, indemnity, communication, tax assessment, etc. Others addressed environmental concerns: restrictions on surface disturbance and the location of wells; environmental remediation agreements; water testing provisions; limits to seismic testing; and prevention of damage to plants and soil, poultry, fish, or livestock. Timing played a key role in these differences; groups organized across the state from about 2006 onward and compensation rates rose until 2008, when the recession forced large cutbacks in leasing. Coalitions forming and negotiating at different periods were subjected to this ebb and flow. Some groups were still in the early stages of organizing when members were interviewed in 2011, while others had already disbanded, their mission accomplished. Coalitions in New York State similarly benefited from the "emerging benefits of collective natural resource management", where landowners in coalitions, working together, "gained sometimes substantial increases in compensation, property-level environmental protections, and legal power acquired for their members" (Jacquet and Stedman 2011, 85). This was a far cry from the early isolation of farmers approached individually by company representatives.

Coalitions may have negotiated as units, but they were not perfectly unified: individual members were driven by different motivations, and politics within the groups shaped and disrupted their collective action. Some landowners were there because they were genuinely excited about gas development; they believed it was an environmental good, would help revitalize the local economy and their own finances, maybe even help save the rural character of the area or specific, expensive-to-maintain properties. Many, perhaps the majority, joined because they did not see anything wrong with natural gas and held essentially populist ideas about being little guys getting a better deal from the big guy if they all banded together. Some were making the best of a situation that they did not feel they could stop, hoping to have a bit more say in the situation by joining a coalition, or just make some money if drilling was going to proceed regardless. A few in that broad latter group later called on their position as coalition members for credibility among anti-gas activists, their membership indicating how personal the stakes were for them, and how much they had learned about the process.

Many coalition members were pro-drilling, focused on the promised economic and even environmental benefits, the opportunity that natural gas and its associated industry might bring to their quiet corners of Pennsylvania. But some were more ambivalent. A leader of one of the most visible groups confessed, "Look, I'm an old fart. If I could push a button right now and stop this whole thing, I would". He was trying to slow and direct changes he saw as inevitable. One landowner, who did sign with a coalition but had strong reservations, expressed the decision to join as a kind of compromise:

> We felt this is probably one of those in-the-real-world compromises that you need to make, between the perfected reality that you'd like to see and the actual reality that you have to live in . . . it's like a poll question; it depends on how you ask it. Are the vast majority of people in the coalition pro-drilling?

If you use the practical definition of advocating for industry, I don't think they are. But certainly, we don't delude ourselves into believing that the vast majority of people in the alliance are somehow anti-drilling either. Most people's reality is a bit more complicated than that.

In short, he and his wife joined because they felt they had to, in order to protect their property and stay involved. In this way, individual members negotiated trade-offs and politics, typically accepting lease terms preferred by the majority.

The different motivations and circumstances of members played out within coalitions. Balancing individual and group concerns, particularly in an issue as risky and polarizing as natural gas development, is an inherent challenge in organizing community groups both efficiently and democratically. And in contrast to measuring success in banning natural gas development, measuring success in lease negotiations was not straightforward. Most individuals probably wanted a high dollar amount for leases, commensurate with the associated environmental damage and risks to their land, with a certain amount of control or oversight over drilling, without spending too much time or money on the negotiation process. But within a group, different individuals had different ideas about appropriate compensation, with different plans and priorities for their land, sometimes complementary and sometimes conflicting. Some landowners did not want surface development, while others wanted to reap the payments associated with siting wells, access roads, pipelines, and other infrastructural components. Environmental concerns differed based on water sources, agricultural easements, wildlife, or any number of other factors. A hunter, a dairy farmer, an absentee landowner – all had different interests. Financial concerns could also be incompatible: the willingness to accept environmental, legal, and other trade-offs for higher dollar amounts could differ, as well as the preferred timing for payments (all at once or over time). In short, successful outcomes for a group as a whole could be different from success for individual members, or for leaders.

Landowners thus needed to negotiate not only with the oil and gas companies, but with other coalition members. Should a landowner with five or more acres have more say in a collective lease than a homeowner with just a house and yard? How much control should an individual give up (e.g., power of attorney, an attractive offer elsewhere) in order to secure a lease acceptable to a broad community of his/her neighbors? Every coalition had a slightly different answer to these dilemmas. Many tried to work it out formally, others ran things more informally, while others yet tried a more dictatorial approach: one group was run by a man called (jokingly) "the supreme commander" whose "cabinet" provided consultation and advice, but who retained authority over final decisions. Such negotiations often played out along informal channels of communication and influence; after all, many groups were composed of long-term neighbors and friends. Pre-existing social networks, reputations, trust, and subtle pressures all played a part. Having more acreage at stake generally made landowners more invested in the process, and a longer local residency conferred more legitimacy.

Although most landowner coalition members were pro-gas development and found themselves allied with the oil and gas industry, not all were. Some individuals joined in order to protect their land and steer the momentum of the ongoing rush, not out of a desire to lease per se. Others were skeptical of information presented in educational meetings that too obviously originated from drilling companies' public relations departments. One member explained:

> Members like us . . . more or less joined out of a concern to get as much protection for our property as possible, because . . . we were looking to get as much legal protection, but also band together with your neighbors in a common interest sort of thing . . . . The way that [coalition] operated in the in the days prior to signing the lease was, was more consistent with that, whereas once the once the lease offer . . . was on the table, it seemed like that the leadership or certain members of the leadership took a very public stance, really pushing a pro-drilling agenda. Now there was always the assumption that there were going to be a lot of people in the alliance that were going to be pro-drilling. But the tenor of the agenda – prior to everyone getting together and signing a lease – was not strongly in that direction. Once it did, it almost seemed like now we're gonna advocate for industry . . . There were a lot of rank and file members in the coalition that not only didn't really agree with the public stance that the [coalition] was taking, but . . . when they tried to speak up within the organization about that, more or less got shut down.

A few members of this coalition were entirely against drilling and had joined in an attempt to protect their land from possible future forced pooling. Initially ambivalent at best, they came to feel misrepresented, as this coalition over time took up pro-drilling political actions. This large and active coalition was in an area polarized by drilling politics, near to several anti-drilling groups, the family property of the director of *Gasland*, and the township of Dimock, where Pennsylvania's Department of Environmental Protection and the federal Environmental Protection Agency were investigating claims of water contamination from drilling. When, after leases were signed, drilling in the area was delayed by a regulatory body, coalition members publicly protested. In 2011, the leadership voted to file a lawsuit, and later met with the governor of Pennsylvania to push against the delays.

Several members were dismayed to learn that their coalition's legal actions were to be uniformly pro-development, with little public recognition of the need for environmental and other regulations. One spoke at a coalition meeting about his concerns and was thereafter contacted by a leader with a response he felt was "hostile". He perceived their actions as bad negotiating tactics, that publically advocating for less regulation was "telegraphing to industry that you're all in on this to start with . . . it weakens your negotiating position, when there's not a lease signed".

Another member had a similar story:

> We thought, this is maybe some security for us, if we join [the coalition] and have these strong leases, this would give us some kind of protection

if something goes wrong. There was talk of having a financial fund in [the coalition] that would take care of issues that would come up. Later, we found out that that was more for issues against suits from anti-drilling people, to fight them rather than to fight the gas companies, if something went wrong environmentally . . . we became more and more disenchanted.

This member felt like the leadership did not want her questions to be heard, and indeed that her pro-regulation emails were not forwarded to the entire listserv, that she was not trusted because of her reputation of being an environmentalist.

It bears repeating that this group was in an area with vocal anti-drilling sentiment and such opposition came to define its work in many ways. Even those members who disagreed with the coalition's later aims agreed that the polarization of the surrounding area tied the leadership's hands:

> The polarization probably undermines the . . . ability of an organization like the [coalition] to play an active role in looking out for its members . . . [it has] been forced into taking a very pro-drilling stance . . . I honestly don't think that the very strident position that you have from, say, a Damascus Citizens [fractivist] organization is effective. I think it actually makes the problem worse, in the sense that it allows the conversation to become so polarized that it makes it impossible for people like us to have conversations with people in the leadership . . . because they can't hear anything other than you're either pro-drilling or you're anti-drilling . . . At the end of the day, even if drilling goes forward, there's still a thousand issues that need to be worked out and it's going to be a question of degree in many cases, not a black-and-white, yes-or-no kind of thing . . . I think that it's really easy to fall into the trap of thinking that, well, if I want to see this resource developed, then I'm going to cast my lot with industry and the enemy is with the chunk of the population who has a different opinion about this. But I think that's how industry often does pull off the divide and conquer thing, and in the end, gets their way. And the interest of both of those groups of local people wind up being undermined, because they've been had by falling into the polarization of the whole thing.

At the time of the interviews, these individuals were considering forming a small group with other disenchanted members to reach out to the leadership: "our short-term goal is to stop the [coalition] from being a lobbyist for the gas companies."

One clear overall finding was that the coalitions did produce real, major results. Over the time period examined here, royalty payments rose to nearly double the minimum and to thousands of dollars per acre (up from the single digits). Many leases also began to specify stronger environmental and landowner protections. These longer and more sophisticated leases for the most part benefited landowners, who, often through coalitions, came to have more say in the terms of the development on their own property and their immediate surroundings.[1] Coalitions may not have been able to stop drilling – even had they wanted to – but they played a major role in deciding *how* and where drilling went forward, from broad lease provisions for exploration, drilling, hydraulic fracturing, and eventual reclamation, to minutiae such as reseeding disturbed land. Even natural gas companies may have found the arrangements attractive, as the organization of coalitions streamlined recruitment and negotiations. While coalitions varied greatly, as detailed earlier, their collective economic and environmental influence was widespread through their lease agreements, educational outreach, and promotion of gas development. Indeed, many groups educated their members and provided a forum for sharing experiences. They became a "force to be reckoned with" both as individual groups and as a whole, as members and leaders were in constant and widespread communication via online forums (Chedzoy n.d., 1; Liss 2011). In the following section, we step back and attempt to theorize this "force" from the perspectives of political ecology and environmental governance.

## Discussion

In this section, we analyze two major themes regarding the landowner coalitions discussed earlier: why they focused their efforts on negotiating the terms of drilling rather than opposing it, and how they functioned as actors in, and terrains of, governance.

### Engagement, benefits, and limitations

Given the outright opposition and resistance that figures so prominently in the scholarly literature regarding extractive industries, it is worth asking why landowner coalitions related to Marcellus Shale drilling in Pennsylvania focused overwhelmingly on the *terms* on which the industry operated, rather than *whether* it operated. At first glance, the answer is deceptively simple: they benefited from it, they needed or wanted those benefits, and they could not have stopped it anyway. These answers demand careful scrutiny, however. There are both critical differences, and important similarities, between the Marcellus Shale region of Pennsylvania and many other extractive regions. These comparative insights have theoretical and policy implications.

Specific property relations were the main reason that coalition members were able to benefit from shale gas drilling. First, the US is highly unusual in that owners of the surface usually control the ground and minerals below their property, the subsurface estate. In many countries, companies do not need to negotiate with individual landowners on the surface at all in order to access subsurface resources. Second, although there is significant state and federal land ownership in the region, the area of Pennsylvania in question is mostly in private ownership, with those landholdings dispersed into small parcels relative to many other places elsewhere in the US and around the world. Drilling companies were thus compelled to reach agreements with not just one, but many, private landowners to access the gas in many locations. Permission to explore, restrictions on industry activities, compensation, requirements for remediation – all stemmed directly from landowners' property rights.

Property relations were also central to two critical limitations of the landowner coalitions and their work. One is that not everyone in the communities and region owned land and had those rights. So, landowners holding significant or critical parcels needed by the gas companies were able to exercise some control and receive some significant benefits, but many in the area subject to the risks and inconveniences associated with the drilling boom did not enjoy those advantages. One leader asked, "What constitutes a landowner?" His group did not accept "homeowners" with smaller parcels of land (roughly 5 acres or less), apologetic that those property owners were "screwed". There are thus serious limitations on the extent to which the landowner coalitions can be considered "community-based organizations" (cf. Carre 2012). The fact that landowners felt that they could not, ultimately, stop drilling from occurring in the region also turned substantially on property relations: the threat of forced pooling – that is, the potential revocation by the state of their right to exclude – functioned as an effective disciplining mechanism that helped keep negotiations focused on the terms under which inevitable drilling would occur. Demonstrating such causality is difficult, but it was abundantly clear in wider discussions in the state at the time that the industry was prepared to strongly and actively pursue legislation in support of forced pooling if necessary, that there were elected officials in the state legislature prepared to act on that agenda, and that landowners involved in the coalitions were acutely aware of that backdrop. Many coalition members were explicit about deciding to focus on getting the best possible deal from drilling (monetarily and environmentally), rather than opposing a process they saw as unstoppable.

In considering why the members of landowner coalitions focused their efforts on the terms of drilling rather than on outright opposition, it is also important to consider the obvious but vital differences and similarities between this case and many other regions dominated by extractive industries. On the one hand, the drilling and responses to it were taking place in an advanced industrialized country with not just strong private property rights, but relatively strong environmental regulations and enforcement; a robust, multi-scalar environmental movement; and substantial scrutiny of companies' activities by the state and NGOs alike. The residents of the region had genuine political voice and representation, a significant social safety net (however diminished by decades of neoliberalism), and at least a limited variety of employment options. Perhaps most of all, the state was far from entirely captured by or dependent upon the revenues associated with extraction, and extraction was not performed or protected by force. In short, residents had less to fear and to lose from the influx of extractive corporations. On the other hand, there are more than trivial or coincidental similarities between rural Pennsylvania and many other resource-dependent regions. The gas-rich Marcellus Shale formation runs, essentially, between the Rust Belt and Appalachia, where stressed rural communities are the norm. Compared to national averages and, more to the point, adjacent metropolitan areas, rates of poverty, unemployment, and outmigration are high, and incomes, education levels, and economic diversification are low (Schafft 2014). Thus, a great many residents in the region felt that they were not in a position to turn down the payments, jobs, and tax revenues associated with drilling. Likewise, as in many other extractive regions, the corporations involved were largely based elsewhere, bringing much of their own workforce and equipment in with them, and taking most of their profits out. While the boom was building, they made substantial campaign donations to candidates and elected officials, and, in direct exchange or not, they received relatively lax and permissive oversight by Pennsylvania state agencies, the level of government with the most authority over their activities. Finally, the boom-and-bust cycle so familiar in fossil fuels and other primary commodities has been playing out: following a massive expansion of production, there is now a glut of gas, prices have plummeted, and many companies have slowed their operations (Conti 2015).

The geographies described earlier make the Marcellus Shale region of Pennsylvania subject to many of the classic dynamics of resource-based, boom-and-bust economies. Yet several of its features – greater wealth and economic diversification than many extractive regions; a strongly functioning state and civil society, including a well-organized environmental movement; and strong private property rights – lend real weight to the argument advanced by some that if fossil fuel extraction is going to happen at all, it might be better for it to happen in these sorts of places than in many other sites of extraction where those conditions do not hold (see Lave and Lutz 2014, 749). A critical question in this respect is whether the extraction of gas really does substitute for fossil fuel extraction elsewhere, or merely adds to the total.

### Landowner coalitions as actors in and terrains of governance

Landowner coalitions emerged, evolved, and operated within a very specific configuration of governance relations around shale gas in the US and Pennsylvania in particular. The shift from government to governance has been widely discussed and theorized, including with respect to environmental governance, which Bridge and Perreault define as "the manner, organisations, institutional arrangements and spatial scales by which formal and informal decisions are made regarding uses of nature" (2009, 475; see also Lemos and Agrawal 2006). The term "governance" emphasizes the increasingly multi-layered nature of rule and management, as well as the presence of more individuals and non-state institutions, in shaping the terrain of permissible activity. Of particular importance is the growing role of non-state entities in governance, including private economic actors such as corporations and industry groups and civil society actors such as NGOs, consumers, and social movements. Some have gone so far as to call this an "effective 'privatisation' of environmental decision making" (Bridge and Perreault 2009, 481). Related to the growing roles of private actors has been a blurring or hybridization of the categories of public and private action and authority. Private actors are taking on many functions historically performed by states, and public-private partnerships and cooperation make such categorization difficult (Himley 2008, 442; McCarthy and Prudham 2004). A critical question is "who participates in decisions large and small, and a sensitivity to the extent to which policies and proposals – i.e., the mechanisms through which environmental futures are enacted – express an elite vision or have 'social depth'" (Bridge and Perreault 2009, 485–6).

Within this framework, it seems clear that landowner coalitions were significant actors in the environmental governance of drilling in the Marcellus Shale. As noted previously, the US federal government has taken a light hand in the regulation of drilling for shale gas. The Pennsylvania state government, in turn, was quite welcoming to oil and gas companies, particularly relative to neighboring New York. Meanwhile, the efforts of municipal governments to ban or severely limit drilling met with substantial opposition and limited, if any, success.

Private actors had an especially important role to play. Firms in the industry promised jobs, tax revenues, and other benefits to the state and affected communities; donated to political candidates; and controlled critical pieces of proprietary information, including geological data, chemical usage, and the terms of leases already signed, about which they were very secretive. Companies were often the only or best source of information for regulatory bodies with urgent demands for data about the risks (Lave and Lutz 2014). Environmental organizations publicized concerns, with state and local level environmental NGOs almost unanimously opposing natural gas and national ones often cautiously supporting it in hopes of reduced carbon emissions (Damascus Citizens for Sustainability 2016; Natural Resources Defense Council 2016).

Coalitions therefore came to play key roles. Some became direct advocates of industrial development, particularly in cases where planned drilling was delayed. Some served as intermediaries, brokers, and diffusers of a growing body of knowledge, regarding not just rates of financial compensation in leases, but about a range of factors to consider and negotiate in leases: well locations, hours and noise levels of operation, remediation of the surface after drilling, etc. These coalitions were hailed as a success story of social and political organizing, providing most of their members a sense of increased ownership over a suite of processes, lower information and transaction costs, and an explicit recognition of local knowledge and interests (Balliet 2008; Jacquet and Stedman 2011; Liss 2011).

Since landowner coalitions emerged as important actors in environmental governance, it is important to consider what sorts of actors they were – a goal made more difficult by their diversity. Most appeared to be genuinely grassroots organizations, composed of residents of the places affected by drilling, and forming in fairly organic, bottom-up ways – through local contacts and organization around an issue of shared local concern. They were for the most part open to any local residents who had property of interest to drillers, contiguous to other members' property. They certainly fit within the definition of "grassroots organizations" as local, small, "membership-based organizations operating without a paid staff . . . which tend to be (but are not always) issue-based and therefore ephemeral" (Mercer 2002, in Horowitz 2011). This is a very different picture than, for example, the frequent charge faced by Wise Use groups in the West that they were 'astroturf' shells formed and controlled by industry-funded hired guns.

A more difficult question is whether is landowner coalitions are "community based organizations," as discussed by Carre (2012) with respect to local advocacy regarding fracking in Colorado. While the coalitions were certainly grounded in broader communities in their areas (notwithstanding the notorious ambiguities of "community" (see Agrawal and Gibson 1999)), they did not purport to represent anyone but their members, and then only in limited ways (i.e., as property owners in negotiations over leases, not as citizens or taxpayers). This is one limitation of privatized environmental governance: area residents who did not own land of interest to drilling companies were not directly included by a category of organizations that came to play important roles in local environmental governance. Landowner coalitions clearly did not meet most definitions of a social movement, but they were forms of collective action, and intersected with broader politics. Beyond the negotiation of specific land deals, the most important and influential function of coalitions was probably the acquisition and diffusion of information regarding the overall process of drilling and potential problems that should be considered in negotiating leases.

Nonetheless, while Jacquet and Stedman noted that the coalitions were seen by some as a "proxy to municipal or community-based regulation of natural resource development [with] the potential to exert greater influence over development than state regulators or local municipalities" (2011, 3), it is vital to point out that the coalitions were not actually involved in the ongoing extraction of natural gas, or its regulation. Leaders' expertise and the thoroughness of many leases deserve recognition and respect, but did not constitute ongoing oversight. Their influence did not result from a deliberate decentralization of governance, so they are neither an example of "authority . . . wrested from the state" in an explicit leveraging of local power (Himley 2008, 435), nor the state ceding that authority in a top-down decision. Even the parameters for drilling and development laid out in these leases may not ultimately have been effective: "to most of the locals, a contract was like the received word of God, an immutable set of commandments set in stone. Big companies . . . saw [leases as] . . . nothing more than a good place to start" (McGraw 2011, 88).

Finally, landowner coalitions were not only actors in politics and governance, but terrains of both. By this we mean that, in a pattern familiar from research on "communities" and other small-scale, largely informal organizations with respect to environmental governance, they were internally heterogeneous, with significant differences and sometimes disagreements among members. Members with particular sorts of resources tended to step up in leadership positions and steer their coalition, typically, towards more drilling (even if responsible drilling). The coalitions were thus not unitary actors, agreeing or disagreeing with others about the desirability and conditions of drilling: they were themselves arenas within which such questions were actively contested. Precisely such dynamics are at the heart of "micropolitical ecology." As Horowitz has argued, we need to better understand these sorts of "intragroup dynamics, which inform grassroots protestors' engagements with other actors and in particular the micropolitics of disagreements among community members about how to respond to industrial development" (2011, 1384). Our analysis of the emergence, evolution, and activities of landowner coalitions as responses to the extraction of natural gas from the Marcellus Shale in Pennsylvania is an effort to analyze one set of such dynamics.

# Conclusion

In this chapter, we have addressed a case that runs counter to most scholarship on the resistance to development along the extractive frontier. While drilling for natural gas in the Marcellus Shale (as well as in other shale formations across the US) certainly engendered a strong backlash, that reaction probably represented a minority of residents in the rural areas of Pennsylvania where drilling took place. Instead of asking what provoked resistance, then, we examined how local landowners contested the terms of drilling and other development, rather than whether it should go forward at all, negotiating the gray area in between outright refusal and total quiescence or a warm welcome.

Much of the answer lay in landowner coalitions, groups of property owners across rural Pennsylvania who banded together to negotiate collective leases with drilling companies. In seeking to better the terms of drilling on their own properties, these landowner coalitions influenced the pace, extent, and overall impacts of drilling across the state, in aggregate and beyond, sharing information and education. Through thousands of volunteer hours and collective compromise, these coalitions successfully raised the prices and protections of lease agreements across the state. Such outcomes may strengthen arguments that it may be preferable to direct fossil fuel extraction to locations where local populations have greater rights and political voice and may be more able to mitigate the impacts of development than those in many extractive regions.

Peering within the coalitions, in response to calls for the micropolitical ecology of environmental governance, (Bridge and Perreault 2009; Horowitz 2008, 2011), we see a familiar flux of politics and personalities, largely based on very real differences among landowners – of acreage, wealth, education, contacts, and more. The coalitions' internal heterogeneity was reflected in the diversity of their external objectives and outcomes. This diversity helps us to broaden our understanding of environmental governance and its hybrid institutions, particularly in the extractive frontier, where the contours of such governance are still being defined. At the same time, however, the landowner coalitions had certain critical features in common: all were private groups with no public oversight and quite restrictive criteria for inclusion (namely, substantial rural landholdings). Even if they experiment with democratic institutions and put in volunteer hours, is it appropriate and desirable that such groups dominate important dimensions of local environmental governance, perhaps in lieu of formal regulation and oversight? These questions have implications well beyond the borders of Pennsylvania's Marcellus Shale.

# Note

1 It should be noted that a truly comparative study to prove the effects of coalition on lease markets would be impossible, given the need to control for variables such as geology and other characteristics of the property in question, as well as the evolution of lease markets and regulations over time. Much relevant information is proprietary or otherwise inaccessible.

# References

Agrawal A. and Gibson C.C. (1999) "Enchantment and Disenchantment: The Role of Community in Natural Resource Conservation" *World Development* 27 4 629–649.

Andrews E. and McCarthy J. (2013) "Scale, Shale, and the State: Political Ecologies and Legal Geographies of Shale Gas Development in Pennsylvania" *Journal of Environmental Studies and Sciences* 4 1 7–16.

Balliet K. (2008) Should You Join a Landowner Group? Pennsylvania State University Extension (http://extension.psu.edu/natural-resources/natural-gas/issues/leases/publications/should-you-join-a-landowner-group) Accessed 21 January 2016.

Brasier K., Filteau M.R., McLaughlin D.K., Jacquet J., Stedman R.C., Kelsey T.W., and Goetz S.J. (2011) "Residents' Perceptions of Community and Environmental Impacts from Development of Natural Gas in the Marcellus Shale: A Comparison of Pennsylvania and New York Cases" *Journal of Rural Social Sciences* 26 1 32–61.

Bridge G. (2008) "Global Production Networks and the Extractive Sector: Governing Resource-Based Development" *Journal of Economic Geography* 8 3 389–419.

Bridge G. and Le Billon P. (2012) *Oil*. Polity Press, Cambridge.

Bridge G. and Perreault T. (2009) Environmental Governance. In Castree N., Demeritt D., Liverman D., and Rhoads B. eds., *A Companion to Environmental Geography* Wiley-Blackwell, Oxford 475–497.

Carre N. (2012) "Environmental Justice and Hydraulic Fracturing: The Ascendancy of Grassroots Populism in Policy Determination" *Journal of Social Change* 4 1 1–13.

Chedzoy B. (n.d.) Wise Gas Leasing Practices for Farmers (http://cce.cornell.edu/Energy ClimateChange/NaturalGasDev/Documents/PDFs/Wise%20gas%20leasing%20practices%20for%20farmers.pdf) Accessed 25 January 2016.

Colaneri K. (2014a) *Corbett says public misunderstands impacts of gas tax*. StateImpact Pennsylvania. September 9. (https://stateimpact.npr.org/pennsylvania/2014/09/09/corbett-says-public-misunderstands-impacts-of-gas-tax) Accessed 25 January 2016.

Colaneri K. (2014b) *Former state health employees say they were silenced on drilling* StateImpact Pennsylvania. June 19. (https://stateimpact.npr.org/pennsylvania/2014/06/19/former-state-health-employees-say-they-were-silenced-on-drilling/) Accessed 25 January 2016.

Considine T.J., Watson R., and Blumsack S. (2011) The Pennsylvania Marcellus Shale Natural Gas Industry: Status, Economic Impacts, and Future Potential (http://marcel luscoalition.org/wp-content/uploads/2011/07/Final-2011-PA-Marcellus-Economic-Impacts.pdf) Accessed 25 January 2016.

Conti D. (2015) "Fracking Decline Slows Business in Marcellus Shale Towns" *The Morning Call*. December 15. (www.mcall.com/news/nationworld/pennsylvania/mc-pa-gas-business-decline-20151213-story.html) Accessed 25 January 2016.

Corbett, T. (2011) "2011–12 budget address" March 8. (http://media.pennlive.com/midstate_impact/other/GovSpeech.pdf) Accessed 25 August 2016.

Damascus Citizens for Sustainability. (2016) Home (http://damascuscitizensforsustain ability.org) Accessed 25 January 2016.

Department of Energy (2009) Modern Shale Gas Development in the United States: A Primer (http://energy.gov/sites/prod/files/2013/03/f0/ShaleGasPrimer_Online_4-2009.pdf) Accessed 25 January 2016.

Fox, J., Gandour, M., Adlesic, T., and Sanchez, M. (2010) Gasland: Can you light your water on fire? New York: Docurama Films.

Galbraith R. (2013) "Fracking and the Revolving Door in Pennsylvania" *Public Accountability Initiative* (http://public-accountability.org/2013/02/fracking-and-the-revolving-door-in-pennsylvania) Accessed 25 January 2016.

Gaventa J. (1982) *Power and Powerlessness: Quiescence and Rebellion in an Appalachian Valley*. University of Illinois Press, Champaign, IL.

Himley M. (2008) "Geographies of Environmental Governance: The Nexus of Nature and Neoliberalism" *Geography Compass* 2 2 433–451.

Hopey D. (2011) "Corbett Repeals Policy on Gas Drilling in Parks" *Pittsburgh Post-Gazette*. February 24, AI–AII.

Horowitz L.S. (2008) "'It's up to the Clan to Protect': Cultural Heritage and the Micropolitical Ecology of Conservation in New Caledonia" *The Social Science Journal* 45 2 258–278.

Horowitz L.S. (2011) "Interpreting Industry's Impacts: Micropolitical Ecologies of Divergent Community Responses" *Development and Change* 42 6 1379–1391.

Howarth R.W., Ingraffea A., and Engelder T. (2011) "Natural Gas: Should Fracking Stop?" *Nature* 477 7364 271–275.

Huber M. (2015) "Review of Klein, This Changes Everything: Capitalism vs. the Climate" *Antipode* (https://radicalantipode.files.wordpress.com/2015/01/book-review_huber-on-klein.pdf) Accessed 25 January 2016.

Jacquet J. (2009) *Energy Boomtowns and Natural Gas: Implications for Marcellus Shale Local Governments and Rural Communities*. Northeast Regional Center for Rural Development, State College, PA (http://energy.wilkes.edu/PDFFiles/Issues/Energy%20Boomtowns%20and%20Natural%20Gas.pdf) Accessed 25 January 2016.

Jacquet J. and Stedman R.C. (2011) "Natural Gas Landowner Coalitions in New York State: Emerging Benefits of Collective Natural Resource Management" *Journal of Rural Social Sciences* 26 1 62–91.

Johnson L. (2015) "On Crises and Peculiar Endurance" *Human Geography* 8 1 92–97.

Klaber K.Z. (2011) Marcellus Shale Coalition: Presentation before the Marcellus Shale Advisory Commission (http://marcelluscoalition.org/wp-content/uploads/2011/05/MSC_Advisory_Commission_Final.pdf) Accessed 25 January 2016.

Klein N. (2014) *This Changes Everything: Capitalism vs. the Climate*. Simon and Schuster, New York.

Lave R. and Lutz B. (2014) "Hydraulic Fracturing: A Critical Physical Geography Review" *Geography Compass* 8 10 739–754.

Le Billon P. (2012) *Wars of Plunder: Conflicts, Profits and the Politics of Resources*. Columbia University Press, New York.

Lemos M.C. and Agrawal A. (2006) "Environmental Governance" *Annual Review of Environment and Resources* 31 1 297–325.

Liss J. (2011) "Negotiating the Marcellus: The Role of Information in Building Trust in Extractive Deals" *Negotiation Journal* 27 4 419–446.

McCarthy J. and Prudham S. (2004) "Neoliberal Nature and the Nature of Neoliberalism" *Geoforum* 35 3 275–284.

McGraw S. (2011) *The End of Country*. Random House, New York.

McKibben B. (2014) *Oil and Honey: The Education of an Unlikely Activist*. Times Books, New York.

Mercer C. (2002) "NGOs, Civil Society and Democratization: A Critical Review of the Literature" *Progress in Development Studies* 2 1 5–22.

Natural Resources Defense Council. (2016) The Role of Natural Gas in America's Energy Mix (www.nrdc.org/energy/naturalgasenergymix.asp) Accessed 25 January 2016.

Obama B. (2011) Remarks by the President on America's Energy Security (www.whitehouse.gov/the-press-office/2011/03/30/remarks-president-americas-energy-security) Accessed 25 January 2016.

Pennsylvania Department of Environmental Protection. (2016) Wells Drilled by County [Well Status: Active] (www.depreportingservices.state.pa.us/ReportServer/Pages/Report Viewer.aspx?/Oil_Gas/Wells_Drilled_By_County) Accessed 25 January 2016.

Pennsylvania Oil and Gas Act. (1984) Title 58: Oil and Gas, Chapter 11: Oil and Gas Act (files.dep.state.pa.us/OilGas/BOGM/BOGMPortalFiles/LawsRegsGuidelines/Act223_uc.doc) Accessed 25 January 2016.

Schafft K. (2014) Busted Amidst the Boom: The Creation of New Insecurities and Inequalities within Pennsylvania's Shale Gas Boomtowns (http://poverty.ucdavis.edu/sites/main/files/file-attachments/davis_marcellus__poverty_paper_schafft.pdf) Accessed 25 January 2016.

Sheppard K. (2012) "For Pennsylvania's Doctors, a Gag Order on Fracking Chemicals" *Mother Jones*. March 23. (www.motherjones.com/environment/2012/03/fracking-doctors-gag-pennsylvania) Accessed 25 January 2016.

Skocpol T. (2013) Naming the Problem: What It Will Take to Counter Extremism and Engage Americans in the Fight Against Global Warming (www.scholarsstrategynetwork.org/sites/default/files/skocpol_captrade_report_january_2013_0.pdf) Accessed 25 January 2016.

US Energy Information Administration (2012) Annual Energy Outlook 2012 (www.eia.gov/forecasts/archive/aeo12/) Accessed 25 January 2016.

Watts M. (2015) "All or Nothing?" *Human Geography* 8 1 109–111.

# Part IV
# Politics

# 10 Accumulating insecurity and risk along the energy frontier

*Michael J. Watts*

## Energy security

In March 2011, the Obama administration released its new 'blueprint' for American energy security. At least since the 2001 September 11 attacks, the very notion of a secure – and securitized – energy supply had once more returned to public consciousness in the wake of almost 15 years of relatively low oil prices and, even with the instabilities surrounding the Gulf War, few supply-side problems driven by rising oil reserves, abundant supplies and serious disagreements within OPEC. Amidst concerns over elevated oil prices, the California electricity crisis in 2000, and regional supply disruptions framed by the massive uncertainties surrounding the launching of the US-led War on Terror, American policy discourse on energy over the last decade – and indeed within and among the trans-Atlantic economies more generally – shifted toward a less sanguine assessment of the energy security landscape. The Cheney Report – more formally the Energy Task Force that formulated the national energy policy (NEP) – released in May 2001 immediately before the al-Qaeda attacks, turned once again on the question of American oil-dependency (a plank of American energy security policy since the Kissinger years), and on oil states, as the vice president famously opined, that did not have US interests at heart. The report's subtitle – *Reliable, Affordable, Environmentally Sound Energy for America's Future* – proved to be a digression, since it pointed to a raft of supply-side offerings with precious little in the way of environmental soundness. Rather the proposed policy would open up federal lands to drilling for oil and gas, notably by reducing restrictions on such drilling, unlock a part of the Alaska National Wildlife Refuge (ANWR) for oil and gas drilling and actively promote drilling in offshore Arctic areas off Alaska. In addition it offered $2 billion for research on clean coal technologies and provide what it termed regulatory certainty to promote investment in coal burning for electricity generation, and it would "support the expansion of nuclear energy in the United States as a major component of our national energy policy." The Cheney plan advocated that the United States should build between 1,300 and 1,900 new electric power plants by the year 2020. On the energy infrastructural front, natural gas, and electricity transmission lines were to be fostered by new legislation granting rights of way on federal lands. As an ex-oil man (Halliburton) working under an ex-oil man president (Harken Energy Corp.), Cheney offered precious little about conservation or alternative sources of energy but was obsessed with getting more oil (and secondarily gas) and getting the politics of oil supply right (in his case the new supply regions in the Caspian and the Gulf of Guinea in West Africa).

The 2011 White House blueprint identified a trio of interventions in a quite different register, each of which could be seen to address the conventional or core elements of energy security, understood as a reliable and adequate supply of energy at reasonable prices. First, to develop and secure American supplies in large measure by providing incentives to enhance United States (and North American) oil and gas potential while simultaneously "leading the world toward safer cleaner and more secure energy supplies" (2011: 2). Second, to provide consumers with energy efficient choices ("more efficient cars and trucks") and more efficient homes and buildings (in short enhanced energy conservation and efficiency). And third, as part of a larger push toward green capitalism to "innovate [the United States] to a clean energy future" through smart-grid innovation, offshore wind development, clean coal technologies, nuclear energy and so on. Running across this trio of policies was a distinctive lexicon of keywords: cleanliness, safety (triggered by the Deepwater Horizon explosion), reliability, and renewability.

Much might be said about the Obama blueprint. For example, the obvious contradictions between the rhetoric of safety and the speed with which the administration resumed drilling in the Gulf of Mexico and endorsed deepwater drilling in the Arctic; the evident tensions between the construal of natural gas as a 'clean transition fuel' and the raging debate over fracking technologies associated with the shale revolution; and the glaring fact that the Obama administration (and the Bush era before it) has shown precious little leadership let alone action on carbon emissions and global warming. All of this might suggest that energy security in its contemporary iteration follows in a long line of failed US energy policy dating back at least to the 1970s. It might also suggest that energy security seems at odds with the necessity of addressing the urgent question of a transition to a post-carbon economy, or at least to alternative forms of renewable energy. Neither of these conclusions suggest that energy security is either a model of consistency, or in light of other pressing political problems in the US (the fiscal cliff, economic recession, deepening income polarization, entitlement defunding) that energy security is high on the political agenda.

How have the meanings of energy security changed over the decade since the Cheney Report? Both reports rested, in different ways, on geopolitics and on the dubious notion of energy (meaning oil) independence. While Cheney looked to drilling more wells (for example to get access to low sulphur sweet oil from West Africa for the US gasoline market), the Obama administration looked to unconventional hydrocarbons: tight gas, the oil bearing shales, the Canadian tar sands and very deepwater offshore, all within the geographical perimeter of North America (in short, they substituted technological for political risk). The fracking revolution and the Deepwater Horizon explosion compelled the safety question onto the Obama energy security agenda that was barely visible in Cheney's; unconventional sources extended as it were the semantic space of security. Global climate change barely registered in Cheney's vision of an energy secure US; by 2011 cap and trade, the global carbon market and the debate over multilateral (the Kyoto protocols) versus sub-national regulation (California's aggressive emission standards) were embedded in the security discourse. The War on Terror, of course, hung like a pall over the larger geopolitics of energy supply in a way that post-dated Cheney's paranoic vision of energy-interdependence. In a sense, the Obama vision of energy security turned inward. Viewed in this way the changing map of energy security has a particular American valency. Viewed from other parts of the world, the content of security appears quite different. From this synopsis one might plausibly conclude that energy security is always situationally specific: it is framed, in short, by place (national politics and national interests in particular) and by time (for example the history of technological innovation, or shifting temporalities of the oil market and oil governance).

Energy security – and especially oil as a biopolitical security question (Campbell 2005) – has a long history almost as deep as the history of commercial oil production itself. It began with Winston Churchill, then First Lord of the Admiralty prior to the First World War, who changed from coal to oil as power source for the Royal Navy. With the UK war machine dependent on Middle Eastern oil instead of British coal, oil turned into a high-level foreign policy and security issue turning on questions of territory, sovereignty and the ability to prosecute war; that is to say it surfaced as a question of the geopolitics of security. In biopolitical terms, oil was a strategic commodity before it became a commercial commodity. The US awareness of energy security changed dramatically during the Second World War. The attack upon Pearl Harbor – triggered by the US which then supplied the vast majority of Japan's oil and responded to the Japanese invasion of Indochina by freezing Japan's US assets and cutting off oil exports – has in fact been described as the first energy war. If Franklin D. Roosevelt brushed off a request from the US oil companies to provide economic support to Saudi Arabia in 1941, only two years later, Roosevelt proclaimed that the preservation of the independence and territorial integrity of Saudi Arabia was vital to the defense of the United States.

The pursuit of energy security gained a new worldwide impetus after the tripling of the international price of crude oil in October 1973. One of the consequences of this shock was to put energy security and, more specifically, security of oil supply at the heart of the energy policy agenda of most industrialized nations. After the 1973 oil price shock and the successful cartelization of world oil by OPEC during the 1970s, Henry Kissinger argued that US security had been very directly affected, indeed that the energy crisis had placed at risk all of the nation's objectives in the world. As oil producers organized themselves and took control over the upstream segment of the industry it was perceived as a fundamental threat to a particular Western way of life. Reducing the dependency on foreign oil – energy security in part secured as energy independence – was given a pride of place at the highest echelons of power. But after the oil price collapse of 1986 oil became just another commodity. Prices fell, oil supply was abundant and oil trade was increasingly handled at, or in connection with, market-based stock exchanges. The oil market took on the features of a global buyers' market; OPEC struggled with lack of internal cohesion and the increasing interaction between the oil market and financial markets saw the oil trade assume the features – securitization, financial-ization, speculation – of other commodity markets.

Energy security is now back on the national and international political agenda with a vengeance. Not since the 1970s has energy been a more prominent political issue than today. Why is energy security back at the top of the agenda? There is no doubt that the terrorist attacks of September 11th are key and the California energy crisis in late 2000 certainly added to the ethos of scarcity but the return of the Peak Oil debate coupled with historically low OPEC surpluses and political instability in key oil-producing states (triggered in part by US militarism) made oil in particular centrally part of the national security debate. A Council of Foreign Relations white paper put energy security front and center in 2006 (CFR 2006: 3–4):

> Put simply, the reliable and affordable supply of energy – "energy security" – is an increasingly prominent feature of the international political landscape and bears on the effectiveness of US foreign policy. At the same time, how-ever, the United States has largely continued to treat "energy policy" as something that is separate and distinct – substantively and organizationally – from "foreign policy." This must change. The United States needs not merely to coordinate but to integrate energy issues with its foreign policy.

The run-up in oil prices over 2007–08 again raised the profile of energy security policies still further. Over 180 bills with the term energy security (Cohen, Joutz and Loungani 2011) in the text of the bill were introduced into the US Congress during the 111th Congress (2009–10) and over 200 bills were introduced during the Congress that preceded it. The seamless integration of the US national secu-rity state and the War on Terror extended to the energy sector producing more calls for deregulating the sector, exploiting unconventional oils (oil shale, tar sands, deepwater) and securing critical oil infrastructures (see Hildyard, Lohmann and Sexton 2012).

## The changing landscape of security

> Energy security would mean the *security of everything*: resources,
> production plants, transportation networks, distribution
> outlets and even consumption patterns; *everywhere*: oilfields, pipelines,
> power plants, gas stations, homes; *against everything*: resource
> depletion, global warming, terrorism, 'them' and ourselves.
> At its maximum, this logic invests every single object of any kind
> with and in security. At least potentially, the result is a panoptic
> view of security that legitimates panoptic security policies.
> (Ciuta 2010: 135)

One of the most striking images to capture the rise of global environmental change as a matter of security depicts Sir Richard Branson and Al Gore in 2007 announcing the Virgin Earth Prize, a challenge comparable, according to Branson, to the competition launched in 1675 to devise a method of precisely estimating longitude. It is a memorable photograph: a global capitalist whose personal wealth is rooted in an industry distinguished by its dependence on petroleum and a substantial carbon footprint, and a Nobel Prize-winning US politician and former vice president honored for his contributions to popularizing the scientific work of the Intergovernmental Panel on Climate Change (IPCC) and relatedly the relations between climate change and human security. Casually tossing the globe into the air, British tycoon Sir Richard Branson offered a $25 million prize for the scientist who discovers a way of extracting greenhouse gases from the atmosphere – a challenge to find the world's first viable design to capture and remove carbon dioxide from the air.

In its own way, the photograph is a *planetary image*, a bookend to the famous NASA planet earth ('whole earth') photograph AS17–22727 taken during the final Apollo 17 mission in 1972. It is a picturing, or rendering, of a certain sort of global nature, global politics and global science all at once – all rooted in the sense of a profound contemporary crisis in which survival and security, for everyone, is at stake. The NASA image came to be the lodestar for the United Nations Convention on the Human Environment held in Stockholm in 1972, and in turn the Branson-Gore photograph captures perfectly not just the policy sentiment in the run-up to the December 2009 UN Climate Conference in Copenhagen (COP 15) but also a wider ethos, namely of the confluence of global environmental change and human security configured in a very particular way. Copenhagen was obviously not the first global forum in which big science, big politics, and big business have joined forces (branded by the Virgin Earth Prize!) to address the conundrum of growth without limits and the consequences of capitalism's massive material wastes and detritus.

The twinning of these images is especially resonant because it links two important moments of crisis thinking. Released in 1972 in the same year as the Stockholm Earth Summit and the Apollo image, the famous *Limits to Growth* report – penned by a quartet of MIT physicists, cyberneticians and business management theorists – represented the apotheosis of a form of catastrophism thinking driven by a deep Malthusianism. What was on offer was a powerful discourse offering the prospect of chaos and collapse rooted in demographically driven scarcity (the five key sub-systems calibrated in their World3 computer model were world population, industrialization, pollution, food production and resource depletion).[1] The language of security – despite the predominant Cold War thinking of the time – was almost wholly invisible. If the global modeling exercise of *Limits to Growth* proved to be flawed in all sorts of ways it nevertheless served as an exemplar of 'limits modeling' that reappeared, in different guise, in the general atmospheric circulation models (GCMs) three and four decades later. As they gained standing and analytical power, the new wave of global climate change models without which there would have been no Montreal or Kyoto Protocols or COP 15 were also draped in the language of crisis and apocalypse, but now thoroughly immersed in the lexicon of security. If 1972–73 witnessed the global food crisis and the oil price boom, the Virgin Prize was launched at a time of a massive run-up in food and oil prices to unprecedented levels, and renewed talk of the 'scramble for scarce resources' by the chattering classes and policy wonks. Into the mix was added something new: the spectacular collapse of the investment banks and the bursting of the financial speculative bubble. By 2012 the discourse is less Malthusian (but the dead hand of Malthus is far from invisible) and is redolent with the language of security, systemic risk, vulnerability, resilience, and adaptive capacity. It is an emergent science of planetary disaster demanding an urgent public response – political, policy, civic and business – of an equal and opposite magnitude and gravity. A war on global warming, says Iain Boal, must be declared as draconian as the global War on Terror: "are we not faced with inhabiting – once again – the rubble of a ruined world?" (Boal 2009: 5).

In a discursive sense, then, climate change – to take one index of environmental security discourse – is a symptom of a planetary emergency. Global warming encompasses, and has direct consequences for, two of the most fundamental human provisioning systems, food and energy but to these one can add war, conflict and militarism, critical infrastructures, systemic financial risk all of which are now seen to be inseparably and organically linked in a complex of networks of tele-connected effects (OECD 2003; World Economic Forum 2012). This worldview mobilizes and enrolls powerful actors around the threat of massive, catastrophic risks and uncertainties. Central to this vision is a construal of the nature of life itself drawing especially upon the molecular and digital sciences – complexity, networks and information are its avatars – which shapes the nature of what is to be governed and how. If life is constituted through complex and continual adaptation and emergence it rests upon a sense of radical uncertainty in which danger and security form an unstable present, what Dillon and Reid (2009: 85) calls "the emergency of its emergence", or a life "continuously becoming dangerous". Ash Amin (2012: 138) sees this as 'the condition of calamity', or catastrophism:

> The recurrence, spread, severity and mutability of the world's natural and social hazards are considered as symptomatic of this state (of permanent risk), and its latent conditions are understood to be too volatile or random and non-linear to permit accurate prediction and evasive action. In the apocalyptic imaginary, hazard and risk erupt as unanticipated emergencies, disarming in every manifestation and in every way.

Three things can be said about this state of emergency. First, while there remain important differences across different domains of life, there are nonetheless close family resemblances between differing forms of purported insecurity (energy, food, biosecurity, finance and so on). For Melinda Cooper (2008) these commonalities share deeper state-led entanglements which conflated and drew together molecular research and the informational sciences, speculative finance and war. As a particular ontology, catastrophism and a life of radical uncertainty has produced a distinctive culture of risk (and fear) and risk (and fear) management, what Berlant (2007) calls an 'actuarial imaginary', an assemblage made up of the institutions, technologies, techniques, and ethics, the goal of which is to maximize security, profitability and well-being. Across these domains, as Anderson notes (2010a: 779–780), each threat is potentially catastrophic, the threat is often vague and spectral, and the disaster is imminent or at least foreseeable. For all such disaster talk, the threat is already present, an incubus that can be discerned and visualized through a series of signs, early warnings and simulations (Anderson 2010a).

Second, the threats are imminent but indeterminate in a way that prioritizes what Jane Guyer (2007) calls the "near future"; anticipatory actions become, as a result, the defining qualities of modern liberalism (everyone, Donald Rumsfeld famously said, needs to be proactive and not reactive, less bureaucratic and more like a venture capitalist). Pre-emption, precaution and preparations are its key deployments – or political technologies – through which a wide range of crises and challenges are to be confronted (Anderson 2010a; Amin 2012). Anderson expresses the matter very well: the question is how to protect certain forms of valued life that revolves around a future – uncertain, life threatening, and full of surprises – that diverges from both the past and present? What constitutes governance and action "in the here and now before the full occurrence of a threat or danger" (2010: 780)?

The third and related point is that these forms of latent catastrophism are, as it were, held together by – more properly, constituted by – the language of security and by processes of securitization (Floyd 2010). The hegemony of 'security talk' is evident in the extent to which virtually any expression of public concern – energy, terror, finance, environment, food, inequality, globalization, health, pandemics – is now attached to the moniker of security. The extraordinary capaciousness of security as an analytic and as a policy frame reached, in one regard, its final apotheosis in the drawing together of three keywords of contemporary modernity – globalization, security and development – in the 1994 *Human Development Report*. Coeval with the rise of neoliberalism and the *privatization* of everything is the long march of governmentality and the *securitization* of virtually everything.

The influential Copenhagen School, especially the work of Weaver (see Buzan and Weaver 2003), have traced the way in which a core logic of security has expanded its referent objects through securitization and has, as a result, widened its circumference from the modern concept of security (modeled in accordance with raison d'état and necessity) consolidated in the 1940s. Questions of threat and survival become the basis for assigning absolute political priority without conventional constraint (Weaver cited in Floyd 2010: 39). This approach, which is at heart discursive, draws upon a strange (and on its face highly contradictory) group of theoretical bedfellows: Austin, Derrida, Schmitt and Walz among them. It is however odd that the work of Foucault does not figure more centrally in this project. After all, it was Foucault who made the point that what distinguished modern rule (over the last four centuries) was a new form of biopower that links freedom and danger, namely *security*. Processes of securitization/desecuritization – an approach most associated with the Copenhagen School (Buzan and Weaver

2009) – explores how in the case of the environment or energy, for example, an expression of some putative ecological threat becomes a matter of emergency politics or security/threat as a result of the actions of powerful securitizing actors. Any form of security is self-referential; it turns on questions of performative speech acts (the securitizing move) and discursive legitimation (complete securitization). The meaning of security in its various forms is a function of what it does.

## Governing through security

Environmental and other securities can be productively located on the larger canvas of biopolitical security derived from Foucault's (2008) discussion of biopower, capitalism and liberal rule. Biopower encompasses a variety of forms of governing associated with the modern technologies of risk and threat management. Foucault (2008: 65) asks the question: what is the principle of calculation for the manufacture of liberal freedom? The principle he says is *security*. In our epoch, biosecurity, or more properly biopolitical security, deploys a vast array of technologies of risk. From the perspective of contemporary neoliberalism and its technologies of rule, there is a close affinity between resiliency thinking and a vision of how a spontaneous market order will be built from and out of an individual and community self-making and self-regulation through means of calculation and commodification shaped by their own peculiar exposure to the necessary and unavoidable contingencies of life. As Anderson properly notes, "through neoliberal logics of governing, the contingency of life has become a source of threat and opportunity, danger and profit" (2010: 29). The strength of political ecology I argue is that it attempts to link its foundational concerns with regimes of accumulation (in our time the dynamics of neoliberalism) with forms of contemporary governing and the operations of liberal governmentality.

Biopolitics in the Foucauldian sense points of course to both a rather different way of thinking about environmental security and about Nature or life more generally both historically and contemporaneously. Nature – or perhaps more appropriately the world of living things – has always provided the ground and substance for economics and politics and in this sense the relations between environment and governance or forms of rule have a long history (Schabas 2009). But it has also provided, as Michel Foucault (2007; 2008) shows, a way of linking security and the apparatuses and rationalities of modern government in the context of the growth of a capitalist economy. Biopower refers to the strategic coordination across a raft of forces that make up life or living beings, and represent a distinctive, and distinctively new, raft of modern governmental techniques and technologies of power. Biopower entails the rendering of life or living people as an object of regulation, and it rests upon forms of intervention aimed at optimizing life against particular threats ('making life live').

It goes without saying, of course, that what passes as life or a living thing (and what is necessary to support it) is a historical question (Jacob 1993; Kauffman 2000) – life is, as it were, a project rather than an accomplishment. Life as a living system and as an emergent system characterized by self-organization – a vision central to our contemporary sense of the life sciences – is central to the constitution of the biopolitical securitization (see Campbell 2005; Dillon 2008, 2007). Biopolitics, in other word, changes in relation to the forms in which life processes are, as Dillon (2008) has shown brilliantly in his work,[2] made transparent to knowledge. If life as a biological phenomenon is the object of biopolitical security technologies then to the same degree the technologies – now dominated by the technologies of risk and the wider actuarial imaginary – are constituted by, and regulated through, the historical forms of circulation of life (what Foucault calls *être biologique*). Currently the modalities through which life reproduces itself are transactional, complex, non-linear, and combinatorial (see Kaufman 2000). Dillon (2007) makes the important point that it is the idea of radical contingency which stands at the heart of this view of life.

Foucault originally drew a distinction between two political technologies of biopower: discipline (an anatomopolitics focused on the body and deployed in institutions like the prison) and biopolitics (especially a state biopolitics applied to humans as living species). In *Security, Territory, Population* Foucault (2007) explored how early biopolitics revolved around the aleatory properties and processes of populations which were normalized through forms of classification, ordering, testing. In this way force is brought to bear less through direct discipline than in "regulating overall conditions of life and naming threats to the balance or equilibrium of life" (Anderson 2010: 32).

Just as populations are aleatory, however, so contingency is said now to be generically constitutive of life as biological existence. As contemporary life scientists offer a view of life as incalculable, non-algorithmic, and beyond our capacity to predict, so the biosphere is, in this account, constructed by the emergence and persistent co-evolution of autonomous agents. The science of complexity, as much as the life sciences per se, focuses now on the emergent properties of living systems. Adaptation within these living systems is unpredictable, self-organizing, and self-engendering. Against this backdrop of the molecular and digital revolutions, biopolitics cannot be achieved solely through the avalanche of statistics alone, nor is the homeostatic goal of biopower possible or even desirable. As Anderson puts it (2010: 33), a productive life can only be secured in relation to threat and danger that resides within life, and securing life must involve a creative relation to the contingent (the free, self-governing subject must be open to and embrace the radical uncertainty of life). Modern life is, says Dillon, governed by laws of emergence and what he calls a distinctive moral and behavioral economy of existence:

> Biopolitically speaking, at the beginning of the 21st century, biological being as emergent being is enjoined to secure itself through securing its future by experimental participation in the engendering and unleashing of its own emergent potential. While allied to other ways of taming chance, risk technologies are also now deeply implicated in this novel biopoliticised securing of the life of emergent entities.

> (2008: 314)

In epistemological terms, contingency is the defining quality of human life to which biopolitics is committed to securing. As a consequence, biopolitical security can only be meaningfully performed *through* contingency not apart *from* it, which is to say that biopolitical security will be conducted through the conduct of shaping our exposure to, and the creative exploitation of, contingent events and processes in nature and from the "independent actions and interventions of biological being itself" (Dillon 2008: 315). As we shall see, these forms of intervention are complemented in our time by other forms associated with high neoliberalism which are consistent with the vision of biological being as emergent, namely the vision of an economy as a living, self-organizing and self-correcting system (Hayek 1988; Cooper 2008).

Radical contingency as a condition of existence and as a form of prescription suggests a new form of biopower that links freedom and danger, namely security. Modern biopolitics of security cannot be formed by safety and protection as such but by cultivating the very principles of adaptive emergence. Contingency and transformation are the means to survive and be safe, or more properly qualitative change in the nature of the living thing itself is the very condition of possibility of security. It is this notion that aleatory events are now perpetually beyond any sense of control – that the objects of security are seemingly an infinite horizon of emergent threats, a sort of paranoid world of permanent emergency – which leads Anderson to suggest that security now has another iteration; as he puts it, "security can be understood as a break with discipline and an *intensification* of biopolitics" (2010: 34 my emphasis). Security poses the prospect of interventions extending to all of life in order to make life live for the market. The question is what technologies of risk management constitute such a security strategy? And what sort of economy provides the "basic grid of intelligibility" for this contemporary historical form of the biosecuritization of politics? If as Foucault (2008) suggests, neoliberalism is "a whole way of being and thinking", a "grid of economic and sociological analysis", what is its relation to the governing of contingency?

One part of this story – the relation between contingency and liberalism – is well understood. O'Malley (2006) shows how risk calculation and uncertainty in the nineteenth century represented not simply something ultimately incalculable but a *dispositif de sécurité* focused on foresight, contract, prudence, and enterprise. In our time risk operationalises the biopolitics of emergent life through the commodification of contingency, which is taken to be constitutive of what it is to be a living, emergent, transactional being (Dillon 2007, 2008). Risk is by definition about the probability of the unpredictable: it speaks to danger but also market opportunity and source of profit by making contingency a fungible commodity. Risk may invoke a device – insurance or underwriting – for offsetting the consequences of injury but it has come to encompass a much larger social and economic ground, indeed it underwrites many orders of governance. It is, in Gramscian terms, the hegemonic practice governing the conduct of conduct; it is now an ontology. Risks multiply and circulate; they are monetized and securitized in a veritable avalanche of forms and norms. Risk technologies which are in the business of underwriting exposure to contingency, are central mechanisms to self-governing – that is to say self-making and self-regulating subjects saturated in, and bound by, a world of calculation and commodification determined by their peculiar profile of exposure to the necessary and unavoidable contingencies of life. Put rather differently, risk is about the governance of threat in an uncertain near future: it speaks to anticipatory action in a contingent world. Anderson notes that this anticipatory governance – the management of risks – is rooted in the calculative and performative actions of preparedness, pre-emption and pre-caution (2010a); that is, stopping events before they happen or reach points of irreversibility and or halting the effects of potential threats and disruptions, all in the name of care and safety. But risk as universal account has come to mean that risk can itself become a risk, potentially producing its own negation (this is the case of Deepwater Horizon and the oil industry to which I shall return).

Risk has become an assemblage of universal account and security as a form of biopower leads inexorably to Foucault's inquiry about the relations between government and the transformations in the circuits of capital. Naturally this takes us deep into the heart of neoliberalism – and Foucault's (2008) astonishingly prescient lectures on German ordo-liberalism and its aftermath – and the twin processes of financialization and securitization associated with the rise of money-manger capitalism. What lies behind the rise of finance capital as a dominant force within capitalism (led by the US restructuring of the 1970s) is neoliberalism as a whole way of life – or as Hayek said of seeing liberalism as "a living thought", as a "utopia". It necessitates generalizing the enterprise forms to the entire social fabric, the economization of the entire social field (Foucault 2008: 242); competition is the measure or norm for all of life while the enterprise form is the model for living a life (i.e. *homo economicus*).

If the neoliberal economy is a self-organizing and self-correcting living system composed of individuals whose life is "a sort of permanent and multiple enterprise" (Foucault 2008: 241), it is rendered actionable says Anderson (2010: 38) by 'environmental technologies'. These technologies address not so much capabilities through discipline or the management of populations as the future-oriented operating environment, the rules of the game rather than the players. That is to say markets and competition as a way of grasping the future or the event before it occurs. This is what is contained in the transformation of risk from a management device to a universal system of account and an entire order of governance. The 'actuarial imaginary' constitutes an assemblage made up of the institutions, technologies, techniques, and ethics the goal of which is to maximize (future) security, profitability and well-being. But if security is to be located within the circumference of a normalized prudentialism resting on the individualized and dispersed risk regimes of the neo-liberal order, there is much to suggest, to return to Foucault, that life has not so much been integrated into forms of governance as it has escaped from them (2008: 143). The governance of risk itself seems to be in crisis in the face of the likes of the meltdown of the financial sector, the scale, and magnitude of the global climate crisis, and the slow death of forms of livelihood in the Global South. The securitization of everything as a form of governance seems to constantly confront the terrifying fact that it confronts (and *produces* from within the larger system of which it is part) events that exceed its capacity to regulate and secure.

## Accumulating insecurity and risk: a case study of the deepwater horizon disaster in the Gulf of Mexico

The Macondo well – named ironically after Garcia Marquez's famous fictional town in *One Hundred Years of Solitude* – was drilled from a semi-submersible mobile rig, Deepwater Horizon, owned by Transocean, while BP as the field operator (as is often the case in the Gulf) shared the field with Anadarko Petroleum and Mitsui Oil Exploration. The well was successful in locating a major reservoir and at the conclusion of the drilling operation the well casing was to be installed and the field sealed with a cement plug to be later opened from a production platform. The cementing of the well was completed by Halliburton but on the day of the explosion there were indications of flow into the well. A large blowout of methane gas traveled up the drilling pipe and ignited the platform leading to an explosion and a fire which sank the rig in 5000 feet of water in late April 2010. It took 87 days to bring the well under control in the wake of the catastrophic failure of the so-called blowout preventer.[3] The disaster happened on the same day that BP executives visited the rig to congratulate management on a job well done. It was coincidentally the fortieth anniversary of Earth Day.

It goes without saying that complex systems fail in complex ways, and this is as true of the blowout as it is of the emergency response and clean-up. Some of the most striking events of the post-blow out period was the extent to which nobody seemed prepared at all. In sum one might say that the biopolitics of energy security – a high-tech industry saturated with risk management, risk aversion, and resiliency talk – seems to have failed, or to return to Foucault to have escaped the techniques that govern and administer. What has to be explained here is not the, dare I say it, well-oiled machine of pre-emption, precaution and preparedness – forms of calculation, imagination and performance aiming to stop the threat before it reaches a point of impact or stopping the effects of an event that disrupts life (Anderson 2010a) – but rather its obverse, the system's inability to function like an adaptive, self-organizing living system. Or to put it differently, to protect and save and care for certain forms of life – perhaps cynically the culture of the SUV – certain forms of life were abandoned (the Gulf coast), destroyed (the killed rig workers) and dispossessed (the livelihoods of the Gulf).

How then do we explain a catastrophic event like the Deepwater Horizon blowout in the context of the securitization of everything (or more specifically within the frame of energy security)? One would start with the resource itself. The Outer-Continental Shelf (OCS) in the Gulf of Mexico is the largest US oil-producing region. Not unexpectedly, the Gulf's oil complex – the assemblage of firms, the state, and communities that shape the character of oil and gas extraction – is massive by any accounting. With over 4,000 currently operating wells, the Gulf accounts for one-third of US crude oil production and over 40% of US refining capacity. Over the past century, companies have drilled over 50,000 wells in the Gulf (27,000 have been plugged), almost 4,000 of them in deepwater (more than 1,000 feet). In the last 15 years more than 60 wells have been drilled in the ultra-deepwater zones – in more than 5,000 feet of water – deploying dynamic positioning systems that use computers and satellites to keep rigs and supply vessels steady in rough seas and high winds. There are 3,020 platforms currently operating, but they represent only a small part of the Gulf's oil and gas infrastructure: 33,000 miles of pipeline on and offshore connected with a network of terminals, plus a huge capital investment of refineries, storage facilities, shipyards, and construction facilities stringing the coast from Mississippi to Texas. The total fixed capital in the Gulf oil complex is now valued at an estimated $2 trillion.

Louisiana is America's own petro-state, a living testimony to the petro-populism and oil-based human and ecological development failures that have typically afflicted oil-producing states in the Global South (Goldberg et al. 2008). Petro-corruption and the shady politics of oil development were there from the beginning as the oil industry emerged on the backs of an extractive economy (timber, sulfur, rice, salt, furs). Local businessmen snapped up land and threw themselves into a chaotic land grab backed by Texas drillers and operators with little regard for the law. Wildcatting sprung up with no regulation; leases, especially along the coast wetlands, were allocated behind closed doors. Huey P. Long famously launched his career with an attack on Standard Oil and then proceeded to build his own subterranean oil empire (Fairclough 1999). While senator, Long and his political cronies established the Win or Lose Corporation, which acquired cut-rate mineral leases through the government and re-sold them at a healthy profit. At the same time he used oil severance taxes to begin a populist program of public service provision, which integrated a white working class into a program of economic modernization (Heleniak 2001). By the 1970s, when oil was providing 40% of state revenues, Louisiana ranked at the very bottom of the heap in terms of basic development indicators. Louisiana currently ranks forty-eigth of the states (only Mississippi and West Virginia are lower) in terms of human development indices, and is marked by massive inequalities between white and black populations along all measures of human well-being; infant mortality and homicide rates are comparable to parts of Central America and sub-Saharan Africa. In some parishes well-being is roughly at the average level of the United States in 1950.

The history of the oil industry in Louisiana and the Gulf more generally is an almost textbook case of frontier dispossession and reckless accumulation running far in advance of state oversight and effective regulation (Gramling 1996). Offshore drilling technology was in effect born and nurtured in Louisiana with an assist from Venezuela – the former along the shallow coastal waters, the latter on lake Maracaibo. Technology quickly developed from oil derricks on piers to stationary, mobile and, by the 1930s, submersible drilling barges. All of this was propelled by new seismic technologies, which uncovered numerous salt domes across the coast and offshore region. Between 1937 and 1977 almost 27,000 wells were drilled in the coastal parishes including shallow offshore. It was the first wave of leases and back-room petro-populism unleashed a torrent of canal construction, dredging and pipeline corridor construction (to say nothing of the emerging petro-chemical complex in what became 'Cancer Alley') which permitted large-scale salt intrusion and rapid coastal degradation.

In practice however the moving offshore frontier was transformed through four giant waves of frontier development, a quartet of land grabs and dispossession. The first was almost wholly unregulated during the late 1940s and 1950s prior to and immediately after the resolution of the state jurisdiction question. A second occurred in the wake of the oil import quotas of 1959, which unleashed another round of major leasing; two million acres were leased in 1962, in water depths up to 125 feet, more than all previous sales combined. Oil production almost tripled between 1962 and 1968 and deepwater operations had by this time reached 300 feet. The first subsea well was drilled in 1966. As the *National Commission on the BP Disaster* noted (2011: 28), this period was associated with massive hurricane damage, and serial accidents including blowouts, injuries and helicopter crashes. A 1973 NSF report noted what was clear to everyone, namely widespread collusion between industry and government and very light government oversight. The USGS freely granted waivers from complying with the limited regulations and inspection demands while the regulatory agencies were hopelessly underfunded and understaffed (12 people in the lease management office oversaw 1,500 platforms).

In the wake of the Santa Barbara spill in 1969, OCS development nationally was stymied but the Gulf of Mexico proved to be a striking exception to the larger national trend. Exploration proceeded apace with the first deepwater (1,000 feet and more) play made by Shell in 1975 in the Mississippi Canyon. The landmark 1978 National Energy Act and the OCS Lands Act Amendments in the same year, fundamentally transformed offshore leasing by vesting expanded power in the secretary of the interior, developing an exploration and production planning process expressly requiring the Secretary of the Interior to demand environmental and safety studies, a requirement however that the secretary could override if "incremental costs" were deemed to be high (National Commission on the BP Deepwater Horizon Spill and Offshore Drilling 2011: 62). In short, the good news was that finally – three decades after the beginning of the offshore boom – there was something like an effort to provide serious government regulatory oversight (though the Oil Pollution Act was not passed until 1990); the bad news was that the Gulf of Mexico was granted an exemption from all of the review and oversight legislation. The 1978 Lands Act Amendments expressly identifies the Gulf of Mexico "for less rigorous environmental oversight under NEPA" (National Commission on the BP Deepwater Horizon Oil Spill and Offshore Drilling 2011: 80); three years later in 1981 the Interior Department categorically excluded from NEPA review applications to drill wells in the central and western Gulf. The 1980s provided in a sense an ideological resolution to the issue: the environmental enforcement capacities were eviscerated and what emerged was a "culture of revenue maximization" as the *National Commission on the Deepwater Horizon Oil Spill* put it (2011: 76).

The election of Ronald Reagan in 1981 marked not just the third round of leasing but an assault on the Carter reforms, and a fully fledged neoliberalization of the Gulf deploying the now expanded powers of the Interior. Under this leadership, Secretary of the Interior James Watt promised to open up the OCS to area-wide leasing and placed 1 *billion* acres on the block. He began by establishing a new agency in 1982 – the Minerals Management Service (MMS) – which created 18 large planning areas rather than the traditional 3-mile square blocks. While Watts subsequently resigned amidst controversy and Congressional opposition to OCS development on the east and west coasts, the Gulf was exempt and the result was a land rush and massive exploration and production which constituted the third deepwater frontier wave (the record lease sale prior to 1982 was 2.8 million acres; the first area-wide lease in the Gulf produced a sale of 37 million acres!). Seven sales between 1983 and 1985 leased more acreages that all previous leases combined since 1962; 25% were located in deep water and the lion's share was captured by Shell, the leading innovator and player in offshore technology and production. At the same time the reforms provided for radically reduced royalties and federal bonus bids with the consequence that companies paid 30% less despite a sixfold acreage expansion (average lease prices per acre fell from $2,224 to $263). In 1987, the MMS reduced the minimum bid for deepwater tracts (from $900,000 to $150,000) enabling a few companies to lock-up entire basins for ten years for almost nothing. The fruits of this frontier expansion were visible a decade later: within that period deepwater (1000 feet and more) wells grew from 4% to over 45% of all Gulf production (Lehner 2010: 88)

The 1990s proved to be a "stampede" (National Commission on the BP Deepwater Horizon Oil Spill and Offshore Drilling 2011: 39). Seismic innovations, a new generation of drilling vessels capable of drilling in 10,000 feet of water and through 30,000 feet of sediments (tension-leg, SPAR and semi-submersible platforms), and new drilling techniques ('downhole steerable motors') pushed the deepwater frontier to the so-called sub-salt plays. Ten years later the Gingrich revolution ushered in another reform to lay the basis for another round of accumulation by dispossession: the OCS Deep Water Royalty Relief Act of 1995 suspended all royalties to be paid by the companies for five years. In turn this produced another land grab in which 2,840 leases were sold in three years. By 2000, deepwater production topped shallow water output for the first time. At the same time the ascendant BP was increasingly displacing Shell's hegemony in the Gulf. By using new 3-D seismic technologies they had made a series of remarkable discoveries and by 2002 BP was the largest acreage holder in deepwater (accounting for over one third of all deepwater reserves). The MMS budget reached its budgetary nadir precisely during this boom (a record number of wells were drilled in 1997). The *Houston Chronicle* reported that over the 1990s there was an 81% increase in offshore fires, explosions and blowouts. In the following decade it increased fourfold.

The final wave of frontier accumulation was triggered by the election of George Bush in 2001 and the events of September 11. On May 18, two days after Cheney's Energy Task Force report was delivered, Bush issued Executive Order 13212 (titled Actions to Expedite Energy related projects) the purpose of which was to "expedite [the] review of permits or other actions necessary to complete the completion of such projects" (Cavnar 2011: 156). The language was, as a number of commentators pointed out, almost identical to that of a memorandum on the 'streamlining' of development in the OCS submitted by the American Gas

Association to the Cheney Task Force. The MMS was already laboring under a congressionally mandated rule to limit permit review to an impossibly confining 30 days, but the new order pushed things much further: in its wake, 400 waivers were granted every year for offshore development. As offshore exploration and production stepped into historically unprecedented ultra-deepwater, the permitting process and enforcement were laughable. MMS was not simply toothless and staffed by the sorts of oilmen it was designed to regulate but according to a 2008 Inspector General report was a hothouse of among other things a culture of substance abuse and promiscuity. To round out the abandonment of anything like supervision, in June 2008 George W. Bush removed the ban on offshore drilling. Oversight deteriorated to the point where NOAA was publicly accusing MMS of purposefully understating the likelihood and consequences of major offshore spills and blowouts. Watt's new system was nothing more than "tossing a few darts at a huge map of the Gulf" (Freudenberg and Grambling 2011: 148).

Shell announced the birth of the new 'neoliberal frontier' in 2009. The Perdido platform, located 200 miles offshore in water 2 miles deep, is nearly as tall as the Empire State Building, drawing in oil from 35 wells in 3 fields over 27 square miles of ocean (Lehner 2010: 92). Sitting atop an 'elephant' field rumored to contain as much as 600 billion gallons of oil, the scramble was on. In a similar fashion BP pushed forward on a hugely ambitious program to develop multiple fields in the most demanding and unforgiving of environments pushing deeper into old Paleogene and Lower tertiary strata. The likes of Thunder Horse – BP's massive semi-submersible production facility almost destroyed by Hurricane Dennis in 2005 – located in the Mississippi Canyon 252 Lease and the Macondo Well (40 miles distant) represented, as the *National Commission on the BP Deepwater Disaster* put it, 'formidable tests'. Viewed on the larger canvas of the *longue durée* of offshore development, Perdido and Macondo were the expressions of what one might call the accumulation of insecurity, and the neoliberal production of systemic risks in the Gulf of Mexico – each rooted in the politics of substituting technological and financial for political risk.

The Deepwater Horizon catastrophe was overdetermined by the vast accumulation of risks fabricated along the shifting neoliberal frontier of offshore accumulation. Nowhere are the links between deregulation and neoliberal capitalism clearer than in the 2011 report by the Deepwater Horizon Study Group (DHSG 2011: 5–10). In their devastating assessment the catastrophic failure resulted from: multiple violations of the laws of public resource development, and its proper regulatory oversight, by a BP safety culture compromised by management's desire to "close the competitive gap" and to save time and money – and make money – by making trade-offs for the certainty of production because there were perceived to be no downsides, BP's corporate culture embedded in risk-taking and cost-cutting, and not least the histories and cultures of the offshore oil and gas industry and the governance provided by the associated public regulatory agencies.

The Deepwater disaster has more than a family resemblance to the 2008 financial crisis. And it is financialization in fact which adds yet another dimension to the production of insecurity along the oil frontier. At the time of the disaster

BP was one of the largest traders in the emerging oil futures and securitization markets. Standing at the heart of this financialization is the shift to oil as an asset class (O'Sullivan 2009; Moors 2011). Oil prices have not always depended on the futures markets. In the 1970s and 1980s, before the advent of active crude oil futures trading in the New York and London markets, most of the oil produced was traded via long-term contracts (Dicker 2011). In the last 20 years oil has broken their relation to 'market fundamentals' and is dominated by the flow of money and by the investment banks seen in unprecedented price volatility. Behind this newfound volatility and the speculative role of paper oil was the fact that "innovations in the financial industry made it possible for paper oil to be a financial asset in a very complete way. Once that was accomplished, a speculative bubble became possible. Oil is no different from equities or housing in this regard" (Parson 2010: 82). The volume of unregulated over-the-counter commodity transactions had grown enormously since 2000; a development was made possible largely by the Commodity Futures Modernization Act of December 2000.

These changes and what Dicker (2011) calls assetization (the rise of commodity index funds and exchange traded funds), financialization (new and mostly over-the-counter customized energy products similar to the derivative markets) and electronic access to oil markets collectively not only made oil into an asset class similar to equities and bonds but also gave the commodities market a massive boost. As a result it was not so much minor speculators as large institutional investors who sought exposure to the commodities market. They regarded commodities as an alternative investment category in their portfolio allocations and invested a significant proportion of their assets accordingly. The new actors in the oil trade have produced a situation in which, according to Moors (2011: 98) 60% of the oil futures market is coming from speculators. Oil has become a source or store of liquidity sometimes preferable to the dollar because the oil market allows a better hedge against the loss in dollar value in foreign exchange. The movement into crude oil and oil product futures contracts as a flight to liquidity, which is a barely a decade old, has decisive implications for oil volatility. This is the heart of the so-called 'oil vega' problem: the increasing inability to determine the genuine value of crude oil based on its market price. The inability to plan, predict and compensate indicates, "we have a developing market (dis) order – a pervasive and endemic disequilibrium masquerading as the "new order" in the oil market" (Moors 2011: 6).

An oil assemblage generating massive new systemic risks of financial and market volatility in one new expression, throws the 'formidable tests' of deepwater oil into sharp relief. Other risks are biophysical and would include of course the potentially catastrophic costs of hurricane damage, which are endemic to the region but seemingly now are rendered even more devastating by the products of the oil industry itself (carbon emissions, global warming, and extreme climatic events). The 2005 hurricane season crippled the Gulf energy sector and left $120 billion in losses. Of course this is what the insurance and reinsurance industries are in theory in the business of protecting. But the 2005 season consumed the entirety of global premiums insurers had collected from energy underwriting

(Johnson 2012: 3). The Gulf 'wind market' – major underwriters already have high rates and have capped coverage – is a big question mark. Gulf oil seems to combine the worst of Wall Street, the worst of corporate rapaciousness, and the worst of technological hubris all running headlong into the global climate crisis. A perfect storm of catastrophic risk (see Hildyard, Lohmann and Sexton 2012).

Energy security in the Gulf is an extraordinary case of how building resiliency within the oil assemblage is undermined by the logic of neoliberal governance and quite specifically the effects of simultaneously deregulating government oversight while unleashing the most rapacious of market forces in a high-risk environment (that is to say pushing into ever deeper water for essentially geopolitical reasons). The Macondo well disaster reveals the deadly intersection of the aggressive enclosure of a new technologically risky resource frontier (the deepwater continental shelf in the Gulf), with the operations of what one can call neoliberalised risk, a lethal product of cut-throat corporate cost-cutting, the collapse of government oversight and regulatory authority and the deepening financialization and securitization of the oil market. The blowout dramatically exposes the internally contradictory and leaky nature of those efforts to integrate, govern, and administer life. Life, as Foucault says, constantly escapes those efforts. In the Gulf the political story ends with class action suits, a reorganization of the regulatory but ultimately the abandonment of Obama's moratorium and the gradual resumption of deepwater drilling. The oil assemblage lurches forward simultaneously advancing the frontier and simultaneously multiplying – and amplifying – the production of profit, risk and insecurity.

## Notes

1   The debate continues. Donnella Meadows, Jørgen Randers, and Dennis Meadows updated and expanded the original version in *Beyond the Limits* in 1993 – a 20-year update on the original material. The most recent updated version was published in 2004 by Chelsea Green Publishing Company and Earthscan under the name *Limits to Growth: The 30-Year Update*. In 2008 Graham Turner at the Commonwealth Scientific and Industrial Research Organization (CSIRO) in Australia published a Working Paper entitled "A Comparison of 'The Limits to Growth' with Thirty Years of Reality", which examined the past thirty years of reality with the predictions made in 1972. He found that changes in industrial production, food production and pollution are all in line with the book's predictions of "economic and societal collapse in the 21st century" (see www. csiro.au/files/files/plje.pdf).
2   This sections draws extensively on Dillon (2007, 2008); see also Anderson (2010, 2010a).
3   There is now a substantial literature including the President's Commission report: see Cavnar (2011), Freudenberg and Grambling (2011), Konrad and Shroder (2011), Steffy (2011). A new report by the Bureau of Ocean Management, Regulation and Enforcement was just released on September 14, 2011, which concludes as follows: The Panel found that a central cause of the blowout was failure of a cement barrier in the production casing string, a high-strength steel pipe set in a well to ensure well integrity and to allow future production. The failure of the cement barrier allowed hydrocarbons to flow up the wellbore, through the riser and onto the rig, resulting in the blowout. The precise reasons for the failure of the production casing cement job are not known. The Panel concluded that the failure was likely due to: (1) swapping of cement and drilling

mud (referred to as "fluid inversion") in the shoe track (the section of casing near the bottom of the well); (2) contamination of the shoe track cement; or (3) pumping the cement past the target location in the well, leaving the shoe track with little or no cement (referred to as "overdisplacement").The loss of life at the Macondo site on April 20, 2010, and the subsequent pollution of the Gulf of Mexico through the summer of 2010 were the result of poor risk management, last minute changes to plans, failure to observe and respond to critical indicators, inadequate well control response, and insufficient emergency bridge response training by companies and individuals responsible for drilling at the Macondo well and for the operation of the *Deepwater Horizon*.

# References

Amin, A. 2012 *Land of Strangers*. London: Polity.

Anderson, B. 2010 Affect and Biopower. *Transactions of the Institute of British Geographers*, 37, 28–43.

Anderson, B. 2010a Preemption, Precaution, Preparedness. *Progress in Human Geography*, 34, 6, 777–798.

Austin, D., Carriker, B., McGuire, T., Pratt, J., Priest, T. and Pulsipher, A.G. 2001 *History of the Offshore Oil and Gas Industry in Southern Louisiana*. Volume I. Center for Energy Studies. Baton Rouge: Louisiana State University.

Berlant, L. 2007 Slow Death (Sovereignty, Obesity, Lateral Agency). *Critical Inquiry*, 33, 7, 762–787.

Boal, Iain. 2009 *Globe, Capital, Climate*. Berkeley: RETORT.

Buzan, B. and Weaver, O. 2003 *Regions and powers: the structure of international security*. Vol. 91. Cambridge University Press.

Buzan, B. and Weaver, O. 2009 Macrosecuritisation and Security Constellations: Reconsidering Scale in Securitisation Theory. *Review of International Studies*, 35, 253–276.

Campbell, D. 2005 The Biopolitics of Security. *American Quarterly*, 57, 3, 943–971.

Cavnar, B. 2011 *Disaster on the Horizon*. White River: Vermont.

Ciuta, F. 2010 Conceptual Notes on Energy Security: Total or Banal Security? Security Dialogue, 41, 2, 123–137.

Cohen, G., Joutz, F. and Loungani, P. 2011 Measuring Energy Security: Trends in the Diversification of Oil and Natural Gas Supplies. IMF Working Paper No. 11/39, Washington, DC.

Cooper, M. 2008 *Life as surplus*. Seattle, WA: University of Washington Press.

Council on Foreign Relations. National Security Consequences of US Oil Dependency. New York: CFR.

DHSG 2011 *Final Report on the Macondo Well Blowout*. Deepwater Horizon Study Group. Berkeley: UC Berkeley.

Dicker, D. 2011 *Oil's Endless Bid*. Hoboken: John Wiley.

Dillon, M. 2008 Underwriting Security. *Security Dialogue*, April, 39, 2–3, 309–332.

Dillon, M. and Reid, J. 2009 *The Liberal Way of War*. London: Routledge.

Dillon, Michael 2007 Governing Through Contingency: The Security of Biopolitical Governance. *Political Geography*, 26, 41–47.

Fairclough, Adam 1999 *Race and Democracy: The Civil Rights Struggle in Louisiana 1915–1972*. Athens: University of Georgia Press.

Floyd, R. 2010 *Security and Environment*. Cambridge: Cambridge University Press.

Foucault, M. 2007 *Security, Territory, Population*. London: Palgrave.

Foucault, M. 2008 *The Birth of Biopolitics*. London: Allen Lane.

Freudenberg, W. and Grambling, R. 2011 *Blowout in the Gulf*. Boston: MIT Press.

Global Risk Report. Davos: WEF.

Goldberg, E., Wibbels, E. and Mvukiyehe, E. 2008 Lessons from Strange Cases: democracy, development and the resource curse in the US. *Comparative Politics*, 41, 4, 477–514.

Gramling, R. 1996 *Oil on the Edge*. Albany: State University of New York Press.

Guyer, J.I. 2007 Prophecy and the near future: Thoughts on macroeconomic, evangelical, and punctuated time. *American Ethnologist*, 34, 3, 409–421.

Hayek, F.A. 1998 *The Fatal Conceit*. Chicago: University of Chicago Press.

Heleniak, Roman 2001 Local Reaction to the Great Depression in New Orleans, 1929–1933. In Edward Haas (ed.), *The Age of the Longs: Louisiana 1928–1960*, Volume Eight in the Louisiana Purchase Bicentennial Series in Louisiana History. Lafayette: Center for Louisiana Studies, pp. 419–433.

Hildyard, N., Lohmann, L. and Sexton, S. 2012 *Energy Security: For Whom? For What?* Sturminster Newton: Corner House.

Jacob, F. 1993 *The Logic of Life*. Princeton: Princeton University Press.

Johnson, Leigh 2012 Financializing Energy and Climate Risks. Unpublished Manuscript, Geography Department, University of Zurich.

Kaufman, S. 2000 *Investigations*. New York: Oxford University Press.

Konrad, J. and Shroder, T. 2011 *Fire on the Horizon*. New York: Harper Collins.

Lehner, P. 2010 *In Deep Water*. New York: OR Books.

Moors, K. 2011 *Oil Vega*. New York: Wiley.

National Commission on the BP Deepwater Horizon Oil Spill and Offshore Drilling 2011 *Deep Water: The Gulf Disaster and the Future of Offshore Drilling*. Washington, DC: The Oil Spill Commission, US Congress (www.oilspillcommission.gov/final-report).

OECD 2003 *Emerging Risks in the 21st Century*. Organization for Economic Cooperation and Development: Paris (www.oecd.org/dataoecd/20/23/37944611.pdf).

O'Malley, Pat 2006 ed., *Governing Risks*, Aldershot: Ashgate.

O'Sullivan, D. 2009 *Petromania*. Petersfield: Harriman House.

Parson, J. 2010 Black Gold and Fools Gold. *Economia* 10, 2, 81–116.

Priest, T. 2007 Extraction not Creation. *Enterprise and Society*, 8, 2, 227–267.

Priest, T. 2005 A Perpetual Extractive Frontier? The History of Offshore Petroleum in the Gulf of Mexico. In Paul S. Ciccantell, David A. Smith, and Gay Seidman (eds.), *Nature, Raw Materials, and Political Economy*. Oxford: Elsevier Press, pp. 209–229.

Schabas, M. 2009 *The natural origins of economics*. Chicago: University of Chicago Press.

Steffy, L. 2011 *Drowning in Oil*. New York: McGraw Hill.

# Index

For Product Safety Concerns and Information please contact our EU
representative  GPSR@taylorandfrancis.com
Taylor & Francis Verlag GmbH, Kaufingerstraße 24, 80331 München, Germany